BEYOND BORDERS

BEYOND BORDERS

Exploring the History of Cornell's Global Dimensions

EDITED BY

ROYAL D. COLLE
HEIKE MICHELSEN
ELAINE D. ENGST
COREY RYAN EARLE

PUBLISHED IN ASSOCIATION WITH
CORNELL UNIVERSITY PRESS
ITHACA AND LONDON

First published 2024 by Cornell University Press

Library of Congress Cataloging-in-Publication Data

Names: Colle, Royal D., editor. | Michelsen, Heike, editor. | Engst, Elaine D., editor. | Earle, Corey Ryan, 1984- editor.
Title: Beyond borders : exploring the history of Cornell's global dimensions / edited by Royal D. Colle, Heike Michelsen, Elaine D. Engst, Corey Ryan Earle.
Description: Ithaca : Published in association with Cornell University Press, 2024. | Includes bibliographical references and index. | Contents: Teaching, Research, and Outreach—Students and Alumni.
Identifiers: LCCN 2023050928 (print) | LCCN 2023050929 (ebook) | ISBN 9781501776991 (cloth) | ISBN 9781501777004 (paperback) | ISBN 9781501777011 (epub) | ISBN 9781501777028 (pdf)
Subjects: LCSH: Cornell University—History. | Cornell University—Influence—History. | Cornell University—Public services—History. | Foreign study. | International education. | Transnational education. | Education and globalization. | Education, Higher—International cooperation. | Education, Higher—Aims and objectives—New York (State)—Ithaca.
Classification: LCC LD1368 .B49 2024 (print) | LCC LD1368 (ebook) | DDC 378.747/71—dc23/eng/20231106
LC record available at https://lccn.loc.gov/2023050928
LC ebook record available at https://lccn.loc.gov/2023050929

CONTENTS

PREFACE

Royal D. Colle

Many people, events, and institutional developments have contributed to Cornell's global dimensions. The stories and accomplishments have been many, but existing books on Cornell's history have given little attention to the significant international involvements of Cornell and Cornellians here and abroad. The importance of creating this book became especially evident from testimony of David J. Skorton, Cornell's twelfth president, in July 2007 before the US House of Representatives Committee on Science and Technology.

Skorton emphasized the value of globalization in higher education, calling international education and research "among our country's most effective diplomatic assets." He remarked: "Cornell's international programs involve all of our colleges and professional schools and nearly every program on campus. Most visibly—and perhaps of greatest interest to the committee—we opened a branch campus of our medical school in Doha, Qatar, in 2001. We offer a joint degree program in Singapore (hospitality) and dual degree programs in China (Asian studies and political science) and India (agriculture). We operate our own study abroad programs in France, Rome, Tanzania, Nepal, Berlin, and Tokyo. About five hundred Cornell students each year enroll in a Cornell study abroad program or at an international university, with assistance from Cornell Abroad, for a semester or a year."[1]

In 2004, recognizing the importance of Cornell's vast experience in international affairs, the Cornell Academics and Professors Emeriti (CAPE) organization launched an effort to document this part of the university's heritage. We began with oral history interviews and discussions, with the audio and video files titled "The International History of Cornell University" and stored in the Cornell University Library's digital repository, eCommons. There, you now can hear such notables as Milton Esman, Norman Uphoff, Randy Barker, John Mellor, David Thurston, and Ronnie Coffman, as well as read more about Cornell's international history.[2]

CAPE's executive council took on the challenge of producing a book on the subject and formed an editorial committee. That committee recognized the enormity of the task of telling Cornell's vast international story. The publication's editors needed to be selective in choosing content in order to avoid producing an encyclopedic work. We reached out to the CAPE and Cornell international community for recommendations of topics and authors and received an outstanding response. This book reflects these results: a collection of fifty-eight short vignettes written by a wide array of Cornellians, many of whom themselves have been part of the university's international history.

We have drawn cases from the university's earliest days up through the beginning of the twenty-first century. They examine the teaching and research programs, the international development projects and programs, the contributions of library and museum collections, and the experiences of students and faculty. The vignettes introduce some of the people involved in these activities and explore the institutional framework that fostered Cornell's global dimensions. They highlight the diversity, accomplishments, and impact of many remarkable and pioneering activities both on campus and abroad. The intent was to produce a readable, popular work that would entertain and inform.

The vignettes are loosely arranged as chapters in two major sections. Part I contains vignettes focused on the teaching, research, and outreach fostered by the university and its colleges. Vignettes in part II highlight alumni and facets of the student experience.

Each vignette is a showcase of how the international dimensions of the university have contributed to Ezra Cornell's goal "to do the greatest good." Whether by educating generations of global citizens; attracting the best international students, professionals, and scholars; producing innovative research and knowledge; or building institutional capacities and forging international mutually beneficial relationships around the world, Cornellians are committed to making the world better for future generations.

In the pages ahead, you can read about Cornell students, faculty, and scholars who have made an impact beyond our borders, individuals from abroad who have contributed to the university's extraordinary global academic and intellectual life, and research and interventions that have made a difference in the world.

Notes

1. *The Globalization of R&D and Innovation, Parts I–IV: Hearings before the Committee on Science and Technology, U.S. House of Representatives, One Hundred Tenth Congress, First Session, July 26, 2007* (Washington, DC: Government Printing Office, 2008), https://www.govinfo.gov/content/pkg/CHRG-110hhrg35857/html/CHRG-110hhrg35857.htm.

2. "The International History of Cornell University," eCommons, Cornell University Library, accessed September 20, 2023, https://ecommons.cornell.edu/handle/1813/2818.

ACKNOWLEDGMENTS

I would like to acknowledge support received for this project from its early stages. Walter Cohen, who chaired Cornell University's International Studies Committee, and Ronnie Coffman, as director of International Programs in the College of Agriculture and Life Sciences, contributed funds. Robert Cooke, administering a grant from Atlantic Philanthropies, pushed us into the modern publishing age by suggesting and giving support to the idea of producing digital material that could be distributed throughout the world. The Cornell Academics and Professors Emeriti (CAPE) executive council has been patient and supportive over the many years that the project has progressed.

Developing this book, attracting authors, and editing contributions were activities accomplished by talented and dedicated Cornellians who joined the book's editorial team. They are Heike Michelsen, former director of programming, Mario Einaudi Center for International Studies; Elaine Engst, the Dr. Peter J. Thaler '56 Cornell University Archivist Emerita; and Corey Ryan Earle, Cornell historian and lecturer. All also served as authors of vignettes.

The editorial team is especially grateful to the many authors who contributed vignettes and cheerfully submitted to the editorial process, and to Jeff MacCorkle for his support. We also appreciate the cooperation of the Mario Einaudi Center for International Studies, its units, and its programs. We are also grateful to the Cornell University Library's Division of Rare and Manuscript Collections and to Cornell University Photography for providing many of the photographs that enhance this book.

Royal D. Colle
International Professor Emeritus

INTRODUCTION

The History of Cornell's Global Dimensions

Elaine D. Engst and Carol Kammen

The Beginnings: The Nineteenth Century

The Founding

From its very beginnings, Cornell has looked both inward and outward. Its founders, Ezra Cornell and Andrew Dickson White, envisioned a new kind of institution, startling at the time for its robust faculty, extensive range of courses offered, and diverse student body. This was achieved despite its newness and its rural and rather isolated setting. White's ideas stemmed from his own experiences. After graduating from Yale, he traveled and studied in England, France, Germany, and Russia. He was excited by the ideas flowering in Paris and Berlin, in Oxford and Cambridge, where some disciplines and some professors had broken from the pattern of class recitations and "given knowledge" to deliver lively lectures based on research in the plentiful source materials in European archives and libraries. This was a new sort of education that tested the accepted truths of the past; it was engaging, it was based on scientific method, and it challenged and expanded what was known. Evidence of White's broad vision is apparent in Cornell's faculty, its curriculum, its students from abroad, the ways that the university provided opportunities for students to study other cultures, and its library and museum collections.

As president of Cornell, White traveled to Europe in 1868 to seek professors for the new university. He hired James Law, a young veterinary professor from Edinburgh, and Goldwin Smith, an eminent Oxford professor of history, who later contributed his personal library to Cornell. In the university's second year, George Behringer and Frederick L. O. Roehrig, both Germans, came to Ithaca as language instructors. Other faculty from abroad followed. The nonresident faculty, assembled by White to enliven the university, also included European lecturers, some more successful than others. In addition to staff, even some of the crews erecting university buildings included laborers from Great Britain, in particular masons, carpenters, and other skilled workers. Cornell has continued to seek and welcome faculty from across the globe.

White continued his international involvements and travel while president. He led the US Commission of Inquiry for the annexation of San Domingo in 1871 and was appointed to the US commission charged with solving Venezuela's boundary disputes in 1895–1896. Taking a leave from the university presidency from 1879 to 1881, White served as US minister to Germany, and after his resignation as Cornell's president, he became US minister to Russia, serving from 1893 to 1894, and US ambassador to Germany from 1897 to 1902. In 1899, he became president of the American delegation to the peace conference in The Hague, which developed international treaties relating to laws of war and war crimes.

Curriculum and Extracurricular Activities

Cornell's early curriculum also represented an international dimension. The early course offerings included modern history and political science. The standard fare at most colleges and universities was to offer Greek and Latin, and sometimes Hebrew for divinity students. Those ancient languages were offered at Cornell, but in addition the curriculum included modern French, German, Swedish, Icelandic, and Persian—offered by Willard Fiske. T. F. Crane offered classes in German, and then in French, Spanish, and Italian. Roehrig, a linguist thought to know twenty-three to twenty-five languages, taught French, which he was hired to teach, adding to that Turkish and Tartar languages, Chinese, Japanese, Malayan, "Mantchoo" (the language of Manchuria), Turanian (the language of Turkestan), and Sanskrit. Roehrig became the professor of living Asiatic languages and assistant professor of French. In 1874, Felix Adler, a nonresident professor, taught Hebrew along with biblical studies. Students expressed pleasure in 1881 when modern French was offered in addition to classical French, and in 1883 when the course was expanded to include modern French literature. This was soon true for German as well. By 1883, students commented in the *Cornell Era* that there was "not a college that can boast better advantages for the study of so many tongues."[1]

There were many opportunities on campus outside the classroom to interest and inform students about the world beyond, including lectures by faculty and visiting speakers. Essays by students studying or traveling abroad appeared in the *Era*, lending an international perspective to that student publication. An *Era* article, contributed by Theodore Stanton (class of 1876 and son of Henry and Elizabeth Cady Stanton), reported that the American University Dinner Club had been founded in Paris in 1897 to enable graduates of American universities and French educators to meet, dine, and get to know each other. Another account reported on an 1898 dinner for Cornell alumni in Puerto Rico that was to "go down in history as a unique pioneer event."[2]

Study Abroad

Many other influences on campus promoted a broad view of the world and the ways that a student could learn in places beyond Ithaca. Charles Hartt, professor of geology, took students on expeditions to Brazil in the 1870s, and after his death some of those students continued his work there. In the 1890s, students accompanied Professor Ralph Tarr on expeditions to Greenland and Alaska. In 1882, Cornell participated in the founding of the American School of Classic Studies in Athens, and in 1894, the American Academy in Rome gave Cornell students with an interest in the classical world opportunities to go abroad for study.

Cornell students went off to investigate Indian ruins in the Amazon, while others explored Peru. In 1877, Cornell sent students on for graduate study in Oxford, Paris, Leipzig, Heidelberg, Halle, Berlin, Brussels, and Vienna, while other students were traveling in France, Italy, and Spain. Women students found it easier to enter graduate study in Europe, and many headed to German and Swiss universities when they found American institutions closed to them. From 1888 on, the number of students from Cornell going abroad increased. That year, the university trustees gave G. A. Ruyter, a "fellow-elect" in modern languages, permission to spend a year in France and Germany, and it also approved a leave to "study in Europe" for Professor Liberty Hyde Bailey.

International Students

Surprisingly, considering the newness of Cornell University and its location, there were international students on campus from its first year, from England, Russia, Bulgaria, and Canada. Writing in his diary at the end of January 1870, Ezra Cornell noted that there were students from eleven foreign countries. Students from the Caribbean, including students of color, came as early as 1869 when William Bowler of Haiti attended. Brazilian students came in the 1870s, through the efforts of Charles Hartt. Cornell's first Japanese student, Kanaye Nagasawa, studied natural history in 1870; the first Japanese graduate, Ryokichi Yatabe, received his degree in 1876.

During Cornell's first forty years, just under seven hundred international students—graduate and undergraduate—earned university degrees. The largest number came from Canada, then Mexico, Brazil, the Philippines, China, Argentina, Puerto Rico, England, India, Peru, Japan, and Russia. In 1894, Jacob Gould Schurman reported that, looking at the range of places from which Cornell students came, compared with other institutions, Cornell was the "most cosmopolitan of American universities."[3]

Libraries, Museums, and Other Collections

On his trip to Europe in 1868, White bought book collections for the library, works of art, and scientific models and instruments to enrich student life and learning. The university received gifts from abroad to create and enhance library and museum collections. White and Willard Fiske, the first university librarian, continued to acquire major scholarly collections, including the Franz Bopp philological library and the Zarncke library of German literature. With the opening of the university library building in 1891, White presented his historical library, including his collections on European witchcraft, the Protestant Reformation, and the French Revolution. Fiske contributed his book collections on Iceland, Dante, Petrarch, and the Swiss language of Rhaeto-Romanic.

White's European purchases included "the Rau models of plows from Hohenheim; the Brendel plant models from Breslau; the models of machine movements from London, Darmstadt, and Berlin; the plastic models of Auzoux from Paris; and other apparatus and instruments from all parts of Europe."[4] Ezra Cornell purchased artifacts and seashells from Central America and the Sandwich Islands (Hawaii) collected by Wesley Newcomb, who served as their curator. Professor William M. Gabb sent fossils from San Domingo. The Brazilian Centennial Commission presented a set of South American ornamental woods. Charles Hartt provided archaeological items that he collected from the Amazon region. In 1884, the American Consul in Cairo donated the mummy of Penpi, a scribe of Thebes from the Third Intermediate Period (ca. 828–625 BCE), along with his sarcophagus. McGraw Hall housed a university museum, with the north wing devoted to zoology and the south wing to geology and geography.

The Twentieth Century and Beyond

International Involvement

Cornell increased its international involvement in the twentieth century. Schurman, who became Cornell's third president in 1892, chaired the US First Philippine Commission in 1899 and served as US minister to Greece and Montenegro during the Balkan Wars in 1912 and 1913. After his long Cornell presidency, which ended in 1920, Schurman became the US minister to China (1921–1925), and then US ambassador to Germany (1925–1930).

International Cornellians served their own countries: Mario García Menocal (class of 1888) as the third president of Cuba (1913–1921); Alfred Sao-ke Sze (class of 1901, MA 1902) and Hu Shih (class of 1914) as ambassadors from China to the United States; M. C. Chakrabandhu (MS 1941) as the director-general of the Department of Agriculture in Siam, president of Kasetsart University, and cofounder of the International Rice Research Institute; Jamshid Amouzegar (class of 1945, PhD 1951) as prime minister of Iran (1977–1978); Lee Teng-hui (PhD 1968) as president of Taiwan (1988–2000); Vaclav Klaus (postgraduate study in 1969) as prime minister of the Czech Republic (1993–1998); and Tsai Ing-wen (LLM 1980) as president of Taiwan (elected in 2016), to name just a few.

During World War I, Cornell provided more commissioned officers to the war effort than any other university, and Cornellians assisted in medical care in France as doctors, nurses, and ambulance drivers. Martha Van Rensselaer and Flora Rose, professors in the School of Home Economics, assisted in reconstruction efforts in Belgium after the war.

While some students had participated in missionary programs in the nineteenth century, in 1922, the Cornell-in-China Club formed "to promote the mutual friendly relations of China and America, in particular of Chinese and American students at Cornell, and to establish and foster a Cornell educational enterprise in China."[5] Cornell-in-China sponsored lectures and fundraising events. The club was instrumental in helping the university to establish an extension program in China. Cornell faculty and graduates joined the Plant Improvement Project at the University of Nanking, Cornell's first major international effort.

The university reacted to the crisis of World War II with a major military presence on campus. The Army Specialized Training Program trained over 3,500 enlisted service men and taught area and language studies, including Russian, German, Italian, Czech, and Chinese. The V-12 Navy College Training Program produced officers for both the US Navy and Marine Corps. The College of Medicine sponsored the army's General Hospital No. 9 in the South Pacific.

More international programs began in 1947 in the wake of the Marshall Plan. Cornell anthropologists worked in Peru, Thailand, and India as part of an experiment in applied anthropology. The College of Agriculture led a major assistance project to rebuild the University of the Philippines. Cornell faculty and staff provided expertise to help reorganize the University of Liberia, and Cornell Law School faculty assisted in the codification of Liberian laws. In 1962, Cornell began a partnership with the newly created Peace Corps. In the 1950s, Thomas Mackesey, professor of city planning and dean of the College of Architecture from 1950 to 1960, participated in the team advising the Brazilian government on the selection of a site for the new national capital of Brasilia, and city planning students helped in the design work. More recently the College of Engineering established the Cornell-Bologna Center for Vehicle Intelligence, a collaboration with the University of Bologna in Italy.

Since 2004, the Office of the Vice Provost for International Affairs has led Cornell's global engagement, overseeing and managing Cornell's global partnerships and supporting and facilitating global activities for colleges, faculty, staff, and students. Following President David Skorton's 2012 white paper "Bringing

Cornell to the World and the World to Cornell," the office spearheaded the Global Cornell initiative.[6]

Curriculum and Extracurricular Activities

Through the twentieth century, the curriculum also diversified. The College of Arts and Sciences began programs focusing on international subjects in many areas. The creation of the Department of Chinese Studies in 1944, later broadened to Far Eastern Studies, strengthened ties to Asia. During World War II, Cornell began a controversial course in contemporary Russian civilization and an intensive Russian language course, in cooperation with the Army Specialized Training Program. A grant from the Rockefeller Foundation led to the founding of the Southeast Asia Program in 1951. A South Asia program began in the 1950s. In 1962, the Department of Asian Studies in the College of Arts and Sciences began coordinating all teaching and research in East Asia, Southeast Asia, and South Asia.

The Latin American Studies Program began in 1961 as an interdisciplinary program. In 1961, the area programs were consolidated under the Center for International Studies, now the Mario Einaudi Center for International Studies, which currently includes the East Asia Program, the Southeast Asia Program, the South Asia Program, the Latin American and Caribbean Studies Program, the Institute for European Studies, the Institute for African Development, the Comparative Muslim Societies Program, and the Reppy Institute for Peace and Conflict Studies.

Language studies continued to grow; currently over fifty languages are offered through eight departments or programs in the College of Arts and Sciences, including Africana Studies, Asian Studies, Classics, Comparative Literature, German Studies, Linguistics, Near Eastern Studies, and Romance Studies. The Language House, a "living-learning community" founded in 1984, helps students achieve fluency in languages including Arabic, French, German, Japanese, Mandarin, and Spanish.

Liberty Hyde Bailey, dean of the College of Agriculture, also had an international perspective, and in 1960 Dean Charles E. Palm added international work to the college's functions of teaching, research, and extension. The 1960s saw the creation of a formal program, the International Agricultural Development Program (later International Programs of the College of Agriculture and Life Sciences). In 1990, Cornell established the International Institute for Food, Agriculture and Development. The new Department of Global Development now integrates many international programs. The Division of Nutritional Sciences, which includes programs in the College of Agriculture and Life Sciences and the College of Human Ecology, now has the Global and Public Health Science Program.

In the early years, the curriculum of the College of Architecture was heavily influenced by its early professors who studied at the French École des Beaux-Arts. Cornell students continued to study at the American Academy in Rome, and several won the distinguished Prix de Rome. The college created the Cornell in Rome program in the early 1980s.

In the 1960s, the School of Hotel Administration began an executive education program that brought students from overseas to take summer session courses. Other Hotel School programs bring industry leaders from across the globe and provide custom-designed programs for corporate clients around the world.

Faculty in the College of Human Ecology (then Home Economics) began to engage in international cooperative teaching and research in the 1920s. After World War II, there were extensive projects in Belgium, Japan, the Philippines, Thailand, Ghana, and Liberia. In 1947, the Voice of America produced a film featuring the College of Home Economics as a model for higher education of women, and women educators from around the world continued to visit.

From its beginnings in 1945, the School of Industrial and Labor Relations has played a key role in developing the field of international and comparative labor relations, establishing the International Institute of Industrial and Labor Relations in 1951 and the Department of International and Comparative Labor in the 1990s.

The Law School has focused on international and comparative law since its founding in 1887, with programs that promote justice on a global scale. It became the first American law school to establish a special degree program in international and comparative law, and developed the International Legal Studies Program in the 1990s. Graduate programs allow international students to pursue advanced work, and visiting scholars, along with specific research institutes, centers, and programs, further enhance the international educational environment.

The College of Veterinary Medicine began its international involvement in the 1930s, and today many faculty work internationally. The Department of Population Medicine and Diagnostic Sciences, with its Wildlife Health and Health Policy Group, engages with national, international, and local governments, as well as nongovernmental partners. Public and Ecosystem Health brings together public health professionals, biophysical and social scientists, and veterinarians. A variety of student programs enhance this presence.

Many of the colleges and schools at Cornell have jointly developed international programs with institutions across the globe. The College of Engineering has a variety of exchange programs, including with the Hong Kong University of Science and Technology, the University of Cantabria and the University of Comillas in Spain, the Technical University of Denmark, and the Technion-Israel Institute of Technology in Israel. The Hotel School hosts an international dual-degree graduate program with the Guanghua School of Management at Peking

University in Shanghai. The ILR School Exchange Programs include partnerships with University College Dublin, the Bocconi Universitat Rovira I Virgili, Queen Mary University of London, the University of Warwick, and Cardiff University. The Johnson Graduate School of Management offers a dual-degree MBA program with Tsinghua University and an Emerging Markets Institute. The Law School partners with some twenty-five law schools on every continent. The College of Veterinary Medicine collaborates with the City University of Hong Kong, the Tata Trust Animal Medical Center in Mumbai, and Obihiro University in Japan.

Weill Cornell Medicine maintains relationships with more than twenty international partners. When Weill Cornell Medicine–Qatar was established in 2001 by Cornell University in partnership with the Qatar Foundation for Education, Science and Community Development, Cornell became the first American university to operate an American medical school outside the country. Other key initiatives include the Haitian Study Group on Kaposi's Sarcoma and Opportunistic Infections Centers in Haiti for HIV/AIDS and tuberculosis; the Open Medical Institute in Salzburg, Austria, to bring medical knowledge to physicians from the former Eastern bloc countries and other "countries in transition"; the Weill Cornell Bugando Program to strengthen the Weill School of Medicine in Tanzania; and the Weill Cornell Medicine Office of International Medical Student Education to oversee the global health education programs. All are now directed by Weill's Office of International Affairs.

In 2011, Cornell and the Technion-Israel Institute of Technology won a New York City competition to build an applied sciences graduate campus on Roosevelt Island. The Jacobs Technion-Cornell Institute at Cornell Tech now offers dual master's degrees in connective media, health tech, and urban tech, along with other programs.

International Students

After 1900, international students came to Cornell in increasing numbers. Alfred Sao-ke Sze, the first Chinese student, graduated in 1901. In 1906, the university trustees authorized six scholarships a year for Chinese students. In 1908, funds authorized by US president Theodore Roosevelt from the Boxer Indemnity, imposed on China after the Boxer Rebellion of 1900, subsidized these scholarships, and many Chinese students came to Cornell. Six Indian students entered the College of Agriculture in 1905, and considerable numbers followed.

The Cosmopolitan Club, founded in 1904, among the first international student organizations in the United States, gave many international students a home at Cornell until 1958 and provided an extensive program of dinners and lectures to which many students, international and American, flocked. In 1970, Cornell founded the International Living Center (now the Holland International Living

Center) to provide housing for international students and American students interested in cross-cultural exchange.

In 1936, Cornell created the nation's first university office for international students, led by Donald Kerr. Now known as International Services in the Office of Global Learning, it also includes Experience Cornell, providing opportunities for students to study, work, and do research in countries across the world, as well as promoting cross-cultural connections on campus and beyond.

Currently, international students compose 25 percent of the Cornell student body. Nearly 150 student organizations have an international flavor and offer international students a chance to network with other students from "home," and to share their cultural heritage with the rest of Cornell and the larger Ithaca community.

Libraries, Museums, and Other Collections

Cornell's library and museum collections continued to grow. Early Chinese students gave books to the library. William Elliot Griffis, a local minister, donated his collection of more than two thousand Japanese-language books, and alumnus Charles Wason bequeathed his library on China and the Chinese. In 1953, the Echols Collection on Southeast Asia was established when Cornell agreed to acquire, if possible, at least one copy of every publication of research value produced in Southeast Asia. The collection is now the premier collection on Southeast Asia in the world. The library holds collections in English literature, including the Wordsworth Collection, considered the best in the world outside of Dove Cottage in England, as well as the Burgunder Shaw Collection, one of the largest collections relating to George Bernard Shaw. Distinguished French holdings were increased when Arthur Dean (class of 1921 and university trustee) purchased the Lafayette Collection, the largest outside Paris, for the library. The Noyes family gave the Lavoisier Collection, the largest collection outside France on chemist Antoine-Laurent Lavoisier (1743–1794), commonly considered to be the founder of modern chemistry.

Cornell's first art museum was established in 1953 in the Andrew Dickson White House and included works from Europe and Asia. Currently, the European collections of the Johnson Museum of Art include works from ancient Greece and Rome to the Middle Ages and the Renaissance, as well as modern painting, sculpture, and photography. The museum particularly specializes in Asian art, but it also holds works from Africa and pre-Columbian America.

Other collections on campus also represent international diversity. Over the years, faculty and others have donated Egyptian, Greek, and Roman artifacts; anthropological items from Zambia; Australian aboriginal pieces; items from the Philippines; and pre-Columbian Andean pottery and textiles to the

Anthropology Collection. The College of Home Economics (now Human Ecology) began the Textile Collection in 1916 when Professor Beulah Blackmore took a world trip to acquire examples of native dress and textiles to illustrate her lectures. Currently, the Cornell Fashion + Textile Collection includes nearly nine thousand items of apparel, accessories, and flat textiles from around the world. The Laboratory of Ornithology houses the Macaulay Library, which includes audio recordings of about three-quarters of the world's bird species, and the Cornell University Museum of Vertebrates, with over 1.5 million specimens of birds, fish, reptiles, and mammals from around the world. The Insect Collection in Comstock Hall, with about seven million specimens dating back to the earliest years of the university, includes specimens from South America, Africa, and Asia to provide a worldwide view of insect diversity. The Bailey Hortorium houses one of the two largest and most representative palm collections in the world, from all areas of the tropics, as well as holdings of other plant specimens from Europe, Asia, New Caledonia, Australia, and New Zealand.

Cornell's international involvements have continued to grow and expand. Through programs on campus and abroad, through students and scholars from across the globe, and through vast and diverse collections, Cornell aims to achieve its mission "to educate the next generation of global citizens . . . and . . . to enhance the lives and livelihoods of students, the people of New York and others around the world."[7] The vignettes presented in this book tells the history of some of those initiatives.

Notes

1. *Cornell Era* 16, no. 6 (October 26, 1883): 51.

2. *Cornell Era* 31, no. 3 (October 8, 1898): 25–26.

3. *Report of the President of Cornell University, 1893–94* (Ithaca, NY: Cornell University, 1894), 64–65.

4. Andrew Dickson White, *Autobiography of Andrew Dickson White* (New York: Century, 1914), 1:338–339.

5. "China and Service," *Cornell Daily Sun*, April 25, 1922.

6. David J. Skorton, "Bringing Cornell to the World and the World to Cornell," presidential white paper, March 2, 2012, https://president.cornell.edu/_files/archives/skorton/20120302-international-studies-engagement-white-paper.pdf.

7. "University Mission," Cornell University, accessed September 20, 2023, https://www.cornell.edu/about/mission.cfm.

PART I

TEACHING, RESEARCH, AND OUTREACH

1. A PIONEERING INTERNATIONAL PROGRAM

The Cornell-Nanking Story

Royal D. Colle

"The first notable example of international technical cooperation in agriculture was the Plant Improvement project carried on from 1924 to 1931 by Cornell and the University of Nanking," said William I. Myers, dean of the College of Agriculture, in 1962 while addressing the first century of agriculture at Cornell. The impact went beyond China. He continued: "The success of the Cornell-Nanking project was one of the basic reasons for the initiation of a more comprehensive program of cooperation between American colleges and their overseas counterparts as an important part of the [USA Point Four] technical aid program." The accomplishments of the Cornell and Nanking programs are especially notable because of the disruptions and wars in China at the time. In 1963, Cornell professor Harry Houser Love and University of Nanking dean John Henry Reisner compiled a report on the project, *The Cornell-Nanking Story: The First International Technical Cooperation Program in Agriculture by Cornell University*, which provided much of the information presented here.[1]

The University of Nanking was established in 1910 in Nanking (now Nanjing), China, by the union of three small Protestant missionary colleges. An agriculture department formed in 1914, and farm and agricultural experiment stations, reforestation projects, and the development of improved crops became important activities of the university.

Famines were a recurring problem in the area, and in 1920, US president Woodrow Wilson set up the Committee of One Hundred for China Famine Relief. When relief work ended sooner than expected, the dean of the College of Agriculture and Forestry at Nanking submitted a proposal to use the remaining $1,000,000 to prevent future famines through crop improvement projects. Cornell president Livingston Farrand was a member of the American Committee for the China Famine Fund. In 1923, the University of Nanking received a multiyear grant of $675,000.

Figure 1.1 Rod rows of wheat hanging in storage shed, Tai Ping Men Farm, Nanking. (H. H. Love and John H. Reisner, *The Cornell-Nanking Story*, New York State College of Agriculture, 1963, provided by Division of Rare and Manuscript Collections, Cornell University Library)

The Cornell-Nanking story began with a letter from Reisner to Love, dated February 24, 1924: "We are looking for a Plant Breeder—a man who is interested in the practical applications of the principles of plant breeding and in getting practical results as quickly as possible. . . . We would like to have a man like you." Reisner noted that his university had already made progress in the improvement of wheat, cotton, and corn but that they wanted "a man who had specialized in the small grains. . . . Assistants are available and one man is able to make his time go a very long way by careful and wise use of them."[2]

A five-year program was approved in 1924 by the two universities, with additional money from the Rockefeller-funded International Education Board, to organize and conduct a comprehensive crop improvement program involving the principal food crops of the famine areas of central and northern China and to train people in the principles, methods, applications, and organization of crop improvement. Each year, for a minimum period of five years, Cornell agreed that a professor from Cornell's Department of Plant Breeding would be associated with the Agronomy Department of Nanking's College of Agriculture and Forestry to help develop their plant breeding work. The University of Nanking, with assistance from the China Famine Fund committee, would cover travel and living expenses and a share of work at cooperative stations (eventually fourteen stations

Figure 1.2 Promising wheat strains in the plots grown at the University Farm, Nanking. (H. H. Love and John H. Reisner, *The Cornell-Nanking Story*, New York State College of Agriculture, 1963, provided by Division of Rare and Manuscript Collections, Cornell University Library)

were associated with the program). The International Education Board provided salaries for Cornell faculty on leave without pay from the university.[3]

The key Cornell professors who went to China during the five-year project were Love (1925, 1929), Clyde Hadley Myers (1926, 1931), and Roy Glen Wiggins (1927, 1930). They lectured at Nanking and worked with students, staff, and faculty there and in the field, stressing crop improvement methods in their teaching and research.[4] The project would concentrate on selecting promising existing varieties through field tests, rather than on hybridization research. Wheat improvement provided the most spectacular results, with a variety called Nanking 2905 becoming the best.[5]

In their report, Love and Reisner discussed some of the challenges of their extension work. They were careful not to appear condescending to the Chinese farmers and concluded that, when considering new methods or seed varieties, "[the Chinese farmer] is not any more conservative by nature than were the farmers of the United States 50–60 years ago. The chief difference is one of economy." Since the average size of Chinese farms was about three to five acres, and frequently less than an acre, farmers were reluctant to try something new, "for if no good result was obtained he would have less food than would have been the case if he had used all his land for his own crops." American farmers, who had larger farms, could afford to experiment without affecting their income. "When the Chinese farmer could see the experiment demonstrated in his neighborhood then he was eager to have it on his own farm."[6]

However, vital as crop improvement was as a focus and goal, the training of people was seen as the most important element in the entire program. By the end of the formal cooperation, it was estimated that well over 125 men who had little or no experience had been trained to the point where they were independently able to conduct crop improvement experiments. When it ended in 1931, the Cornell-Nanking program could boast the training of students, faculty, and other professionals, many of whom "became associated with the remarkable advances in agriculture and agricultural education that took place in China after 1931."[7]

Institutes became a key part of the Cornell-Nanking program. Cornell professor Norman Scott, speaking at the ninetieth anniversary celebration of Nanjing Agricultural University in 2014, observed that the first Summer Institute of Crop Improvement was held at Nanking in the summer of 1926, followed by summer institutes in 1929, 1930, and the last in 1931. Led by Cornell professors, the students, experiment station staff, and Nanking faculty participated in courses on topics such as genetics, plant breeding, plant pathology, and biological statistics.[8]

Some of the Chinese students continued their education in crop improvement on the Cornell campus, especially the extraordinary T. H. Shen (Shen Zonghan), probably China's preeminent agronomist. He interrupted his graduate work at Cornell to accompany Clyde Myers to Nanking in 1926 but completed his PhD in plant breeding in 1928, the first Chinese student to do so. Shen returned to China as professor of plant breeding at Nanking, teaching and continuing his own plant breeding research. He helped found the National Agricultural Research Bureau with the help of Cornellians Love, Myers, and John Lossing Buck, who would marry noted author and Cornellian Pearl S. Buck. Shen went to Taiwan in 1949, where he continued his agricultural work and became a leader in the Sino-American Joint Commission on Rural Reconstruction.[9]

Research was also an important part of the Cornell-Nanking story. Professor Scott, in his ninetieth anniversary talk, reported, "Soon after arriving in China, Dr. Love and interested Chinese sought to encourage the development of a government plan research. The National Agricultural Research Board was established and based in Nanking for the purpose of developing research in all important phases of agriculture as rapidly as possible."[10]

The Cornell-Nanking story also shows that teaching can be learning. In their report, Love and Reisner recounted "the Wong barley story," which involved not only Chinese farmers but also New York State farmers and an adviser's (Love's) learning experience. When Love returned from China, he was asked "whether it was not a situation of all give and no return." He answered that it was not and that "he gained much from the new experiences, and especially from some new plant types." While in Nanking, he had observed "a large field of hybrid barley plants and was happily surprised to see some bearing their heads erect even when the plants were nearly ripe." At this time, barley varieties in the United States had a weak straw. He asked his Chinese colleague for a few seeds and was given four heads of winter barley. Back at Cornell, he found interest in developing winter barley varieties. While he was concerned that the climate in China was less severe than in New York State, he still planted the seeds in the garden of the Department of Plant Breeding. Two of the heads survived the winter and grew better than the others. "These were grown in other winters and finally the plants from one line did much better and this line was kept, the seed was multiplied further, and the variety named Wong. This new sort was grown by a number of farmers of New York and was the stiffest strawed type then available to United States growers. It yielded well compared with the other varieties then grown in New York." Love and Reisner concluded that "the result obtained from the Wong barley is definite proof that when staff members go from their institutions in the United States to some institution abroad it is not always 'a give, no take effort,' especially if the visiting staff member is a keen observer."[11]

Shen summarized the results of the Cornell-Nanking relationship:

> The most significant results of the Nanking-Cornell-International Education Board program for Crop Improvement in China were: (1) training a group of Chinese plant breeders for carrying on a national program of crop improvement; (2) developing better varieties of wheat, barley, rice, kaoliang, millet and soybeans showing increased yields from 10–20 percent more than native varieties; (3) stimulating the Chinese government to establish the national Agricultural Research Bureau of the Ministry of Industry in 1931 which made great improvements in agricultural production in China up to 1949 through scientific research and agricultural extension services. Dr. H.H. Love, of Cornell, served as Advisor to the Bureau in 1931–1934.[12]

The University of Nanking underwent many trials through 1950, including the surrounding battles of warlords, the destruction of its campus during the Sino-Japanese War, and its disruption with the nation's takeover by a Communist government. In 1952, the University of Nanking became the government-operated Nanjing Agricultural College, and in 1984 it became Nanjing Agricultural University. The success of the Nanking program would lead the Cornell University College of Agriculture to undertake the extensive program in cooperation with the College of Agriculture at the University of the Philippines at Los Baños after World War II and many other international projects.[13]

Notes

1. Harry Houser Love and John Henry Reisner, *The Cornell-Nanking Story: The First International Technical Cooperation Program in Agriculture by Cornell University* (New York: Internet-First University Press, 2012), iv, https://ecommons.cornell.edu/handle/1813/29080/.

2. Love and Reisner, 1.

3. The International Education Board was established in 1923 by John D. Rockefeller Jr. for the purpose of cooperating with foreign institutions and agencies in the conduct and promotion of education. Cornell College of Agriculture dean Albert R. Mann (BS 1904) took a leave of absence from Cornell to serve as the director of the board's agriculture program in Europe.

4. See Harry H. Love Papers, #21-8-890, Division of Rare and Manuscript Collections, Cornell University Library. Finding aid online at https://rmc.library.cornell.edu/EAD/htmldocs/RMA00890.html.

5. Randall E. Stross, *The Stubborn Earth: American Agriculturalists on Chinese Soil* (Berkeley: University of California Press, 1986), 156–157, https://publishing.cdlib.org/ucpressebooks/view?docId=ft2g5004m0.

6. Love and Reisner, *Cornell-Nanking Story*, 41.

7. Love and Reisner, 4.

8. Norman Scott, personal communication with author, referencing "Cornell-Nanjing: Past, Present and Future, 90th Anniversary Celebration, October 20, 2014." Scott was invited to speak as a representative of not only Cornell University but similar US and land-grant universities. His remarks were a part of the ninetieth anniversary celebration, which was attended by thousands assembled in an outdoor stadium.

9. Stross, *Stubborn Earth*, 188–199.

10. Scott, "Cornell-Nanjing: Past, Present and Future."

11. Love and Reisner, *Cornell-Nanking Story*, 58–59.

12. Love and Reisner, 60.

13. For more about Cornell's work in the Philippines, see chapter 17, Institution Building Abroad: Cornell in the Philippines.

2. A WORLD OF KNOWLEDGE FOR A WORLD OF GOOD

The Mario Einaudi Center for International Studies

Heike Michelsen

Collaborations that advance knowledge, advocacy, and thought leadership to inform global publics, as well as teaching and learning that open doors to new worlds, have been core commitments of the Mario Einaudi Center for International Studies for over sixty years. Whether on issues of migration, climate change, international relations, inequalities, cultural traditions, or nuclear disarmament, the center has been "Cornell's hub for campus engagement and global thinking and action."[1]

Mason Woods, a class of 2020 undergraduate, said, "There are numerous resources at the university to help you. . . . For me that was the Einaudi Center. A place to grow, both academically, professionally, and personally. No matter what part of the world you might be interested in, whether that be traveling there, whether that means studying it, whether it means just talking to academics who know more about it, the Einaudi Center has it for you."[2]

The Origins

The Center for International Studies came into existence upon the recommendation of the Cornell University Faculty Committee on International Affairs. A resolution calling for the creation of a center "to facilitate and encourage research and teaching activities dealing with International Affairs" was approved by the faculty council on May 3, 1961. On July 1, 1961, President Deane Malott appointed Mario Einaudi, then chair of the Department of Government, as its first director. John Mellor from the College of Agriculture and Steven Muller from the College of Arts and Sciences were appointed as associate directors along with an advisory committee of distinguished faculty and administrators.[3]

Cornell's Social Science Research Center and the Ford Foundation influenced the creation of the Center for International Studies. The Social Science Research Center had been established in 1949 to stimulate research activities in social

Figure 2.1 Professor Mario Einaudi, founding director of the Center for International Studies. (Photo by University Photography, provided by Division of Rare and Manuscript Collections, Cornell University Library)

science departments and colleges and to help faculty members explore arrangements for effective work. The center's agenda included an international dimension from the beginning, and its initiative to create an international professorship was chaired by professor of anthropology and Asian studies Lauriston Sharp. Although an external funding proposal was not successful, Sharp was asked to lead the newly formed Faculty Committee on International Affairs. Sharp's committee introduced a proposal to establish not only an international professorship but the Center for International Studies at Cornell.[4]

The Center for International Studies immediately assumed responsibility for a proposal to the Ford Foundation's program in support of non-Western studies, which aimed to make international studies a permanent part of university programs on a competitive footing with other academic studies. During the summer of 1961, many components were proposed by a wide range of Cornell groups and the center's executive committee discussed the scope of the proposal as well as the priorities for the university. The negotiations with the Ford Foundation resulted in a grant of $3.2 million awarded in March 1962, to be administered under the general supervision of the center. It included ten-year grants for the Southeast Asia Program and the China Program as well as five-year grants for the center itself in support of other non-Western programs and for the College of

Figure 2.2 Cornell International Fair 2017 on the terrace of Uris Hall, the home of the Einaudi Center. (Photo by Annika Tomson, provided by the Einaudi Center)

Agriculture's international programs. Grant funds were available for faculty positions, faculty research, travel, compensation for visiting scholars, research assistants, library expansion, fellowships, publications, and administrative support.[5]

Steven Muller, professor of government who became director of the center in spring 1962, concluded in the first annual report, "There can be no question that the international studies have found a significant and distinguished place in the permanent program of Cornell University. The Center is pledged to achieve maximum benefit for Cornell's commitment to this vast new area of undertakings."[6]

Six Decades of International Studies

1960s

In its first decade, the center helped to bring international studies at Cornell into full relief. The center inherited three programs—the Southeast Asia Program, the South Asia Program, and the China Program (now East Asia Program)—and soon established the Latin American Program (now Latin American and Caribbean

Studies Program). All of these programs, university-wide in their scope, were interdisciplinary associations of faculty members whose academic base was in the departments of the university's various colleges but whose interests and research intersected with one or more of these programs.

In 1962, Einaudi was appointed as Walter S. Carpenter, Jr. Professor of International and Comparative Politics, a chair newly endowed by a major contribution to the university's Centennial Campaign.[7] He assumed leadership of the center in 1966 and envisioned international studies going beyond courses in area studies and foreign languages to include academic efforts to deal with economic, social, and development problems around the world. During his tenure, he raised over $11 million to fund and endow international studies at Cornell. The university matched these grants and created three professorships of international studies, named for Aaron Binenkorb, John S. Knight, and Carl Marks.

By the end of the 1960s, the center was recognized nationally as the best-organized and most generously financed center of international studies. It served as an intermediary entity able to help bring together people interested in exploring questions that lie astride the normal disciplinary boundaries.[8]

1970s

Despite a difficult economic climate throughout the 1970s, the center developed a vision of academic innovation, particularly through interdisciplinary and comparative endeavors and increased student involvement. The center founded the Peace Studies Program (now the Judith Reppy Institute for Peace and Conflict Studies), the Western Societies Program (now the Institute for European Studies), the African Studies Program (now the Institute for African Development), and the Rural Development Committee. Several college-related international programs (in agriculture, law, planning, and nutrition) maintained loose relations with the center.

"These programs multiplied the participation of Cornell faculty in organized international studies," stated former Einaudi Center director Milton Esman, professor of government. "Its field studies and published works established Cornell as a major player in international rural development."[9]

The center's Rural Development Committee, for example, drew together scholars with an interest in adapting modern technology to benefit the rural poor in developing countries—small farm families, tenants and sharecroppers, agricultural laborers, rural women, and disadvantaged ethnic groups—who have been outside the mainstream of their nation's development. There had been a lot of interest in Cornell's research that stressed the importance of a close relationship between technology, government policies, and local participation for successful development. Chaired by Norman Uphoff, professor of government and international agriculture, the committee won a substantial grant from the United States Agency for International Development. According to Gilbert Levine, professor of biological and environmental engineering, who would serve as interim director of the center on several occasions, Cornell was way ahead of development thinking at that time and provided the opportunity to put theories into practice around the world.[10]

1980s

The 1980s saw a great expansion of the center's role and prominence. Several initiatives addressed the sponsorship of undergraduate activities during this decade. At the request of the university's board of trustees and the International Programs Committee of the Cornell University Council, in 1983 the center undertook the development of Cornell Abroad, the undergraduate study abroad program.[11] In 1984, the center inaugurated the Henry E. and Nancy Bartels World Affairs Fellowship, a prestigious public event involving a visit by eminent international public figures.[12] The center also developed its first cross-college undergraduate international relations minor, which continues to attract students across campus.

In addition, the US Department of Education began funding all of Cornell's five area studies programs simultaneously as Title VI National Resource Centers: East Asia, Latin America, South Asia, Southeast Asia, and the Institute for European Studies. These grants supported a wide range of activities and provided support for faculty and student research, the teaching of languages and area studies, programming, library and museum collections, and outreach. Through this designation, these programs could now offer government-funded Foreign Language and Area Studies fellowships.[13]

1990s

In 1991, the center was renamed in honor of its founding director, Mario Einaudi, in recognition of his influential leadership and engagement with the center until his retirement in 1972. During this time, the center played a greater role in national organizations and initiatives and became highly visible in international higher education in the United States. It integrated the management and coordination of international programs, the International Students and Scholars Office, and study abroad under an overall strategy and umbrella, and it assumed responsibility for the Fulbright Program.

Faculty engaged with the center's myriad programs and initiatives valued its role as a place that liberated faculty and students from both geographical and disciplinary silos. Its regional and topical diversity in terms of scholars, students, and resources allowed them to think in new ways. Ron Herring, Einaudi Center director during this time, stated that the center had facilitated some significant contributions. It not only "re-grooved a generation of researchers steeped in disciplinary practice but also expressed discoveries in ways comprehensible to public discourse, without becoming simplistic and trained a new generation of students with better interdisciplinary contacts, skills, and inclinations than their teachers."[14]

2000s

During the first decade of this century, the center went through several institutional changes, particularly the disaggregation of administrative responsibilities. Cornell Abroad and the International Students and Scholars Office were moved out of a reporting relationship with the center, as was its responsibility for international alumni affairs. In 2007, the Office of the Vice Provost for International Relations (now Office of the Vice Provost for International Affairs), created in 2004, resumed oversight of the center. At the same time, the center engaged in a series of initiatives to foster collaborations and share information across campus, such as a new international gateway website, which became the largest collection of links to international resources at the university at the time.

The center established the Comparative Muslim Societies Committee (now the Comparative Muslim Societies Program) in 2001 and supported new faculty initiatives such as the Global Health Program. The Einaudi Center director during this time, Nicolas van de Walle, started the Foreign Policy Initiative in 2004, expanding international affairs awareness and global competence on campus through a variety of speaker series, debates, and other events. He reasoned that "the events of 9/11 only underscored the importance for Americans to pay attention to the politics, history, and cultures of the rest of the world."[15] Finally, the center launched a postdoctoral fellowship program to attract outstanding junior scholars from around the world in the fields of foreign policy, security studies, and diplomatic history.

2010s

When celebrating its fiftieth anniversary in 2011, the center invited experts from across the country to discuss the future of international studies in American research universities. It also welcomed Cornell president David Skorton to present his vision of a global Cornell. Skorton's white paper titled "Bringing Cornell to the World and the World to Cornell" focused on the internationalization of Cornell's curriculum and opportunities to regain its global competence. Pledging $15 million over five years, he appointed a faculty task force to develop a series of recommendations to strengthen the university's international standing and improve its global standing among peer universities.[16]

The Global Cornell Initiative was launched in 2013, signaling a new era of internationalization at Cornell with profound influence on our teaching, research, and engagement. Fredrik Logevall, director of the Einaudi Center at that time, was appointed vice provost for international affairs to spearhead the initiative. The vice provost's office took responsibility to develop strategic leadership for global engagement and internationalization at Cornell. Strengthening the Einaudi Center and its international programs was a key priority. It provided additional support to faculty whose research and teaching were international in nature, offered professional development opportunities for faculty, and created meaningful international experiences for students. It also launched the international faculty fellowship program, providing three-year support to a total of twelve faculty from across campus.

Today

Over its sixty years of existence, the center has never ceased to be a faculty-driven organization that serves as Cornell's crossroads for research, teaching, and learning about the world. Its area studies and thematic programs are places where students, scholars, and practitioners come together to explore, exchange, debate, and expand their global understanding. Its research priorities and initiatives (currently identified as Democratic Threats and Resilience; Inequalities, Identities, and Justice; and Migrations) bring people together from across the university and around the globe, empowering and inspiring them not just to deepen their knowledge but to make positive change.

Today, over 350 faculty across Cornell have an active engagement with the center and its programs, and many more participate in hundreds of events organized throughout the year. The center supports the teaching of over fifty languages and offers eight academic minors, numerous seminars, and training opportunities. Annually, more than four hundred undergraduate and graduate students receive grants from the center for research, travel, language study, and internships.

Einaudi Center director Rachel Riedl stated, "The Einaudi Center is at the heart of Cornell's mission to do the greatest good—for the next generation of global citizens and for the world. Our innovative research, thought leadership, and global student opportunities are helping Cornell make a world of difference."[17]

Notes

1. "Mario Einaudi Center for International Studies," Cornell University, accessed March 17, 2023, https://einaudi.cornell.edu/discover.

2. Global Cornell, "Welcome to the Einaudi Center: For Students," August 30, 2021, YouTube video, 4:59, https://www.youtube.com/watch?v=s_E3N6FYdXA&list=PLrQWZABeqo_t-rOKIMqfz_ANVDP6_rKik&index=1.

3. Cornell University Center for International Studies, *First Annual Report*, July 31, 1962.

4. Larry Zuidema, "The Origin of the Mario Einaudi Center for International Studies" (unpublished manuscript, June 2, 2015).

5. Cornell University Center for International Studies, *First Annual Report*.

6. *First Annual Report*.

7. Cornell University Center for International Studies, *Second Annual Report*, July 31,1963.

8. Mario Einaudi Center for International Studies, "Reflections on the Past from Cornell Leaders in International Studies," prepared for the Einaudi Center 50th Anniversary Symposium on International Studies in the American Research University: The Path Ahead, November 14–15, 2011.

9. Mario Einaudi Center for International Studies, "Reflections on the Past."

10. Cornell University Center for International Studies, *The International Dimension*, August 1980.

11. For more about Cornell's study abroad programs, see chapter 49, Sending Students Overseas: The History of Cornell Abroad.

12. For more about the Bartels World Affairs Fellows, see chapter 12, The Bartels World Affairs Fellows: Bringing the Internationally Distinguished to Cornell.

13. For more about the Title VI grants, see chapter 9, Title VI Grants to Cornell: A Demonstration of Strength in International Studies.

14. Mario Einaudi Center for International Studies, "Reflections on the Past."

15. Mario Einaudi Center for International Studies, *Mario Einaudi Center for International Studies*, program brochure, November 2005.

16. David J. Skorton, "Bringing Cornell to the World and the World to Cornell," presidential white paper, March 2, 2012, https://president.cornell.edu/_files/archives/skorton/20120302-international-studies-engagement-white-paper.pdf.

17. Mario Einaudi Center for International Studies, *Cornell's Hub for Global Thinking and Action*, program brochure, 2022.

3. BUILDING THE FOUNDATIONS OF A CAMPUS-WIDE INTERDISCIPLINARY EAST ASIA PROGRAM

Tsu-Lin Mei

While relations between the United States and China may now be strained, Cornell has long had many constructive interactions in East Asia and particularly in China. These activities and events have invited the enthusiastic attention and analysis of countless scholars, resulting in the interdisciplinary teaching, research, extraordinary academic resources, and professional contacts that compose the East Asia Program.

In 1946, after teaching at Yenching University in Beijing for almost twenty years, Harold Shadick joined the Department of Far Eastern Studies at Cornell, teaching Chinese language and literature. He worked with Knight Biggerstaff, the department chair, to plan a center for Chinese studies in upstate New York. China and the Chinese language were then still regarded as exotic subjects, and only Harvard University had a center of Chinese studies. In 1950, Shadick founded the China Program and served as its director until 1966. During this time, with generous support from the Ford Foundation and the Rockefeller Foundation, he established Cornell as one of the major centers of Chinese studies in North America. In order to attract distinguished faculty to an isolated location like Ithaca, he worked with a succession of able curators to make the Cornell University Library's Wason Collection one of the five best Chinese collections in America at that time.[1] He also helped recruit such distinguished scholars as Liu Ta-chung and John Fei in Economics, William Skinner and Arthur Wolf in Anthropology, John Lewis in Government, and Nicholas Bodman in Linguistics. As a result, during his tenure as director of the China Program, Cornell became preeminent in the Chinese-related social science subjects.

From 1970 to 1972, David Mozingo from the Government Department served as director of the China Program. The next director, Martie Young from History of Art, made two major innovations. He invited Robert J. Smith in Japanese anthropology and Eleanor Jordan in Japanese language and linguistics to join the program, thus expanding the China Program to the China-Japan Program and eventually the East Asia Program.

Figure 3.1 Chunnuan Liu (*right*) and Jun Dai (*left*) of the New York Chinese Traditional Art Center perform a Beijing Opera combat scene from *Havoc in Heaven* in 2012. (Provided by East Asia Program)

While the Japan part of the China-Japan Program initially had only two professors and limited resources, beginning in the 1970s, additional scholars joined the Cornell faculty: T. J. Pempel (Japanese government), Karen Brazell (premodern Japanese literature), Brett de Bary (modern Japanese literature), David McCann (Korean and Japanese literature), John Whitman (Japanese linguistics), Victor Koschmann (modern Japanese history), Naoki Sakai (Japanese philosophy and intellectual history), and Ted Bestor (Japanese anthropology). Together with Smith and Jordan, Cornell's 1970s Japan program boasted ten tenured professors concurrently.

At the same time, the China part of the China-Japan Program added the following scholars: Tsu-Lin Mei (premodern Chinese literature and Chinese historical linguistics), Edward Gunn (modern Chinese literature), Charles Peterson (premodern Chinese history), Sherman Cochran (modern Chinese history), Vivienne Shue (government), John McCoy and James Huang (Chinese linguistics), Thomas Lyons (economics), Paul Steven Sangren (anthropology), Thomas J. Christensen (government), and Victor Nee (sociology).

From the 1980s onward, the China-Japan Program consisted of a community of scholars equally divided between China and Japan, and between modern and premodern eras.

Figure 3.2 Inaugural Wong Chai Lok Calligraphy Fellow Becky Wong Wai Ching, 2013. (Provided by East Asia Program)

As his second innovation, Martie Young initiated an ambitious and necessary program of fundraising. Shadick had put all the money from the Ford Foundation grant into growing the Wason Collection, leaving little for the day-to-day operation of the program, and now neither Ford nor Rockefeller was interested in supporting Chinese or Japanese studies. The most likely source of funding was Cornell's far-flung alumni in East Asia.

When I became the director of the China-Japan Program in 1977, I spent several summer and winter vacations traveling to Hong Kong, Singapore, Taiwan, and Honolulu, meeting Cornell alumni and asking for their help. During my first trip I had the good fortune of meeting Bob Miller (class of 1955, Hotel School, and cofounder of Duty-Free Shoppers) in Hong Kong. When Miller returned to Ithaca for the Cornell University Council annual meeting, he interacted with faculty of the East Asia Program. Karen Brazell, as director of the program, established an alumni advisory council for the program and asked him to join, thus ensuring yearly contact between Miller and the program. Throughout the years, Miller continued to be our steady friend and generous benefactor.

In Taiwan, I met alumnus Robert C. T. Lee (PhD 1962), then head of the Sino-American Joint Commission on Rural Reconstruction. Lee gave us a gift on behalf of Cornell alumni in Taiwan. Ed Gunn and Brazell also saw Lee in Taiwan, but our fundraising efforts could go no further. Eventually our Taiwan contact led to Lee Teng-hui, who also worked for the commission before coming to Cornell to get his PhD.

Lee Teng-hui received his doctorate in agricultural economics in 1968, studying with Daniel Sisler, Kenneth Robinson, and Liu Ta-chung. When he returned to Taiwan, Republic of China president Chiang Ching-kuo, the son of Chiang Kai-shek, promoted him as a Taiwan-born politician in order to deflect popular criticism about rule by mainlanders and to lend the regime legitimacy. Lee was appointed in 1972 to a ministerial portfolio. By 1978, he was mayor of Taipei and by 1984 Chiang's vice president. When Chiang died four years later, Lee assumed the presidency.

Cornell University president Frank Rhodes led a delegation of Cornell professors to visit East Asia (Taiwan, Japan, and Hong Kong) in November 1990. Since this was the year following the Tiananmen Square incident of June 4, 1989, the United States' relations to the People's Republic of China had taken a nosedive, but Lee Teng-hui's succession as president of the Republic of China made 1990 a good time to visit Taiwan.

The Cornell delegation consisted of Frank and Rosa Rhodes, vice president for alumni affairs and development Richard Ramin, vice president for research Norman Scott, and faculty members Greg Galvin, Alfred Kahn, Walter LaFeber, Randy Barker (who had driven to the Ithaca airport in the 1960s to first welcome Lee Teng-hui to Cornell), Brazell, Catheryn Obern from Alumni Affairs and Development, and me.

The Cornell delegation was in Taiwan for four days, from Tuesday, October 30, to Friday, November 2. On the first day, we visited National Taiwan University (NTU), where Rhodes and NTU president Sun Chen discussed Cornellian Hu Shih and past collaboration between Cornell and NTU.[2] A dinner with Cornell alumni was held that evening at the Fu Hua Hotel.

On Wednesday morning, Scott, Brazell, Galvin, and I visited Cheng Kung University, where we were greeted by university president Ma Tse-ru and given a tour of the medical school and aerospace lab. Dinner was hosted by minister of education Mao Yu-kang, with Y. S. Chiang, Mayor Huang Ta-chou (PhD 1971), and Pao Yih-hsing, Cornell professor of applied mechanics. During dinner, Ramin arranged a visit to the Chiang Ching-kuo Foundation the next day.

On Thursday, Ramin, Brazell, and I went to the foundation and chatted with its president, Lee Yi-yuan. We returned for a symposium that included remarks by Fred Kahn and Walter LaFeber, followed by a visit with premier Hao Po-chun. Lunch was hosted by Mayor Huang.

The climax of the 1990 trip came on the final day, Friday, November 2. Earlier that year, the Cornell University board of trustees had created the Distinguished International Alumni Award and bestowed it on Lee Teng-hui. He was invited to return to campus to receive the award, but the US State Department denied him entry. Since Lee was unable to return to Cornell to receive the award, Cornell went to Taiwan and President Rhodes presented a framed copy of the award in person to Lee. Representing Taiwan, President Lee was flanked by Vice President Lee Yuan-tsu and Chief of Staff Y. S. Chiang. On the Cornell side, President Rhodes was flanked by professors Kahn, LaFeber, and Tsu-Lin Mei, as well as vice presidents Ramin and Scott. There were about one hundred attendees in the audience, consisting of Cornell alumni, university leaders, and government officials. President Lee hosted a dinner for the Cornell delegation that evening. Laden with gifts, I was ready to head home. The rest of the party went on to Hong Kong.

The 1990 trip laid the foundation for trips to Taiwan by President Rhodes in 1994 and 1995. It was these trips and the relationships they built that resulted in the Lee Teng-hui Professorship and Graduate Fellowship in World Affairs, presented anonymously by friends of Lee in Taiwan, as well as the East Asia Program's Hu Shih Professorship in Chinese Studies, made possible by a gift from the Cornell University Alumni Association of the Republic of China.

Since its founding, Cornell's East Asia Program has provided campus-wide interdisciplinary research, teaching, and engagement with contemporary and historical East Asia, with over fifty affiliated faculty members, visiting scholars, and more than one hundred graduate and undergraduate students. Current activities include the Cornell Contemporary China Initiative for research on current Chinese economy, politics, and society; East Asia+, combining programming, mentorship, and digital publishing in media studies and digital humanities; the Hu Shih Distinguished Lectures, which are also made available online; the Cornell Classical Chinese Colloquium for scholars interested in premodern Sinographic text; the Translation Studies Initiative, which deals with critical issues relating to translation; and the Wong Chai Lok Calligraphy Fellowship, which provides an opportunity for an artists' residency and exhibit. The program also publishes the Cornell East Asia Series, an award-winning scholarly imprint of Cornell University Press.

Notes

1. For more about the Cornell University Library's Asia Collections, see chapter 41, Asia Collections in the Cornell University Library.

2. For more about Hu Shih, see chapter 47, Hu Shih: Forging a US-China Alliance.

4. THE SOUTHEAST ASIA PROGRAM

Global Cornell from the Beginning

Thomas Pepinsky

The Southeast Asia Program (SEAP) at Cornell University is one of the world's preeminent centers for the study of Southeast Asia, a region of nearly seven hundred million people living in eleven independent states that lie between China, India, and Australia. SEAP faculty members past and present include some of the most prominent scholars of the region and its people, and its alumni can be found in teaching and research positions around the world. The program's rich history of engaged scholarship serves as a model of Global Cornell in its fullest sense: introducing students and scholars from the region to the Cornell community and bringing Cornell research and teaching to bear on key issues, events, and problems around the world.

Although the roots of SEAP can be found in Cornell's strengths in research on China and what was then generally termed "the Far East," before the establishment of SEAP the university's main connections to the region were anthropologist Lauriston Sharp's research in Thailand and the personal papers of Jacob Gould Schurman, Cornell's third president, who chaired the first US Philippine Commission in 1898. SEAP was formally established in the 1950s after the university secured a major gift from the Rockefeller Foundation to support Southeast Asian studies. Cornell's was the second major center of Southeast Asian studies in the United States (Yale came first), but SEAP grew rapidly in the first twenty years of its existence to cover the states that today form Southeast Asia: Cambodia, Indonesia, Laos, Malaysia, Myanmar, the Philippines, Singapore, Thailand, and Vietnam. As Brunei Darussalam and Timor-Leste achieved independence in the 1980s and 1990s, they too joined the ambit of SEAP.

Three features of SEAP are of particular note. The first is its political engagement: many of the program's most prominent founding faculty were unabashedly committed to ensuring that the US foreign policy community had a more sophisticated understanding of the region and its peoples than they had earlier. Faculty such as Sharp, an expert in Thailand; Frank Golay, an economist with particular

Figure 4.1 Lauriston Sharp leads a Thailand seminar in 1962. (Provided by Southeast Asia Program, published in *SEAP Bulletin*, Fall 2007)

expertise in the Philippines; and John Echols, who had developed the Foreign Service Institute's first program in the Indonesian language, had either rotated through Washington, DC, in temporary government positions or come to Ithaca after having completed government or military service. These scholars were by no means beholden to US national policy—far from it, they were unabashed critics of US policy under both Democratic and Republican administrations. Nevertheless, SEAP's early leaders viewed Southeast Asian studies as having an important voice in informing government policy decisions and also contributing to the public debates and the policy discourse about the region more generally.

Second, the SEAP faculty institutionalized a model (now common in the United States, if less so elsewhere around the world) of Southeast Asian studies as functionally linked to specific disciplines, yet nevertheless interdisciplinary in essence. Students would enroll in PhD programs through a department like Government or Music, and program faculty would be appointed and tenured in these departments as well. The role of SEAP was to build an interdisciplinary space—both literally and figuratively—in which students and faculty could learn from one another. SEAP's comprehensive approach to Southeast Asian area studies, encompassing the social sciences and the humanities as well as the applied sciences, combined with the program's commitment to studying the entire region to produce

Figure 4.2 Sri Mulyani Indrawati (*center*), the Republic of Indonesia's minister of finance, meets with Gamelan musicians after giving the Bartels 2019 World Affairs Lecture. (Cornell University Photography, provided by Einaudi Center)

an unusually rich and eclectic body of research on the region and its human and natural environment.

Third, and perhaps most importantly, because SEAP was founded at a time of great need for training in Southeast Asian studies, it relied heavily on visiting faculty and scholars in its early years due to the shortage of knowledgeable US-based experts on the region. This outward orientation also meant that from its earliest days SEAP welcomed students from around the world who were interested in pursuing graduate training with a focus on Southeast Asia. A large portion of those students were from the countries of Southeast Asia, and many returned to their home countries after graduation to found or lead their own academic communities. Such robust connections between SEAP and what was then an emerging global community of Southeast Asian studies—with centers in Kyoto, Leiden, London, and Sydney, not to mention the new universities being established in the region itself—ensured that SEAP was globally engaged from the very beginning.

Nearly seventy-five years after SEAP's founding, these foundations for an engaged interdisciplinary, global Southeast Asian studies are plain to see. In the ensuing decades, SEAP faculty, students, and alumni have played important roles in Southeast Asian studies and current Southeast Asian affairs, establishing the program as one of the most dynamic and interesting area studies centers in the world. During the war in Vietnam, for example, SEAP faculty member George Kahin was a keynote speaker at the first national teach-in in Washington, DC. At about the same time, Ruth McVey, Benedict Anderson, and Fred Bunnell authored what has come to be known as the "Cornell Paper," an analysis of the 1965 coup in Indonesia and its bloody aftermath. Even as geopolitical events led the United States to turn its attention away from Southeast Asia, a trend that began in the 1970s, SEAP faculty continued to produce important scholarship on Southeast Asia, both intense studies of particular places and events and broad comparative work that looked beyond the region itself to see its connections with a changing global landscape. As the first generation of SEAP faculty retired, subsequent generations have provided new energy and given new intellectual direction to the program, continuing SEAP's tradition of cross-border and transregional research while also embracing new forms of critical scholarship in the humanities, exploring renewed collaboration between the social and natural sciences, and most recently exploring how Southeast Asian American and other diasporic perspectives can enrich SEAP as a program and as a community. SEAP also enjoys the good fortune of being the only continuously funded Title VI National Resource Center on campus, with programming that helps to train the next generation of globally engaged experts on Southeast Asia and its wide connections.[1]

As a Title VI center, SEAP has a special role in supporting Southeast Asian studies in the public interest in the United States. The Echols Collection is one of the world's most extensive collections of primary source material, scholarly research, media, and other material on Southeast Asia.[2] SEAP offers regular classroom instruction in six Southeast Asian languages (Burmese, Indonesian, Khmer, Tagalog, Thai, and Vietnamese), more than any other university in the United States. The program also helps to promote language study in Lao, Javanese, and other important regional languages through teaching partnerships beyond Cornell. Cornell Southeast Asia Program Publications, now an imprint of Cornell University Press, has published dozens of landmark contributions to Southeast Asian studies. And today, Cornell is a central node in several cross-university consortia that bring together multiple Southeast Asia centers around the United States, including the Graduate Education and Training in Southeast Asia consortium, the Southeast Asia Language Council, and the Southeast Asia Digital Library. Through its intellectual leadership, SEAP helps to strengthen Southeast Asian studies in postsecondary institutions around the country.

As a prominent intellectual community in Ithaca, SEAP brings scholars and students together from across campus and from around the world—it is Global Cornell in miniature. The George McT. Kahin Center for Advanced Research on Southeast Asia—colloquially known as the Kahin Center—is a dedicated space for scholars and students affiliated with SEAP to work and to gather for regular weekly research seminars and other program events. The program has hosted hundreds of visiting scholars from Southeast Asia over the years, as well as hundreds of alumni who are all part of SEAP's global network. Especially in recent years, SEAP has also been a vocal advocate for undergraduate foreign language study at Cornell, capitalizing on the fact that SEAP offers regular instruction at all levels in six Southeast Asian languages. Although there have been many changes to the faculty and to the student population over the years, SEAP continues to maintain its position as one of the most prominent area studies centers in the world.

Notes

1. For more about Title VI grants, see chapter 9, Title VI Grants to Cornell: A Demonstration of Strength in International Studies.

2. For more about the Cornell University Library's Asia Collections, see chapter 41, Asia Collections in the Cornell University Library.

5. A CENTER OF THE PERIPHERY

The South Asia Program

Daniel Bass, Iftikhar Dadi, and Bonnie G. MacDougall

From 2016 to 2017, T. V. Sekher, professor in the Department of Population Policies and Programs, International Institute for Population Sciences, Mumbai, spent a year at Cornell as a Fulbright-Nehru Fellow. He wrote that he "was looking for a vibrant, conducive and multi-disciplinary environment with a lot of scope for interdisciplinary interactions and academic exchange," which he was happy to find in the South Asia Program (SAP) at Cornell University.[1]

SAP was established in 1954 to serve as an interdisciplinary hub for Cornell students, faculty, staff, community members, and academic visitors engaged in the study of South Asia (Afghanistan, Bangladesh, Bhutan, India, the Maldives, Nepal, Pakistan, and Sri Lanka). SAP is not a degree-granting unit but facilitates the development and regular offering of undergraduate and graduate courses across campus, campus activities about South Asia, and overseas learning opportunities.

SAP's mission is to offer a comprehensive curriculum of undergraduate and graduate education on historical and contemporary South Asia; enable the circulation of ideas among an international community of South Asia scholars; encourage connections among faculty and students from South Asian institutions and Cornell University; provide a wider public exposure to South Asia through lectures, conferences, exhibitions, publications, and performances; and mobilize resources at Cornell and externally to support these efforts.

SAP grew out of the Comparative Studies in Cultural Change Project, an initiative that was organized in the 1940s in the Department of Anthropology with generous support from the Carnegie Corporation, which also spurred the development of the Latin American and Southeast Asia programs. Morris E. Opler, professor of anthropology, was the founding director of SAP and the face of its organization and expansion for its first twenty years.

During the early years, the aims of post–World War II South Asian studies at Cornell were somewhat different from those of the multidisciplinary

Figure 5.1 First director of SAP, Morris Opler, with student, Mildred Stroop Luschinsky (MA 1954, PhD 1962), 1953. (Provided by South Asia Program, published in *South Asia Program* newsletter, Summer 2014)

campus-wide area program that SAP is today, with sixty-four core and associated faculty across twenty-eight departments and nine colleges. It began as a training ground and leadership program in anthropology and closely related disciplines for graduate students and postgraduate scholars from Cornell and elsewhere. Scholars focused their research on new issues facing the postcolonial world. In a project in India, for example, researchers took up residence in village communities that were seen as the fundamental unit of study through which national change and development could be understood and introduced. This era had wide-ranging influence on a broad literature in the social sciences on South Asia. It brought Cornell students into a relationship with students and established scholars in India, some of whom became visiting faculty in Ithaca.

Since 1983, the US Department of Education has designated SAP a National Resource Center for South Asia, in a consortium with the South Asia Center at Syracuse University, one of just eight currently active in the United States. What makes SAP distinctive among other South Asian studies centers in the United States is its focus on the breadth of South Asia, and not just India. SAP is renowned for being a "center of the periphery," due to its long-standing focus on Sri Lanka, Nepal, and Bangladesh, including teaching the languages of those otherwise peripheral South Asian lands. In addition to these National Resource Center grants,

Figure 5.2 Indian architect and educator Brinda Somaya participates in a graduate seminar at the Johnson Museum as part of her tenure as an A. D. White Professor at Large, 2018. (Photo by Lindsay France, University Photography)

SAP has received Foreign Language and Area Studies grants, allowing SAP to provide fellowships for South Asian language and area studies to Cornell students.

These four-year, multimillion-dollar grants, given as part of the Title VI International Education Program, are the largest grants for international higher education from the US government. "The National Resource Center designation is a hard-earned honor," said Wendy Wolford, Cornell's vice provost for international affairs, in 2018, adding that "it is really a testament to the world-class faculty, students and staff" of SAP.[2] These funds support SAP programming at Cornell plus South Asia–related educational outreach to schools of education and community colleges in upstate and central New York State. The funds also provide Foreign Language and Area Studies Fellowships for Cornell graduate and professional students who are US citizens for the academic year and summer study of South Asian languages. One cannot underestimate the importance of these awards, as they allow Cornell to recruit competitive graduate students researching South Asia.

SAP currently has sixty-four affiliated faculty from across Cornell's colleges and schools, working in the humanities, social sciences, and natural sciences. This multidisciplinary expertise and tradition of collaboration across disciplines allows Cornell's SAP faculty to tackle the most complex problems related to the South Asian region. Its academic depth provides state-of-the-art research and professional preparation for students on the politics, economics, international agriculture, food security, global public health, architecture and urban planning, anthropology, visual and performing arts, religious studies, and literature of South Asia. SAP faculty represent twenty-eight graduate-degree-granting fields across the university's colleges and professional schools. SAP possesses a proven capacity to innovate across the scale of research engagement, from experimental small-scale research projects to macro-level research shaping scholarship, policy, and economy in South Asia and beyond.

Although SAP prides itself on being "the center of the periphery," the university embraces the study of India—its history, people, and politics—as well as the scholarly understanding of South Asia as a region. Among its North American peers, SAP possesses the greatest geographic breadth in South Asian studies. While any strong South Asia research center must include research and teaching expertise on India, SAP is unique for incorporating expertise in all geographic areas of South Asia (though Bhutan and the Maldives are underrepresented in relation to other areas). SAP provides an unusual geographic breadth of expertise that includes Afghanistan, Nepal, Sri Lanka, Bangladesh, India, and Pakistan.

This geographic breadth is reflected in the range of South Asian languages available at Cornell. Eleven are taught at the university, most of them in full curricula running from introductory to advanced levels: Bangla/Bengali, Hindi, Nepali, Pali, Persian, Punjabi (video-conferenced from Columbia to Cornell), Sanskrit, Sinhala (video-conferenced from Cornell to Columbia and Yale), Tamil (video-conferenced from Columbia to Cornell), Tibetan (modern Tibetan video-conferenced from Columbia to Cornell and classical Tibetan taught on campus), and Urdu.

These language offerings reflect Cornell's status as a global leader in Sri Lankan studies, as well as Nepal and Himalayan studies. Cornell is the only institution in North America to offer a full curriculum in Nepali and the only institution outside Sri Lanka teaching a full curriculum in Sinhala. SAP is the leading publisher outside Sri Lanka for Sinhala-language teaching materials, and its library collection in Sinhala is unmatched. SAP has also been a publisher of Nepali-language materials. The commitment to Bangladesh is supported by being one of only four US universities to offer Bengali at all levels (elementary, intermediate, and advanced).

Undergraduate students associated with SAP undertake semester-long overseas study in Kotagiri, Tamil Nadu, India, via the Nilgiris Field Learning Center, and in Peradeniya, Sri Lanka, through the Intercollegiate Sri Lanka Educational Program. In addition, students and faculty participate in winter- and summer-break study programs in Mysore, India, and other sites focused on agriculture and development, labor relations, global health, and disability studies. Following the

2015 earthquake in Katmandu, the Cornell-Nepal Study Program became inactive after many decades of supporting students at Cornell and Tribhuvan University.

Undergraduate students typically speak of their experiences abroad as "life-changing" and count their international experience as one of the most rewarding features of their college careers. Read Barbee, an environmental and sustainability sciences major who participated in the Nilgiris Field Learning Center in 2019, wrote, "The program has pushed me to grow in ways that I never expected and in ways that I think only time will allow me to truly appreciate."[3]

The Cornell University Library includes a collection of over four hundred thousand materials on South Asia in multiple languages. The South Asian collection at Cornell's Kroch Asia Library is overseen by a dedicated full-time curator and a three-quarter-time assistant, who devote their time exclusively to the South Asian collection. Furthermore, the libraries hold collections that are of service to scholars of South Asia at Cornell and elsewhere.[4] About half of the South Asia collection is in English, with the remainder in one of the eleven languages taught at Cornell, as well as additional materials in Marathi, Oriya, and Malayalam. Cornell's Klaus Ebeling Ragamala research collection, which consists of more than 3,500 slides of South Asian art, is freely available online. The Bombay Poets Archive includes personal papers of Arvind Krishna Mehrotra, Adil Jussawalla, Dilip Chitre, and other major midcentury modernist Indian poets. The library also has emerging archival collections of visual materials including colonial trade labels and Indian political posters.

SAP maintains an active program of weekly lectures, performances, and conferences. It sponsors a weekly seminar series with presentations by world-class scholars, Cornell faculty, and students. SAP also partners with Cornell student organizations to bring South Asian musicians, dancers, and other artists for campus performances, such as the Cornell Cinema for film screenings. A signature event, begun in 2009, is the Rabindranath Tagore Lecture Series in Modern Indian Literature, made possible by a gift from Cornell professor emeritus Narahari Umanath Prabhu and his wife, the late Sumi Prabhu. Inspired by Rabindranath Tagore's expansive imagination, unbounded by geopolitical boundaries, the series has regularly featured prominent writers from across South Asia and its diasporas, including Amit Chaudhuri, Manjushree Thapa, Mohammad Hanif, Shyam Selvadurai, Neel Mukherjee, Anuradha Roy, and Cheran.

Every year, several visiting scholars from South Asia come to Cornell and affiliate with SAP. Some come on Fulbright fellowships, others as SAP's Tamil Studies Visiting Scholars to teach a course, or as our South Asian studies fellows. These emerging scholars and artists have contributed greatly to SAP and used their time in Ithaca as springboards for further research, publications, and other academic accomplishments.

SAP is committed to the central and upstate New York region and performs outreach to K–12 teachers, community colleges, and schools of education to foster engagement with South Asia. This includes bringing speakers and performers to their campuses, holding pedagogical workshops, and supporting the inclusion of new South Asia–related components in their curricula. These projects increase collaboration across campuses interested in South Asia, sharing Cornell's financial and intellectual resources with partners in the central New York region.

For decades, SAP's outreach efforts focused on K–12 schools, including a lending library of South Asian books, videos, and culture kits for teachers to use in their classrooms, as well as the Afterschool Language and Culture program, in which volunteers taught six-week language courses in underfunded school districts. Since the 2010s, outreach efforts, following the lead of the US Department of Education, have increasingly focused on community colleges in New York State, chiefly Tompkins Cortland Community College in Dryden, Onondaga Community College in Syracuse, Monroe Community College in Rochester, and Corning Community College in Corning. Nearly seventy years after its founding, SAP continues its founding mission of supporting students and scholars through a range of activities and programs.

Notes

Portions of this chapter are excerpted or adapted from "The SAP Celebrates 60th Anniversary: The Early Years," published in the South Asia Program's summer 2014 newsletter (https://hdl.handle.net/1813/67053) and written by the late Bonnie G. MacDougall, professor emerita of architecture.

1. T. V. Sekher, "2016–17 Visiting Scholars," *South Asia Program 2017 Bulletin*, p. 28, https://hdl.handle.net/1813/67050.

2. Jonathan Miller, "Cornell's South and Southeast Asia Programs Named National Resource Centers," *Cornell Chronicle*, September 5, 2018, https://news.cornell.edu/stories/2018/09/south-and-southeast-asia-programs-named-national-resource-centers.

3. Read Barbee, "NFLC Student's Blog: Everything Is Connected," *Nilgiris Field Learning Center: A Project of the Keystone Foundation & Cornell University* (blog), March 25, 2019, https://blogs.cornell.edu/nflc/2019/03/25/nflc-students-blog-6-everything-is-connected/.

4. For more about the Cornell University Library's Asia Collections, see chapter 41, Asia Collections in the Cornell University Library.

6. THE BENEFITS OF INTERDISCIPLINARY UNDERSTANDING

Cornell's Latin American and Caribbean Studies Program

Debra A. Castillo

Many of Cornell's earliest students and faculty, including some very distinguished Latin Americans, were from distant places. In 1873, Puerto Rican–born civil engineer Estevan Antonio Fuertes was attracted to Cornell by the exciting promise of "any person . . . any study." A longtime advocate of practical, field-based learning, he became one of the first professors of civil engineering (and later dean) at Cornell, bringing a devotion to practical, laboratory-based learning. Fuertes had previously worked in Puerto Rico, on the Croton aqueduct for New York City, and on early Panama Canal surveys. His students spent their summers in the field surveying the Finger Lakes in upstate New York. Throughout the fall term, engineering seniors used the telescopes of Cornell's observatory to measure stars for calculations of time and position. The campus observatory would be named for Fuertes in 1904, as would its successor that opened in 1917. I like to imagine that Cornell's long relationship with Puerto Rico's Arecibo Observatory (from 1963 to 2011) speaks to that legacy of exchange with Puerto Rico as well.

Recruited by geology professor Charles Hartt, who traveled in Brazil, Brazilian students arrived at Cornell, attracted by the promise of Cornell's originality in structure and mission.[1] Elias Fausto Pacheco Jordão became the first Brazilian graduate, with a degree in civil engineering in 1874. He and other Brazilian students were part of the Club Brasileiro, the first international student group at Cornell, which also published *Aurora Brasileira*, the first international newsletter in Portuguese, from 1873 to 1875. In 1878, Francisco de Paula Rodríguez y Valdés from Cuba became the first Black student to graduate from Cornell.

These individuals long predate the founding of Cornell's Latin American Studies Program (LASP); however, their early presence in our university reminds us that Cornell from its very first years was in conversation with Latin America, in both its faculty and its student body. Spanish was taught at Cornell from the very beginning as part of a "modern languages" curriculum. Indeed, José Martí, the famous apostle of the Cuban Revolution, visited Cornell in the late nineteenth century

Figure 6.1 Cornell and Chiapas students participating in "Experience Latin America, Chiapas Edition," 2009. (Provided by Latin American and Caribbean Studies Program)

and wrote several tributes to its unique mission between 1885 and 1889: "There is much to fear, much to reject, much to despise in the selfish and harsh civilization of North America. . . . In this respect, as in all respects, one college stands out, the living college, Cornell. . . . Cornell, in Ithaca, is a magnificent university. It is the modern university. . . . Hispano American youth should be sent . . . to Cornell University, based on the knowledge and necessities of modern life without disdain for the good that comes from the ancients; to Cornell University, where they will achieve the universal elements of a new life through interesting and rich work."[2]

In 1890, Latin American students created Alpha Zeta, a fraternity that the *Cornell Daily Sun* reported was "intended solely for the benefit of persons born in the western hemisphere and who speak either Spanish or Portuguese."[3] In 1894, the Club Latino-Americano flourished, with Professor Fuertes serving as its *presidente honorio*. A graduate student from Argentina, Modesto Quiroga (MS 1905), organized the Cosmopolitan Club, Cornell's first international student group, in 1904.[4]

LASP was formally established in 1961 after five years of effort by a planning committee helmed by anthropology professor Allan Holmberg, and under the leadership of Joseph Stycos, professor of development sociology, as its first director. Initial funding came from the Rockefeller Foundation, Ford Foundation,

Figure 6.2 Michael Manley, former prime minister of Jamaica and Bartels World Affairs Fellow in 1994, speaks to a journalist. (University Photography, provided by Einaudi Center)

and Carnegie Corporation to support the creation of the program and its graduate minor. The original proposal named a group of twenty enthusiastic professors in the College of Agriculture and Life Sciences; School of Industrial and Labor Relations; College of Architecture, Art, and Planning; and College of Arts and Sciences and mentioned a group of eighty graduate students as the core body. The project built specifically on the concentration of expertise in the highland Andes with the Cornell-Peru (Vicos) Project and in Brazil.[5]

During my second term as director of the program, at the fiftieth anniversary of LASP in 2011, we were teaching a total of 375 courses a year with representation in every college of the university, with a total enrollment of over 9,000 students, of whom 2,000 were graduate students and 7,500 were undergrads. During the commemoration events, former director Tom Holloway (1982–1987) commented, "LASP's history shows that there is much to be gained from an interdisciplinary understanding of Latin America," not only for its diverse cultures but for "the historical, social, political, economic and environmental aspects that may be studied in the isolation of the traditional academic disciplines, but which cannot be adequately understood without making the interconnections among them."[6]

In 1966, with the National Defense Education Act, Cornell became one of the premier programs in the country, and in 1984, through a consortium with the University of Pittsburgh, a Title VI National Resource Center for Latin

America with a grant from the US Department of Education. Holloway noted that in the 1960s, "Cornell was already well placed to move in these directions, and the existence of LASP was important in the creation of new faculty positions focused on Latin America in history, government, economics, literature, city and regional planning, and other fields."[7]

Indeed, when I met with fellow directors at National Resource Center meetings, they always marveled at the exceptional reach of our program. Most programs nationally focus heavily on humanities and social sciences; it was very unusual to see so much leading research and engaged field practice coming from engineers building bridges in Bolivia or water filtration systems in Honduras, to see faculty and students studying crop rotation in Nicaragua and horticulture in Chile, to learn of the groundbreaking work done in collaboration with the Universidad Autónoma Chapingo in Texcoco de Mora, Mexico, on improved varieties of potatoes and maize.

Later support came from the National Endowment for the Humanities, the Venezuelan Fundación Gran Mariscal Ayacucho, and others. Support for student fieldwork and research has always been at the heart of the program. Through the years, I have seen Cornell-sponsored programs in Brazil, Bolivia, Chile, Costa Rica, Cuba, the Dominican Republic, Ecuador, Guatemala, Honduras, and Peru (and maybe others) in collaboration with scholarly research in fields ranging from the Cornell-sponsored study abroad program originally housed in anthropology to urban planning, international agriculture, engineering, public health, political science, and arts and humanities research.

The grandfather of all these courses, the venerable course Agriculture in the Developing Nations (IARD/LATA 4010/6010), started in 1967. The courses ran continuously for forty-eight years in Puerto Rico, the Dominican Republic, Costa Rica, Honduras, Ecuador, and Mexico. Over the years, the courses have frequently been supplemented by a Spanish discussion section for students with basic language skills, supported by additional readings in Spanish. Students come from crop science, tropical agriculture, watershed management, regional planning, nutrition, assorted health careers, hotel administration, government, and linguistics, along with a few from literature or performance studies.[8]

With its hundreds of alumni over the years, there have naturally been many published articles deriving from this IARD/LATA fieldwork, as well as undergraduate honors theses, master's theses, and PhD dissertations. The one-year experience includes a semester-long preparatory course, followed by an intense research experience that includes a two-week living laboratory in the field and an optional eight-week internship, followed by a subsequent on-campus agenda of analysis and reporting. The highly contextualized encounters, especially the incorporation of the field laboratory, have been powerful keys to real learning. William B. Lacy, vice provost for university outreach and international programs at the University of California, Davis, from 1999 to 2014 and director of Cornell Cooperative Extension from 1994 to 1998, summarized the achievement at the 2001 Millennium Conference on Agricultural Development: "[Experience Latin America] is one of the richest learning experiences I have seen in higher education. The dynamic international learning environment is greatly enhanced by bringing together undergraduates and graduates with diverse backgrounds and international experiences with a multidisciplinary, intergenerational group of faculty, administrators, and extension educators. Each of the participants becomes an active learner and teacher."[9]

Indeed, students who have traveled with Cornell programs in Latin America echo Lacy on the life-changing effects of these experiences. Kimberly Cárdenas, a government major in the class of 2017, says, "This is by far the most important Cornell experience I have had thus far. I saw the importance of going abroad, but in particular, going abroad to a disadvantaged region in the world as opposed to an area resembling the United States; it is in this way that one can truly be immersed in an entirely different context from where personal growth results." Urban planning graduate Alia Fierro adds, "I ended my first year of graduate school at Cornell wondering, What am I doing here? Is there a space for me within the field of planning? Do I want to do international work? Why should I be working in communities abroad? Fast-forward to today, week one of my second and final year as a graduate student at Cornell. My summer experience in Chiapas and with Foro gave me a taste of what working in Latin America is like, it made me realize that there is a space for me."[10]

Our conversations at Cornell have been enriched by the perspectives of heads of state—presidents and former presidents of many Latin American countries whom we brought to campus. These include Carlos Andrés Perez, the controversial president of Venezuela; Michael Manley, prime minister of Jamaica; Fernando Henrique Cardoso, president of Brazil; Michelle Bachelet, president of Chile; and Sergio Rámirez, prize-winning novelist and vice president of Nicaragua. We also brought to Cornell the expanding perspectives of activists like Rigoberta Menchú; scholars like Arturo Escobar, Walter Mignolo, and Santiago Castro Gómez; and writers from Isabel Allende and Carlos Fuentes to Valeria Luiselli and Giovanna Rivero.

In addition to the familiar activities of the program today that provide support for research and exchange in many formats, early iterations of the program also had a standing publications committee responsible for putting out the international journal *Andean Past* and a working-paper book series, as well as the monumental Quechua dictionary compiled by former Cornell Quechua professor Luis Morató in 2016.

Leadership also came from close collaboration with our libraries. For instance, David Block, former curator of Latin American Studies and a onetime acting director of the program, was a sought-after expert in the field and president of the Seminar on the Acquisition of Latin American Library Materials, a crucial digitization resource. Along parallel lines, the Latin American Journals Project established by Tom McEnaney, former assistant professor of comparative literature at Cornell, in collaboration with the library, provided "a hub for scholars across the globe to more easily access literary and cultural journals published in the Hispanophone Caribbean and Latin America during the late nineteenth and early twentieth centuries. Many of these journals are difficult to find in their printed form, and/or hard to access in private collections, including in many of the countries where the journals first appeared."[11]

Student activism has spurred conversations about inclusivity in the name of the program, and in 2021 the Latin American Studies Program officially changed its name to Latin American and Caribbean Studies to more formally indicate its openness to research in that region. It is, perhaps, a reminder of the historic role that the Caribbean has always played in Cornell: all the way back to Estevan Antonio Fuertes, Francisco de Paula Rodríguez y Valdés, and José Martí in the nineteenth century.

Notes

1. For more about Charles Hartt, see chapter 39, Exploring Our World: Cornell Expeditions.

2. José Martí, *Escenas norteamericanas* (New York), June 12, 1885. Translation from Spanish by the author.

3. "Alpha Chapter of Alpha Zeta," *Cornell Daily Sun*, January 7, 1890.

4. For more about the Cosmopolitan Club, see chapter 55, Above All Nations Is Humanity: The Cornell Cosmopolitan Club.

5. For more about the Cornell-Peru Project, see chapter 25, Applied Anthropology in the Andes: The Cornell-Peru Project.

6. "Latin American Studies Program Celebrates 50 Years," *Cornell Chronicle*, November 3, 2011, https://news.cornell.edu/stories/2011/11/latin-american-studies-program-celebrates-50-years.

7. "Latin American Studies Program."

8. See "Experience Latin America," course website, Cornell University, accessed September 21, 2023, https://courses.cit.cornell.edu/iard4010.

9. Robert W. Blake, "Tradition and Transition: INTAG 602 and the Graduate Field of International Agriculture and Rural Development," *Millennium Conference on Agricultural Development in the 21st Century* (2001): 36–40.

10. Student reflections cited in 2015 reports to Kellogg Foundation. Not publicly available.

11. See Latin American Journals Project website, accessed September 21, 2023, https://latamjournals.library.cornell.edu.

7. THE INSTITUTE OF EUROPEAN STUDIES

A History of Stability and Change

Susan Tarrow

Although Cornellians had traveled to Europe for studies and research for decades, there was no program at Cornell specifically dedicated to European studies until 1973. That was when the Western Societies Program (WSP) was founded. It received generous support from professor of government Mario Einaudi, Cornell's Center for International Studies, and a three-year Ford Foundation grant for research and training on Western Europe.

The major players in WSP were Sidney Tarrow and Peter Katzenstein from the Department of Government, Davydd Greenwood from the Department of Anthropology, Steven Kaplan from the Department of History, and Gardner Lindsey from the School of Industrial and Labor Relations. The program covered Western Europe and Canada, and its biweekly lunch seminar focused on the social sciences. Further grants afforded opportunities for research in Europe for faculty and graduate students, and for international meetings held at Cornell. A series of occasional papers was published featuring authors from the United States and Europe, and funds were allocated to Olin Library to increase holdings on European subjects.

A major focus of WSP has always remained support for student research and foreign language acquisition. In 1984, under professor of history and director John Weiss, WSP created the first program at Cornell for undergraduate summer research in Europe. Funded by the Kellogg Foundation, students spent four to six weeks in Europe conducting research approved by their department adviser; many of them produced a senior thesis; and of the first one hundred students, only one failed to fulfill the requirements. When Kellogg funds were exhausted, a generous endowment was established in 1993 by Mario Einaudi's daughter-in-law, Meredith Wood Einaudi, in honor of her father and Cornell trustee Frederick Conger Wood (class of 1924). In recent years, the Harum Prize and the Susan Tarrow Fellowship have offered grants for work in Russia and France or Italy, respectively.

Figure 7.1 Mario Einaudi (*center right*) and Manon Michels Einaudi (*center left*) with Professors Sidney (*right*) and Susan (*left*) Tarrow. In 1990, Einaudi's contributions to political sciences were honored in the publication *Comparative Theory and Political Experience: Mario Einaudi and the Liberal Experience*. (Photo by University Photography, provided by Division of Rare and Manuscript Collections, Cornell University Library)

Graduate students also saw increased funding for Europe-based research. In 1981 the Sicca Foundation trust, named for Michele Sicca, an antifascist physician who worked closely with Mario Einaudi during his exile from wartime Italy, supported summer grants for graduate students in all fields for research in Europe. The Manon Michels Einaudi summer fellowship for graduate students in the humanities was created in 1991.

The 1980s were probably the most prosperous decade for the program, with major sources of funding from the US Department of Education, the Mellon Foundation, and the Luigi Einaudi Foundation. Applications for the Department of Education Title VI National Resource Centers (NRCs) were cumbersome; in those days there were few computers to help us fill out all the forms required. The Kaypro computer we were using had no auto-save function, and there were last-minute crises when we discovered that whole sections had been lost and needed to be retyped. WSP applied for an NRC for Western Europe, and in 1985 it was awarded its first three-year grant. It allowed us to supplement staff salaries, initiate seminars and conferences, develop new courses, and run outreach programs in the Ithaca and upstate community. Foreign Language and Area Studies Fellowships made it possible to offer tuition support to graduate or undergraduate students

Figure 7.2 Institute for European Studies Einaudi Chair Luigi Spaventa (*left*) and Professor Mario Einaudi, who continuously worked during his career to explain Europe to America and America to Europe. (Photo by University Photography, provided by Division of Rare and Manuscript Collections, Cornell University Library)

for training in a modern European language, for either the academic year or the summer. We were also able to contribute to the support of library collections, as well as lecturers of less commonly taught languages, thus increasing the number of foreign language offerings in the College of Arts and Sciences.

In the spring of 1986, late on a Friday afternoon, a quiet gentleman appeared in the WSP office and asked a few casual questions about the program. Apparently satisfied with what he heard, he identified himself as a program officer of the Mellon Foundation; he was inviting proposals from a few universities for a five-year grant in support of European studies. Could we produce an application within a week? Yes, we could, and with prudent management made it last for seven years! It enabled us to put resources into the development of the Slavic and East European Studies Program, a vital need since interest in the area was growing fast as the Soviet Union disintegrated. We were able to invite visiting scholars from the area, and their lectures were packed with students eager to meet these strangers from a forbidden realm. More Eastern European language classes were developed, and several departments hired faculty to inaugurate new area courses. The Slavic and East European Studies Program was awarded its first undergraduate NRC for Eastern Europe and Russia, thanks to the leadership of Valerie Bunce, professor of government.

During the same period, the Luigi Einaudi Chair in European and International Studies was inaugurated. Named in honor of Mario's father, Luigi Einaudi, the first president of the Republic of Italy after World War II, and endowed with funds raised by Mario Einaudi and a gift from the Italian government, the chair brought a European visiting scholar each year to teach two courses at Cornell, as well as shorter-term visiting fellows. It supported graduate student research in Europe, enabled international conferences, and strengthened Cornell's relationships with Italian and other European universities. If the Einaudi name features prominently in this chapter, it is because Mario offered his wisdom, generosity, and friendship to European studies until his death in 1994. His son, Luigi Einaudi, former ambassador and secretary general of the Organization of American States, continues the family tradition, and the program owes the family a great debt.

The fall of 1992 saw a major realignment of European studies at Cornell. In late October, the board of trustees approved the creation of the Institute for European Studies (IES), uniting the former WSP and Slavic and East European Studies Program. Cornell was the first to merge its European programs and to apply for an all-Europe NRC. The divisions of postwar Europe drawn during the Cold War were fast becoming outdated; IES was committed to training a new generation of Europeanists who could respond quickly to the need for an integrated approach in government, business, and academia. Foreign Language and Area Studies support for students also provided opportunities for them to focus on many more areas of the continent. In 2003, a renewal of Title VI funding for the upstate New York Consortium for Trans-European Studies with Syracuse University made it possible to continue development of courses and to resume outreach programs to schoolteachers in the region. Although virtual learning was then still in its infancy, language courses could be shared between the two campuses.

At the same time, IES was expanding its horizons within Cornell. Historically attached to the College of Arts and Sciences, the program began interacting more frequently with colleagues in programs like architecture, city and regional planning, engineering, the Atkinson Center for Sustainability, and the Law School. Issues such as immigration, climate change, and landscape architecture crossed the old academic boundaries between established fields. A perfect example of this cross-field and cross-cultural activity is the Mediterranean Studies Initiative, developed by Gail Holst-Warhaft. In 2002, in cooperation with the Department of Near Eastern Studies, and with seed money from the mayor of Kefalonia and the Onassis Foundation, Holst-Warhaft organized events around her own field of expertise, Mediterranean and especially Greek music and literature. She arranged many thrilling musical performances with leading artists from the region. With persistence and gentle diplomacy, she continued to raise money for instruction in modern Greek and Turkish, and in 2006 she began a long-term research project on the environmental issues associated with water in the Mediterranean basin. With a colleague in the Department of Biological and Environmental Engineering, Tammo Steenhuis, Holst-Warhaft led several groups of students to study water storage and rain collection on the Greek islands of Crete and Santorini, drawing on her diverse contacts in the region to collaborate with local environmental scientists. She also taught courses on Mediterranean water issues in the Law School and in biological and environmental engineering with diverse faculty colleagues.

IES has remained on the cutting edge of international studies in the twenty-first century. It has maintained exchange agreements with numerous European universities, enabling faculty and students to participate in research projects in the field, and to collaborate with scholars in their own countries. One example is the Abraham and Henrietta Brettschneider Oxford Exchange Fund, endowed by alumnus Michael Borkan in honor of his grandparents; it facilitates annual visits between Cornell and Merton, New, and Nuffield Colleges at Oxford University. Another lively relationship, with the University of Turin, includes a six-week summer course for undergraduates in the College of Arts and Sciences and the Department of Policy Analysis and Management, with visits to the Einaudi family's hometown of Dogliani and the Luigi Einaudi Vineyards. Funds from the San Giacomo Charitable Foundation supported international exchange and institutional development, and a Ford Foundation grant awarded to longtime institute director Davydd Greenwood introduced us to the serious questions facing institutions of higher education in the United States and Europe.

Contemporary issues of migration have forged links with Ottoman and Turkish studies, the Law School, the Atkinson Center, and the College of Architecture, Art, and Planning. Under the leadership of director Esra Akcan, professor of architecture, a multidisciplinary academic minor in migration studies has attracted students from across the university, and in 2020 a series of online workshops dealt with a wide range of issues, such as the cultural heritage of Hagia Sophia in Turkey; the repatriation of museum objects; and the transformation of Germany, Bosnia, and Russia and the subsequent migration; as well as problems of climate change and its impact on the movement of peoples. Now that virtual meetings have become commonplace, conferences and seminars can reach a large global audience at a considerably reduced cost.

IES is also engaged with addressing the increasing need for support for scholars at risk, and in 2018 it created a scholar hardship fund for those under threat, hosting several scholars from Turkey and Russia. The current IES director, Mabel Berezin, professor of sociology, continues to support these opportunities and since

2022 has hosted Russian dissident writer and journalist Dmitri Bykov, in collaboration with the Open Society University Network.

For almost fifty years, WSP/IES has remained at the cutting edge of international scholarship and contemporary political, social, scientific, and literary areas of research and student instruction in Europe. With the advent of advanced technology and greater opportunities for close collaboration with colleagues and their students across the continent, IES will continue to be a vital worldwide force in the study of Europe, and to contribute to international understanding in the United States.

8. CREATING CONNECTIONS WITH AFRICA

Cornell's Institute for African Development

Muna Ndulo and Heike Michelsen

An African proverb advises, "If you want to go fast, travel alone. If you want to go far, travel together." This could readily apply to Cornell's establishment in 1987 of the Institute for African Development (IAD) to address critical development issues in Africa by mobilizing the university's substantial teaching, research, and technical assistance capabilities. At the time, Cornell faculty and administration saw the need to educate the Cornell community about Africa, to sponsor serious discussions that would include African academics and other knowledgeable colleagues, and to contribute as an educational institution to the improvement of the education and related environment on the African continent. A faculty committee, led by Milton Esman and including Norman Uphoff and James Turner, recommended the establishment of IAD. It quickly became a magnet for Cornell scholars and practitioners in the humanities, sciences, and social sciences and continues to maintain substantial student and faculty interest today.[1]

With fifty-four countries, Africa is characterized by ethnic, cultural, economic, environmental, and political diversity. The continent's challenges are well documented. Health emergencies, armed conflict, corruption, bad governance, domestic and international terrorism, and hunger and malnutrition tend to dominate the headlines. But Africa has great promise, with extraordinary natural resources unmatched anywhere else in the world, 1.3 billion people, and the world's youngest population. African countries need strategies to promote growth and reduce poverty, to overcome the limitation of Africa's small and fragmented economies through regional integration, to give the continent a greater voice in the management of international economic processes, to strengthen institutions and build capacity for development, and to maintain an environment of peace and security. The growing importance of African issues and increasing trade and political ties between Africa and the United States require a better understanding of African societies, cultures, and economies.

Figure 8.1 Professor Muna Ndulo (*center*) and LLM graduates and Institute for African Development Fellows Mapange Nsapato (Zambia) (*right*) and Lebina Phukuile (South Africa) (*left*) in 2018. (Photo by Jackie Sayegh, provided by Institute for African Development)

For over thirty years, Cornell's IAD has worked to expand the depth and breadth of teaching, research, and outreach in and about Africa, building knowledge and interest among faculty and students in a wide range of disciplines. It has brought together individuals and communities across continents in ways that illuminate Cornell's global engagement and commitment to African development. It has established strong partnerships with African institutions, developed human and institutional capacity in Africa, and, through its fellowship programs, attracted and facilitated the training of many young African scholars. Today, IAD is a mature, campus-wide, interdisciplinary, problem-focused, collaborative, policy-driven, development-focused part of Cornell.[2]

"With its twin focus on policy and development, IAD is a very distinctive area studies program, successfully attracting faculty from a wide range of disciplines," said Nicolas van de Walle, Maxwell M. Upson Professor of Government. "It takes full advantage of Cornell's unique strength of combining a top-notch liberal arts college with an exceptional applied policy tradition in its land-grant colleges."[3]

N'Dri Assié-Lumumba, professor in the Africana Studies and Research Center and director of IAD (2020–2022), aimed to expand IAD's partnerships in Francophone countries—from Senegal to Madagascar—building on IAD's existing strengths. "Through my work with pan-African development, continental, and

Figure 8.2 Students visiting the women's craft cooperative in Limpopo during the Law and Social Change course at the University of Johannesburg in 2017. (Photo by Jackie Sayegh, provided by Institute for African Development)

diasporic organizations, I've been able to build networks from Egypt to South Africa, from Senegal to Ethiopia," Assié-Lumumba said. "Cornell is in a unique position as a land-grant institution to reach outside of academia."[4]

At Cornell, the institute supports and offers courses on Africa; language instruction in Yoruba, Swahili, Tumbuka, Twi, Wolof, Zulu, Arabic, French, and Portuguese; seminars and symposia; and meetings with academics, practitioners, and institutions on the African continent. The seminar series has a specific theme for each semester covering a variety of topics including financing development in Africa, natural resources, climate change and its impact on development, governance and constitution making, and regional integration. The series provides a forum for participants to explore these and other topics and exchange ideas; it has become a de facto introductory course on Africa for many Cornell students. For many, the seminar series was an eye-opener. "The [IAD] seminar series . . . transformed my life," stated Samuel Adarkwah, Cornell law student and 2011 IAD fellow from Ghana. "I have never had the chance to sit in with people of such caliber who are knowledgeable of what is going on in Africa and who give first-hand accounts of what is actually happening on the ground."[5]

Each year, IAD brings a distinguished African scholar to campus in collaboration with departments in various schools at Cornell. Scholars are nominated by departments, which house them, in collaboration with IAD. These scholars give a public presentation open to the university community, participate in classes, and interact with students and faculty in the host department. Recent distinguished African scholars have included Sophie Oldfield (2018), a geographer at the University of Cape Town in South Africa and internationally recognized expert on urbanization; Charles Midega (2015), from the International Center for Insect Physiology and Ecology in Kenya; and Akin Adesina (2010), former vice president of the Alliance for a Green Revolution in Africa and current president of the African Development Bank.

IAD also has an impressive publication program, including the *Institute for African Development Bulletin* newsletter and the IAD Occasional Paper Series with multidisciplinary, policy-oriented, and development-oriented articles in all fields of African studies. The Cornell Institute for African Development Series, a book series published by Cambridge Scholars Publishing, currently includes a dozen titles, written, edited, or translated by IAD faculty.[6] These publications serve as a communication channel and a repository of important research enabling IAD to disseminate knowledge to the academy, development practitioners, and policy makers.

IAD has established significant networks and partnerships with African institutions, such as the Southern African Institute for Policy and Research in Zambia, as well as with academics and practitioners.[7] Across the continent, IAD supports faculty research and faculty-led courses, as well as research and internship opportunities for students in collaboration with partner institutions and alumni in Africa, creating a wide range of meaningful experiences in Africa for Cornell students. Other Cornell programs such as International Agriculture, Global Health, the Johnson Graduate School of Management, and the School of Industrial and Labor Relations have collaborated with IAD in support of their engagements in Africa.

In 2020, IAD received a three-year grant from the US Department of Education to strengthen engagement with undergraduate students by focusing on establishing cohesive and multilayered Cornell "hubs" in Zambia and Ghana. These will serve as anchors for broader programming throughout the region, creating a network of African-based alumni mentors offering research and internship opportunities to students of diverse disciplines, as well as new, innovative on-campus language and cultural predeparture courses and reflection seminars.[8]

The core of IAD's graduate studies operation is the Tuition Fellowship Program, one of few programs in the United States, if not the only one, that specifically targets capacity building in Africa. The program has engendered significant positive outcomes in Africa and serves as a source of great pride for IAD and Cornell. Since 1988, more than four hundred midcareer professionals from over twenty countries in sub-Saharan Africa have received advanced degrees from

Cornell in a wide range of disciplines. IAD selects these fellows based on their merit, commitment to return to Africa, proven record of public service, and geographic and gender diversity. The fellowship program has now been changed to a tuition waiver in collaboration with other Cornell units.

IAD alumni become catalysts for development and form an extensive network across Africa that enriches field courses, research activities, and internship opportunities for current Cornell students. "Cornell alumni in Africa carry on the university land-grant mission in myriad ways that show the remarkable imprint of what it means to be a part of the Cornell global community," said Jackie Sayegh, IAD's program manager. "Our alumni network is an invaluable resource to Cornell and to advancing African development."[9]

Former IAD fellows include Charles Kajimanga (LLM 1993), a judge on the Supreme Court of Zambia; Amina Abdalla (MPS 2000), the only politician ever nominated for three successive terms as a member of the Parliament of Kenya; Omar Abdi (MRP 1989, PhD 1992), the deputy executive director of UNICEF; Ragendra Berta de Sousa (MS 1996, PhD 2003), Mozambique's minister of industry and commerce; Anthony Akunzule (MPS 1999), executive director of the Ghana Poultry Network and coordinator of Veterinarians Without Borders/Vétérinaires Sans Frontières Canada projects in Ghana; Justin Chola (MBA 1999), CEO of Bayport Financial Services, a microfinance and credit firm in Zambia; Dunia Prince Zongwe (LLM 2008), associate professor at Walter Sisulu University in South Africa and head of the Mercantile Law Unit; and Naalamle Amissah (MS 2003, PhD 2006), head of the Department of Crop Science at the University of Ghana.

When IAD fellows reflect on their experiences at Cornell, they express a profound appreciation for the breadth and depth of the educational offerings that transformed their lives. "Being an IAD Fellow opened my eyes to the different issues that impact the African continent. As the continent with the lowest human development indexes overall despite having the world's richest natural resource endowment, Africa faces issues that are uniquely diverse, multifaceted, and seemingly intractable," said Dunia Prince Zongwe (2007 IAD fellow from Namibia).[10]

Naalamle Amissah (2003 IAD fellow from Ghana) described her experiences at Cornell as "parallel to none. IAD fellows all over the world are a testament to the institute's great achievements in training scholars from Africa. . . . IAD brought together fellows and distinguished scholars to network with great minds while deliberating on issues pertinent to the development of Africa. . . . There was no question in my mind after graduating that I needed to return home to make a difference after having received such a rich experience."[11]

Every year IAD alumni work with IAD to find internship placements for Cornell students in Ghana, Namibia, Senegal, Zambia, Liberia, and Tanzania. For example, Akunzule, who won the 2019 World Veterinary Association Animal Welfare Award, remains in contact with both IAD and the College of Veterinary Medicine's Expanding Horizons program. "Giving student interns placements in Ghana provides them with an international perspective," Akunzule said. "I was once a Cornell student, and when I see these students come to Ghana, it reminds me of my student days at Cornell, and I feel proud of that."[12]

A summer internship program reinforces academic learning by providing undergraduates the opportunity to actively engage with individuals and organizations directly involved in policy and program development in Africa. The institute and its partners view placements as an integral part of the students' education, immersing them in field experiences that seek to achieve awareness of developmental challenges and intercultural understanding. Interns work closely with a supervisor, colleagues, and peers on development-related challenges including court efficiency, labor, gender, land tenure, nutrition and food security, migration, and conservation.

ILR major and 2020 IAD intern Georges Batoussi (class of 2019) worked with IAD fellow Justin Chola, CEO of Bayport's operation in Zambia. "There are so many incredible minds on campus, and the same holds for alumni," Batoussi said. "Bridging that gap for undergraduates who have an idea of what they want to pursue, with people who are doing that kind of work and were in their shoes ten years ago—I think it's a perfect fit, and IAD is doing just that."[13]

It comes as no surprise that IAD has received several national and international recognitions. According to Michigan State University professor David Wiley, former president of the African Studies Association and speaker at the institute's twenty-fifth anniversary in 2014, Cornell's IAD may be "the most distinguished center in African development in the United States."[14]

Notes

1. A study on Cornell dissertations related to international agriculture and rural development confirms faculty engagement. The number of dissertations in the Department of International Agriculture and Rural Development about countries in sub-Saharan Africa rose sharply from thirteen in the 1960s to fifty-six in the 1970s, peaked at seventy-five in the 2000s, and remained relatively high at sixty-one in the 2010s. See Larry Zuidema, "Cornell Dissertations Related to International Agriculture and Rural Development: Report of a Study" (unpublished draft manuscript, April 27, 2018).

2. For details, see IAD's annual reports available at "Mario Einaudi Center for International Studies Annual Reports," eCommons, Cornell University Library, accessed September 21, 2023, https://ecommons.cornell.edu/handle/1813/49812.

3. Nicolas van de Walle, Maxwell M. Upson Professor of Government and former director of the Mario Einaudi Center for International Studies, interview with the author, December 17, 2015.

4. Sheri Englund, "Assié-Lumumba Leads Institute for African Development," *Cornell Chronicle*, July 8, 2020, https://news.cornell.edu/stories/2020/07/assie-lumumba-leads-institute-african-development; N'Dri Assié-Lumumba, "Director's Message," *Institute for African Development Bulletin*, 2020.

5. Samuel Adarkwah '2016 and 2011 IAD fellow, interview with the author, December 18, 2015.

6. For a list of recent IAD publications, see "Publications," Mario Einaudi Center for International Studies, website, accessed September 21, 2023, https://einaudi.cornell.edu/publications?program=4.

7. Heike Michelsen, "Institute for African Development," *Institute for African Development Bulletin*, Spring 2017.

8. Melanie Lefkowitz, "IAD Grant Will Support Learning Hubs in Ghana, Zambia," *Cornell Chronicle*, October 29, 2020, https://news.cornell.edu/stories/2020/10/iad-grant-will-support-learning-hubs-ghana-zambia.

9. Priya Pradhan, "Ithaca Roots Growing in Africa," *Cornell Chronicle*, March 28, 2019, https://news.cornell.edu/stories/2019/03/ithaca-roots-growing-africa.

10. Dunia Prince Zongwe, "My Experiences as an IAD Fellow," *Institute for African Development Bulletin*, 2020.

11. Naalamle Amissah, "Alumni Update: Former IAD Fellows Report Back," *Africa Notes*, Institute for African Development, Cornell University, Fall 2014.

12. Pradhan, "Ithaca Roots Growing."

13. Pradhan.

14. David Wiley, remarks at IAD's 25th anniversary celebration, November 4, 2014.

9. TITLE VI GRANTS TO CORNELL

A Demonstration of Strength in International Studies

Heike Michelsen

A 187-pound, basketball-sized, orbiting satellite, the Soviet Sputnik 1 brightened the night sky on October 4, 1957. The wave of public hysteria in the United States started not only a space race to compete with the USSR and its allies but also a science and education race. As a key component of the "Sputnik response" and to address the need to better understand the world beyond US borders, Congress passed Title VI of the National Defense Education Act, offering grants to universities to become centers of excellence in area and language studies.[1] Cornell was able to provide such expertise. The Title VI investments made by the US government are deeply intertwined with Cornell's impressive foundations in international studies today.

History of Title VI

The act signed into law by US president Dwight Eisenhower in 1958 became the largest program in the world for international education in foreign language, area, and international studies.[2] Initially, Title VI, administered by the US Department of Health, Education and Welfare, offered grants to a university for serving as a National Resource Center (NRC), along with Foreign Language and Area Studies (FLAS) fellowships for students. International Research and Studies grants were also available under the original legislation. In 1979 Title VI was moved to the newly established US Department of Education. Over the years, the goals expanded to include grants for Undergraduate International Studies and Foreign Languages, Centers for International Business Education and Research, Language Resource Centers, and American Overseas Research Centers, among others. In 1961, the Mutual Educational and Cultural Exchange Act, or Fulbright-Hays Act, established programs for overseas study, research, and training, which were placed

Figure 9.1 Teachers at the Einaudi Center's International Summer Studies Institute view art on global inequalities at the Johnson Museum, 2022. (Provided by South Asia Program)

alongside Title VI to be administered as complementary international programs.

Federal funding for Title VI was not always a given. Annual appropriations and authorizations varied significantly, but overall, Title VI provided a long-term source of continuous support for the institutional base of modern international, foreign area, and foreign language studies. It was highly successful in building more than one hundred centers of excellence in more than fifty leading US universities.[3]

Title VI at Cornell

Title VI grants are highly competitive and prestigious. To be successful, a program must prove excellence in areas critical to the national interest. Excellence manifests in the depth and breadth of faculty expertise in the region, courses focusing on the region, programs for less commonly taught languages, library collections, and strong regional and international relationships. Success also requires significant financial support from the university for the program's operation.

Figure 9.2 Mary Moroney (*center*), a doctoral student in linguistics, received a Foreign Language and Area Studies grant in preparation for her research in Thailand in 2018. (Provided by Southeast Asia Program)

"The National Resource Center designation is a hard-earned honor," said Wendy Wolford, Cornell's vice provost for international affairs. "It is really a testament to the world-class faculty, students and staff of these extraordinary programs."[4]

Since the launch of the Title VI program, Cornell has received over 150 multiyear grants, and it is ranked among the top ten recipients for these grants, in total numbers as well as grant funding.[5] The number of grants to Cornell has decreased over time. While Cornell was one of a few universities with institutional expertise to apply for the grants in the 1960s, today, most major American universities compete for them. Other universities have made major institutional investments leading to new programs across a broad range of issues, languages, and regions of the world and increased their internationally oriented capacities.

The following Cornell programs have been successful in competing for Title VI funding: the Southeast Asia Program (SEAP): fifty grants; the East Asia Program: forty-two grants; the South Asia Program in collaboration with Syracuse University: twenty-four grants; the Institute for European Studies: eighteen grants, of which several were in collaboration with Syracuse University; the Latin American and Caribbean Studies Program: eighteen grants, of which several were in collaboration with the University of Pittsburgh; the International Programs of the

College of Agriculture and Life Sciences: four grants; and the Institute for African Development: two grants.[6]

Most of the grants were received by Cornell's area studies programs. Since 2000, they have received a total of $44 million for forty-four grants.[7] The Asian studies programs lead the list, accounting for over 80 percent of funding received. SEAP has received Title VI grants continuously since the inception of Title VI in 1959, the East Asia Program from 1960 to 2014 with just a few gaps, and the South Asia Program continuously since 1985 as a consortium with Syracuse University. European studies has represented 12 percent, Latin America 9 percent, and Africa 1 percent of Title VI funding received since 2000.

In 1985, the US Department of Education expanded Title VI programs to include global issues, thereby going beyond language and area studies. The International Programs of the College of Agriculture and Life Sciences successfully submitted a proposal focused on food issues. The original three-year grant was renewed three times for a total of twelve years.

Activities Supported by Title VI

Title VI grants to area studies programs supported a wide range of activities and provided critical support to Cornell for the teaching of languages and area studies, programming, library and museum collections, outreach, and student fellowships.[8] In the International Programs of the College of Agriculture and Life Sciences, it supported the creation of the Center for the Analysis of World Food Issues, including a speakers bureau for outreach to other colleges and universities, a dedicated library, MPS degree student support, and campus seminars by experts from the United States and abroad.

Fellowships

FLAS fellowships support students who wish to acquire a high level of competence in languages critical to national needs of the United States and a fuller understanding of the areas, regions, or countries in which those languages are used. FLAS awards allow programs to support graduate students for stipends and tuition during the year and summer tuition and stipends for intensive language instruction. A total of 3,344 Cornell students have obtained Title VI fellowships.[9]

Languages

Title VI grants provide significant support for Cornell's language programs, mostly supporting the salaries of language teachers. Over the years, Title VI has supported the development and teaching of thirty-three least commonly taught language programs at Cornell:

- East Asia: Chinese-Cantonese, Chinese-Mandarin, Japanese, Korean, Tibetan
- South Asia: Bengali, Hindi, Nepali, Sinhala, Tamil, Urdu
- Southeast Asia: Balinese, Burmese, Hmong, Indonesian/Malay, Javanese, Khmer, Lao, Tagalog, Thai, Vietnamese
- Europe: Catalan, Dutch, French, German, Hungarian, Italian, Polish, Portuguese, Russian, Serbo-Croatian, Swedish
- Latin America: Quechua

Until 2014, Cornell was the only university to offer four levels in Cantonese, and it remains the only university outside Asia to offer four levels of study in all six major Southeast Asian languages (Burmese, Indonesian, Khmer, Tagalog, Thai, and Vietnamese) and four levels of Nepali and Sinhala.

"Language training for undergraduates, graduate students and, on occasion, faculty members is critical to all facets of the research and teaching mission of the Southeast Asia Program," said Abby Cohn, former director of SEAP and professor of linguistics. "Cornell has taken a leadership role through its commitment to teaching the least commonly taught of the less commonly taught languages."[10]

Title VI funding for offering language programs at Cornell was crucial. When the Institute for European Studies lost its National Resource Center funding in 2009, it forced the elimination of Hungarian and contributed to the loss of Dutch, Swedish, and modern Greek.[11] In the summer of 2011, the US Department of Education slashed its funding in the middle of a grant cycle, putting at risk the continuation of eleven critical language programs (Bengali, Burmese, Hindi, Indonesian, Khmer, Nepali, Persian, Sinhala, Tagalog, Thai, and Vietnamese). Only emergency funding from the Office of the Provost bridged this shortfall and saved the programs during this crisis, showing strong university support and commitment.

Programming

Title VI funding significantly widened the range of initiatives, activities, and collaborations and strengthened the resources available to researchers, students, and teachers. Examples of these include the following:

- organization of weekly seminars and lectures open to the public with presentations by Cornell faculty and invited outside scholars

- organization of international symposiums and conferences on key academic issues
- development of new courses and student programs about the regions, resulting in the internationalization of Cornell's curriculum
- publication of monographs, language textbooks, and journals
- support to faculty for joint projects, research, travel, and conferences
- establishment of new and maintenance of existing collaborations with scholars and institutions globally, regionally, and locally
- development of faculty-led study abroad opportunities and other meaningful international experiences for students such as internships or research projects

Funding from Title VI also contributed to the salaries of the core staff of the area studies programs for coordination and management of these activities.

Library

National Resource Center grants helped the Cornell University Library's area studies collections primarily to finance acquisitions and specialized staff. Considered by scholars to be among the largest and best-integrated collections in North America, the Asian studies collections hold nearly a million printed volumes that chronicle the growth of cultures throughout the Asian continent since the beginning of civilization. The grants ensure that graduate students and top researchers in international studies will continue to be able to examine the collections for their research.[12]

Outreach

Finally, National Resource Centers have a commitment to share Cornell's financial and intellectual resources with partners in the central New York region, which dovetails with Cornell's land-grant mission. Programs offer professional development for K–12 teachers, including teacher-training workshops and an annual International Studies Summer Institute. They also support faculty at nearby community colleges and schools of education to become Regional Visiting Fellows. Collaborating faculty receive funding and access to Cornell expertise and resources for projects aimed at internationalizing their curricula. In some cases, the faculty fellows have the opportunity to travel to the region or even build their own study abroad program for students at their home institution. Teachers and faculty have access to area-specific resources including books, films, and culture kits from a lending library. Programs also offer the opportunity to partner with Cornell's faculty to develop and pilot curricula.

Lasting Impact

Cornell combines the intellectual breadth of one of the world's leading research universities with the professional, applied, and outreach missions long associated with New York's land-grant university. Title VI grants recognized and contributed to Cornell's breadth and excellence in world areas deemed critical to US national interests.

"Cornell's international and regional reputation and visibility are substantially enhanced by these grants," stated Nicolas van de Walle, former director of the Einaudi Center. "The FLAS awards significantly increase Cornell's ability to attract top graduate students in international studies. In addition, K–12, and community-based outreach activities play an important role in shaping state and local perceptions of the university."[13]

Despite the strong national competition, Cornell has remained successful in applying for Title VI funding. According to professor of government Peter Katzenstein, "Area studies have been Cornell's way of dealing with globalization and internationalization. This has been our preferred way of conducting interdisciplinary work (research and teaching) and thus stem, to some extent, the powerful parochialism that has come with the reassertion of disciplinary insularity across many fields in the social sciences."[14]

Recently, SEAP and the South Asia Program successfully safeguarded their recognition as National Resource Centers for another four years, until 2026, and the Latin American and Caribbean Studies Program and the Institute for African Development each received Undergraduate International Studies and Foreign Languages grants. There is no doubt that Title VI funding continues to affect international studies at Cornell and provides important resources to develop and maintain Cornell's area studies programs, increasing their reputation and vitality.

Notes

Thanks to Miriam A. Kazanjian of the Coalition for International Education, as well as former colleagues at the Einaudi Center, particularly T. Joshua Young, Thamora Fishel, and Daniel Bass, for their comments, insights, and reflections.

1. See Gilbert W. Merkx, "Gulliver's Travels: The History and Consequences of Title VI," in *International and Language Education for a Global Future*, ed. David S. Wiley and Robert S. Glew (East Lansing: Michigan State University Press, 2010).

2. See David S. Wiley, "Introduction: Seeking Global Competence through the Title VI and Fulbright-Hays Act," in Wiley and Glew, *International and Language Education.*

3. See Wiley.

4. Jonathan Miller, "South and Southeast Asia Programs Named National Resource Centers," *Cornell Chronicle*, September 5, 2018, https://news.cornell.edu/stories/2018/09/south-and-southeast-asia-programs-named-national-resource-centers.

5. See US Department of Education, International and Foreign Language Education, International Resource Information System (IRIS), accessed June 25, 2022, https://iris.ed.gov/iris/ieps/search.cfm.

6. Based on information from IRIS (2022); Miriam A. Kazanjian, email message to the author, April 28, 2022; Miriam A. Kazanjian, Coalition for International Education, "HEA-Title VI and Fulbright-Hays—Funding History in Current $ FY 1959—FY 2022," unpublished data, June 2022; Mario Einaudi Center for International Studies annual reports and historical websites (various years).

7. This figure includes funding for the consortium partner universities. Funding for before 2000 as well as for 2022 is not available.

8. Heike Michelsen, "Cornell's Area Studies Programs NRC and FLAS Grants," internal memo, Mario Einaudi Center for International Studies, May 2009; Heike Michelsen, "Cornell's Area Studies Programs Receive Prestigious NRC and FLAS Grants," internal memo, Mario Einaudi Center for International Studies, August 11, 2006.

9. This figure also includes the Fulbright-Hays Doctoral Dissertation Research Abroad fellowships, Faculty Research Abroad, and Group Projects Abroad, representing about 10 percent of all fellowships.

10. Miller, "South and Southeast Asia."

11. Cornell Institute for European Studies, *Annual Report 2010–11*, 2011.

12. For more about the Cornell University Library's Asia Collections, see chapter 41, Asia Collections in the Cornell University Library.

13. Nicolas van de Walle, "Some Basic Data about Current Department of Education Support for Area Studies at Cornell University," internal memo, Mario Einaudi Center for International Studies, September 10, 2004.

14. Mario Einaudi Center for International Studies, "Reflections on the Past from Cornell Leaders in International Studies," prepared for the Einaudi Center 50th Anniversary Symposium on International Studies in the American Research University: The Path Ahead, November 14–15, 2011.

10. LAUNCHING PEACE STUDIES AT CORNELL

The Air War in Indochina

Judith Reppy

When Cornell's Peace Studies Program was established in the fall of 1970, it took as its purpose "to sponsor teaching and research on the moderation or avoidance of war, and on the political, economic, technological, and social implications of such progress toward peace."[1] Early activities included a biweekly seminar, a conference on controlling the proliferation of nuclear weapons, and an ambitious program for the publication of working papers, journal articles, and books.

In the last category, the program had the good fortune of being approached by a group of faculty who were embarking on an interdisciplinary study of the air war in Indochina, which was expanding at the time with very little public knowledge of its conduct, its impacts, or its broader implications. The faculty were prepared to do this on a pro bono basis but sought an institutional home for their project and some modest funding for operational costs. Peace Studies was quite willing to be involved as a sponsor because the project exemplified everything that the new program hoped to encourage, especially in its commitment to evidence-based analysis and its engagement with important policy issues, issues that unfortunately remain pertinent today.[2]

The publication of *The Air War in Indochina* in 1972 was the culmination of this project. In brief, the group used open sources to make well-informed estimates of the number of tons of bombs dropped in the US bombing campaigns in Vietnam, Laos, and Cambodia between 1965 and 1971; wrote up their findings to include assessments of the economic, ecological, and legal implications of the air war; and found a publisher in Beacon Press.

Origins of the Air War Study Group

The longer history is more interesting.[3] Starting in the mid-1960s, Cornell, like many other American universities, had seen an increase in student demonstrations

Figure 10.1 Members of the Technical Arms Control Study Group, 1983–1984. *Left to right:* Zellman Warhaft (Engineering), Nariman Mistry (Physics), Herbert Lin (Peace Studies Program), Franklin A. Long (Chemistry, Peace Studies Program), Peter Auer (Engineering), Peter Stein (Physics), and Lorri Staal (research assistant). (Provided by Judith Reppy Institute for Peace and Conflict Studies)

protesting the US role in the ongoing war in Vietnam.[4] At Cornell, the atmosphere was further inflamed by the demonstrations led by Black students protesting the racism they faced at Cornell, protests that culminated in the occupation of Willard Straight Hall in April 1969 and the subsequent resignation of the university's president. The campus was deeply divided on these issues, and the teach-ins and protest events were attended by hundreds and sometimes thousands of students.

Antiwar organizations and counterorganizations proliferated on campus. Among the antiwar groups was the Faculty Anti-War Group, which brought together faculty from across the university who in quieter times might never have met each other. Cochaired by Raphael Littauer, chair of the Department of Physics, and Norman Uphoff, assistant professor of government, the Faculty Anti-War Group also included notable faculty like Chandler Morse (economics), Frank Rosenblatt (neurobiology), Paul Feeny (entomology, and ecology and systematics), and Carl Sagan (astronomy).

Uphoff describes the origins of the Indochina Air War Study Group this way:

> Some time in the spring of 1971, Raphael [Littauer] came to me and asked: How much do we (meaning anyone) know about the air war in Indochina? My answer was, as I recall: Not very much. He asked: Shouldn't we (meaning everyone) know a lot more about it? My answer was, of course: Yes. And he asked: Shouldn't we try to get information on this air war into the public domain (or something to that effect)? And my answer was yes.

Figure 10.2 Meeting of Women in Military project, codirected by Judith Reppy (*fourth from right in back row*), professor emerita, Science and Technology, and Mary Katzenstein (*first from left in front row*), Stephen and Evalyn Milman Professor of American Studies, emerita. (Provided by Judith Reppy Institute for Peace and Conflict Studies)

> He asked me to join in an effort to study the air war. I explained that I had already a pretty full plate, being an assistant professor and responsible for getting a new Rural Development Committee up and running, a task given me by Milt Esman.[5] His response was that he was serving as the Physics Department's chair. How could I top that? He said he would do most of the work, but he wanted to add the perspective of a political scientist.[6]

Littauer was the driving force for the study, making frequent trips to Washington, DC, to gather data and conduct interviews.[7] The group members had to educate themselves on the history of US involvement in Indochina, the arcana of US strategic doctrine, types of military aircraft and their payloads, and the various problems for targeting that arise in actual combat. In addition to the estimates of tons of bombs dropped, they also analyzed the institutional practices that supported a triumphalist account of success in contradiction to the facts on the ground.

The study group was determined to create as objective an account as possible, one that rested on publicly available data and avoided doctrinaire arguments, because they knew that their report would not be taken seriously if it could be dismissed as one-sided propaganda. Their data assembly and assessment were vindicated when the *Pentagon Papers* were published in June 1971, and the data through 1968 (the last year covered in the *Papers*) agreed quite closely with those the Air War Study Group had collected and pieced together from unclassified sources.

The Findings

The numbers are stunning. Combining information about the number of sorties flown and average payloads for the different types of aircraft, the study group estimated that between 1965 and 1971 the allied forces had dropped 6,320,195 tons of aerial munitions on the four Southeast Asian countries involved in the conflict (South Vietnam, North Vietnam, Cambodia, and Laos). US forces were responsible for the vast majority of this tonnage, with the South Vietnam Air Force accounting for less than 10 percent in the final four years of the period under the policy of "Vietnamization" of the war's conduct.[8]

In a bitter irony, more than 60 percent of this tonnage was dropped on South Vietnam, which was the United States' ally in the conflict.[9] These numbers may be compared with data from World War II, during which the United States dropped about 2,000,000 tons of air ordnance across all the theaters of that war.[10] Indochina was a tiny fraction of the area of these theaters in Europe and Asia.

Some things are easier to count than others. While the data on bomb tonnage drew the most attention, the air war report included a sensitive discussion of the damage inflicted on the peoples who were bombed. The effects included a large number of civilian casualties, mass internal displacement of population, loss of livelihood in the agricultural sector, destruction of established social relationships and cultural capital, and extensive environmental damage that lingers on.[11]

The report also considered the economic costs of the air war and its status under international law, especially regarding the criterion of proportionality, which holds that the military value of an action should be proportionate to the damage caused. The report's descriptions of the many instances in which US air bombardments destroyed entire villages, based on only weak evidence of enemy presence, documented the violation of the proportionality standard.

Analysis of the special features of air warfare is a constant theme running through the report. The study group noted the psychological aspects of killing from a distance, a distance that protected the pilots from any personal experience of the carnage below. The relatively small number of pilots and their remote bases also rendered the war less visible to the public as bombing was substituted for more boots on the ground.[12] The report describes the ways in which the failure to achieve the original goals of destroying the morale of the North Vietnamese and interdicting the flow of supplies to the National Liberation Front in South Vietnam led to shifting rationales in favor of escalation in the bombing campaigns, rather than to questioning their effectiveness.

Impact

A draft of *The Air War in Indochina* was circulated to a limited number of reviewers in late fall 1971, and a slightly revised version with a preface by Neil Sheehan was then published by Beacon Press in 1972. The *New York Times* put a long review of the book on page 1 of its Sunday Book Review section for August 13, 1972.[13] This was a major event in an age in which most people still got their news from reading a print newspaper.

While the public attention to the book's conclusions did not lead directly to any change in US policies, the book attained the status of being a standard treatment of the issues that were involved in the air war, and for some years it was included in the curriculum at the National War College and the Air Force Academy. More recent studies cite it as the standard source for understanding the complexities of the air war and the effects of new technologies on the conduct of war.[14]

The book holds a special place in the history of the Peace Studies Program, now the Peace and Conflict Studies Program. Its scope and high standards for evidence-based argument have informed subsequent research supported by the program. The topics treated, especially the effects of advanced technology on war fighting and the application of international humanitarian law principles to civilian casualties, are well represented in the research agendas of past and current program members.

Relevant publications supported by the Peace Studies Program include *Do the Geneva Conventions Matter?* (2017), edited by Matthew Evangelista and Nina Tannenwald; *The American Way of Bombing: Changing Ethical and Legal Norms, from Flying Fortresses to Drones* (2014), edited by Matthew Evangelista and Henry Shue; *New Wars, New Laws? Applying the Laws of War in 21st Century Conflicts* (2005), edited by David Wippman and Matthew Evangelista; and *Weapons Choices and Advanced Technology: The RPV* (1978), by Samuel L. Hall.

Notes

1. Cornell University Peace Studies Program, *First General Report (September 1970–July 1972)* (unpublished report, 1972).

2. See Azmat Kahn, "Hidden Pentagon Records Reveal Patterns of Failure in Deadly Airstrikes," *New York Times*, December 18, 2021, 1.

3. I thank Norman Uphoff for his considerable help in understanding the origins of the Air War Study Group.

4. For a detailed history of student activism at Cornell during this period, see chapter 6 in Glenn C. Altschuler and Isaac Kramnick, *Cornell: A History, 1940–2015* (Ithaca, NY: Cornell University Press, 2014).

5. Milton Esman was the director of the Mario Center for International Studies and a professor in the Department of Government.

6. Norman Uphoff, email message to the author, May 20, 2022.

7. The 2009 obituary for Raphael Littauer in the *Ithaca Journal* summarized the extraordinary range of his interests and talents. It concludes thus: "Outraged by the US involvement in the Vietnam War, Raphael, Alexandra, and their children were regular marchers in demonstrations. He was the lead author and editor of 'The Air War in Indochina,' a quantitative study of the amount and effects of bombing in Southeast Asia. He was disappointed that he was not mentioned on Nixon's Enemies List." *Ithaca Journal*, October 21–24, 2009, https://www.legacy.com/us/obituaries/theithacajournal/name/raphael-littauer-obituary?id=28500294.

8. Raphael Littauer and Norman Uphoff, eds., *The Air War in Indochina*, rev. ed. (Boston: Beacon, 1972), 179–180.

9. Littauer and Uphoff, 10.

10. Neil Sheehan, preface to Littauer and Uphoff, *Air War in Indochina*, v.

11. Littauer and Uphoff, *Air War in Indochina*, 62–67.

12. The US Air Force was quick to claim a leading role for its B-52 bombers. See Robert M. Kipp, "Counterinsurgency from 30,000 Feet: The B-52 in Vietnam," *Air University Review* 19, no. 2 (1968): 10–19, https://www.airuniversity.af.edu/Portals/10/ASPJ/journals/1968_Vol19_No1-6/1968_Vol19_No2.pdf.

13. Robert Kleiman, "The Air War in Indochina," *New York Times*, August 13, 1972, BR1.

14. See, for example, Mark Clodfelter, "The Limits of Airpower or the Limits of Strategy: The Air Wars in Vietnam and Their Legacies," *Joint Force Quarterly* 78 (July 1, 2015): 111–178.

11. THE STUDY OF MUSLIM CULTURE, SOCIETY, AND HISTORY AROUND THE WORLD

The Comparative Muslim Societies Program

Eric Tagliacozzo

Our Origins and Ambit

In February 2017, the Comparative Muslim Societies Program (CMS) joined the Near Eastern Studies Department and scholars from across the university in decrying the new "Muslim ban" that had been promulgated by the administration of US president Donald Trump, preventing those from several countries with Muslim-majority populations from traveling to the United States. Lecturing to packed spaces at Cornell, several scholars affiliated with the program spoke with students about the dangers of this legislation, and the chilling impact it would have on the country. Students listened: one told the *Cornell Daily Sun* that the teach-in offered "a more constructive solution to participants" than just raging at the administration. A second said that the forum provided "an opportunity to make a powerful statement."[1] Either as a statement or as a discussion, the event provided a salient teaching moment to let students know that Muslims were part and parcel of the contemporary United States.

CMS has served as a forum for faculty and students on campus who are engaged in the study of various aspects of Muslim culture, society, and history. It has sought to encourage comparison internally within the world of Islam and externally between Muslim and non-Muslim spheres. We have done this through a variety of interrelated disciplines, moving across "ways of knowing" Muslims in the world and the many contexts in which they find themselves. We study two groups: Muslim-majority communities found in Africa, the Middle East, South Asia, Central Asia, and Southeast Asia and Muslim communities found in the United States, Europe, China, and elsewhere where Muslims are a minority.

The program was formed in spring 2001 to promote the comparative study of Muslims and Muslim societies between and across the boundaries of traditional area studies programs and departments. It is important to note that the program came into being before the September 11 attacks; its origin was not in the

Figure 11.1 The 2017 Teach-In on Islam, the Middle East, and America. (Photo by Jason Koski, University Photography)

so-called war on terror but rather in an interest in Muslims and Islam that preceded this era-defining event.

For two decades, we have annually hosted a number of seminars and other events every term, as well as a fellowship competition at both the undergraduate and graduate levels for students going off into the world to do research. Finally, we have engaged with constituents on campus who are interested in the lives of Muslims worldwide. Many faculty have been involved in keeping the program vital and contributing to its health over the past few decades and represent a broad range of departments including Africana Studies, Anthropology, Asian Studies, Comparative Literature, Food Science, Global Development, Government, History, History of Art, Law, and Near Eastern Studies.[2]

Our Speaker Series

The main feature of CMS has been our speaker series. We usually bring about fifteen faculty and scholars to campus each year to speak in the seminar series. The COVID-19 pandemic has necessitated that we bring in everyone virtually for over two years. Speakers normally have come from all over, though usually from North America because of costs, and they cross all academic disciplines and geographic boundaries in their pursuit of knowledge about Islam. Our seminars have been advertised widely and have also been open to the public; the audience for these meetings changes weekly, depending on who the speaker is, where they come from, what they are speaking on, and where in the world their topic explores.

According to our surveys, we usually have had around twenty or so participants per seminar, always changing in composition, but during the pandemic some online events have attracted over eighty participants, mostly faculty and students. In the past, we tried to maintain a salon-type atmosphere, with discussion around a table as the spirit of our program, rather than outright lectures. However, the movement to an online format allowed us to experiment with a different structure, and it also allowed a larger audience to tune in than normally attends our events in-person. The move to the virtual environment also allowed us to include more speakers from abroad—Japan, India, Germany, Belgium, parts of Africa, and even Hawaii. In the future, we hope to keep some aspects of this new online presence, so that we operate in a more hybrid way, with events of both kinds happening every term—in-person seminars, with their friendly and relaxed feel, and the newly incorporated online lectures.

We have tried to assemble an eclectic mix of topics, disciplines, eras, and people in our speaker slates, in order to bring in as large and as varied an audience as we can. Talks have focused on a remarkable array of topics: a West African Muslim who came to help build the Panama Canal in the early twentieth century, fatwas (religious edicts) on drinking coffee in early modern Arabic commentaries, Islamic libraries from Spain to India, the growth of the environmental Muslim movement in contemporary Indonesia, the spread of madrasas in Uzbekistan in central Asia, women and the transmission of Islamic knowledge in Kenya, migrant workers in the Arab gulf, and the writings of Malcolm X after his conversion to Islam, among many others. Seminars have also annually included a session about rare Islamic books in the Cornell University Library's collections.[3] In some instances, we have had special series of talks: in one academic year we hosted several seminars on Islam and gender. In other semesters, we explored topics more regionally, with a daylong conference on Islam in China or a special afternoon on Islam in Africa.

We also typically have funded six to eight other events on campus per year by way of cosponsorship, primarily student initiatives, if those events have an Islam-related theme. These might be student-led events such as Eid Mubarak celebrations, or the hosting of speakers not on our own slate but whom students wish to hear. We have always offered a set amount of money for these sorts of occasions, with the support of the program in the background. In 2017, the group helped support a lecture and roundtable, organized by the Collective of Concerned Students on Global Issues, addressing the crisis of Rohingya Muslims living in Myanmar.

Supporting Students

Supporting students has also been important to CMS over the years. As has been the case with all of the other Einaudi Center programs, we participate every year in a funding competition for students—at both the graduate and the undergraduate levels. Most funding goes to graduate students who are looking to head abroad over their summers and to build research findings into their master's or PhD projects.

One student, Brita Lorentzen, who earned her PhD in 2015, went to study tree ring dendrochronology in Lebanon to learn about droughts a millennium ago in the medieval Levant. She was able to combine her interests in archaeology, geology, and ecology. "It's a unique resource for Cornell students to engage in international interdisciplinary research," said Lorentzen.[4] Her project on the southern Levant (i.e., southern Lebanon, Israel, Jordan, and Egypt) has expanded to encompass several veins of research, and she managed the Cornell Tree-Ring Laboratory after graduation.

An art history student, Holiday Powers, who became an assistant professor at Virginia Commonwealth University School of the Arts in Qatar after earning her PhD in 2015, used CMS funds to go to Paris to work in the collections of the Institut du Monde Arabe. "My time in Paris was key for accessing a variety of archives and library resources. I was able to extend my time there through a second grant which supported Arabic classes in Paris. The support was important for me in giving me the time to explore as I continued to refine my doctoral project," she said. "I appreciate the commitment to understanding not just histories of Europe but histories that have been impacted by European colonialism. It is one of the realities of colonialism that some archives remain in the metropole. Supporting research into these archives allows research into the imbricated and globalized histories wrought by colonialism."[5]

A third student received funding to go to western China, speaking to Muslims there about how Islamic and Chinese legal traditions intersected (and sometimes collided), while a fourth used CMS funding to head to West Africa to examine the development of Islamic finance and the regional forms this sort of banking takes on in an African context. Every year the projects are different, and the recipients head off in different directions, studying different topics, with different methodologies, and in different time periods.

Program Publications and Projects

CMS has compiled a forthcoming volume with Cornell University Press that showcases the kinds of work accomplished by our program over the past twenty years. Titled *Islamic Ecumene: Comparing Global Muslim Societies*, the volume includes twenty-two short essays by a selection of scholars who have presented their work at Cornell in the CMS program over the years. We asked each of these scholars to send us a four-thousand-word essay on a topic of their choice, pertaining to either Islam or the Muslim societies in which they work. These selections were then arranged thematically and accompanied by an introduction. Our goal is to showcase the comparative approach to the study of Islam and Muslim societies. By keeping the essays short, we hoped to include as many authors in the volume as possible. Since no single scholar could possess the range of languages, archival experience, or fieldwork needed to cover the range of societies included in the book, it needed a collective effort.

In January 2020, just before the start of the COVID-19 pandemic, CMS hosted a two-day workshop at the Weill Cornell Medicine campus in Doha, Qatar. Titled "Parallel Waters: The Persian Gulf and the Red Sea," it examined the two vital maritime conduits, together and in a comparative way. An eclectic and international group of scholars participated, including historians, art historians, anthropologists, and sociologists. We hope to publish a compendium based on the presentations.

Another project taking shape is titled "The Pacific Horizon," which will examine how both Islam (coming via Asia) and Catholicism (coming from the Americas) met and mingled in the islands and seas of the Pacific. An international workshop is intended to take place at Cornell Tech campus in New York City, in cooperation with the Latin American Studies Program.

These three projects exemplify the kind of cutting-edge, comparative work that has been a hallmark of CMS since its very beginning, more than twenty years ago.

Notes

1. Meg Gordon, "Near Eastern Studies Department Shows Support through Teach-In on Islam," *Cornell Daily Sun*, February 18, 2017, https://cornellsun.com/2017/02/18/near-eastern-studies-department-shows-support-through-teach-in-on-islam.

2. Current faculty include Jonathan Boyarin, Magnus Fiskesjo, and Saida Hodzic (Anthropology); Sandra Greene, Mostafa Minawi, and Eric Tagliacozzo (History); Seema Golestaneh and David Powers (Near Eastern Studies; the latter is the program's founder); Begum Adalet and Allen Carlson (Government); Ben Anderson, Iftikhar Dadi, Salah Hassan, and Kaja McGowan (History of Art); Chiara Formichi (Asian Studies); Gail Holst-Warhaft (Comparative Literature); Fouad Makki (Global Development); Joe Regenstein (Food Science); and Chantal Thomas (Law School).

3. A listing of past offerings is available at "Past Events," Comparative Muslim Studies Program, Cornell University, accessed September 25, 2023, https://einaudi.cornell.edu/programs/comparative-muslim-societies-program/events/past-events.

4. Melanie Lefkowitz, “Crossing Boundaries: Cornell’s Thriving Research Ecosystem,” *Ezra*, May 6, 2020, https://news.cornell.edu/stories/2020/05/crossing-boundaries-cornells-thriving-research-ecosystem.

5. Holiday Powers, email correspondence with the author, October 2, 2022.

12. THE BARTELS WORLD AFFAIRS FELLOWS

Bringing the Internationally Distinguished to Cornell

Heike Michelsen

Peeking out of the green room, I could not see an empty seat left in the Statler Auditorium. Colleagues guarded the doors, photographers were ready, the lights were dimmed, and participants talked in high anticipation. Cornell president Hunter Rawlings and Fareed Zakaria, host of CNN's *GPS* public affairs show, stepped onstage. During the next ninety minutes, Zakaria shared his insights and knowledge on international affairs, addressing political, military, financial, and economic developments. Before and after his lecture, he also signed an endless number of books and addressed many students and faculty in more intimate settings. Zakaria was the 2011 Bartels World Affairs Fellow.

Since 1985, thousands of students and faculty from across the campus have attended the annual public lectures given by Bartels Fellows during their campus visits to gain firsthand insights on important global issues. It has become one of the most memorable aspects of being at Cornell for many students and faculty, providing them the opportunity for face-to-face meetings with Nobel laureates, presidents, leading UN officials, religious leaders, and other distinguished global thinkers.

The list of Bartels speakers, their professional titles, and the topics of their lectures is more than impressive. Since the beginning, the Mario Einaudi Center for International Studies has named forty-one Bartels Fellows and organized thirty-nine major public Bartels lectures as well as hundreds of seminars and meetings on campus. Previous Bartels Fellows included His Holiness, the 14th Dalai Lama Tenzin Gyatso; Archbishop Desmond Tutu; former leaders of countries including Nigeria, Brazil, Venezuela, and Chile; leaders of international institutions such as UN agencies, the World Bank, the International Monetary Fund, and UNICEF; members of the diplomatic corps in the United States and other countries; academic leaders; distinguished journalists and writers; leaders of US institutions; and politicians. Fewer than half were US nationals with international careers, while others were from a variety of world regions. What most have in common

Figure 12.1 The visit of the 1991 Bartels Fellow, the Fourteenth Dalai Lama of Tibet, with President Frank H. T. Rhodes in front of Olin Library, attracted over twelve thousand people. (Photo by University Photography, provided by Einaudi Center)

is not only outstanding reputations and exceptional international careers but also dedication to public service and to addressing major global challenges.

It was Cornell president Frank H. T. Rhodes in the early 1980s who wanted an international perspective to become a key element of education, particularly for undergraduate students. He wanted to encourage students to be sensitive to worldwide needs and views. Accordingly, the Center for International Studies (renamed after its founder, Mario Einaudi, in 1991) developed a proposal for a lecture series and related activities that would "create a stronger awareness of a particular international topic, provide an open forum for discussion of these issues, and familiarize all segments of the university population with the vital social issues that may influence the future of mankind."[1]

Henry E. and Nancy Horton Bartels, both class of 1948, supported the proposal and endowed the Bartels World Affairs Fellowship program. "Nancy and I feel that the world is getting smaller all the time. As a result, in order to make a mark in this world, our young people will need to consider the international perspectives of their actions. Having the opportunity to meet and listen to people who are internationally prominent will broaden their horizons."[2]

The thematic focus of the Bartels public lectures has intentionally been very broad—from the international debt crisis and challenges to democracy, to the

Figure 12.2 Students presenting a drawing of the "chinita chilena" and the "gaucho chileno" to honor Michele Bachelet, executive director of UN Women and president of Chile (2006–2010), 2012. (Photo by University Photography, provided by Einaudi Center)

post-American world and cyber diplomacy. The lectures have attracted huge audiences over the years from across campus. About half of the lectures have addressed multiregional or global issues, and the other half have focused on specific world regions, particularly Europe, the Middle East, Latin America, Asia, and Africa. Thematic foci have included the following:

- international relations such as the transatlantic alliance, the Cold War, and US foreign policies vis-à-vis Russia, the Middle East, and Asia
- international issues such as the global environment, global health, the role of religion in global relations, the role of UN agencies, new development paradigms, the new world order, a fact-based worldview, cyber diplomacy, and gender issues
- issues in international economics such as the global financial and debt crisis, globalization, trade policies, international investments, and the roles of central banks, the World Bank, and the International Monetary Fund
- national policies such as challenges to democracy, human rights, institutional changes, economic reforms, structural adjustment programs, good governance, human capital development, reconciliation, and peace negotiations

In collaboration with university leadership, departments, programs, faculty, and students across the campus, the Einaudi Center annually selects the topic and speaker and develops and organizes the program. Each Bartels Fellow delivers a major public lecture for the entire university and spends about two days on campus in close interaction with faculty and students, especially undergraduates. In classes, seminars, and informal gatherings, they discuss major issues of global concern as well as their own personal international experiences and careers.

Four Bartels Fellows exemplify the caliber of those who have contributed to the Cornell community. Archbishop Desmond Tutu was one of these. When Nelson Mandela was elected as president in South Africa, he appointed Tutu in 1995 to chair the newly formed Truth and Reconciliation Commission. Tutu had been one of the leading figures in changing South Africa's inherently racist paradigm and was awarded the Nobel Peace Prize in 1984 for his contribution to racial justice. Tutu came to Cornell in 2000 and his lecture was so in demand that it was moved from the Statler Auditorium to the Newman Arena in Bartels Hall. More than 1,500 people welcomed him with a standing ovation. Tutu shared unbelievable testimonies of murders, abductions, and lynchings under apartheid. But instead of prosecutions, South Africa granted amnesty to those who came forward with information about their crimes. Tutu conveyed a message of forgiveness and reconciliation: "We have seen the potent power of truth to help people heal. . . . We want a new kind of society that is gentle and caring . . . transparent and open."[3] He also thanked students at Cornell and across the country for their tireless effort to support the fight against apartheid.

In 2006, Ambassador Lakhdar Brahimi, former special envoy for Afghanistan and adviser to the UN secretary-general, gave a sobering analysis of the situation in Iraq, predicting escalating tensions. Brahimi is highly respected throughout the world as a statesman and for his skill as a negotiator. He noted that the peace process aimed at the rebuilding of the Iraqi state did not seem to be working. "The new constitution and the security forces being trained under US and British leadership are not producing the national institutions that can bring peace back and keep the country together."[4] As we know now, he got it right. Participants deeply appreciated Brahimi's insights and wide experience in international diplomacy and the Middle East. He returned several times to campus as an Andrew Dickson White Professor-at-Large. During his residency as the Einaudi Center's inaugural Diplomat-In-Residence Fellow, he offered a course on conflict resolution and organized a trip to New York City to introduce students to the leadership of the UN and several countries' permanent representatives to the UN.

A group of Chilean students asked the Einaudi Center in early 2012 to invite Michele Bachelet, the former president of Chile and head of the newly created UN Entity for Gender Equality and the Empowerment of Women (UN Women). She was known as one of the most popular presidents of Chile (and was returned to office when allowed to run again) and a champion of women's rights. "There is a rising awareness that we cannot solve the great challenges of our time unless we unleash the potential of full and equal participation of women."[5] Bachelet noted the groundbreaking role of Cornell in the empowerment of women. The first woman to graduate from Cornell, Emma Eastman, received her degree in 1873, forty-seven years before American women had the right to vote. Bachelet called for a new development paradigm to implement policies and reforms that promote gender equality. "That the right of a woman to decide if and when and how many children she wants to have is still up for debate is a sign of the work that still lies ahead of us."[6]

A faculty group nominated Svetlana Alexievich, the winner of the Nobel Prize in Literature in 2015 and former resident of the Gothenburg City of Refuge, to become the 2016 Bartels Fellow. Born in Ukraine and growing up in Belarus, she became a teacher, journalist, and writer in the Russian language. She had chronicled the Soviet Union for over thirty years, a history of the rise and fall of the Russian-Soviet dream told by the people themselves during conversations about life. "I learned how to listen, how to turn myself into one big ear."[7] The audience in the packed Statler Auditorium gave Alexievich a spontaneous round of applause when she stated, in reference to war, "Ideas should be killed, not people."[8]

Each of these high-level visits to the Ithaca campus, involving so many constituencies, required long-term and meticulous planning and preparations, from the identification of the speakers and the organization of the visit to the post-event evaluation. While it is not possible to measure the full impact of the fellowship on the Cornell community, the feedback received from students and faculty has always been very positive and continues to justify these efforts. Debra A. Castillo, professor of Hispanic studies and comparative literature, wrote to former president of Brazil Fernando Henrique Cardoso, the 2010 Bartels Fellow, "It is certainly unusual in academic discussions for the speaker to be mobbed as if he were a rock star! No rock star, however entertaining, has left us with such a rich and complex message, such a tremendous combination of modesty and wisdom, such a grounded analysis of national realities and global vision. We are greatly in your debt."[9]

Andrew Key (class of 2015), who attended a lunch meeting with Zakaria in 2011, exclaimed, "Absolutely incredible experience today. I give my greatest appreciations to you for the opportunity and my deepest congratulations to all of the individuals at the Einaudi Center who made this event the success that it was."[10] Hassan Saleem (class of 2020), who attended a first-year writing seminar with Alexievich in 2016, wrote, "If art can inspire change in the world, perhaps Svetlana Alexievich could be a catalyst, in her works and in her words. Despite the darkness she has experienced, she has somehow brought forth some of the most enlightening literature the world has known. Her final piece of advice for us was never to settle for remaining average, and always to strive to be the best. That is the sort of thing that successful people always tell students, but I think her meaning was deeper. 'Only one who stays above the water,' she said, 'avoids being swept away by the waves.'"[11]

There is no question that the goals of the fellowship remain as relevant today as they were over forty years ago. Students and others benefit from the extraordinary opportunity to interact directly with leaders of international stature to learn about global issues and facets of an international career.

Notes

This chapter is adapted from Heike Michelsen, "The Bartels World Affairs Fellowship Program: Bringing the Internationally Distinguished to Cornell," April 29, 2022, eCommons, Cornell University Library, https://hdl.handle.net/1813/111315.

1. "Proposal for a Global Perspectives Program in the Center for International Studies at Cornell University Presented to Henry E. Bartels," internal memo, Mario Einaudi Center for International Studies, December 5, 1983.

2. "Bartels Fellowship to Focus on International Perspectives," Cornell University, *Communiqué Fall/Winter* (1984).

3. Cornell University, "Truth and Reconciliation: Toward a Just Society." Video of Desmond Tutu, Archbishop of Johannesburg, South Africa, Bartels World Affairs Fellowship Lecture, April 10, 2000, https://www.cornell.edu/video/desmond-tutu-truth-reconciliation-toward-just-society.

4. Mario Einaudi Center for International Studies, "Brahimi Talks on the Current Crisis in Iraq," website, March 6, 2006, https://web.archive.org/web/20060907135937/http://www.einaudi.cornell.edu/news/headlines.asp?id=1182.

5. Lianne Bornfeld, "At Cornell, Former Chilean President Advocates Women's Rights," *Cornell Daily Sun*, September 4, 2012, https://cornellsun.com/2012/09/04/at-cornell-former-chilean-president-advocates-womens-rights/.

6. Steven Mark, "Bartels Lecturer Examines Status of Women Worldwide," *Cornell Chronicle*, September 6, 2012, https://news.cornell.edu/stories/2012/09/former-chile-president-focuses-women.

7. "Nobel Laureate Alexievich Created Her Own Literary Genre," *Cornell Chronicle*, September 13, 2016, https://news.cornell.edu/stories/2016/09/nobel-laureate-alexievich-created-her-own-literary-genre.

8. "Alexievich Created Her Own Literary Genre."

9. Debra Castillo to former Brazilian President Cardoso, March 2010 (unpublished letter).

10. Andrew Key (class of 2015) to Fredrik Logevall, April 25, 2011 (unpublished email).

11. Hassan Saleem, "Svetlana Alexievich Find Light in the Darkness," website, Einaudi Center for International Studies, 2016, https://web.archive.org/web/20170106000601/http://einaudi.cornell.edu/svetlana-alexievich-finds-light-darkness.

13. INSTITUTIONALIZED INTERNATIONALIZATION

International Programs in CALS

Larry Zuidema

In 1963, the New York State College of Agriculture at Cornell University, today known as the New York State College of Agriculture and Life Sciences (CALS), made a commitment to internationalize. Although many Cornell faculty had participated in international research and education activities, the magnitude of this college-level decision was and remains unprecedented at Cornell. Today, this commitment has two primary dimensions: (1) research and education activities with and on behalf of professionals and institutions abroad; and (2) a comprehensive academic program consisting of over fifty international courses and degree options differentiating Cornell from other US universities.

In the early 1960s, famine in India and elsewhere brought back the idea of a Malthusian dilemma: that population growth would outstrip the world's ability to provide food for all. Although they received outside famine relief, countries like India did not have transportation systems capable of delivering food where it was needed. This prompted Western governments, relief agencies, nongovernmental organizations, foundations, and universities to take short-term and long-term action. With United States Agency for International Development (USAID) funds, US universities were matched with universities in poor countries to build their capacity to conduct research for long-term remedies. In addition, the Ford and Rockefeller Foundations took the lead in creating thematic international research institutions throughout the developing world through the sixteen institutes in the Consultative Group on International Agricultural Research to address critical food production issues.

CALS had institution-building experience and partnered with the University of the Philippines College of Agriculture on a massive graduate education program in 1963, sponsored by the Ford Foundation.[1] Management of this long-term project, and the possibility of developing an academic program focused on agricultural development abroad, led the faculty and administration of CALS to establish in February 1963 the International Agricultural Development Program

Figure 13.1 Professor Kenneth Turk, the inaugural director of international agricultural programs. (Photo by University Photography, provided by Division of Rare and Manuscript Collections, Cornell University Library)

(later known as International Programs of CALS, or IP-CALS) with a strong academic focus. In February 2013, Cornell celebrated the fiftieth anniversary of the establishment of IP-CALS, and its core elements continue today as part of the Department of Global Development.

Genesis of IP-CALS

Several interlinked events converged between 1960 and 1963 that laid the path to the establishment of IP-CALS. The establishment of International Agricultural Development involved the combination of a dynamic foundation leader (Forrest F. "Frosty" Hill of the Ford Foundation), a development theorist (John W. Mellor), an enlightened administrator (Charles E. Palm), an experienced visionary (Richard Bradfield), an energetic program leader (Kenneth L. Turk), and substantial financial support.

Hill was a professor and chair of the Department of Agricultural Economics in CALS from 1943 to 1952, university provost from 1952 to 1955, and vice president of the Ford Foundation from 1955 to 1967, where he had primary responsibility for their overseas programs. In 1957, he presented a paper at Cornell titled "The Human Factor in Economic Development." As a conclusion to this talk, he said, "There is a need for specialization plus the more important kinds of political, social, economic, and technological changes that must take place in a country as it moves from a less to a more economically developed stage."[2] Following the foundation's announcement of a new international program in 1960, Cornell made a broad proposal for international studies in 1962, to which Ford responded with a $3.25 million grant, including $800,000 for the appointment of six international professors in international agriculture. A stipulation of this grant to CALS was the establishment of IP-CALS with New York State funding.

Mellor, who received three degrees in agricultural economics from Cornell, became an assistant professor in that field in 1954, focusing on the role of agriculture in economic development. He was one of ten members of the Cornell International Affairs Committee, which in the spring of 1961 recommended the creation of the Center for International Studies at Cornell. In the Ford Foundation proposal, Mellor wrote the IP-CALS section and proposed that it have a director and advisory committee to handle the various segments of the program.

Palm, professor of entomology, became dean of CALS in 1959. In 1960 and 1961, the American Association of Land-grant Colleges and State Universities in Washington, DC, focused on the need for an emphasis on international activities, which resonated with Palm. In May 1961, Palm appointed a fourteen-person committee chaired by professor of agronomy Richard Bradfield, with assistance from Mellor, and later asked them about the advisability of developing a program as a college responsibility. With a positive response, Palm and a faculty committee identified international agriculture as a "fourth dimension" of CALS—meaning that international work would be equal to the functions of teaching, research, and extension, with four directors in leadership positions under the dean.

Bradfield had a distinguished international career, including serving as adviser to the Rockefeller Foundation and member of its board of trustees. The Bradfield Report, which defined the role of CALS in international agricultural development, was presented to Dean Palm in June 1961. The major recommendations were summarized as follows: (1) that a program director be named by the dean to be responsible for any administrative aspects of international agricultural development programs and that an advisory committee be appointed; (2) that the college provide a comprehensive, quality graduate program for training international and American students for service in international agricultural development; (3) that cooperative contract arrangements be developed with one or two foreign universities for the purpose of developing these institutions into regional centers; and (4) that the college take special interest in the University of the Philippines College of Agriculture at Los Baños and explore further cooperation.

Turk, professor and former chair of the Department of Animal Science, was appointed to the Bradfield Committee in 1961 and therefore became involved with organizing international agriculture at Cornell. After approval and financial support was obtained from New York governor Nelson Rockefeller and the New York State Legislature (as required by the Ford Foundation), Turk was officially appointed inaugural director of IP-CALS on February 1, 1963. During his first year, he had already established both the undergraduate and graduate programs of IP-CALS. He helped lay the foundation of IP-CALS and contributed significantly to its viability, growth, accomplishments, and enduring quality. His total dedication, energetic leadership, bold initiatives, and insistence on quality were as equally applied to the newly established program in the Philippines as they were to the establishment of a first-class, on-campus international education program at Cornell.

The Ford Foundation funded six positions as "international professors" in the social sciences within CALS for five years: three agricultural economists (Mellor, Solon Barraclough, and Tom Poleman), two rural sociologists (Robert Polson and Frank Young), and one education professor (J. Paul Leagans). Being an international professor in CALS meant that a faculty member's activities would be 100 percent international. A short time later, the Ford Foundation also started funding international faculty in soils (Armand van Wambeke), plant breeding (Loy Crowder), plant pathology (David Thurston), and animal science (Robert McDowell). Ford Foundation support was for a ten-year period. International professors taught many of the international courses and became the backbone of the IP-CALS academic program.

Components of the IP-CALS Program

On-campus activities include the academic program that has been the constant centerpiece of the IP-CALS program, as well as several other types of activities:

- a strong interdisciplinary academic program including a MPS degree option in international agricultural development, which has been attractive to returning and outgoing Peace Corps volunteers
- numerous and often sponsored professional development activities, including the Norman E. Borlaug International Agricultural Science and Technology Fellowship Program and the Hubert H. Humphrey Fellowship Program
- numerous publications in the early years, including three distinct series allowing faculty to share their knowledge and research: IA Bulletins (37 publications), IA Mimeographs (116 publications), and IA Reprints (journal articles only)

- conferences and workshops focused on worldwide food and agricultural issues—most conferences included experts and participants from outside Cornell; two large conferences dealt with Chinese agriculture when China became accessible and second-generation issues from the Green Revolution
- hosting activities, the most notable of which are the Hubert H. Humphrey program to bring midcareer professionals in agriculture and the environment from developing countries to Cornell for a year and the Peace Corps recruiting contract that enables Cornell graduating students who become Peace Corps volunteers to gain valuable international experience before making advanced graduate degree or employment choices[3]
- coordination of study abroad and student exchange opportunities for undergraduate students since 1966

The international activities of CALS have often been multidimensional and interdisciplinary, involving both faculty and graduate students. The most notable institution-building projects were the Nanking plant breeding and agricultural economic program between Cornell and the University of Nanking from 1924 to 1931; the two University of the Philippines College of Agriculture education and research projects from 1952 to 1973; the South Pacific Regional Agricultural Development project in Samoa with the University of Hawaii from 1980 to 1992; and education projects at the agricultural universities at Nitra in Slovakia and Gödöllő in Hungary, launched in 1992 and focused on the introduction of the principles of a market economy.[4]

Education-oriented activities of IP-CALS have included the management of advanced education and training programs of Ugandan professionals in US universities funded by USAID under contract with the Ohio State University; the hosting of the International Service for the Acquisition of Agri-biotech Applications, which shares benefits of crop biotechnology with resource-poor farmers; the CALS Transnational Learning program, which leverages experience and resources from CALS to work with partners, mainly in Africa, to increase food security; the Agricultural Innovation Partnership, which enhances agricultural education and extension systems in the Indo-Gangenic Plains of India; and Advancing Women in Agriculture through Research and Education, which seeks to ensure that gender is considered in all IP-CALS activities.

Numerous research-oriented activities have included several USAID-funded projects such as the Soils Management and Bean Cowpea Collaborative Research Support Programs and the Agricultural Biotechnology Support project, as well as projects supported by the Bill and Melinda Gates Foundation such as the Durable Rust Resistance in Wheat project, the Next Generation Cassava Breeding project with African institutions, and genomic selection focusing on variety improvements in maize and wheat for small farmers.

Technical assistance projects of IP-CALS have included Farming Systems Development in the Eastern Visayas of the Philippines, Communications for Technology Transfer with the Academy for Educational Development, and the Eastern Europe Economic Transition project, which provided funds for several Eastern European scientists to spend a year at Cornell to work with Cornell scientists on common problems.

In 1990, Cornell established the Cornell International Institute for Food, Agriculture and Development (CIIFAD) with funding from Cornell alumnus Charles F. Feeney (class of 1956) of $15 million in grants over fifteen years. CIIFAD's focus was on the promotion of sustainable agriculture and rural development in the poorer countries of the world. Its goals were (1) knowledge generation, adaptation, and dissemination; (2) human resource development; and (3) institutional strengthening for sustainable development. While housed in IP-CALS, CIIFAD operated separately to encourage university-wide participation. Major CIIFAD projects abroad involved numerous faculty and graduate students, primarily from CALS.[5]

Factors of Success

Several program characteristics contributed to the success of IP-CALS from the beginning and remained relevant over time.

Clear Objectives: The established objectives mirrored the recommendations of the Bradfield Committee, with the addition of, "Develop a program of basic and applied research in the biological, natural, and social sciences applicable to agriculture in low-income countries."[6]

Integrated Structure: The "fourth dimension" designation gave the program high visibility and status and sent a message to all that CALS was fully committed to internationalization.

International Professors: The ten new faculty members in seven departments—a distinguishing feature of IP-CALS—were a dean's dream. The Ford Foundation grants not only covered these ten faculty salaries but also provided each professor support that included student assistantships, travel, and staff salaries. By 1972, with the cooperation of Governor Nelson Rockefeller and the New York State Legislature, nine faculty lines were shifted to state support as international positions.

Education Focus: Kenneth Turk often said that the Cornell international program is right here on campus and what we do abroad is meant to feed into this program in the form of international experience for faculty and education and research opportunities for students. Other universities defined their international activities as a series of projects abroad.

Student Research Abroad: A hallmark of IP-CALS was encouragement and support for research in the developing world. The idea was to focus American students on development issues abroad and allow international students the opportunity to address the agricultural problems of their own countries. In the first twenty-five years, the number of graduate students conducting research abroad increased from 38 to 102.

Faculty Involvement: IP-CALS was a faculty-driven and faculty-monitored activity of CALS. Comprehensive faculty participation, beyond the international professors, was the key ingredient to its success.

Diversified Funding: IP-CALS received substantial support from Ford, Rockefeller, and other foundations; New York State; the US government; CALS (return of indirect costs); and private donors. USAID funded at least twenty projects over the years.

IP-CALS was the very first international program in an American college of agriculture. While several other universities followed with programs of their own, many defined "international" as a project abroad, leaving out the important on-campus academic program for students. At agricultural conferences and meetings, Cornell was often cited as the model international agricultural program.

Notes

This chapter is adapted from *Cornell University Meets the Challenge of World Agriculture* by Larry Zuidema (Ithaca, NY: International Programs, College of Agriculture and Life Sciences, Cornell University, 2014), https://hdl.handle.net/1813/112751.

1. For more about Cornell in the Philippines, see chapter 17, Institution Building Abroad: Cornell in the Philippines.

2. Forrest F. Hill, "The Human Factor in Economic Development," October 14, 1957, Hill Papers, 003698, Ford Foundation Archives.

3. For more about the Humphrey Fellows and the Peace Corps, see chapter 23, The Cornell Humphrey Program: A Catalyst for Cooperation and Understanding; and chapter 54, Cornell and the Peace Corps: A Valuable Partnership.

4. For more about Cornell in the Philippines, in Nanking, and in Eastern Europe, see chapter 17, Institution Building Abroad: Cornell in the Philippines; chapter 1, A Pioneering International Program: The Cornell-Nanking Story; and chapter 21, After the Berlin Wall: Cornell in Postsocialist Europe.

5. For more about CIIFAD, see chapter 15, CIIFAD: Unique Funding for Collaborative Approaches to International Development.

6. Richard Bradfield, "The Role of the College of Agriculture in International Agricultural Development," *The Bradfield Report*, internal report submitted to the Dean of the College of Agriculture, Charles E. Palm, June 1961.

14. OVER FIFTY YEARS OF TEACHING AGRICULTURE IN THE DEVELOPING NATIONS

Ronnie Coffman

It was a cold night in early January 1969 when Trans-Caribbean Airways lifted off from John F. Kennedy International Airport bound for San Juan, Puerto Rico. Thus began my association with IARD 602: Agriculture in the Developing Nations (now IARD 6020). I was a Cornell plant breeding graduate student at the time, delighted to escape from the Ithaca winter. This was the second year of operation of the course, which was destined to persist for fifty years and beyond, exposing generations of Cornell students to the challenges of international agricultural development.

The course was established and led by David Thurston, international professor of plant pathology, and Robert McDowell, international professor of animal science, with support from their fellow international professors, including Loy Crowder of the Department of Plant Breeding and Matthew Drosdorf of the Department of Agronomy. As the years progressed, nearly every faculty member associated with international agricultural development at Cornell contributed their expertise to the course. It became the flagship of the International Agriculture and Rural Development curriculum.

"Life-changing" was an expression often used by students to describe the impact of the course on their lives and careers. In my case, I decided to do my PhD research with Norman Borlaug in Mexico. After graduation, I opted for a job breeding rice at the International Rice Research Institute in the Philippines. In 1981, I returned to Cornell as a member of the faculty and found myself responsible for leading the course at the request of Dean David Call. I was delighted with the assignment. In this chapter, I have attempted to describe the evolution of the course in terms of geography, content, and the participants.

Geographic Evolution

During my absence, the course had migrated from Puerto Rico to Mexico, with a couple of interim years in the Dominican Republic. Mexico offered more diversity

Figure 14.1 Students from India and Cornell with an Indian extension faculty member who is explaining cucurbit growing, 2020. (Photo by Chris Knight, Global Development, Cornell University)

and the opportunity for student exposure to socioeconomic issues, but a lot of time was spent on buses moving among agro-ecological zones. The extensive bus trips were a safety issue, with a bus turning over near Mexico City in the late 1970s. Miraculously, no one was seriously injured, but many needed medical attention. The students and faculty were taken by ambulances to hospitals all over Mexico City and it fell to Professor Thurston, a fluent Spanish speaker and leader of the course, to account for them. He spent the night moving from hospital to hospital, confirming the well-being of each participant. Famously, he recalled encountering Douglas Hogue, professor of animal science, who had injured his back when the bus overturned. Professor Hogue was infamous for his jokes. He greeted Professor Thurston with a question: "Did you hear the story of the young Mexican bus driver who approached St. Peter's gate?" Hogue continued, "He was immediately waved through the gate to heaven, while many others waited in line, including a priest, who protested that he had been serving the Lord his entire life, and should certainly be favored over a young bus driver. However, St. Peter was quick to inform the priest that the young bus driver had put the fear of God in every passenger who had ridden with him."

When I took over the course, I decided that the long bus trips in Mexico were no laughing matter. In consultation with my mentors, Professors Thurston and

Figure 14.2 The class visits the Earth Trust, Coonoor, Tamil Nadu, 2020. (Photo by Chris Knight, Global Development, Cornell University)

McDowell, I decided to move the course to Costa Rica, where travel distances would be considerably shorter. The three of us did a scouting trip in the summer of 1982. I remember it well, as I had to do all the driving and I was issued a speeding ticket by the Costa Rican police. The fine was only three dollars, but it took me half a day to pay it!

We first operated the course in Costa Rica in January 1983. It was a wonderful place where we could move easily among the various ecological zones. The people were very hospitable and welcomed the students into their homes, where they would often spend the night. Cornell alumni were extremely generous, especially the Rojas family, which had sent four sons to attend Cornell.

After eight years in Costa Rica, I decided to move the course to Honduras for a couple of reasons. First, we had imposed on our Costa Rican hosts for a long time. Second, development issues in the social sciences were limited in Costa Rica. The country was prospering. In Honduras, on the other hand, challenges to development were widespread, with rural people migrating to Tegucigalpa and other urban centers. I had done some consulting in Honduras, and I knew it would be an ideal laboratory for the course, but I had a major concern about security. While working as a consultant to revise the curriculum at Zamorano University, I was in a meeting in the Kellogg Center just across the road from the university when suddenly the building was raked by gunfire from a heavy machine gun. Bullets were hitting the wall—whump, whump, whump—as my colleagues and I lay flat on the floor. Eventually, a terrified woman crawled into the building and said to me in trembling Spanish, "They are robbing the bank!" It turned out that a pickup truck of twelve robbers disguised as Zamorano students (who traditionally dressed in distinctive blue denim) had attempted to rob the bank next door. However, the Honduran army had been tipped off about it and had set up a machine gun in bushes behind the bank. When the robbers arrived and shot the bank guard, they were slaughtered. This weighed on my mind as I explored moving the course to Honduras, but I was assured that the situation had changed. Indeed, that seemed to be the case, so we decided to make the move.

After a couple of years in Honduras, I accepted a position as associate dean for research in the College of Agriculture and Life Sciences and relinquished my teaching responsibilities. Robert Blake (McDowell's successor in animal science) took over the course and sustained it in Honduras for around seven years. However, security resurfaced as an issue when a student was wounded by gunfire during a robbery attempt. The course was subsequently shifted to Ecuador, which had its own set of problems, with an attempted coup stranding the class there at one point. The course moved back to Honduras for a couple of years, but risk seemed to be increasing.

In 2001, I became director of international programs in the College of Agriculture and Life Sciences, and Professor KV Raman and I began to explore the opportunity to shift the course to India. Our first year operating in India was 2003. We enlisted the help of Sathguru Management Consultants, which became an essential partner in operating the course, developing it into a wonderfully organized turnkey operation. Over the years, Raman assumed full responsibility for leadership of the course as I became involved in major development grants. The course operated very successfully in India through 2020, with a one-year stint in Burma in 2017. Earlier, we also operated the course in both India and Thailand, with approximately ten days in each country.

Content Evolution

In the beginning, the course was essentially exposure to production agriculture in the tropics at every scale. In Puerto Rico, we circled the island visiting the various ecological zones with the associated cropping and livestock production systems, large and small. Plantation crops such as sugar cane, pineapple, and oil palm were also included. The emphasis was more on production constraints, as opposed to issues related to development and livelihoods. Slowly but steadily, this changed as students and faculty from the social sciences began to participate. Eventually, to meet the needs of all the students, the course became modular, organized around several relevant themes that included agricultural systems, value addition, food processing, global marketing, and rural development. Under Professor Raman's leadership, learning objectives were formalized for each theme. The following are some examples:

- Understand the complexities of selected agro-ecosystems of India and reflect on what improvements can be made.
- Understand how farmers obtain information, knowledge, and recommendations for their farming practices from public and private sources.
- Evaluate the role of diet and nutrition in public health and ways to ameliorate malnutrition. How are the various crops and livestock used in human diets?
- Understand how value addition practices on a small scale can be enhanced and recommendations for technologies can be used.
- Examine the issues of global trade in value-added products as well as farm products, international policies, and domestic needs.
- Understand the social organization and structure in India at various levels (households, relatives, villages, etc.) and how they relate to livelihood strategies for various social groups of farmers.
- Explore the various marketing channels for farmers' surplus production, including local, national, and international markets, and the role of middlemen, self-help groups, auction centers, and policy interventions.
- Understand the importance of various credit sources for farmers, including with national and state banks, private banks, moneylenders, cooperatives, and micro-credit schemes.
- Visit and explore alternative rural programs to understand the complex nature of how farmers fulfill their livelihood needs. This includes home-based products, agricultural wage incomes, nonagricultural wage activities, and the role of diversification in supplementing farm household incomes.
- Explore the links between human nutrition and agriculture and the issue of nutritional disorders among various social groups in India and how agriculture can help alleviate these problems.

Participant Evolution

For the first three decades of the course, the participants were Cornell students led by Cornell faculty, with the occasional inclusion of someone from the Cornell Cooperative Extension system. When the course evolved to India, we had appeals for the inclusion of Indian students. We began allowing a few students from selected Indian universities to join the field trip. From this experience we observed tremendous mutual benefits to both Cornell and Indian students. They learned from each other technically but also culturally. The cultural exposure was so valuable to Indian students that course participants commanded, on graduation, salaries that were more than 50 percent higher than those of nonparticipating students.

During 2005, the structure of the course was modified to bring Indian students to Cornell during the fall semester to interact with Cornell students in the preparatory IARD 402 course. This enabled the Cornell and Indian students to get to know each other, participate in classes and field trips in upstate New York, and start focusing on their term paper. During the early part of January, selected Cornell students and faculty traveled to India to join with their counterpart Indian students and faculty on field visits related to their chosen theme. After the completion of the India field visits, Cornell students returned to Ithaca the third week of January. Cornell and Indian students worked on their group paper using remote learning tools such as Zoom, Teams, Skype, and Google Docs. The final presentations of the group projects and the term papers were submitted to the respective faculty mentors from India and Cornell.

Both the fall and spring courses provided students a unique exposure to different cultural, educational, and social practices that augmented their learning and stimulated their performance. Students benefited from resources at Cornell University and visits to various industries in the agri-processing sector. This program helped students not just in their academic endeavors but also in understanding different cultures, enabling them to improve their level of confidence and their outlook toward a better career.

Some fifty-four years after its inception, this course continues to be the flagship of our international curriculum. I hope it will be sustained as one of the most life-changing courses ever offered by Cornell University.

15. CIIFAD

Unique Funding for Collaborative Approaches to International Development

Terry Tucker and Heike Michelsen

In 1990, Cornell received a $15 million gift with very unusual and favorable conditions from an anonymous donor—later revealed to be philanthropist and alumnus Charles Feeney (class of 1956, died 2023)—to deal with problems of poverty and hunger, low agricultural productivity, environmental degradation, and human deprivation.[1] This led to the establishment of the Cornell International Institute for Food, Agriculture and Development (CIIFAD). According to Professor Dan Sisler, who spearheaded the proposal, "This kind of funding was never before available for development work."[2] Only ten years later an external review team concluded, "At this point in history, no other institution has the same ability [as CIIFAD] to address issues of agricultural and natural resource sustainability in developing countries through multidisciplinary, participatory research."[3]

To match the generous gift, Cornell agreed not to charge overhead costs and to contribute faculty time to this endeavor (i.e., faculty could voluntarily make CIIFAD activity part of their teaching, research, and outreach responsibilities where they had expertise and both professional and personal involvement). The gift supported program costs such as student and faculty research, training at Cornell and overseas, publications, travel, seminars, and workshops.

While CIIFAD was set up as a university-wide entity, it was based in International Programs of the College of Agriculture and Life Sciences (CALS) and given administrative support and facilities by the college. Faculty, students, and staff from other colleges were welcome to participate in CIIFAD and did. While two CALS deans, then dean David Call and former dean and provost Keith Kennedy, can be credited with creating CIIFAD, CALS faculty led the actual planning and design. They addressed the question of how Cornell's knowledge and human resources could best contribute to advancing and ensuring sustainable agricultural and rural development in developing countries.

Interdisciplinary, problem focused, and collaborative were the three essential qualities that characterized CIIFAD's engagements. CIIFAD's creators understood

Figure 15.1 Li Bo, a master's degree student in natural resources (*center*), looks on while villagers of Tong Dui Sui in Yunnan Province draw a map of the various natural resources in and around their community, 1999. (Photo by James Lassoie)

that no single discipline or perspective could solve the challenges of increasing the capacities of developing countries to deal with sustainability issues on a long-term basis rather than attempting "quick fixes." Remedies would require cooperation between countries and institutions rather than any simple transfer of technology or prescription from abroad. Instead of defining specific objectives, activities, outputs, and outcomes and implementing the planned projects—the usual approach in international development cooperation—CIIFAD worked to diagnose and plan together with partners overseas, using partnerships and learning processes as basic modes of operation. Because there were so many evident and serious problems that needed to be tackled, the intention was to start by utilizing what was already known, rather than undertake "basic" research.

As a university institution rather than a development agency, CIIFAD and its partners supported activities that had three modes of action: (a) to generate more and more relevant knowledge for sustainable development; (b) to train and strengthen human resources, both at Cornell and overseas, for the advancement of sustainable development; and (c) to enhance institutional capacities for generating knowledge, improving human resources, and solving problems, including analysis and advocacy.

Figure 15.2 Professor James Lassoie (*left*) monitors ecological change in northwest Yunnan Province assisted by Wu Ning (*right*), graduate student from Beijing University, 2004. (Photo by Ruth Sherman)

The gift supported CIIFAD's operations and activities for fifteen years, from 1990 to 2005.[4] During this time, CIIFAD's director, Norman Uphoff, was supported by a nine-faculty program committee, reported to a university governing board including four college deans, and was advised by an international advisory committee made up of eminent people from the public and private sectors who had broad development experience.

CIIFAD developed a series of problem-focused, interdisciplinary partnerships, which usually involved some combination of universities, nongovernmental organizations, government agencies, and community representatives, as well as international research institutions or private-sector partners. These partnerships were defined as open-ended, flexible, two-way, and mutually beneficial.[5]

CIIFAD's activities were organized through thirteen country collaborative programs in Africa, Asia, and Latin America and fourteen thematic collaborative programs.[6] Most faculty involved with CIIFAD were members of at least one country program, which allowed them to apply current knowledge while also learning new things, and one thematic program, which allowed them to learn more about broad comparative experience and synthesize new knowledge.

Participation in these programs varied between groups and over time in terms of numbers of participants and the intensity of involvement by faculty, students, and staff. In 2000 alone, for example, there were about sixty faculty and sixty students plus another fifteen staff participating on a voluntary basis in the various CIIFAD programs. They represented twenty-seven Cornell departments or units in six of Cornell's colleges. While most came from CALS, the Colleges of Arts and Sciences; Architecture, Art, and Planning; Human Ecology, Industrial and Labor Relations; and Veterinary Medicine were also represented. Over its first fifteen years, more than two hundred students and ninety faculty were involved in different approaches to achieving sustainable agricultural and rural development.

Country Collaborative Programs

CIIFAD engaged in a broad range of programs. These were distributed among Latin American, African, and Asian countries to foster diverse experience and engage a wide range of Cornell faculty and students. The respective programs had different focuses and structures to best suit the country, problem, and institutional characteristics. There was no set formula or format. Some programs had a national purview, while others had a specific regional or area focus. The respective multidisciplinary Cornell faculty teams, together with their counterparts in a particular country, worked out the design of their programs. Most of the programs diversified over time as experience was gained and as new opportunities became apparent. All programs had one or more primary partners in the country, but cooperation was undertaken with a variety of partners depending on the problem focus, as the following highlights demonstrate.

In the Dominican Republic (DR), Cornell faculty worked with DR university colleagues, government agencies, and communities located around the Los Haitises National Park. The program strengthened knowledge about the national park's soil, natural resources, and biodiversity and proposed ways to reconcile the competing interests of park and people. Additionally, it made a lasting contribution by helping the national government establish an interagency management committee for the national park, with membership and the voice of representatives of the local communities, something unprecedented in the DR. One of the DR students participating in the program, Rhadames Lora Salcedo, who completed MS and PhD degrees at Cornell as part of the program, became a leading administrator for environmental protection in the DR.

At the initiative of the Indonesian government's deputy minister of agriculture, CIIFAD worked with staff of the Indonesian Agency for Agricultural Research and Development over a twelve-year period. CIIFAD collaborated with the Center for Agro-socio-economic Research in Bogor to reorient thinking and policy in different sectors and institutions to make sustainability a more dominant consideration along with productivity and equity. The program also worked with Cornell alumni who had important positions in the National Planning Agency on food and nutrition policies.

Collaborative work with Leyte State University (now Visayas State University) in the Philippines and its Farm and Resource Management Institute developed the national Conservation Farming in the Tropical Uplands consortium. The group grew to sixteen members ranging from local government units and nongovernmental organizations, to departments of national and regional agencies (Department of Agriculture, Department of Environment and Natural Resources) and universities, to international research centers (International Rice Research Institute and International Centre for Research in Agroforestry). That collaborative work provided a functioning model for interorganizational collaboration in which organizations of diverse sizes, structures, mandates, and focuses, but shared interests, have interacted and cooperated to improve the situation of upland rural communities.

Thematic Collaborative Programs

These programs brought together faculty, students, and staff having a common interest in a subject that could contribute significantly to sustainable agricultural and rural development. These interdisciplinary groups constituted pools of knowledge that the country programs could draw on, and country program experiences in turn added to those pools. Some of these groups lasted for a decade, some for only several years, depending on the level of faculty and student interest. They served as means for accumulating and assessing knowledge so that country programs did not operate in isolation, as the following examples demonstrate.

The Agroforestry Working Group taught an interdisciplinary graduate course on agroforestry (now Horticultural Sciences 4940), covering both US and international agroforestry experiences. At its peak, the group had over forty faculty and students from ten departments involved. Its collaborative activities and research led to publications and a new extension focus on sustainable agriculture and agroforestry.

The community-based Natural Resource Management Group evolved over a ten-year period. Its faculty, student, and staff members had interests and involvement that cut across CIIFAD programs in the DR, Central America, Ghana, Madagascar, Indonesia, and the Philippines. It sponsored speakers and discussions to share what was being learned in different parts of the world. This grouping also contributed to the National Science Foundation–supported graduate program on conservation and sustainable development, which trained dozens of graduate students in cross-disciplinary ways.

Several CIIFAD programs addressed farmer-centered research and extension, starting with the Philippine Conservation Farming in the Tropical Uplands program. This focus on discussions and field experience led to an interdisciplinary course that is still taught today as Global Development 7830.

The Intensive Rice Management group supported research, evaluation, and dissemination for the System of Rice Intensification (SRI) developed in Madagascar in the 1980s, which became part of CIIFAD's Madagascar program. This knowledge, once validated, spread and now benefits as many as twenty million farmers in fifty-eight countries.[7] It led to the establishment of the SRI International Network and Resources Center under CIIFAD in 2010. Thesis research on SRI was done in agricultural economics, agricultural engineering, and crop and soil sciences.

Factors of Success and Impact

CIIFAD achieved many notable accomplishments in the first fifteen years following its 1990 establishment. Overall, its contributions to agricultural research and development have helped to improve the lives of millions of people in developing countries, promoted sustainable food systems, generated new knowledge, developed human resources, and built capacity in partner institutions. It also had an important impact on Cornell's capabilities by

- substantially improving the quality and realism of teaching provided in development-related courses to graduate and undergraduate students through faculty engagement in CIIFAD's collaborative, interdisciplinary, problem-solving activities around the world
- increasing the sophistication, experience, and capability of over two hundred Cornell graduates at master's and PhD levels through their involvement with CIIFAD's country or thematic programs in association with their professors and overseas collaborators
- producing and publishing influential research that extended the breadth and quality of Cornell's outreach and engagement related to farming systems, farmer-centered research and extension, agroforestry, watershed management, local knowledge and Indigenous technology, agroecological innovation, and many other subjects relating to sustainable agricultural and rural development
- creating a vigorous and challenging intellectual environment at Cornell for faculty, students, and staff through various activities, seminars, lectures, forums, and reports from the field that inspired them to think,

speculate, and investigate new ideas and opportunities, new subjects, and new domains

CIIFAD's unique and flexible funding structure contributed significantly to its achievements by enabling faculty and students to work more actively and effectively together with institutions in developing countries that shared concerns and interest in advancing the cause of sustainable agriculture and rural development. Funding also could be deployed to areas of most evident opportunity and value without complicated processes of proposal and review. Faculty treated Charles Feeney's gift as enabling and catalytic, and they used it to achieve agreed-on objectives with their partners. It also enabled them to take advantage of new knowledge and new opportunities that were not yet known within established circles. In the end, the initial ten-year program period was stretched out to support activities for fifteen years because CIIFAD was successful in mobilizing financial resources from other sources. Importantly, the donor's generous and flexible gift enabled faculty to work within programs as opposed to short-term projects, fostering the emergence of longer-term collaborations, the pursuit of development objectives and activities not possible within time-bound projects, and far more attention to learning and adaptation.

Another key factor of success was CIIFAD's reliance on partnerships as its main mode of operation. While not all of CIIFAD's experiences with partnerships in Africa, Asia, and Latin America were equally successful, overall the partnership approach has changed the quality and philosophy of work in desirable directions. As Norman Uphoff concluded, "Development becomes better understood as not just doing things *for* or *to* people but as doing things *with* them, with an emphasis on increasing their own understanding of possibilities and their own performance capacities."[8]

Notes

1. See Henrik N. Dullea, "Cornell President's Statement Regarding Charitable Support," *Cornell Chronicle*, January 23, 1997; and Norman Uphoff and Gilbert Levine, "Norman Uphoff Discusses the Early Days of CIIFAD with Gil Levine," eCommons, Cornell University, June 21, 2013, https://ecommons.cornell.edu/handle/1813/33730.

2. Daniel G. Sisler and Edwin B. Oyer, "Dan Sisler and Ed Oyer Discuss the Creation of CIIFAD," eCommons, Cornell University, June 21, 2013, https://ecommons.cornell.edu/handle/1813/33732.

3. Cornell International Institute for Food, Agriculture and Development, *Annual Report 2000–2001* (Ithaca, NY: CIIFAD, 2001).

4. After the initial gift, CIIFAD was led by Alice Pell (2005–2007) and then Ralph Christy until it closed in 2017. During this time, core support from CALS and the central

administration was constrained and programming was reoriented and limited. However, several programs and activities initiated by CIIFAD continue until today. These include food marketing research and educational programs in emerging markets and a weekly seminar series with scholars and practitioners exploring the complexity of global development from diverse perspectives, attracting faculty and students across the campus.

5. Heike Michelsen, *Learning from Partnerships: Experiences from the Cornell International Institute for Food, Agriculture and Development (CIIFAD)* (The Hague: International Service for National Agricultural Research, 2003).

6. For detailed descriptions of programs, see Cornell International Institute for Food, Agriculture and Development, *Annual Reports* (Ithaca, NY: CIIFAD, 1993–1994 to 2000–2001).

7. For more about the System of Rice Intensification, see chapter 16, Transforming Global Rice Production: The System of Rice Intensification.

8. Norman Uphoff, "A Message from CIIFAD's Director," in Michelsen, *Learning from Partnerships*.

16. TRANSFORMING GLOBAL RICE PRODUCTION

The System of Rice Intensification

Erika Styger

Origins of the SRI Method in Madagascar

When the rainy season came early to the highlands of Madagascar in 1983, rice seedlings in the nursery at the agriculture school in the upland town of Antsirabe were still too few and too small. The agronomist in charge, French Jesuit Henri de Laulanié, decided of necessity to transplant the young seedlings that were available by planting them farther apart. To everyone's astonishment, the yield from this plot far outperformed all others in the area. Father de Laulanié and his team of young farmers began experimenting. Over the next five years, they continued to obtain higher yields, from the usual one ton per hectare to two to three tons per hectare. They used new practices: planting single, young seedlings (eight to fifteen days old), widely spaced (twenty-five to forty centimeters between plants) with only minimal irrigation. This differed from the conventional system whereby older seedlings (thirty to forty-five days old) were planted in clumps of three to five plants closely spaced (ten to fifteen centimeters apart) and kept continuously flooded throughout the season. De Laulanié synthesized the combination of these practices into a new method called the Système de Riziculture Intensive (System of Rice Intensification, SRI).[1]

Rice is a staple food for four billion people, more than half of the world's population. It is grown in more than one hundred countries, and 80 percent of rice producers are smallholders who farm less than two hectares of rice. Global rice consumption was 440 million tons in 2010. It is estimated to increase to 650 million tons by 2050, a 48 percent increase. But both the amount of land available for rice and the yield growth rates are in decline, and between 2010 and 2050, irrigated rice yields in developing countries are forecast to decrease by 15 percent due to climate change. Rice has an enormous environmental footprint. Twenty-five to 33 percent of global freshwater resources are withdrawn to irrigate rice fields. Pesticide overuse is causing harm to soil, plants, animals, and humans.

Figure 16.1 Py Phal, System of Rice Intensification (SRI) farmer from the Prasat village, Takeo Province, Cambodia, is happy about her harvest of SRI-grown organic Jasmine rice, 2010. (Photo by author)

Rice is a large greenhouse gas emitter, with 12 percent of the human-made methane emissions, second largest in agriculture, after dairy.

Conventional solutions to address these multiple challenges focus on input-related technologies, such as the use of new germplasm, chemical fertilizers, and pesticides to boost rice yields. These solutions are expensive, force farmers to become dependent on input suppliers, produce considerable environmental damage, and yet remain highly vulnerable to climate change. They also increasingly show their limits: yield improvements are slowing, while the average rice yields remain well below their potential. But there is another way. A climate-resilient rice production alternative has been proved to work for millions of farmers in over sixty countries.

The SRI method remained unknown outside Madagascar until the mid-1990s when an agricultural project team led by Glenn Lines from the Cornell International Institute for Food, Agriculture and Development (CIIFAD) learned of it. The Cornell team tested SRI over three years, also obtaining consistently higher yields. Recognizing the potential benefit for farmers in other countries, CIIFAD director Norman Uphoff began to share information about SRI with rice researchers outside Madagascar.

Figure 16.2 SRI farmer Bouba Boureima from the village of Morikoira, Timbuktu region of Mali, shows two plants: on the right, a plant from his SRI plot; on the left, a plant from his conventionally grown rice plot, 2008. (Photo by author)

While SRI was originally developed for the irrigated rice systems in the highlands of Madagascar, as it has spread across the world, practitioners and farmers have adapted it to different climate zones and rice systems with a suite of additional practices.[2] To integrate the various adaptations, we synthesized the SRI method with four guiding principles: (1) encourage early and healthy plant establishment, (2) minimize competition among plants, (3) build up fertile soils rich with organic matter and beneficial soil biota, and (4) manage water carefully to avoid both flooding and water stress.[3] These principles remain the same wherever the SRI method is used, but how these are implemented can be adapted to a given local environment. This approach allows everyone to share the same understanding of the method, while encouraging innovation adapted to local conditions.

The SRI system teaches us to work with the plants and the environment so that each individual plant can express its genetic potential. Implementing the four principles together creates synergy. Plants become more robust and more productive, producing more and deeper roots, an increased number of tillers (shoots) and panicles (grain heads), and bigger and heavier grains. Yields increase by 20 to 50 percent or more and use of irrigation water and the resulting methane emissions are reduced by 30 to 50 percent, seed by 90 percent, and use of agro-chemicals such as fertilizers and pesticides by 30 to 100 percent. The vigorous SRI plants with their deep roots show an increased resilience to drought, flooding, and strong winds, as well as toward pest and disease.

Since 2005, farmers in India, Nepal, Ethiopia, Mali, and other countries have begun to apply the four SRI principles to other crops: wheat, barley, sugarcane, finger millet, Ethiopian teff, West African fonio, mustard, legumes, and vegetables, all showing excellent results and remarkable yield increases. We call this application the System of Crop Intensification.[4]

Spreading the Word (Late 1990s to 2010)

More researchers and farmers in different countries began testing SRI each year. Their field reports confirmed the improved productivity and performance of rice fields when using the SRI method, even across varied environments. CIIFAD quickly became the global hub for SRI as partners from many countries reported their field results back to Uphoff, aided by Olivia Vent and Lucy Fisher of the CIIFAD communications team. During this early period, Uphoff collected and synthesized the incoming information and data and shared it with interested people through lectures, seminars, personal visits (both domestic and international), emails, and publications.

In 2001, Fisher set up the CIIFAD SRI website to collect and organize field reports, media coverage, and research publications, which soon expanded to include videos, photos, and social media accounts.[5] In addition, she started the bimonthly Global SRI Newsletter and SRI research database, which includes more than two thousand entries: research articles, technical reports, book chapters, and student theses. The website is updated daily and has become the single largest and most comprehensive archive and collection of SRI information available. Vent added another dimension. She focused on marketing SRI rice through her collaboration with Lotus Foods, which distributes imported SRI-grown rice through US grocery stores. She has also been researching the effect of SRI practices on women farmers' health and well-being.

During the decade beginning in 2000, partners in forty-one countries tested and validated the SRI method. These wide-ranging efforts confirmed that SRI can apply to varied climate zones, from humid to semiarid climates, and can be used for different rice systems, from irrigated to rainfed lowland and rainfed upland systems. SRI testing and validation began by working with farmers. In time, a community of practice emerged. SRI "champions" from different locations in a country would meet to learn from each other and draft location-specific SRI manuals in local languages. Eventually, informal networks coalesced into more formal national SRI networks. Several such networks, each with its own organizational structure and way of functioning, developed in Bangladesh, Cambodia, India, Indonesia, Japan, Nepal, Malaysia, the Philippines, Sri Lanka, and Vietnam.[6]

Providing Global Support through SRI-Rice (2010 to 2016)

As worldwide interest in SRI continued to grow, the Cornell team secured start-up support from the Los Angeles–based Better U Foundation to found the SRI International Network and Resources Center (SRI-Rice) in 2010, which I led for six years. Since I had been involved in introducing SRI to Mali from 2007 to 2010, when I joined the Cornell team as a tropical agronomist, SRI-Rice could expand beyond its existing knowledge-sharing and networking functions to include direct technical assistance, reaching thirty countries in Asia, Africa, and Latin America. Two examples are introducing SRI to Haiti in 2010, followed by multiyear technical advice, and providing technical training to US Peace Corps volunteers, counterparts, and staff of five West African countries over a period of three years.

As SRI adoption expanded, SRI-Rice worked to help set up regional networks, which would make it easier for practitioners from neighboring countries to work together, sharing the same climate conditions and rice production systems, and to allow them to coordinate their efforts in a more decentralized way.

From its beginning, SRI-Rice attracted frequent requests for SRI training from numerous partners in West Africa. To meet this burgeoning demand, SRI-Rice teamed with Gaoussou Traore, coordinator for the Mali-based Regional Center for Specialization in Rice, to design and implement the World Bank–funded regional project Improving and Scaling-Up SRI in 13 Countries of West Africa. Working in Benin, Burkina Faso, Côte d'Ivoire, the Gambia, Ghana, Guinea, Liberia, Mali, Niger, Nigeria, Senegal, Sierra Leone, and Togo over three years (2014 to 2016), the project reached 50,048 farmers (33 percent women) using SRI on 13,944 hectares at 1,088 locations, trained 30,000 farmers and 1,032 technicians, and increased the number of local institutions working with SRI from 49 to 215. SRI yields under the project (as compared with conventional rice production) were greater by 56 percent for irrigated rice and by 85 percent for rainfed lowland rice. This increased rice production was worth an estimated value of $10 million in US dollars per season.[7] For this project, West Africa specialist Devon Jenkins joined the SRI-Rice team to provide technical, communication, and project management assistance.

Until 2010, the SRI method had found little uptake in the Latin America and Caribbean region, although a few promising but unconnected smaller-scale projects were underway. To strengthen these local initiatives and help form a regional community, SRI-Rice, together with the Better U Foundation and Costa Rica's Earth University, co-organized the first workshop on SRI for Latin America and the Caribbean, bringing together SRI practitioners from eleven countries. In addition, SRI-Rice supported the development of Spanish language training and outreach material and worked with the Inter-American Institute for Cooperation on Agriculture as it took on regional leadership to support SRI initiatives.[8]

Appropriate mechanization for agriculture increases efficiency, so SRI-Rice prioritized access for farmers and practitioners to expert information about planters, weeders, threshers, and other farm equipment suited to SRI. Such activities included organizing international workshops for SRI practitioners attending the 2014 International Rice Congress in Bangkok, establishing an equipment innovators Facebook page, facilitating ad hoc equipment sharing in different countries and continents, and giving presentations at the 2015 Agritechnica fair in Germany, the world's largest agricultural equipment trade exhibition.

SRI-Rice organized SRI-specific workshops alongside the International Rice Congresses in Hanoi (2010), Bangkok (2014), and Singapore (2018), providing a rare opportunity for SRI researchers and practitioners from Asia, Africa, and Latin America to meet and learn from each other.

SRI-Rice hosted more than thirty Cornell students as interns both at the SRI-Rice office on campus and in assisting partner organizations overseas. This provided students with opportunities to undertake research within the global SRI network.

From 2010 to 2016, uptake of SRI increased from forty-one to fifty-five countries, and SRI-Rice was instrumental in this by collecting and sharing the ever-increasing amount of information and providing direct technical support, thus helping to maintain worldwide dialogue and exchange through its global network.

Two Cornell Programs: SRI-Rice and Climate-Resilient Farming Systems

To expand on SRI-Rice's mission, I started a new program in 2017 called Climate-Resilient Farming Systems, working with other crops and other agro-ecological methods.[9] Both Cornell programs continue their work. SRI-Rice focuses on knowledge sharing and networking, and the Climate-Resilient Farming Systems program on technical implementation and scaling-up of SRI. Climate-Resilient Farming Systems is currently involved in three large projects: the Scaling Up Climate-Resilient Rice Production in West Africa Project, the Jubilee Justice Black Farmers SRI Rice Project, and Project ClimateRice.

As of this writing, we estimate that about twenty million farmers in sixty-two countries grow SRI rice on 6.7 million hectares, a remarkable result, but still covering only 4 percent of the global rice-growing area. There is still great potential for SRI to further enhance global food security, save water, and reduce methane emissions.

Notes

1. Henri de Laulanié, "Le système de riziculture intensive malgache," *Tropicultura* 11, no. 3 (1993): 1–19.

2. Erika Styger and Norman Uphoff, *The System of Rice Intensification (SRI): Revisiting Agronomy for a Changing Climate*, Climate-Smart Agriculture Practice Brief (Copenhagen: CGIAR Research Program on Climate Change, Agriculture and Food Security, 2016), https://ccafs.cgiar.org/resources/publications/system-rice-intensification-sri-revisiting-agronomy-changing-climate.

3. "A New Conceptual Framework for the System of Rice Intensification (SRI) for Research and Practice," Climate-Resilient Farming Systems, Cornell University, March 2017, https://www.climateresilientfarmingsystems.org/single-post/2017/03/26/new-conceptual-framework-for-sri.

4. SRI International Network and Resources Center, *SCI: The System of Crop Intensification* (Ithaca, NY: SRI International Network and Resources Center; Wageningen, Netherlands: Technical Centre for Agricultural and Rural Cooperation, 2014), http://sri.ciifad.cornell.edu/aboutsri/othercrops/SCImonograph_SRIRice2014.pdf.

5. "SRI-Rice," SRI International Network and Resources Center, Cornell University College of Agriculture and Life Sciences, accessed September 26, 2023, http://sri.ciifad.cornell.edu.

6. "Discussion Lists, On-line Communities and Websites Focusing on SRI," SRI International Network and Resources Center, Cornell University College of Agriculture and Life Sciences, accessed September 26, 2023, http://sri.cals.cornell.edu/listservs/index.html.

7. SRI West Africa homepage, accessed September 26, 2023, https://sriwestafrica.org; Erika Styger and Gaoussou Traoré, *50,000 Farmers in 13 Countries: Results from Scaling Up the System of Rice Intensification in West Africa; Achievements and Regional Perspectives for SRI; SRIWAAPP Project Summary Report 2014–2016* (Dakar, Senegal: West Africa Agriculture Productivity Program and West and Central Africa Council for Agricultural Research and Development, 2018), https://sriwestafrica.files.wordpress.com/2018/04/sri-waapp-book-single-p-8mb.pdf.

8. "SRI Is Taking Off in Colombia," Climate-Resilient Farming Systems, Cornell University, January 2019, https://www.climateresilientfarmingsystems.org/single-post/2019/01/16/sri-is-taking-off-in-colombia-regional-workshop-to-share-sri-experiences.

9. Climate-Resilient Farming Systems homepage, Cornell University, accessed September 26, 2023, https://www.climateresilientfarmingsystems.org.

17. INSTITUTION BUILDING ABROAD

Cornell in the Philippines

Larry Zuidema

In the 1960s donors and universities that wanted to assist developing countries improve their education and research institutions adopted the old adage "Give a man a fish and you feed him for a day; teach a man to fish and you feed him for a lifetime." With fears of famine in Asia and other affected areas in the world, they originally focused on expanding agricultural universities in countries with high population growth rates and an unproductive agricultural sector. In the same period, the Ford and Rockefeller Foundations developed and supported several agricultural regional and topical research institutions in developing countries, including the International Rice Research Institute at Los Baños, Philippines. In 1971, the World Bank's International Bank for Reconstruction and Development, with the United Nations Food and Agriculture Organization and the United Nations Development Programme, founded the Consultative Group on International Agricultural Research system to coordinate funding and programs for an international network of sixteen agricultural research centers. Many Cornell and other US university faculties have been involved in long- and short-term research with these centers, as well as with national agricultural research organizations abroad.

The Cornell University College of Agriculture was already a leader in agricultural institution building abroad, having previously supported the development of plant breeding and agricultural economics at the University of Nanking in China in the 1920s and an eight-year institution-building project with the University of the Philippines College of Agriculture (UPCA) in Los Baños in the 1950s.[1] Both involved long- and short-term assignments for Cornell faculty members and graduate students in these countries. These two Cornell activities were said to have influenced the United States Agency for International Development to launch several other agricultural institution-building projects in the developing world involving long-term contracts with dozens of US universities from 1960 to 1980, a massive and expensive investment. Cornell's initial US government-funded

Figure 17.1 Banaue rice terraces—a World Heritage site in the Philippines, 1967. (Photo by author)

institution-building project in the Philippines in the 1950s was followed by a Ford Foundation–supported University of the Philippines–Cornell Graduate Education Program (UPCO) in the 1960s. These two projects constituted Cornell's largest single international activity by far.

Professor Kenneth L. Turk, the first Cornell director of international agriculture (now global development), participated in the first Philippines-Cornell project for a year in 1954–1955 and supervised the second Philippines project from 1963 to 1972. In 1974, he authored *The Cornell-Los Baños Story*, comprehensively describing and documenting both Philippines projects.[2]

The Cornell–Los Baños project had two phases. In phase 1 (1952–1960), Cornell partnered with the University of the Philippines to rebuild its College of Agriculture, which had been almost completely destroyed during World War II. The United States Mutual Security Agency (later the International Cooperation Administration and now the Agency for International Development) and the National Economic Council of the Philippines largely funded the project, with leadership provided by Dean Leopoldo B. Uichanco of the University of the Philippines and Dean William I. Myers of Cornell. During the eight-year project, fifty-one American professors (thirty-five from Cornell) served in the Philippines for one-to-three-year terms and 188 staff members from the Philippines were trained either at home or in the United States. "When the program was terminated by mutual agreement in 1960, the physical plant of the College had been largely

Figure 17.2 Preparing a rice paddy with a carabao (water buffalo) in the Philippines, 1975. (Photo by author)

rebuilt, the Central Experiment Station was established and functioning, and teaching programs had been improved over their previous standards. Enrollments had reached an all-time high and procedures were established to stabilize enrollment and improve the quality of students. . . . Los Baños was rapidly becoming recognized as a teaching and research center extending far beyond the boundaries of the Philippines."[3]

Beginning in 1957 and later extended to 1965, Cornell also developed a concurrent project with the University of the Philippines College of Forestry at Los Baños to expand its programs and operations "in accordance with the rapidly growing needs of the nation for professional foresters and trained forestry technicians."[4] The New York State College of Forestry at Syracuse University provided most of the faculty.

An interim period from 1960 to 1963 saw significant developments, including the inauguration of the International Rice Research Institute in 1962 on the campus of UPCA by the Rockefeller and Ford Foundations. The International Rice Research Institute expanded support for graduate scholarships in the United States for younger Filipino staff. In this period, UPCA Dean D. L. Umali asked the Ford and Rockefeller Foundations to continue their financial support for UPCA. A review committee then recommended a "mutual and integrated approach in graduate education and research" between Cornell and the Philippines. At the same time, Dean Charles E. Palm and associates at Cornell established its Program in

International Agricultural Development, with a full-time director, the first at an American university, in order to "maintain linkages and cooperation with universities and research institutes in developing countries, such as the University of the Philippines."[5]

Phase 2, UPCO, ran from 1963 to 1972, largely supported by the Ford Foundation. The objectives of the first grant included cooperation in campus development and expanded graduate educational, research, and extension programs at the University of the Philippines and strengthening the International Agricultural Development Program at Cornell. "Mutual efforts will be directed toward the education and training of people for leadership in the development of agricultural potentials of the Philippines and other low-income countries."[6]

The program focused on six areas: animal sciences, plant sciences, physical sciences and natural resources, food and nutrition, sociology/economics and communications, and plant and animal protection. Graduate assistants were active participants on both campuses. Other services and activities included "library development, [a] scientific supply house, [a] computer center, campus development, [the establishment of the] Association of Colleges of Agriculture in the Philippines (ACAP), and the training of extension workers and non-academic personnel."[7]

There was significant participation from Cornell. Thirty-two visiting professors and twenty-three graduate assistants from Cornell worked at Los Baños as colleagues with their Filipino counterparts, with an additional twenty-six short-term visiting professors and consultants, plus several administrators from Cornell. Nineteen graduate assistants, three visiting professors, and three short-term visiting professors from UPCA came to Cornell and sixteen staff members studied at other universities in the United States. Five visiting professors from Southeast Asia at Los Baños and approximately seventy-five Filipino and other Asian graduate students received UPCO support for studies at Los Baños. Almost all UPCA faculty were involved in some way with UPCO.

The impact of the institution-building efforts was significant for all institutions and individuals involved. According to Turk, this success was based on the mutual trust and confidence of administrators of the University of the Philippines, Cornell University, the Ford Foundation, the Rockefeller Foundation, and US and Philippine government agencies. He concluded, "It has been a satisfying and thrilling experience to work closely together for the mutual benefit of all and especially to have been a part in the building of a strong educational resource capable of world-wide leadership, the College of Agriculture, University of the Philippines at Los Baños."[8]

By all accounts, the 1950s and 1960s projects helped UPCA in Los Baños become the premier agricultural education and research university in all of Southeast Asia. In fact, the Southeast Asian Ministers of Education Organization, representing the eleven Southeast Asian countries, chose Los Baños in 1966 as the home of the Southeast Asian Regional Center for Graduate Study and Research in Agriculture. It has grown in scope and size and remains very active today.

Among the many scholars who were associated with this project and received advanced Cornell University degrees were two outstanding Filipino agricultural leaders: Emil Q. Javier and Gelia T. Castillo. Javier earned his PhD in plant breeding and genetics from Cornell University in 1969. He returned to Los Baños, where he became dean of UPCA and later chancellor of the university. In the late 1980s, he worked at The Hague in the Netherlands as senior research fellow for the International Service for National Agricultural Research and went to Taiwan to direct work on vegetable research and development. After a few years abroad, Javier returned to his country at the request of former Philippine president Fidel V. Ramos to lead the University of the Philippines as its president. In 2000, he became chair of the Consultative Group on International Agricultural Research's Technical Advisory Committee and from 2005 to 2012 headed the National Academy of Science and Technology. He received many major national and international honors, including the Philippines' highest honor for men and women of science, the rank of National Scientist.

Castillo came to Cornell from the Philippines during the 1950s as part of the Los Baños program. She studied in the College of Agriculture and Life Sciences, earning her doctorate in rural sociology in 1960. Her dissertation, "A Study of Occupational Evaluation in the Philippines," provided a foundation for the study of Filipino farmers that she used in her 1975 book *All in a Grain of Rice*, the first book written by a Filipino about Filipino farmers' responses to new agricultural technology. After her graduate studies at Cornell, Castillo returned to the Philippines, where she gained recognition as an international authority in agriculture and rural development and pioneered the concept of participatory development. She was a consultant for the International Rice Research Institute and held more than a dozen important science and technology administrative positions during her productive career.[9] Like Javier, Castillo was conferred the rank and title of National Scientist by the president of the Philippines in 1999.

Unfortunately, the United States Agency for International Development and other donors grew tired of the expensive and perceived "elitist" institution-building activities involving graduate education and research. Consequently, they shifted to activities that focused more on education at the primary and secondary levels.

When International Programs of the College of Agriculture and Life Sciences celebrated its fiftieth anniversary in 2013, its director, Ronnie Coffman, declared that the College of Agriculture and Life Sciences–Los Baños cooperation was "perhaps one of IP-CALS' greatest success stories."[10] Cornell has continued ties with the Philippines in the College of Agriculture, especially, beginning in the

1970s, with an interdisciplinary Philippine studies program in the College of Arts and Sciences.[11]

Notes

1. For more about Cornell at Nanking, see chapter 1, A Pioneering International Program: The Cornell-Nanking Story.

2. Kenneth L. Turk, *The Cornell-Los Baños Story* (Ithaca, NY: New York State College of Agriculture and Life Sciences, 1974), https://ecommons.cornell.edu/handle/1813/34479.

3. Turk, vii–viii.

4. Turk, viii.

5. Turk, ix.

6. Turk, x.

7. Turk, x.

8. Turk, xi.

9. Castillo tells her story on eCommons: "An Interview with Dr. Gelia Castillo," Oral History Collection on Cornell's International Dimension, eCommons, August 5, 2013, https://ecommons.cornell.edu/handle/1813/33697.

10. Linda McCandless, "CALS Seeks to Meet Needs of the World's Poorest," *Cornell Chronicle*, March 4, 2013, https://news.cornell.edu/stories/2013/03/cals-seeks-meet-needs-worlds-poorest.

11. Clare Cororaton, "History of Philippine Studies at Cornell," Mario Einaudi Center for International Studies, December 7, 2021, https://einaudi.cornell.edu/discover/news/history-philippine-studies-cornell.

18. ASIA'S LAST SHANGRI LA

Cornell's Engagement with Bhutan

James P. Lassoie

Cornell's College of Agriculture and Life Sciences (CALS) has long attracted international graduate students dedicated to addressing challenges in agriculture, environmental conservation, and rural development. Most have professional experience and are seeking advanced education before returning home to assume leadership positions in government agencies, nongovernmental organizations, academic institutions, or the private sector. They not only learn while on campus but also contribute to Cornell's ever-expanding stature as a center for international applied scholarship. By advising such students, faculty expand their research and teaching horizons, leading to new ideas, innovative initiatives, and often remarkable professional contributions both on and off campus.

This vignette is set within such a context, specifically my experience while advising four Bhutanese graduate students between 2001 and 2014. Often considered one of the world's most isolated and least developed countries, Bhutan offered a unique cultural and ecological setting for expanding my interests in sustainability, which strives to balance socioeconomic development and environmental protection. I first visited Bhutan in the summer of 2002 to work with my first Bhutanese MS student, Chukey Wangchuk, and as an interdisciplinary conservation scientist, I found the country intriguing.

Land of the Thunder Dragon

Nestled between India and China in South Asia, Bhutan has been called the "Last Shangri-La" owing to its mountainous topography and mystical persona.[1] Small geographically, Bhutan has a population of only 760,000, with about 60 percent living in rural areas where most practice subsistence agriculture based on a combination of crop and livestock production. Due to its rugged terrain, only 3 percent of the country is arable and, depending on elevation, farmers grow rice, potatoes,

Figure 18.1 Bhutanese farms surrounded by protected conservation areas. Farmers often stay overnight in foreground structure to protect crops from wildlife damage, 2007. (Photo by author)

wheat, and corn and herd yak or cattle primarily for their dairy products, draft power, and manure. With abundant water resources, hydroelectricity is the largest contributor to Bhutan's GDP, followed by tourism and agriculture.

Generations of benevolent kings have promoted policies protecting Bhutan's traditional culture, national identity, and unique biodiversity. In 1972, Bhutan's fourth king, Jigme Singye Wangchuck, initiated the unique concept of gross national happiness for developing a sustainable economy that also preserved Bhutan's unique culture. Based on Buddhist spiritual values and the preservation of nature, it was grounded on four pillars: good governance, environmental conservation, sustainable economic development, and cultural promotion.

With such a comprehensive framing for society and government agencies, Bhutan has placed a very high priority on nature protection. More than 71 percent of the country is forested, and Bhutan's park system is considered one of the most comprehensive in the world, with over half of the country in protected areas. In contrast to US national parks, Bhutan's park system must also support residents who are allowed to continue livelihood activities, including crop and livestock production and the controlled harvesting of timber and the many native plants used in traditional medicine. The government's work to simultaneously promote rural livelihoods and nature conservation has led to growing human-wildlife conflicts.[2]

Figure 18.2 Park rangers with Cornell research associate Ruth Sherman (*far left*) and PhD candidates Phuntsho Thinley (*second from left*) and R. Jamie Herring (*right*), 2007. (Photo by author)

Despite its size, Bhutan's topography, ranging from high mountains in the north to subtropical lowland forests and bamboo jungles in the south, provides a diversity of habitats for an astounding array of plants and animals, making it one of the world's most valuable biodiversity hotspots. Bhutan hosts over 5,350 species of plants, almost 130 species of mammals, and about 740 species of birds, which include endangered keystone carnivores, such as the Royal Bengal tiger, many endangered bird species, two bear species, and numerous native herbivores that serve as important prey for wild predators.[3]

Owing to its intriguing culture and stunning natural resources, Bhutan has become an attractive destination for ecotourists. International tourism officially began in 1974 with only 287 visitors. Fearing cultural and environmental impacts, the state has carefully controlled tourist numbers, first using a principle of "high value, low volume" to regulate government-licensed tour operators who arrange and control itineraries and logistics. This made visiting Bhutan notoriously expensive.

To stimulate tourism development, however, the government changed its operating principle to "high value, low impact" in 2008. Despite the high tariff, the number of tourists continued to increase, reaching over 315,000 in 2019. Additional trekking routes have been developed and new hotels and resorts have been built and upgraded to accommodate more tourists and their varied interests in the future.[4] Fortunately for me, those sponsored by the government or a citizen in "good standing" can visit more cheaply, and in 2002 I was officially invited by Chukey Wangchuk. While supporting his MS research project examining the failure of governmental livestock development programs to mitigate the exploitation of traditional grazing lands, I gained valuable on-the-ground insights that proved useful to my continued work in Bhutan.

Graduate Student Research

Many rural people had grown comfortable over the thirty-five-year reign of the benevolent fourth king and were worried about a new democratic future after his abdication. I returned to Bhutan in July 2007 and personally observed some of the excitement, confusion, and concerns associated with citizens now being responsible for their government. Specifically, government officials responsible for protecting Bhutan's natural resources realized that rural people would now have a say in their management activities through the democratic process. Of special concern were the growing conflicts arising from managing wild carnivores and herbivores that often damaged crops, livestock, and humans in and around Bhutan's protected areas. I had returned to assist two Bhutanese who completed graduate degrees with me: Sonam W. Wang and Phuntsho Thinley. Both held key positions in the Nature Conservation Division in the Department of Forests and Parks and were committed to finding interdisciplinary solutions to Bhutan's human-wildlife conflicts.

Wang and Thinley worked in two large national parks, Jigme Singye Wangchuk and Jigme Dorji, respectively, where they collectively advanced knowledge about the ecology and prey-predator dynamics of key carnivores and herbivores, as well as their damaging impacts on crops and livestock in and around the parks. Since their research projects were sanctioned by the government and they both maintained governmental appointments while conducting fieldwork, they were able to use park rangers as field technicians, which facilitated the collection of exceptionally comprehensive data sets. Among many accomplishments, their development of camera trap methods to estimate wildlife abundance led to the first national assessment of Bhutan's Royal Bengal tiger population in 2015.[5] Both returned to government service to continue conservation work before moving elsewhere to further their conservation careers: Wang to a professorship in Korea and Thinley to a research position in Australia. Both have published widely, and in 2020 Thinley won the prestigious Whitley Award for his work to save Bhutan's endangered Alpine musk deer.[6]

Near the end of his Cornell PhD fieldwork, Wang was appointed chief forest officer for the Nature Conservation Division and began developing a five-year strategy for addressing Bhutan's human-wildlife conflicts. In that capacity he invited me to a stakeholders' meeting during my July 2007 visit in preparation for my returning in December as an international delegate at the National Strategy Development Workshop to Address Human-Wildlife Conflicts in Bhutan. I was further tasked with writing the introductory chapter for the national strategy report that appeared in 2008.[7] Though likely needing revision, Wang's strategy report was featured in Bhutan's 2020 National Environment Strategy and continues to frame the management of human-wildlife conflicts across the country.[8]

During my July visit, I also worked with another Cornell doctoral student, R. Jamie Herring. He was on a multicountry trip to develop an innovative multimedia, internet-based platform, Conservation Bridge, to support interdisciplinary education based on real-world sustainable development dilemmas.[9] This new project was beginning to build collaborative working relationships between universities and conservation practitioners, including government agencies responsible for managing protected areas, to create dynamic case studies that connected field professionals facing real management problems to college students seeking experientially based insights into conservation and sustainable development. With assistance from Wang and Thinley, a video and written documentation on human-wildlife conflicts in Bhutan were added to Conservation Bridge in early 2008.[10]

Between my 2002 and 2007 trips to Bhutan, Wangchuk had completed his master's degree and returned to the Bhutan Trust. He is now a private consultant leading a nonprofit affiliated with the Global Water Partnership.[11] His thesis research examined the reluctance of farmers to adopt government-sponsored crossbreeding and forage improvement programs for reducing migratory livestock practices that were damaging upland grasslands and affecting biodiversity. Among other useful results, he found that Bhutanese farmers, because of their strict adherence to Buddhism, would not perform necessary culling of unproductive cattle for herd improvement, thereby maintaining large herds that produced less milk per unit of feed.

During my 2002 visit, I met Karma Tenzin, who was working as an ethnobotanist in the Nature Conservation Division. He completed a master's degree with me at Cornell and interviewed farmers about their knowledge of local plants, documented their many uses, and found that loss of traditional knowledge was most pronounced in younger villagers who had access to modern amenities that older, poorer individuals did not. Unfortunately, traditional knowledge about plants, including those used in socioreligious activities and as traditional medicines, is continuing to be lost before it can be properly documented.[12] Tenzin returned to the Department of Forest and Park Service to head its anti-poaching and surveillance section and became the chief forestry officer of Wangdue Territorial Forest Division.

Bhutan in the Classroom

I struggled to incorporate realism into a new international conservation course I had launched in 2004 in which students sought dynamic, real-world examples to support abstract concepts and theories. Published case studies initially proved helpful but were static and quickly dated, which led to new frustrations and the impetus to develop a series of international case studies and launch Conservation Bridge with Herring.[13] Later I used the platform's diverse set of case studies in designing courses supporting undergraduate majors in natural resources, environment and sustainability, and international agriculture and rural development. As an open-source resource with many different case studies, Conservation Bridge found its way into many courses at Cornell and elsewhere.

I adapted the Bhutan case for use in a variety of educational settings focused on addressing the general question, Why and how might the government of Bhutan protect wildlife biodiversity while also enhancing rural livelihoods? This experience was incorporated into a comprehensive instructional case study for the National Socio-environmental Center in 2014.[14] There I detailed pedagogies for using the case in different educational settings, including an intensive problem-based learning experience where student teams collaborated directly with field-based practitioners over an entire term.[15]

Impact

Reflecting on my almost forty-five years at Cornell, Bhutan and Conservation Bridge provide an illustrative context for my entire career. With a PhD in forest ecology, I joined the faculty as New York's Cooperative Extension forester in 1976. As such, I learned the importance of connecting university research to varied publics facing complex real-world problems. This commitment to applied scholarship grew as I realized that students in interdisciplinary fields like natural resources, sustainable agriculture, and environmental conservation also sought relevance in their educations and I designed new pedagogies to do so. My ability to transition to an international conservationist was possible because of the vibrant international development community and encouragement, as well as support from noteworthy program leaders at Cornell like Edwin B. Oyer, Norman T. Uphoff, and W. Ronnie Coffman.

As I neared retirement, my department's 2019–2020 seminar series was dedicated to hearing from several of my past PhD students. The fall's first outside speaker was R. Jamie Herring, who talked about the challenges of educating the public about climate change and concluded by announcing his endowment of the James P. Lassoie Global Conservation Travel Fund to support future graduate students for exploratory research trips like his during the summer of 2007.

A long-term Bhutan-Cornell partnership was ensured in 2022 with the establishment of two King's Scholarships for undergraduate Bhutanese students admitted to CALS or to the Dyson School of Applied Economics and Management in the SC Johnson College of Business. These were inspired by Jigme Khesar Namgyal Wangchuk's commitment to strengthening Bhutan's human capital by educating future leaders for the country's civil service.[16]

Notes

1. In Dzongkha, Bhutan is called Druk Yul, or the Land of Dragon; leaders are known as Druk Gyalpo, or Thunder Dragon Kings, in recognition of the country's violent thunderstorms. Many locations in the Himalayas have claimed to be the Shangri-La identified in James Hilton's novel *Lost Horizon* (New York: William Morrow, 1936).

2. Phuntsho Thinley and James P. Lassoie, "Promoting Biodiversity Conservation and Rural Livelihoods in Bhutan" (Cornell University, 2013), 14; "Human-Wildlife Conflicts in Bhutan," multimedia case study, Conservation Bridge, 2011, http://www.conservationbridge.org/casestudy/human-wildlife-conflicts-in-bhutan.

3. Choki Gyeltshen, Karuyna Prasad, and Sangay Dema, "Number of Species in Bhutan," *Conservation Science and Practice* 2 (2020): e146, https://conbio.onlinelibrary.wiley.com/doi/pdf/10.1111/csp2.146.

4. "International Tourism, Number of Arrivals—Bhutan," World Bank, 2020, https://data.worldbank.org/indicator/ST.INT.ARVL?locations=BT.

5. Phuntsho Thinley et al., *Counting the Tigers in Bhutan: Report on the National Tiger Survey of Bhutan 2014–2015* (Thimphu, Bhutan: Department of Forests and Parks Services, Ministry of Agriculture and Forests, 2015), 60.

6. Phuntsho Thinley, "Stepping Up Patrols to Preserve the Endangered Alpine Musk Deer," Whitley Fund for Nature, 2020, https://whitleyaward.org/winners/stepping-up-patrols-to-preserve-the-endangered-alpine-musk-deer.

7. James P. Lassoie, introduction to *Bhutan National Human-Wildlife Conflicts Management Strategy* (Thimphu, Bhutan: Nature Conservation Division, Department of Forests, Ministry of Agriculture, Royal Government of Bhutan, 2008), 1–13. Note that government policy does not allow identified authorship in official reports.

8. Sonam W. Wang, personal communication to author, July 5, 2022; "Human-Wildlife Conflicts," Grantham Research Institute on Climate Change and the Environment, 2020, https://www.climate-laws.org/geographies/bhutan/policies/national-environment-strategy-2020-the-middle-path.

9. James P. Lassoie, R. Jamie Herring, and Karim-Aly S. Kassam, "Conservation Bridge: Enhancing the Management of National Parks and Protected Areas through Collaborative, Real-World Learning, Research, and Practice," *Proceedings—Education for Sustainable*

Development through National Part Experiences, 2012 IUCN World Conservation Congress, Jeju, Korea, 56–81.

10. Thinley and Lassoie, "Human-Wildlife Conflicts in Bhutan."

11. "Ensuring Safe Water and Sanitation for Remote Villages in Bhutan," Global Water Partnership South Asia, 2022, https://www.gwp.org/en/gwp-SAS/WE-ACT/change-and-impact/News-and-Activities/2022/bhwp-story.

12. Karma Tenzin, personal communication to author, July 7, 2022.

13. Conservation Bridge homepage, accessed September 28, 2023, https://www.conservationbridge.org.

14. James P. Lassoie, *People, Pigs, and Tigers in Shangri-La: Case Study* (Annapolis, MD: National Socio-environmental Center, 2014), https://www.sesync.org/resources/people-pigs-and-tigers-shangri-la.

15. For example, Ugyen Namgyel, Stephen F. Siebert, and Sonam Wang, "Shifting Cultivation and Biodiversity Conservation in Bhutan," *Conservation Biology* 22 (2008): 1349–1351.

16. "2 King's Scholarships in Cornell University," *Bhutanese*, August 20, 2022, https://thebhutanese.bt/2-kings-scholarships-in-cornell-university.

19. BT EGGPLANT

Improving Lives with Biotechnology in Asia

Anthony M. Shelton

Working in developing countries requires patience. In March 2018, I was in a minivan on my way from Dhaka to Shibganj, Bangladesh. Traveling a distance of about 180 kilometers would take more than seven hours on paved and dirt roads in stop-sit-and-go traffic through villages typical of rural Bangladesh. We were going to an extension meeting to discuss eggplant, or brinjal, as it is called in Bangladesh and India, that had been genetically engineered.

As an entomologist with research and extension responsibilities at Cornell, I have attended my fair share of extension meetings and was eager to participate in one in Bangladesh. Remarkably, the meeting was similar but more exotic, and in a language (Bengali) I could not understand. The local extension leader gathered about seventy-five farmers under a colorful tent for a meeting about a new line of brinjal, named Bt (*Bacillus thuringiensis*) brinjal, resistant to the eggplant fruit and shoot borer (EFSB). This insect is the main constraint to brinjal production in Bangladesh, India, and many other countries in Asia.

The meeting was held on the farm of Mohammad Abul Hossain, who had grown traditional brinjal for years. After recently seeing Bt brinjal production in a relative's field, he decided to try it himself, a typical adoption scenario seen worldwide. After formal introductions, Hossain took us to one of his fields. His enthusiasm for Bt brinjal was infectious. He told the audience, "I have sold about 8,056 kg of Bt brinjal," and "there was no [borer] infestation in my crop. I am expecting to harvest another 400 kg of brinjal from the field with the same result." In six months, he had earned about $1,600 growing Bt brinjal on 0.6 hectares of land and still had fruit in the field to harvest and sell for a higher price during the holy month of Ramadan. This was a princely sum for a smallholder Bangladeshi farmer. In addition to the money, he was pleased that he did not spray for the borer.

Back under the colorful tent during the meeting, Hossain and others told their stories about growing Bt brinjal to the rapt audience. At the end of the meeting,

Figure 19.1 Non-Bt brinjal fruit infested by the eggplant fruit and shoot borer, *Leucinodes orbonalis Guenée*. (Photo by author)

one of the organizers asked for a show of hands of those who wanted to grow Bt brinjal next year. Nearly all hands went up.

How the Bt Eggplant Project Began

In 2005, I became a member of Cornell's Agricultural Biotechnology Support Program II (ABSPII), funded by the United States Agency for International Development (USAID). The goal of ABSPII was to use bioengineered crops to help boost food security, economic growth, nutrition, and environmental quality in selected countries. Project partners identified pest problems that warranted biotechnology approaches, and eggplant was chosen because it is an important vegetable in the targeted countries (India, Bangladesh, and the Philippines), and its main constraint is the EFSB.

EFSB larvae bore into the petiole and midrib of brinjal leaves and tender shoots, resulting in wilting and desiccation of stems. Larvae also feed on flowers, leading to flower drop or misshapen fruits. But the most serious economic damage is caused by larvae tunneling in fruits and contaminating them with frass, which makes the fruit unmarketable and unfit for human consumption. Despite decades of traditional breeding, no brinjal lines with sufficient resistance to these borers had been produced.

During ABSPII's first year, I visited brinjal fields in India and heard how farmers tried to control EFSB, using frequent, sometimes twice a day, insecticide spraying. Thinking I had misunderstood the frequency, I asked the farmer again and again in different ways, but each time the answer was the same. The farmer further explained that he often sprayed on the day of harvest. When asked what insecticides he used, he replied it was usually a cocktail of insecticides. I learned later that this farmer's practices were not unusual for the 1.4 million small-scale, resource-poor brinjal farmers in India who incur losses of 60 to 70 percent even with frequent spraying.[1] The spraying costs were high, but so were the health and environmental costs.

During my visits to Bangladesh and the Philippines, I heard similar stories and found them documented in the literature. In Bangladesh, farmers usually sprayed their crops barefooted, and as a result of widespread exposure, they reported experiencing multiple health effects, including headaches, eye and skin irritation, vomiting, and dizziness.[2] In the Philippines, exposure of young children was of particular concern. They are often employed in vegetable production as young as six to nine years old.[3] After the use of pesticides, children reported health symptoms including headaches, skin irritation, and abdominal pain.

Development of the Bt Eggplant Project

Given the constraints of spraying insecticides to manage EFSB, ABSPII partners focused on eggplant as a crop for which biotechnology might provide part of the solution. Development of the Bt eggplant technology was initiated in 2000 by Mahyco using the *cry1Ac* gene that had already been widely used in Bt cotton in India and many other countries. This gene produces a protein that, when ingested by an EFSB larva, causes it to stop feeding and die. However, this protein is harmless to humans and most other organisms, including beneficial insects. A partnership was formed in late 2003 between Mahyco, Cornell, USAID, and public-sector partners in India, Bangladesh, and the Philippines under ABSPII. All three countries used the resistant Mahyco gene and incorporated it into local eggplant lines.

When the ABSPII project ended, it was followed in 2015 by a cooperative agreement between Cornell and USAID that focused on eggplant and created the Feed the Future South Asia Eggplant Improvement Partnership. This program included capacity building, seed production, stewardship, and postcommercial communication, and I became its director.

Regulatory Systems, Politics, and Bt Eggplant

For farmers to grow a biotech crop, a country must first have biosafety laws and regulations in place. India, Bangladesh, and the Philippines had a national biosafety framework in place when Bt eggplant was being developed, but each country varied dramatically in its laws, local challenges, and experiences with biotech crops.

In India, anti-biotech activists forced the government to delay commercial release of Bt eggplant until public discussions were held. Opposition groups showed up in force at public discussions, leading the Indian minister of environment and forests, the last gatekeeper on the regulatory road to commercialization, to impose a moratorium, which remains active at the time of writing this chapter. In the Philippines, anti-biotech activists interrupted government approval processes, which has delayed the development and commercialization of Bt eggplant in that country.

It was different in Bangladesh. Bangladesh has a national biosafety framework that provides the regulatory basis for the management of biotechnology products. However, unlike India and the Philippines, Bangladesh had no prior experience with biotech crops before Bt brinjal. Bt brinjal lines were tested under confined and open-field conditions for seven consecutive seasons before the Bangladesh government granted approval of four brinjal lines in 2013.

Why was Bt brinjal approved in Bangladesh while it is still under a moratorium in India after thirteen years? Two important leaders in Bangladesh, Prime Minister Sheikh Hasina and Minister of Agriculture Begum Matia Chowdhury, provided strong support to move Bt brinjal toward commercialization through the Bangladesh regulatory framework. Such high-level political support, absent in India, was vital to commercialization of Bt brinjal in Bangladesh.

I first met Matia Chowdhury in June 2011 when she visited Cornell. She spoke of the importance of brinjal in Bangladesh, where 150,000 farmers grow it and the public consumes it daily. We discussed the Bt brinjal project, and she requested continued cooperation with Cornell. This was just a year after India had placed a moratorium on Bt brinjal's cultivation. When I mentioned this to her, she acknowledged it but added that Bangladesh is an independent country with its own rules. When I pressed the issue of anti-GMO groups that might disrupt the project, she responded, "My job as minister of agriculture is to feed 160 million people and protect the environment, and if Bt brinjal will help us achieve this, we will move forward with it. Besides, we do not have strong anti-GMO groups in Bangladesh because we are a poor country, and these groups have difficulty raising funds."

Meanwhile, back in Bangladesh, things were ramping up for the first commercial planting of Bt brinjal. Seeds were being multiplied, agencies were being assigned various responsibilities, and farmers were being trained.

Bt Brinjal in Bangladesh

In January 2014, Matia Chowdhury distributed Bt brinjal seedlings to twenty Bangladeshi farmers in four districts. This was a major milestone for the project and biotechnology. However, as the plants were growing in the field, challenges soon appeared. A Bangladeshi newspaper article published in 2014 claimed the reporter had visited some of the Bt brinjal fields and found that "25 to 30 percent of the plants were dead" and that the "field now required more pesticides."[4]

Joe Huesing from USAID and I were in Bangladesh when the article appeared, and we scrambled to visit one of the fields. At first sight, we were concerned when we saw about 10 to 15 percent of the plants dying. However, it soon became apparent that they were not suffering from EFSB but from bacterial wilt, caused by *Ralstonia solanacearum*, a common disease of brinjal in Bangladesh. Other fields we inspected had similar levels of diseased plants, but it was a discouraging beginning for our project.

During this initial year, Bt brinjal became the target of increasingly active anti-biotech organizations, both domestic and international. Project partners pushed back on their false claims. An important advocate was Mark Lynas, a journalist and former anti-biotech activist, who published articles and blogs based on his visits and interviews with Bt brinjal farmers in Bangladesh, including an opinion piece in the *New York Times*.[5] These and other educational efforts were especially important during the early phases of the project to document the benefits of Bt brinjal.

By 2021, more than sixty-five thousand farms grew Bt brinjal in Bangladesh, compared with the initial twenty farmers in the 2014 season. This rate of adoption over seven years is truly remarkable. A study conducted in 2020 confirmed the enhanced performance of the four Bt eggplant lines in the field and their increased acceptability in the market.[6] Compared with non-Bt brinjal lines, the Bt lines had a 20 percent higher yield and obtained 22 percent improved revenue. Furthermore, 80 percent of the 195 Bt brinjal farmers were satisfied with the quality of their fruit, compared with 28 percent of the 196 non-Bt farmers whose fruit was infested by the borers.

The Future

The Feed the Future South Asia Eggplant Improvement Partnership ended in 2020, but work continues under a new five-year $10 million cooperative agreement from USAID led by Cornell. It will take up the complex challenge of science and policy. The work will empower scientists in Bangladesh and the Philippines to develop new, locally adapted varieties of eggplant while engaging with policymakers on clear regulatory pathways for their release.

Bt brinjal has helped transform the lives of resource-poor farmers in Bangladesh and improved the environment in which they farm. This should be an indication of the benefits it can bring in other countries. In the Philippines, Bt eggplant was approved for food, feed, and processing and final approval for cultivation was granted in 2022. These regulatory dossiers were developed not only to meet the specific requirements of the Philippines but also to serve as templates to meet international standards for other countries. India, which produces a quarter of the world's eggplants, remains a challenge because of the current political climate.

Bt crops have revolutionized agriculture, but their benefits have largely been confined to field crops such as maize, cotton, and, more recently, soybeans and chickpeas. I believe we need to move forward and use biotechnology—including Bt, other insecticidal proteins, and gene editing—to improve integrated pest management in other crops, such as fruits and vegetables. These are high-value cash crops essential for farmers' income, but with high cosmetic standards and hard-to-manage pest complexes. These crops are also essential for a healthy and diverse diet, a major problem in developing countries like Bangladesh. However, farmers of these crops have historically relied on intensive insecticide treatments for their production, with negative effects on humans and their environment. I hope the success of Bt brinjal in Bangladesh will help pave the way for other insect-resistant, genetically engineered food crops that can serve as cornerstones in integrated pest management programs.

Notes

This chapter is adapted from one published in *American Entomologist* 67, no. 3 (2021): 52–59.

1. Bhagirath Choudhary and Kadambini Gaur, "The Development and Regulation of Bt Brinjal in India (Eggplant/Aubergine)" (ISAAA Brief No. 38-2009, International Service for the Acquisition of Agri-biotech Applications, January 16, 2009), https://www.isaaa.org/resources/publications/briefs/38/executivesummary/pdf/Brief%2038%20-%20Executive%20Summary%20-%20English.pdf.

2. Susmita Dasgupta, Craig Meisner, and Mainul Huq, "Health Effects and Pesticide Perception as Determinants of Pesticide Use: Evidence from Bangladesh" (Policy Research Working Papers, World Bank, November 2005), https://elibrary.worldbank.org/doi/abs/10.1596/1813-9450-3776.

3. Jinky Leilanie Lu, Katherine Z. Cosca, and Jocelyn Del Mundo, "Trends of Pesticide Exposure and Related Cases in the Philippines," *Journal of Rural Medicine* 5, no. 2 (2010): 153–164.

4. Yasir Wardad, "Pest-Resistant Bt Brinjal Comes under Pest Attack," *Financial Express*, April 7, 2014, https://web.archive.org/web/20140424174343/http://www.thefinancialexpress-bd.com/2014/04/07/27497.

5. Mark Lynas, "How I Got Converted to G.M.O. Food," *New York Times*, April 24, 2015.

6. Anthony M. Shelton et al., "Impact of Bt Brinjal Cultivation in the Market Value Chain in Five Districts of Bangladesh," *Frontiers in Bioengineering and Biotechnology* 8 (2020), https://doi.org/10.3389/fbioe.2020.00498.

20. CORNELL EXPANDS THE DIGITAL WORLD

Communication Technology Abroad

Royal D. Colle

At the beginning of the twenty-first century, the term "digital divide" appeared frequently in professional literature. It referred to the fact that while many people had access to and used information and communications technologies for work, school, and recreation, 95 percent of the world's population lacked access to this part of the modern world. The "divide" issue presented a challenge that Cornell faculty and graduate students began to address even before the emergence of low-cost digital technologies.

The simple audio cassette started Cornellians on the way to bringing modern communications technologies to many people around the globe, beginning with rural women in Essex County, in upstate New York. When cassette playback units (without recording capability) became affordable in the late 1960s, we at Cornell began to use them to communicate with rural women in New York State's antipoverty program. The cassette, which had been introduced by the Dutch firm Philips in the mid-1960s, became a relatively inexpensive communication tool for our experimental antipoverty effort. Department of Communication graduate student Robin Whittlesey (MPS 1977) and her colleagues worked with Essex County homemakers to produce health- and nutrition-related tape recordings that mixed entertainment (soap operas) with information and education. Then we provided various women with cassette playback units and a collection of these tapes to play and replay at their convenience. In our post-project research, we discovered that many women played the tapes not only for themselves but also for family and friends. Our research revealed that the women learned from the experiment, as did we!

Taking Cassettes Abroad

What we learned in Essex County we applied to other counties and other countries, including a World Bank development program in the Dominican Republic.

Figure 20.1 Professor Royal Colle (*center*) seeking information for a rural communication project in India. (Photo provided by author)

In a 1974 agricultural radio project in Guatemala supported by the United States Agency for International Development, we introduced audio cassettes as an extension of conventional rural radio programs. Typically, farmers had to listen to the agricultural broadcasts developed by the local extension staff at a time decided by the radio station, and that time often was not convenient to farmers whose schedules were dictated by conditions in their fields. We introduced a system whereby extension agents took cassette recordings of the broadcasts to groups of farmers as they came off the field. They sat with the farmers and played the taped radio programs, discussed the content, and answered questions. And they replayed parts if necessary.

We further expanded the idea in order to reach women on a coffee farm in Guatemala. A Guatemalan graduate student in communication at Cornell, Susana Fernandez Colle, used the cassette in working with rural women as they washed family clothes in an outdoor laundry (pila). Her thirteen-year-old assistant hung a cassette player in the pila every morning, where it played music and stories with development-related content that addressed issues such as the value of inoculating baby chicks. The project attracted the attention of the Ford Foundation, which published a small booklet describing the project. It also earned Susana Fernandez Colle an MPS degree in communication in 1976.

Figure 20.2 Staff of a rural telecenter in Vietnam that Cornellians helped to establish meeting with Professor Royal Colle (*center*), 2006. (Photo provided by author)

From Cassettes to Digital Technology

The audio cassette was soon overtaken by the computer and other digital technologies. This led us to research in Canada as part of the Community Access Program, a Canadian government initiative that aimed to provide Canadians with affordable public access to the internet and the skills needed to use it effectively. One of its goals was to establish ten thousand computer and internet sites across the nation. In Europe, we studied the Hungarian government program that supported a robust eight-year-old telecenter program (supported by the United States Agency for International Development), which resulted in more than 150 "telecottages" throughout Hungary in the late 1990s. However, in a paper we presented at an international meeting in 2005 in Dublin, Ireland, we admitted that higher education's role in engaging digital technologies for development had been dismal.[1] Universities were widely perceived as irrelevant—if they were considered at all—in regard to supporting and helping sustain community telecenters.

Based in part on our experience in helping the G. B. Pant University of Agriculture and Technology in India modernize its practice of providing agriculture programs for All India Radio, we raised this relevance issue when India's National Alliance for Information and Communication Technologies for Basic Human

Needs came into being in the early 2000s. The alliance set a goal of bringing all of India's six hundred thousand villages into the modern "information society" by 2007, the sixtieth anniversary of the nation's independence. India hoped to achieve its "Mission 2007" primarily through the creation of a network of Rural Knowledge Centres (telecenters) across the country. When we proposed to an alliance leader that the agricultural universities in India be explicitly included in the planning as partners for the knowledge centers, we received this terse response: "The universities have failed miserably in many respects. Most university faculty have no clue to life outside the campus nor have they any social concerns. Sorry for being very forthright or even blunt."[2]

About the same time, a two-year study commissioned by the World Bank and UNESCO concluded that the contribution of higher education to social and economic development in developing countries has been "disappointing to date"—including a failure to advance the public interest. One of the major obstacles was that "the social and economic importance of higher education systems is insufficiently appreciated."[3]

Getting Universities Involved

In 2005, we had the opportunity to get universities involved. We arranged a project start-up grant from the Asia-Pacific Economic Cooperation Education Foundation for the Thái Nguyên University of Agriculture and Forestry (TUAF) in Vietnam. The grant was designed to get the university involved in rural telecommunications interventions as part of the Information and Communications Technologies for Development (ICT4D) project. The goal was to reduce poverty for poor, natural-resource-dependent people living in rural areas in Vietnam's northern mountainous area. The project was specifically dedicated to improving the capacity of disadvantaged youths to access information and communications technologies that could help them improve their lives and their futures, especially given that young people have a strong affinity for the new information technologies.

In the final report of the project, lead author Tran Van Dien noted that Vietnam had made great achievements in poverty reduction over the previous decade but that ethnic minority groups generally received the fewest benefits.[4] The ICT4D project was therefore implemented in the northern mountainous area, which was considered to be the poorest and most disadvantaged region of Vietnam, with young people having difficulties in their economic and cultural lives as well as fewer opportunities for accessing education, training, recreational activities, and technology. The goal was to demonstrate the viability of Vietnamese universities as incubators and institutional supporters of community information centers (telecenters) to promote agricultural and rural development and to institutionalize these capabilities in a group of Vietnamese universities. With financial support from the ICT4D project and the contributions of local communities and Nguyen University, six telecenters were established in six target communes, and a communication center was set up at TUAF to serve the disadvantaged students.

An unpublished final evaluation conducted by an independent consultant and summarized in Tran Van Dien's *Final Report* showed that the telecenters in the communes had positive impacts for local communities. These included increasing the number of youths who could access information from either the e-library or the internet and the number who could use a computer (at least for typing). Further, 90 percent of youths interviewed responded that telecenters were useful for livelihood development and other welfare efforts in rural areas. The impact went beyond young people: "Commune authorities (now) know how to use E-library and access information from the internet[,] . . . a reasonable number of people from local communities accessed the telecenters[,] . . . and people [are] accessing the new technologies in agriculture production based on the technical guidelines in E-library and Internet."[5]

In addition, the ICT4D project strongly influenced the university's curriculum. The application of ICT4D has been accepted by TUAF to be a compulsory subject for students in agriculture extension and rural development. Further, the model of linkage between university and disadvantaged communities in creating opportunities for disadvantaged youths to access updated information sources has been considered successful in Vietnam and appears to be highly appreciated by local government and other information and communications technologies projects. The evaluation report observed that "television has broadcast programs several times to disseminate the model of the ICT4D project."[6]

Tran Van Dien's *Final Report* indicated that the project had been well planned and well implemented by TUAF planners, Cornell partners, and local community participants. The report further indicated that the project had "great impacts" on the socioeconomic development of local communities and contributed to reducing the digital gaps between remote people and those in urban or more favorable areas.

Reaching Out to Other Universities

The TUAF activity led Cornell into another involvement, this one with the United Nations Asia and Pacific Training Centre for ICT for Development (APCICT). Based in Incheon, South Korea, the center's objective is to build and strengthen the capacity of Asian and Pacific nations to use information and communications technologies for development (ICTD). Cornell faculty served as advisers on how to get universities and their students more involved in ICTD. We helped develop three demonstration projects in Thailand, Nepal, and the Philippines. We also helped APCICT organize informal conferences dedicated to producing teaching materials focused on getting students engaged in ICTD in communities outside the university walls. An important product of these activities was two publications that I authored for APCICT, *Engaged Learning Toolkit for Faculty: Using ICTs for Community Development* and *Engaged Learning Guidebook for Students: Using ICTs for Community Development*, designed to help universities expand the digital world. These publications continue to be available online.[7]

Faculty at Cornell were involved in other international projects related to universities and development communication. For example, soon after I joined Cornell in 1966, I was invited to go to India for a Cornell–Ford Foundation program at the G. B. Pant University of Agriculture and Technology to modernize its extension activities for farmers. We revamped its audio recording and reporting system and started preparing weekly agricultural radio broadcasts for All India Radio. It was the first instance in India of the production of radio programs by a nongovernmental body. I later became a consultant for the Food and Agriculture Organization of the United Nations on the development of the Centre for Advanced Studies in Agricultural Communication, a PhD program, for the G. B. Pant University.

In another example, the early 1990s saw a delegation of representatives from the private and public sectors in Singapore come to Cornell in search of models for a new program of communication studies at the young Nanyang Technological University (NTU). While the delegation initially focused on journalism, they were attracted by the Cornell model of a more broadly focused department of communication. They invited me to Singapore to study the issue and advise them on a model for NTU, which resulted in today's Wee Kim Wee School of Communication and Information. In 1993, Cornell and NTU signed a memorandum of understanding, leading to a joint training program on communication planning and strategies for development professionals from ten countries, including Indonesia, the Philippines, Senegal, Thailand, and Zimbabwe. In 1995, I became the first Wee Kim Wee Professor at NTU.[8]

Cornell's involvement with information and communications technologies in rural and developing areas significantly benefited many people who had been left behind in the new information age. Perhaps equally important, these kinds of initiatives show opportunities for universities to help bridge those digital divides as even newer technologies emerge.

Notes

1. Prepared for Working Group 3 of the Eighth Meeting of the UN Information and Communication Technologies Task Force, "On Harnessing the Potential of Information

and Communication Technologies (ICTs) for Education," Dublin, Ireland, April 13–15, 2005.

2. The program was described by MS Swaminathan, chairman of the National Commission of Farmers, at the Fifth Annual Baramati Initiative on ICT and Development, Baramati, India, March 3–6, 2005.

3. Task Force on Higher Education and Society, *Higher Education in Developing Countries: Peril and Promise* (Washington, DC: World Bank, 2000), 93.

4. Tran Van Dien, *Final Report: ICT4D and Disadvantaged Populations in Vietnam's Northern Mountainous Area* (Thai Nguyen University of Agriculture and Forestry, 2007).

5. Tran Van Dien, *Final Report.*

6. Tran Van Dien, *Final Report.*

7. The ICT toolkit and guidebook are available for download at Sustainable Development Goals Helpdesk, accessed September 28, 2023, https://sdghelpdesk.unescap.org/e-library/engaged-learning-toolkitguidebook-using-ict-community-development/.

8. The early history of NTU and Cornell's involvement in developing its communication program is reported by Lu Sinclair in *The NTU Story* (Nanyang Technological University, 1992). My recollections about those beginnings in which I played a role appear in a piece I wrote for its fifteenth anniversary commemorative book: *Coming of Age 92:07* (Wee Kim Wee School of Communication, 2007).

21. AFTER THE BERLIN WALL
Cornell in Postsocialist Europe

David L. Brown, James E. Haldeman, and Larry Zuidema

Hungary, Czechoslovakia, East Germany, Poland, and most other East-Central European nations were one-party socialist states from around 1949 until 1989–1992. After the fall of the Berlin Wall in 1989, these countries emerged from the USSR's sphere of influence and began their transformations from state socialism toward market capitalism and democracy. While these social, economic, and political changes occurred at the national level, their effects were experienced in cities, regions, and rural communities throughout society. All institutions were affected, including academia.

The postsocialist transformations stimulated new scholarly interest in Central and Eastern Europe among researchers and educators in the "West," including at Cornell. Foundations and national governments funded research and scholarly engagement projects in Hungary, Slovakia, Poland, East Germany, and other nations in the former socialist region. As a result, many Western scholars boarded planes for the region, enthusiastic at the prospect of developing new research collaborations with scholars and academic institutions there. Cornell's engagement with Eastern Europe was initiated and initially managed by Larry Zuidema, associate director of International Programs of the College of Agriculture and Life Sciences. After his retirement in 1995, the program was managed by James Haldeman. Rather than supporting ad hoc activities, a Central and Eastern Europe Coordinating Committee was established to integrate grant writing and program management. Zuidema chaired the committee until 1995, after which it was chaired by Jerry White in the Dyson School of Applied Economics and Management.[1] Cornell's teaching, research, and engagement activities with Central and Eastern Europe focused mainly on rural economy and society with a particular emphasis on agriculture, environment, and rural community development. Cornell's engagement with Central and Eastern Europe was most active during the 1990s and the first half of the 2000s.[2]

Figure 21.1 Slovak University of Agriculture in Nitra, Slovakia, 1992. (Photo by Larry W. Zuidema)

The Andrew W. Mellon Foundation provided Cornell's initial funding for scholarly activities in postsocialist Central and Eastern Europe supporting collaborative educational and research programs with the University of Agriculture in Gödöllő, Hungary, and the University of Agriculture in Nitra, Slovakia.[3] In 1992, former dean of the College of Agriculture and Life Sciences W. Keith Kennedy, representing Atlantic Philanthropies, encouraged Cornell to contact the foundation about the prospects for establishing new programs in Slovakia and Hungary, in partnership with the University of Limerick in Ireland. Subsequently, major grants were obtained from the Alfred Jurzykowski Foundation and the US Department of State. The Farm Foundation, the US Department of Agriculture, and the Trust for Mutual Understanding provided smaller grants. All of these grants supported collaborative scholarly activities in five interrelated substantive areas for almost a decade.

Programs on Agriculture and the Environment

The Mellon-sponsored project focused on assisting the professional development of the economic and social science faculty of the Slovak Agricultural University (SAU) in Nitra. A total of twenty-one Cornell faculty members, mostly from the Dyson School, participated in the program, which was originally led by Olan Forker, professor of agricultural marketing, followed by Dyson School professor

Figure 21.2 National Agricultural Research and Innovation Center, Agricultural Biotechnology Institute in Gödöllő, Hungary, 1992. (Photo by Larry W. Zuidema)

Loren Tauer. Fourteen SAU faculty visited Cornell University for study leaves of eight weeks to a full semester during the academic year, and a series of workshops were held in Nitra on economic research topics. During the visits to Cornell, SAU faculty attended regular academic classes and seminars. Many worked on new courses to be taught at SAU, while others worked on research reports. They also had opportunities to visit rural and urban communities outside Ithaca.

Eight workshops were held at SAU on various topics. Teams of two Cornell faculty members taught weeklong workshops. Besides SAU faculty and graduate students, these workshops were available to faculty from other Central and Eastern European countries. Opening up the workshops to the region not only provided a professional development opportunity to all regional faculty members but also provided opportunities to these visiting faculty to meet and work with the SAU faculty. Although the project focused mainly on teaching, it recognized the need for additional activities focused on enhancing the research capabilities of SAU economists.

With funding from the Alfred Jurzykowski Foundation, Cornell's Central and Eastern Europe Coordinating Committee initiated a wide range of agriculture and food-related activities in the postsocialist region, including ones focused on food quality and safety, environmental management, market agricultural economics, biotechnology, and rural development.

Food Quality and Safety Group

The Food Quality and Safety Group conducted a workshop in Poznan, Poland, in October 2000 with representatives from thirty-seven Polish meat, poultry, and dairy companies in attendance. Presentations explored food deterioration and spoilage, microbial food safety, good manufacturing practices, and prerequisite programs; the seven Hazard Analysis and Critical Control Points principles; and a case study on the principles' implementation in a small meat processing plant. Conference organizers visited six dairy, meat, and poultry processing plants to assess conditions in these operations.

Environment Group

The environmental component of the Central and Eastern Europe initiative was led by Harold van Es in the Department of Crop and Soil Sciences and Rebecca Schneider in the Department of Natural Resources, and it incorporated both research and outreach activities. With funding from the Trust for Mutual Understanding, the group held a workshop in September 2000 in Podbanské, Slovakia, producing a concept paper for a "Healthy Landscapes Initiative" in the four Visegrád Group countries (the Czech Republic, Hungary, Poland, and Slovakia) and publishing the workshop proceedings. A second workshop was held in Nitra, Slovakia, several months later to develop a specific project proposal and seek funding for implementation. The proposed project focused on creating a training program on the concepts and techniques of conducting outreach programming on environmental management issues.

Additional environmental activities included a collaborative research project with the Research Center for Agricultural and Forest Environment of the Polish Academy of Sciences and August Cieszkowski Agricultural University (now the University of Life Sciences), both located in Poznan, Poland. The project involved research and outreach activities related to sustainable landscape management, including flood and drought management, onsite sewage disposal, use of landscape buffers for biodiversity, and soil and water management.

Agricultural Market Economics Group

In many Central and Eastern European countries, agriculture still employed a large percentage of the rural population, and other employment opportunities were needed for these workers as opportunities for agricultural work diminished. Research challenges also existed in understanding the structural changes occurring in the dairy industry in particular. Individual countries needed to determine how they could compete in a global dairy industry and encourage that development. To be competitive, new investment would be necessary, and correct assessments of those investment opportunities would be critical for a viable dairy industry in Central and Eastern Europe.

In response to this challenge, the Agricultural Market Economics Group conducted a NATO Advanced Research Workshop titled "Economics of the Dairy Industry in Central and Eastern Europe" in Polanica-Zdrój, Poland, from June 5 to 7, 2000, to determine the current state of the dairy industry in the region and to identify the researchable economic issues facing that industry. Participants included dairy economists, dairy industry representatives, and government personnel.[4]

Biotechnology Group

In October 1999, the Biotechnology Group organized a NATO Advanced Research Workshop in Hungary, "Use of Agriculturally Important Genes in Biotechnology." The workshop's proceedings were published in 2000.

Because of the acrimony toward and widespread rejection of genetically modified organisms in Europe, the Biotechnology Group's activities were limited. Since environmental activists were better organized in Europe than in the United States and therefore had a stronger hold on public opinion, the group considered the promotion of agricultural biotechnology issues to be counterproductive at this time. The group did sponsor a visit to Hungary by Geza Hrazdina of Cornell AgriTech in October 2001, where he met with Istvan Marton of the Ministry of Agriculture and Rural Development to set up a program for three PhD students or postgraduates for a one-year rotation at Cornell to work at a modern genomics or plant biotechnology lab.

Rural Development Research

The Mellon project's rural development component focused on the well-being of rural people and households during the transition from state socialism in Hungary. David Brown, professor of development sociology, led the project in collaboration with Gödöllő University of Agriculture professor Laszlo Kulcsar to develop an original research program that examined livelihood strategies, including informal economic activities, deployed by rural people and households during a time of labor displacement and high official unemployment in rural Hungary. They also examined rural-urban migration and population redistribution, finding that rural areas were absorbing urban out-migrants displaced by economic restructuring.

The rural development project had three main impacts: scientific publications, the training of PhD students at both Gödöllő and Cornell, and the formation of an international network of scholars conducting research on rural development in postsocialist Central and Eastern Europe. An international conference on rural development in the region was held in 1999 at Podbanské, Slovakia, that involved fifty scholars from twenty-six institutions in twelve nations. Among other products, the delegates developed an agenda for future research. A follow-up conference to examine rural change in the region was held in 2013 at SAU, which published a proceedings volume titled *Social and Economic Transformations Affecting Rural People and Communities in Central and Eastern Europe since 1990.*[5]

With funding from the Alfred Jurzykowski Foundation, the Central and Eastern Europe Coordinating Committee's Rural Development Project also conducted a transdisciplinary international comparative analysis of rural community adaptation to the transformation from state socialism. The "three nation study," which involved scholars from Poland, Hungary, Slovakia, and Cornell, promoted international research cooperation among Eastern European scholars and institutions.

Mellon-Sawyer Seminar: Toward a Transnational and Transcultural Europe

With funding from the Mellon Foundation, four Cornell professors conducted a four-semester Mellon-Sawyer seminar titled Toward a Transnational and Transcultural Europe, facilitated by the Einaudi Center's Institute for European Studies. The seminar was organized into four semester-long components: religious practices, the media, contentious politics, and rural community transformations. From twenty to twenty-five professors and PhD students from across the university attended the monthly seminars. A capstone conference was held at the Central European University in Budapest in 2004.

Special Education Partnership with Rousse, Bulgaria

In 2003, Cornell received a grant from the US State Department's Bureau of Educational and Cultural Affairs to collaborate with Rousse University in Bulgaria to establish educational programs focused on regional development management in the Rousse Region. David L. Brown and Jerry White were Cornell's principal investigators, along with Bulgarian counterparts Vasil Penchev and Stoyanka Smaikarova. Twelve Cornell faculty participated in the program along with eleven colleagues from Rousse University. The project operated from 2003 to 2006, pilot-testing three master's degree programs and five certificate programs. All these programs were developed in collaboration with local and regional governments. In addition to establishing an entirely new curriculum for the university, the project enhanced the university's role in development management in the Rousse region. Three Rousse PhD students spent a semester at Cornell, where they participated in David Lewis's regional planning seminar in the Department of City and Regional Planning. During their stay at Cornell, the seminar designed a development strategy for Rousse, part of which was subsequently implemented. The new regional management curriculum was still being offered by the university as of this writing. In 2007, David L. Brown was awarded an honorary doctorate by Rousse University.

Central and Eastern Europe Coordinating Committee Program Impacts

The program's most lasting impact was the mutually beneficial and durable scholarly partnership formed between Cornell faculty members and counterparts in Central and Eastern Europe. Cornell scholars modeled contemporary research and pedagogical methods and philosophies, while colleagues in Hungary, Slovakia, Bulgaria, and other countries provided deep knowledge of diverse national and cultural contexts relevant to the design and conduct of scholarship on social and economic transformations in the region. Both sides benefited greatly from this decade of scholarly collaboration.

Faculty members who participated in the Nitra-based Mellon Foundation project developed a better appreciation for the skills that their students would need to succeed in the world economy. These students became increasingly capable of good decision-making in business and in politics. Participants identified ways to use economic concepts to analyze economic problems. They observed that major US universities not only teach students but also perform significant research. The program enhanced SAU's subsequent economic research activities.

The rural development activities have had a concrete impact. Scholarly publications have had a lasting influence on the scholarship on postsocialist rural transformations. The project's articles continue to be cited in research publications a decade later. However, perhaps the project's most enduring legacy is the young scholars who began their careers by participating in it and who are now influential midcareer scholars in both Hungary and the United States.

Notes

1. During the period in which these activities took place, the Dyson School was known as the Department of Agricultural Economics (until 1993); the Department of Agricultural, Resource and Managerial Economics (1993 to 1995); and the Department of Applied Economics and Management (2000 to 2010).

2. In addition to the College of Agriculture and Life Sciences–based activities described in this chapter, scholars in Cornell's Department of Government (Valerie Bunce and

Sidney Tarrow) and Department of Modern Languages (Wayles Browne) have long-term scholarly programs focused on the region, with the help of the Einaudi Center's Institute for European Studies.

3. The University of Agriculture in Gödöllő, Hungary, became part of the new Szent István University in 2000. The University of Agriculture in Nitra was renamed the Slovak University of Agriculture in Nitra in 1996.

4. The workshop's proceedings were published in *Roczniki Naukowe Stowarzyszenia Ekonomistow Rolnictwa i Agrobiznesu / Journal of the Association of Polish Agricultural Economists and Agribusiness* 7, no. 2 (2000).

5. Barbara Babjaková et al., eds., *Social and Economic Transformations Affecting Rural People and Communities in Central and Eastern Europe since 1990*, conference proceedings (Nitra: Slovak Agricultural University, 2013).

22. A CORNELL-JAPAN PARTNERSHIP

The Food Industry Connection

Gene A. German

The Food Industry Management Program in the Dyson School of Applied Economics and Management has developed a long-standing relationship with the Japanese food industry. This relationship began in the 1970s and includes activities with Japanese university faculty, supermarket chains, food manufacturing companies, and both graduate and undergraduate students from Japan. One of the most active programs in this relationship is the Cornell National Supermarket Association of Japan Retail Management Program for Japanese managers aspiring to gain insights and knowledge that will make them more effective managers. In July of each year, thirty management executives from the leading Japanese supermarket companies come to Cornell's Ithaca campus as the final step in this yearlong management development program.

This program begins in the fall when the participants are selected by their companies and approved by the board of directors of the National Supermarket Association of Japan. This prestigious association has been a sponsor of this program with Cornell for more than twenty years. The first meeting of this group is a two-day seminar in Tokyo, Japan, at which several Cornell faculty members from the Food Industry Management Program in the Dyson School are featured speakers. In addition to the Cornell faculty, industry leaders from Japanese supermarket companies, as well as faculty from prominent Japanese universities, are invited as speakers for the opening seminar.

Following the seminar, participants gather each month for a two-day meeting with faculty from various Japanese universities to discuss current issues facing the food industry and food distribution system in Japan. At these sessions, topics are assigned for study before next month's meeting. During the year, faculty from Cornell's Food Industry Management Program visit one or more of the monthly two-day sessions to observe and to provide updates on recent developments that are taking place in the US food distribution system. These meetings provide an opportunity for Cornell faculty to share information about food distribution in

Figure 22.1 Professor Gene German meets with Takeo Onodera (class of 1970), president of the Megmilk Snow Brand company, at Cornell in 1994. (Photo provided by Jean German)

the United States and to learn about trends taking place in the Japanese food system.

The Connection between Cornell and the Japanese Food Distribution Industry

The connection between Cornell's Food Industry Management Program and the food distribution system in Japan began in the early 1970s when Nissin Foods sent two of its promising young managers to Cornell. Both were enrolled in the College of Agriculture and Life Sciences as graduate students, and both completed the necessary requirements for an MS degree. One of the students eventually became president and CEO of Nissin Foods. When they returned to Japan, they shared information about their experience at Cornell with others in the food industry, and soon a number of Japanese food companies began sending managers to study at Cornell.

In 1976, Gene A. German, professor of agricultural economics, made a trip to Japan to meet with food industry executives and to encourage companies to send young executives to attend Cornell and its Food Industry Management

Program. During this first visit to Japan, German met a young writer for *Chain Store Age*, the leading publication for the supermarket industry in Japan. This writer, Satoshi Nishimura, wrote several articles describing the participation by Japanese executives in the Food Industry Management Program. This led to greater interest throughout the Japanese food system in the educational opportunities at Cornell that existed for Japanese managers. Nishimura later spent a year studying at Cornell in the Department of Agricultural Economics to learn more about the Cornell program and to broaden his knowledge of the food distribution system in the United States. This experience led him to start a new career in Japan as a consultant to the food industry, during which he continued to promote the idea of an educational connection between Cornell and the Japanese food industry.

During the 1980s, several other factors contributed to strengthening the relationship between Cornell and the Japanese food distribution industry. The number of Japanese managers who had completed a master's degree and returned to their companies in Japan continued to grow. This group formed their own Cornell alumni association and met periodically to talk business and to socialize. Also, Japanese faculty at several leading universities became aware of Cornell's prominence in the field of food distribution and requested the opportunity to spend sabbatical leave time to do research at Cornell and interact with Cornell faculty. This resulted in a number of joint research papers and projects between faculty in Cornell's food industry program and faculty from Japanese universities. This in turn opened up a dialogue that has grown over the years and continues today between faculty at Cornell and faculty in various Japanese universities.

In 1984, Professor German was invited to spend a sabbatical leave in Japan to study Japan's food distribution system, which is remarkably different from that in the United States. During his sabbatical leave, he was able to spend time gathering data by working directly with several major Japanese supermarket chains and food manufacturers, which was made possible by the relationships that had been developed with former Japanese graduate students and especially with the help of Nishimura through his contacts in the food industry as a consultant. This sabbatical leave experience led to the establishment of an annual food industry seminar held in Tokyo and featuring faculty from Cornell, faculty from Japanese universities, and executives from the Japanese food industry. These early seminars were sponsored and funded by various Japanese and multinational food marketing companies. As the popularity of the seminar grew, guest speakers were also invited from prominent international organizations such as the Food Marketing Institute, a US-based trade association, and the Paris-based CIES, a global food business network. These early seminars were the forerunners to the current executive program that brings promising Japanese managers to Cornell each summer and sends members of the Cornell faculty to Japan several times each year to participate in the Cornell-Japan food industry management program.

The Cornell food marketing alumni group in Japan still meets periodically to socialize and to share memories of their days studying at Cornell, and some have stayed engaged with Cornell through alumni leadership roles. In 2019, this group invited Professor German and his wife to Japan for a weeklong visit to renew memories of their sabbatical leave time in Japan and to thank them for the role they played in their educational experience at Cornell. This international outreach that began with a few graduate students attending Cornell through sponsorship by their company has grown and developed into a formal management development program that involves a wide range of faculty from Cornell interacting with faculty from Japanese universities and now has strong financial support from a major Japanese supermarket trade association. The thirty or more Japanese managers who participate in this program each year will always remember their Cornell experience and consider themselves Cornell alumni.

23. THE CORNELL HUMPHREY PROGRAM

A Catalyst for Cooperation and Understanding

Peter Gregory, Matt Hayes, and Polly Endreny Holmberg

Program History

In March 1978, US president Jimmy Carter announced the creation of the Hubert H. Humphrey Fellowship Program to honor the late US vice president and senator Hubert Humphrey for his exemplary leadership, his tireless devotion to public service, and his sincere hope for greater understanding among nations.

The specialized nondegree program that bears his name is a Fulbright exchange activity that is currently conducted at Cornell and twelve other US universities. It provides professionals from countries with developing and emerging economies an opportunity to enhance their leadership capacity. More than 6,400 men and women have been honored as Humphrey Fellows across the country since the program began, with more than 400 of those at Cornell. The program provides intensive training for an academic year across a broad range of international development fields and impact areas.[1] Primary funding is provided by the US Congress through the Bureau of Educational and Cultural Affairs of the Department of State. Cosponsors include other governmental agencies, multinational organizations, and private donors. The Institute of International Education assists the Bureau of Educational and Cultural Affairs in administering the Humphrey Fellowship Program and provides valuable logistical support to Humphrey campuses.

Cornell's Humphrey Program focuses on agriculture (improving agricultural yields and food security), rural development (improving the quality of life and economic well-being of rural communities), and natural resource management (managing conservation challenges from social, ecological, and cross-disciplinary perspectives). Since its inception in 1979, Cornell has enriched the professional experience of more than 400 people from 115 countries who have come to Ithaca for a yearlong exchange and returned to their home countries with new skills to make profound development changes back home.

Figure 23.1 Vice Provost for International Relations Fredrik Logevall (*left*) and Humphrey Fellow 2011–2012 Pratim Roy (*right*), director of the Keystone Foundation, sign a memorandum of understanding for the establishment of the Nilgiris Field Learning Center in Kotagiri, Tamil Nadu, India, in 2013. (Photo by Jason Koski, Cornell University Photography)

Shortly after arriving at Cornell, Humphrey Fellows prepare individual program plans for their professional development, detailing their goals and objectives for the year, including courses, seminars, special projects, and professional and community activities.[2]

Forging partnerships is a key objective at Cornell. Our fellows are seeking collaboration to accelerate efforts to improve rural peoples' livelihoods and lands in their countries. The bold thinking and innovation from our Humphrey alumni are transforming development in areas such as food safety, trade, environmental safety, and poverty alleviation. Some work on resettlements in conflict areas, while others have launched foundations and businesses to stimulate the economy, teach youth and women, and protect the environment.

Bilateral cultural exchange is a crucial part of the program. Each year, fellows work with faculty, students, and US residents or organizations on plans to address challenges in their fields. Those collaborations lead to profound and lasting changes around the world. The fellows share their culture, skills, and professional experience with US counterparts by teaching classes and working with Cornell faculty and students on projects. Placements around New York State are facilitated by Cornell Cooperative Extension and Alfred State College, our associate campus.

Figure 23.2 National TV news reporter interviews Humphrey Fellow 2017–2018 Emmanuel Ajani after the solar installation training in Nigeria in 2018. (Provided by Emmanuel Ajani)

Featured Alumni

Pratim Roy, Indian alumnus of the Cornell Humphrey Fellowship class of 2011–2012 and founder and director of the Keystone Foundation, was instrumental in setting up the Keystone Foundation, which since 1993 has worked to enhance the quality of life and environment of Indigenous communities using eco-development approaches. He is currently responsible for Keystone's donor relationships and plans its programs and projects. His knowledge on bees and their service to biodiversity and the ecosystem in the mountains has been of immense value to the organization, as has his interest in water, which has led to wetlands projects in the Nilgiris, a mountainous district in the southern Indian state of Tamil Nadu.

The Nilgiris Field Learning Center, launched in 2014 as a partnership between the Keystone Foundation and Cornell, helps students conceive our world anew through a field-based learning experience. The fifteen-week program aims to build conscious leadership among the youth of the Adivasi (Indigenous tribal people) community and undergraduate students from Cornell. It is an opportunity for young people from opposite parts of the world to interact and learn from one another.

During the first several weeks of training, theoretical models of research covering various topics are taught and demonstrated in a classroom setting. The remaining weeks are all about practical experience and continuously exchanging views with their fellow researchers and most importantly meeting diverse people. Themes in the course are community-based conservation, social-ecological systems, forest-based livelihoods, community wellness, Indigenous worldviews, governance, urbanization, and trade and markets.

The course, as envisaged, aims to build narratives that will make sense on a long-term basis. This ensures that the students who succeed the previous group are not initiating something that they cannot conclude at the end of the course but are rather picking up the baton from where it was left.

The Adivasi students have begun pursuing higher studies on topics ranging from conservation to development studies; some have joined Keystone and are coordinating program implementation with communities across different regions.

Emmanuel Ajani, Nigerian alumnus of the Cornell Humphrey Fellowship class of 2017–2018, is deputy director at the National Agency for Science and Engineering Infrastructure in Nigeria. He is pioneering a new approach to adoption of solar energy in rural areas of his country and beyond. He acknowledges the key role in the project of Alfred State's School of Applied Technology, where he gained hands-on experience with solar installations.

In 2014, a Center for Global Development report showed that six hundred million Africans had no reliable access to electricity.[3] Even urban areas with high electrical grid coverage are plagued by several hours of blackouts and power outages per day. Solar energy has emerged as a popular alternative source of energy in Nigeria, but the supply of qualified solar installers has proved unable to meet the growing demand.

To address this gap and deliver a solar installation training program, Ajani led a team from Cornell, Alfred, and the National Agency for Science and Engineering Infrastructure. Solar electricity is growing very fast, but the activities of fake solar installers in the past marred the integrity of solar energy systems. Capacity in solar installation skills must be built at a rate equal to or greater than the demand. If this is not done, it will lead to poorly installed solar systems, which will discourage others from installing solar in the future.

With Tarig Ahmed, a class of 2017–2018 Cornell Humphrey alumnus from Sudan, and Joseph Abu, a graduate student in the Cornell Institute for Public Affairs, Ajani was awarded a summer project grant issued by Cornell's Institute for African Development at the Mario Einaudi Center for International Studies. The initial proposal was intended to cover training for twenty students, but Ajani and his team expanded the program to train fifty-three students from July 30 to August 10, 2018.

Toko Village, a rural community close to Abuja, Nigeria's capital, served as the pilot site for the training's practical activities. The village lacked basic infrastructure such as electricity and potable drinking water. Training participants worked with community members to drill a fresh borehole and install a solar water pump to supply water to the community. Fifty-three solar installers were trained. Monthly monitoring and evaluations indicated that the installation has made a positive impact on the community's health and water consumption. Trainees from the program have gone on to mentor solar installers in other communities and start up their own solar installation businesses. Ajani has been working with Ahmed to launch similar programs in Liberia and Sudan.

Ajani is also working on the establishment of a solar cell manufacturing plant in Nigeria. There is already a solar module and panel factory, but the factory uses imported solar cells. With this new factory, Ajani and his colleagues will be able to increase the local content of the solar panels, bring down the cost of installation of solar energy systems, and possibly increase the solar penetration in Nigeria. At the time of writing, ninety-nine scientists, engineers, and technicians are being trained on various aspects of solar cell manufacturing technology. Ajani sees the possibility of exporting the products.

Eugenia Saini, Argentinian alumna of the Cornell Humphrey Fellowship class of 2009–2010, has served as executive secretary of the Regional Fund for Agricultural Technology (FONTAGRO) since 2018, leading an international team of about thirty people. She is the first woman to lead the fund. FONTAGRO is a unique cooperation mechanism among Latin American countries and Spain that promotes innovation in family farming, competitiveness, and food security through regional platforms. Comprising fifteen Latin American countries, FONTAGRO has $112 million invested in 160 international projects with 230 public-private organizations and spillover in at least twenty-nine countries. The organization is sponsored by the Inter-American Development Bank and the Inter-American Institute for Cooperation on Agriculture. FONTAGRO also functions as a discussion forum on agricultural and rural innovation.

Saini says, "The most important impact of my Humphrey Fellowship experience is that it prepared me for leadership of a $100 million program comprising 15 Latin American and Caribbean countries in agricultural research and development."[4]

Much of her time is spent monitoring the investments of the fund promoting partnerships among public and private organizations. Saini's top leadership position at FONTAGRO is closely aligned with her passion for agriculture, feeding people, and making life better for farmers. Her professional background enhances her ability to work in multicultural and interdisciplinary teams, sharing knowledge from basic and applied sciences, portfolio financial management, and agribusiness policy design.

Indeed, this has been the hallmark of her almost twenty-five years of work in strategic planning and execution of regional cooperation projects. Her focus is on science and development, technological innovation, and sustainable agribusiness for small farming in Latin American and Caribbean countries. Her vision is establishing stronger strategic alliances among public and private organizations that enhance governance and increase investments in research and development.

Recently she was honored with an Abshire-Inamori Leadership Academy award at the Center for Strategic and International Studies in Washington, DC, an award that aims to empower the center's young professionals and external audiences to make positive contributions to their communities and the world at large.

Impacts of the Cornell Humphrey Program

The Cornell experience has empowered Humphrey Fellows to become leaders and agents of change. The fellows have applied their new skills, advanced in their careers, developed capacity in their organizations, created and nurtured new organizations, and influenced national and even international policies and implementation practices, all in accordance with the program goals. The range of Cornell fellows' impacts in their countries and regions is illustrated in the stories of alumni that have been featured in this chapter.

The fellows also have considerable impact in the United States—at Cornell, in Ithaca, and beyond. For example, they all conduct professional affiliations on and off campus. Typically, these involve a six-week full-time, mutually beneficial placement at an organization (e.g., international development bank, university, or corporation, etc.) related to the Humphrey Fellow's professional field. Fellows also cowrite articles for publication with US authors and accept invitations to speak in classes, seminars, conferences, and workshops on and off campus. They also volunteer with local humanitarian organizations, serve as expert panelists and speakers at the annual World Food Prize New York Youth Institute event at Cornell, and participate in cultural exchange activities, including trips, events, and social gatherings. A recent exciting venture is fellows' participation in the implementation of the City of Ithaca Green New Deal, a novel initiative that has attracted the attention of many, including the White House.

"Friendship Partners" catalyze the integration of fellows into US cultures and experiences. These are families and individuals in the Ithaca community who graciously volunteer their support. Many of the local partners are Cornell University faculty and staff members. These individuals offer their time and friendship to fellows to help them with everything from moving into their new Ithaca-based homes to exploring the local outdoors to experiencing US holidays and celebrations.

Future of the Cornell Humphrey Program

Global production of food, agriculture, and fisheries is on track to meet rising global demand, but a key challenge is whether continued growth in production can be achieved sustainably. Agriculture has a considerable environmental footprint as the largest user of the world's land and water resources and an important source of greenhouse gas emissions. Fish stocks are under increasing pressure from overfishing, while aquaculture raises concerns about the degradation of ecosystems. The food, agriculture, and fisheries sector can be expected to continue to underperform with respect to sustainability, climate, and resilience goals set by governments.

Depending on future funding, the Cornell Humphrey Program will place even more emphasis on raising fellows' awareness of these issues and on the constantly evolving technological innovations and policy measures intended to address them.

Notes

1. For more about the Humphrey Fellowship impact areas, see "Impact Areas," Humphrey Fellowship, accessed September 29, 2023, https://www.humphreyfellowship.org/impact-areas/.

2. For detailed Humphrey Fellowship components, see "Fellowship Components," Humphrey Fellowship, accessed September 29, 2023, https://www.humphreyfellowship.org/prospective-applicants/fellowship-components/.

3. Ben Leo, Vijaya Ramachandran, and Robert Morello, "Shedding New Light on the Off-Grid Debate in Power Africa Countries," Center for Global Development (blog), October 14, 2014, https://www.cgdev.org/blog/shedding-new-light-grid-debate-power-africa-countries.

4. "Eugenia Saini," Global Development, Cornell College of Agriculture and Life Sciences, accessed April 28, 2023, https://cals.cornell.edu/global-development/our-work/our-initiatives/hubert-h-humphrey-fellowship-program/alumni/eugenia-saini.

24. THE TANG CORNELL-CHINA SCHOLARS PROGRAM

Connecting with CALS

Norman Scott

"The program is wonderful and has had impacts on my work in China. A long-term relationship was established. Techniques and ideas have benefited our students." "The most important element in development of my scientific career in China has been the Tang Cornell-China Scholar program." These are comments from two Tang Cornell-China Scholars about their experiences as scholars in the program, which was established in 1999.[1]

The Tang Cornell-China Scholars Program was an outcome of annual visits by Cornell president Frank Rhodes and other senior Cornell administrators to China in the early 1990s. The Jack C. Tang (唐驥千) Family Foundation provided a generous endowment of $2 million. President Rhodes had formed an advisory group to provide guidance on how Cornell might better engage with China. Norman Scott, Cornell vice president for research and advanced studies, and Ray Wu, a revered biochemistry professor, were asked to develop a systematic plan to engage Cornell and Chinese universities and agencies to advance cooperation for improving the agriculture and food system in China. Rhodes and Scott met annually with several Cornell trustees, including Martin Y. Tang (class of 1970), during the spring meetings of the university's board of trustees.

As a result of the activities between Cornell and numerous Chinese universities, Tang and his sisters Leslie and Nadine suggested to Scott that Cornell consider developing a programmatic initiative to enhance collaboration through a formal process with a focus in agriculture. Martin Tang shared with Scott a similar initiative that was funded by the Tang family at the University of California, Berkeley (where Leslie and Nadine were graduates), in a different scientific area.[2] Scott, with the Berkeley example in hand, prepared the proposal for the Tang family. It was readily accepted, and the first scholars began coming to Cornell in 2001.

Figure 24.1 *Left to right in front row*: Mrs. Jack Tang (seated); Leslie Tang, Ruqian Zhao (scholar), CALS Dean Susan Henry, Gonyou Chen (scholar), Martin Tang; *left to right in second row*: Paul Soloway (faculty advisor), Norman Scott (program director), Allan Colmer (faculty adviser). (Photo provided by author)

Program Goal

Scott served as the founding director through 2012, when Ping Wang, professor of entomology and current director, succeeded him. The program aspires to enhance scientific and technological collaboration throughout the world by developing cooperative relationships between the best scholars at the threshold of their careers in China and established research and education leaders at Cornell University in the College of Agriculture and Life Sciences. It was designed to provide opportunities for the most distinguished scholars from the People's Republic of China—those in the early stages of careers in the agricultural and biological sciences and biological engineering—to spend up to two years at Cornell undertaking research in their field of specialty. Scholarly research areas were made broad to reflect emerging or priority areas deemed worthy of collaborative research efforts to capitalize on the strengths of each partner institution and the qualifications of the scholar.

Those chosen to be Tang Cornell-China Scholars were expected to have demonstrated, at the time of their nomination, a track record of extraordinary capability in research, significant potential for research leadership, and outstanding teaching abilities. During their stay at Cornell, they would be able to enhance their research and teaching skills.

Figure 24.2 Martin Y. Tang speaks at the dedication event for the new Martin Y. Tang Welcome Center, located in the renovated Noyes Lodge, 2018. (Photo by Lindsay France, University Photography)

Through participation in the program, the Tang Cornell-China Scholars would expand their research proficiencies, build lasting research relationships with Cornell colleagues, and develop their ability to lead research and technology developments and educational advancements in their home institutions and in China at the highest levels. While the program was adjusted to the needs of the individual scholars and their respective institutions, it was envisioned that those selected would spend a minimum of one year—all at once or in two study periods—working as colleagues in research in an appropriate laboratory or program at Cornell.

In order to enhance the quality of education in the scholars' special field of study upon their return to China, while at Cornell the scholars would actively participate in the teaching and learning environment, teaching at least one course during their time here. Once the scholars returned to their home institutions in China, they would continue their collaborative efforts with Cornell researchers. Through these associations, the links between the scholars and their Cornell colleagues and between Chinese institutions and Cornell University would remain strong and lasting.

Selection of Scholars

Cornell's president Hunter R. Rawlings contacted the presidents of the best universities in China and asked them for up to two nominations from different fields of agricultural and biological sciences and biological engineering within their institutions. The list of institutions contacted included Peking University, the Chinese Academy of Sciences, Fudan University, Shanghai Jiao Tong University, Nanjing University, Tsinghua University, Nanjing Agricultural University, China Agricultural University, Southwest Agricultural University, Northwest Science and Technology University of Agriculture and Forestry, Huazhong Agricultural University, Zhejiang University, Shenyang Agricultural University, Chinese Academy of Agricultural Sciences, University of Science and Technology of China, and Shanghai Academy of Agricultural Sciences. Because the objective was to build leaders for the future in China, the program sought candidates between the ages of thirty and forty-five.

The Cornell selection committee, chaired by the director of the Tang Cornell-China Scholars Program, included distinguished Cornell faculty representing, as much as possible, the expertise of nominees. Members of the selection committee were asked to choose two or three scholars from the nominees strictly on the basis of their extraordinary capacity in research and education, their potential to participate effectively in programs at Cornell, and their potential for leadership of the research and educational enterprise in China in the long term.

Financial Support

Since the program's support comes from the interest on the endowment, scholars were selected every other year based on available funding. Originally the program selected two scholars every other year, but in 2017 and 2019 the program was able to support three scholars biennially. The Tang Cornell-China Scholars receive an annual salary during their stay at Cornell to pay living costs for them and their families, as well as round-trip travel costs from China to Cornell, any Cornell fees, and a small research budget during their stay. In an effort to advance communication and to build a community, once the scholars returned to China, the Tang Family Foundation supported several biennial symposiums in China.

Program Assessment

Over the two decades of the Tang Cornell-China Scholars Program, which had its first on-campus scholars in 2001, Cornell has hosted twenty-seven scholars to date.

To assess the value of the program, Norman Scott developed a survey to seek input from the scholars, Cornell faculty advisers, and presidents of the participating Chinese universities. Responses to the survey illustrate the program's impact.

Scholars highlighted the impact on their skills, expertise, and professional development. One noted that the "program widened my scope and the research technologies and methods are valuable to us in China" and it "increased my scientific strategy, experimental skills and fluency in English," describing it as "not only a high honor but an opportunity to work with a community of world-class scientists." Another wrote, "Technologies learned at Cornell such as bioinformatics and gene cloning have been useful in my work." Many scholars noted the honors and opportunities that resulted from the program, such as "four international collaboration projects and . . . a major grant for a national center," "the Excellency Youth Award from NNSFC [National Natural Science Foundation China]" and recruitment "as leading scientist to academic scientist program at CAAS [Chinese Academy of Agricultural Sciences]."

Cornell faculty described the program as a "wonderful opportunity to grow a lifelong friendship and collaboration. Furthermore, our institutions and students have become well acquainted." Another faculty member claimed that scholars "helped broaden our perspective." Another stated, "It is important that we have this kind of short-term exchanges over a period of several years to move forward and to provide a foundation for working in different institutional environments."

Finally, Chinese university presidents were enthused about the program. One stated that the "impact of the program has been significant at our university because: 1) the momentum from study at Cornell has been important to their laboratories and college as they play a role as leading scientists, 2) during stay at Cornell they had the opportunity to meet Cornell scientists which has generated useful ideas and have led to numerous peer-reviewed publications and 3) as a result of the collaborative relationships, Cornell advisors have visited our university and staff and students have benefited from their lectures and interactions during their stay." A second wrote, "The program has impacted our organization by increasing international collaborative projects and academic exchanges. Specifically, three international collaborative projects have been funded with Chinese funds." A third noted, "The Tang Scholars program has benefited our university and the scholar has gained new skills and knowledge," and a fourth university president stated that "the program is very influential in China. This recognition adds credibility to the scholar's nominations for award and prizes. Specifically our two faculty have received awards from the [Ministry of Education] and China State Council since their return."

The Tang Cornell-China Scholars Program continues to be successful as an exemplary model to engage distinguished faculty at Cornell and at numerous Chinese universities in science and technology related to agriculture and food systems.

It has promoted collaborative and cooperative relationships between faculty members through significant interactions during a year or more of participation in research and education. Beyond the joint research and education collaborations, personal relationships have evolved as an important benefit of the program. The scholars, Cornell faculty, and participating Chinese universities have each expressed the value of major outcomes and benefits to each group as a result of the Tang Cornell-China Scholars Program. Chinese universities, science agencies, and national, provincial, and local governments widely recognize the program as an influential initiative.

Notes

1. Quotes throughout this chapter were obtained from a self-study survey conducted by Norman Scott, then director of the Cornell-Tang program, in 2007. The survey was sent to Cornell-Tang scholars, Chinese University presidents of the respective universities from which the scholar came, and Cornell faculty advisers/mentors for the scholars. The survey was designed to evaluate the program and therefore adjust the program character accordingly.

2. The UC Berkeley Tang Distinguished Scholarship focuses on biological sciences, mathematics, physical sciences, engineering, and chemistry.

25. APPLIED ANTHROPOLOGY IN THE ANDES

The Cornell-Peru Project

David Holmberg

The Cornell-Peru Project (Proyecto Perú-Cornell) was a unique undertaking in the history of Cornell, in the history of anthropology, and in the history of the subfield of applied anthropology.[1] Modern anthropology began at Cornell under the leadership of Lauriston Sharp, who was originally appointed to the Department of Economics in 1936 after receiving his PhD in anthropology from Harvard University. Sharp also founded the Southeast Asia Program and the Department of Asian Studies, and he was instrumental in the establishment of the Center for International Studies. In the late 1940s, Sharp led an effort at Cornell to expand anthropology as part of a combined Department of Sociology and Anthropology. He wanted to develop anthropology in a distinctive way and not just replicate the kinds of programs found at major centers of anthropology at that time, including Columbia, Yale, Harvard, Chicago, and Berkeley. He decided to direct Cornell's efforts to applied anthropology and received financial support from the Carnegie Foundation. Anthropology at Cornell initially focused almost exclusively on studying social change and applying anthropology. Four applied anthropology projects were initiated in four locales: Latin America, Thailand, India, and the American Southwest. This departmental focus continued until the mid-1960s.

Allan Holmberg initiated the Cornell-Peru Project after joining the faculty at Cornell in 1948. Having visited Andean communities before coming to Cornell, he developed an interest in exploring processes of social change diverging from his doctoral research among the Sirionó, an isolated group of hunters and gatherers in the Amazonian region of eastern Bolivia. Once at Cornell and in collaboration with colleagues in Peru, his interest in social change evolved into an unusual—even radical—project both to induce as well as study processes of social change.

The Cornell-Peru Project officially began in 1952 and continued until 1962, although Cornell's involvement in the area continued until the untimely death of Holmberg in 1966. The project centered on the community of Vicos in the Callejón de Huaylas. Vicos was a hacienda, a large estate owned by the Public

Figure 25.1 Pay day at Hacienda Vicos: Allan Holmberg (*center*) observing Enrique Luna and Mario Vasquez distribute shares to community members, 1950s. Allan R. Holmberg Collection on Peru, #14-25-1529. (Photo by Abraham Guillén, provided by Division of Rare and Manuscript Collections, Cornell University Library)

Benefit Society of Huaraz, the provincial capital. The income generated from renting the hacienda went to supporting a regional hospital. At the outset of the project, there were some 361 households and 2,250 people in the community of Vicos. The *patrón*, or the one who rented and managed the hacienda, had rights to the land of the hacienda and to the labor of the residents. The people of Vicos were required to provide three days of labor per week to the patron of the hacienda and had a host of other obligations to the manor house or other work around the hacienda. They worked in the fields, in the gardens, and in the pastures of the hacienda, but the patron could also in turn rent them out as laborers to work in towns, other haciendas, or mines nearby.

The situation for Vicosinos was oppressive and on the margins of subsistence. Households on the hacienda did have ownership over small individual plots of land in varying amounts on which they could grow subsistence crops of maize and potatoes. These rights, of course, depended on their performance of required labor. One Vicosino remembered the hacienda system in these terms:

> The landlord exploited us a lot. . . . Like a contractor does now, just like that, they made us work fourteen hours, all the same, men and women. The [patrons] rented us out with everything, as if we were a tool for work, to

Figure 25.2 The new school at Vicos, 1953. Allan R. Holmberg Collection on Peru, #14-25-1529. (Photo by Abraham Guillén, provided by Division of Rare and Manuscript Collections, Cornell University Library)

> the coast or to the south coast. Since we were illiterate, we didn't know anything. For that reason they mistreated us. With the *patrón*'s threats one couldn't go wherever one wanted, and when he rented [out] one's work by the day, the *patrón* or hacendado himself received [the pay]. We peasants just took advantage of what we possessed, a little land, where one lived from a certain amount.[2]

Land-poor households had to labor on others' land and glean or steal what they could to subsist. Wealth tended to be accumulated in cattle and other livestock that Vicosinos could put to pasture in highland grazing lands. Education was almost nonexistent, and only 10 percent of the population could speak Spanish. Public health facilities and infrastructure were nonexistent. The average Vicosino had numerous parasites, and nutrition was often substandard. Vicosinos were subject to the whims of their overseers and often physically abused. Moreover, women were subject to harassment by the patrons and their functionaries.

After visiting the region of Vicos for the first time, Holmberg came up with an idea that now strikes most of us as audacious. He approached the Cornell president and board of trustees with the proposal that Cornell rent the hacienda and act as the patron to institute a program of improvement of life and human dignity of the Vicosinos and to study those processes of change. As Holmberg put it,

> In 1952, quite by design, although unexpectedly and suddenly, I found myself in the delicate position of having assumed the role of *patrón* (in the name of Cornell University) of a Peruvian *hacienda* called Vicos, for a period of five years, for the purpose of conducting a research and development program on the modernization process.
>
> As you can readily imagine, such action on my part clearly shook (or perhaps I should say shocked) the Board of Trustees—to say nothing of the some 2,000 residents of the *hacienda* and no few of my anthropological colleagues.[3]

More often than not, anthropologists are brought into development projects to help facilitate the projects after they have been designed by economists, engineers, agricultural specialists, or government officials. It was a rare project indeed that was conceived and directed largely by social scientists. Carlos Monge of the Instituto Indigenista Peruana worked with Holmberg in procuring the lease on Vicos, and the project proceeded with an official collaboration with the institute. Mario C. Vásquez became codirector of the Vicos project after conducting graduate studies in anthropology at Cornell. Vásquez was a key figure in the project and was essential in gaining the confidence of the people of Vicos. His fluency in the Quechua language was instrumental to the successes the project achieved. Many other scholars and graduate students participated in the project over the years.

In a comprehensive overview of the Vicos project, Barbara Lynch highlights several areas of intervention. Much effort was focused on the increase in agricultural productivity and improvement in agricultural technique, particularly in the cultivation of potatoes. Similarly, the project introduced programs relating to agricultural credit, livestock management, barley, and reforestation. Much effort was extended to develop institutions for Vicosinos to become self-governing at the local level. These innovations would serve to strengthen a local economic base that would not only improve nutrition in the community but generate income for the community as well as integrate them in the greater Peruvian economy. Moreover, education, in Holmberg's view, was also central to the efforts of the project. A new school was built, new teachers recruited, and a new curriculum established. Attendance at the school increased dramatically and, despite difficulties with sustaining a corps of dedicated teachers, the school played a key role not only in Vicos but in surrounding communities. As Lynch notes, "There can be no doubt whatever the broader consequences of education, the school had a strong, immediate impact on Vicos with strong attendance and significant increases in literacy."[4]

Although the effects of these interventions can be debated, in retrospect, the most telling accomplishment of the project was the transformation of a community of people bound under an exploitative feudal-like hacienda system—a legacy of Spanish colonial transformation of Indigenous civilization—into a self-governing independent community in control of its own lands. Holmberg's overall ethos was driven by a fundamental belief in the dignity of all humans and the natural ability of humans to achieve progress. The goal of the project from the very beginning was to work toward the dissolution of the hacienda system and have the people of Vicos control their own lands and destiny. As Lynch noted, this effort coincided with the realization on the part of the Peruvian elite that the hacienda system could no longer be sustained. Peasant communities like Vicos were making demands as well. Florencia Zapata has recorded the voices of Vicosinos on their memories of the project. She notes that in her interviews, "the abolition of the hacienda system and purchase of the lands of Vicos were especially commented upon and discussed." For example, one Vicosino commented, "When the gringos arrived in Vicos they brought us many changes. That is, from that date we no longer served the hacendados but rather Vicos. Every one [of us was] liberated from the patrones. The peasant worker had very little land to cultivate before; rather he served the *patrón*." Another Vicosino noted that the project "was good in parts, but bad in parts," and particularly noted the introduction of agricultural techniques based on synthetic fertilizers that disrupted the organic farming of the past.[5]

The first efforts to facilitate the purchase of the hacienda by the community of Vicos occurred early on in Cornell's first five-year tenure, but these efforts were stymied by the resistance of the Public Benefit Society of Huaraz and other political forces. It took a second Cornell term as patron of Vicos to achieve the transfer of Vicos lands to the Vicosinos themselves. On July 13, 1962, the community of Vicos obtained title to the hacienda and was no longer subject to the oppressive patron of the past, nor the more benevolent patrons of the Cornell era. The project continued for another four to five years, but political forces in Peru coinciding with Holmberg's death led to the cessation of the project in 1966.

Vicos sustains a strong sense of identity and remains an independent and collectively organized community. In the summer of 2007, the Casa de los Abuelos (House of the Ancestors) opened as part of a local memory project undertaken by the Mountain Institute. Included in the Casa are the memories of the Proyecto Perú-Cornell from the perspective of Vicosinos along with numerous photos. Moreover, the Cornell University Library houses an extensive archive on the Vicos project, including more than two thousand photographic images.[6]

Notes

1. An overview of the project and its impact from the perspective of numerous scholars involved as well as others can be found in Tom Greaves, Ralph Bolton, and Florencia Zapata, eds., *Vicos and Beyond: A Half Century of Applying Anthropology in Peru* (Lanham, MD: AltaMira, 2011).

2. Florencia Zapata, "Remembering Vicos: Local Memories and Voices," in Greaves, Bolton, and Zapata, *Vicos and Beyond*, 325–326.

3. Allan R. Holmberg, "The Research and Development Approach to the Study of Change," *Human Organization* 17, no. 1 (1958): 12.

4. Barbara Lynch, *The Vicos Experiment: A Study of the Impacts of the Cornell-Peru Project in a Highland Community* (Washington, DC: Bureau for Latin American and the Caribbean, US Agency for International Development, 1982), 38, https://pdf.usaid.gov/pdf_docs/PNAAJ616.pdf.

5. Zapata, "Remembering Vicos," 326–328.

6. For more information about the Vicos Collection in the Division of Rare and Manuscript Collections, Cornell University Library, see the Allan R. Holmberg Collection on Peru, #14-25-1529, as well as the Henry F. Dobyns Papers, #6803; Paul L. Doughty Collection of Vicos Photographs, #6734; Norman Pava Photographs of Vicos, #14-25-3837; William W. Stein Papers Relating to Vicos, #14-25-1603; Steven R. Nelson Photographs and Papers Relating to Vicos, #14-25-4356; and William Mangin Papers, #8413. A virtual tour of the Vicos project can be found online at "Vicos: A Virtual Tour," Cornell University, accessed October 2, 2023, https://vicosperu.cornell.edu/cornellperu_page_1.htm, and the collection's main website can be found at Vicos Collection, Cornell University, accessed October 2, 2023, https://vicos.library.cornell.edu/en/index.html.

26. SOUTHEAST ASIAN LANGUAGES AND THE BIRTH OF MODERN LANGUAGE STUDIES AT CORNELL

John Wolff

Before World War II, Southeast Asia was of peripheral interest to American scholars. Even the Philippines, at the time a commonwealth under US dominion, aroused meager scholarly interest. Aside from a few popular books and magazine articles that described exotic places and strange peoples, the Southeast Asian nations and their peoples were hardly written about or brought to the attention of the American public.

The war and Japanese occupation of much of the area changed that. The war effort brought into focus the importance that an understanding of these lands and their peoples had for defeating our enemy. This realization led the government to support the development of expertise in Southeast Asian matters, and that was the beginning of Southeast Asian area studies in the United States.

However, basic to the development of expertise in Southeast Asia was the knowledge of languages. It is impossible to learn what makes a culture tick and how a people think if you cannot talk to them in ways that are familiar to them and inspire trust. To develop military personnel who could deal with the local populations in Southeast Asia as the United States pushed the Japanese back, we needed to help these personnel develop language competence.

To meet the need for military personnel who knew the languages of the countries Americans would occupy, the US Army turned to the scholarly community to provide the pedagogical materials and instruction. The secretary of the American Council of Learned Societies (ACLS), F. Mortimer Graves, administered the project and chose Leonard Bloomfield, the foremost linguist of the day, to give the intellectual guidance for developing materials aimed at inculcating the languages of places where Americans were likely to go, including the countries of Southeast Asia.

The problem was that there was no tradition in America for teaching basic language competence in an effective way—not even in the widely studied European languages, much less in the languages of countries that were not within our ken.

Figure 26.1 Huynh Sanh Thong conducts Vietnamese class, 1953. (Provided by author)

Bloomfield understood that the almost universal practice of the time, teaching language by focusing on grammar and translation, hardly developed language competence and most certainly was wholly inappropriate for the learning of languages considered exotic at that time, such as Chinese and Japanese. It was no more appropriate for the languages of Southeast Asia. Under Bloomfield's direction, materials were prepared that were a sharp departure from the literature-oriented language pedagogy that was the norm throughout the United States.

Bloomfield's methods involved linguists who directed native speakers. The native speaker's job was to drill dialogues that the students were supposed to memorize, and to focus on conversing with the students, using the words and phrases that they had learned in the memorized dialogues. The focus was on oral use—reading and writing were secondary, in most cases totally left out. Materials were prepared for Burmese, Thai, Vietnamese (called Annamite in those days), and Malay, among the languages of Southeast Asia.

As American scholarship became more sophisticated and Southeast Asia became the focus of scholars in a wide range of fields, the basic need for language competence became far better understood. In 1950, when Lauriston Sharp, an anthropologist with research in Thailand, applied for funds for the establishment of a program of Southeast Asian studies at Cornell University, a strong part of the

Figure 26.2 John Wolff conducts Indonesian class, 1964. (Provided by author)

proposal was that Cornell at the time had the reputation of being the center of the most advanced and successful language teaching in America.

The ACLS had funded the Chinese and Japanese Language Institute at Cornell in the summer of 1941, and Cornell created the Department of Slavic Languages and Literatures in 1942, thanks in part to support from the Rockefeller Foundation. Intensive Russian language instruction began in fall 1942, in cooperation with the ACLS and under the auspices of the US Army Area and Language Program. Using Bloomfield's methods, the program brought in native speakers to aid in instruction. This program impressed the dean of Arts and Sciences, Cornelis W. de Kiewiet, and inspired him to propose establishing a new division of modern languages at Cornell using this method for teaching languages. De Kiewiet's proposal was accepted, and he hired a member of the ACLS team, J. Milton Cowan, as the division's director in 1946.

Cowan brought to Cornell University linguists specializing in French, Italian, German, Spanish, Chinese, Russian, and later a number of others, who oversaw programs in these languages and also other languages, which they may not have known but for which they found native speakers whom they could train in the Bloomfield method and direct. By 1949, Cornell's Division of Modern Languages could boast of offering instruction (using the "Cornell Method") in nine modern languages, including Arabic and English as a foreign language. Thai (Siamese) was added in 1951 with the advent of the Southeast Asia Program (SEAP).

When the Rockefeller Foundation funded a grant to form a program of Southeast Asian studies at Cornell, language instruction was a key part of the envisioned curriculum.[1] The first regular faculty member hired under the Rockefeller Foundation grant was George McT. Kahin, a specialist in Indonesian political history and international relations, who joined the faculty in 1951. Funds had been allocated for a linguist and a specialist in Thai language and literature. An offer was made to William Gedney, a well-known specialist in Thai language and literature, but he did not accept. For one year, J. Marvin Brown, a PhD candidate specializing in Thai at the University of California, Berkeley, came to Cornell to teach Thai.

In 1952, the first linguist specializing in a Southeast Asian language was appointed to the position of professor. A specialist in Indonesian, John M. Echols, introduced regular instruction at multiple levels in Indonesian, as well as Dutch reading. The following year, Vietnamese was taught, although without input from a linguist. In 1955, R. B. Jones was hired to develop courses in Thai, Burmese, and Vietnamese. In 1963, Javanese was added to the Southeast Asian language offerings under the direction of visiting professor Anthony Johns from the Australian National University, in later years taken over by me.

The funding for language instruction was never entirely covered by the university, and expansion and institutionalization of language instruction ultimately hinged on the program's access to federal funding through the 1958 National Defense and Education Act.[2]

Echols was heavily engaged in helping develop the library collection of materials pertaining to all Southeast Asian countries. With his extensive connections throughout the region, he was in a position to gather materials exhaustively and thus founded one of the world's premier research libraries for scholarship on Southeast Asia.[3] Accordingly, a position was opened for another specialist in Indonesian, for which I was hired in 1963. In the following years, two additional faculty positions were created for the teaching of the mainland Southeast Asian languages. Jones continued directing Thai and Burmese, Franklin Huffman was brought to Cornell to supervise Khmer and Vietnamese, and later Robert Quinn was hired to direct Vietnamese study. In 1965, I introduced instruction in Tagalog and, on occasion, regional languages of the Philippines.

The linguistic faculty saw it as their mission not only to supervise language instruction but also to prepare pedagogical materials. Over the course of more than twenty years, dictionaries for Indonesian, exhaustive revisions of the Indonesian dictionary, and materials for all levels of Indonesian (two different versions for the first two years of instruction), Vietnamese, Khmer, and Tagalog were published. These materials were a significant contribution to putting instruction in the Southeast Asian languages on a firm footing, not only at Cornell but at other institutions of higher learning. The materials proved largely effective. Although they are now several decades old, they are still in widespread use.

Developments at Cornell outside SEAP strengthened language instruction. In 1965, with the addition of two Arabic specialists in the Department of Near Eastern Studies, Arabic language instruction was introduced. Further, the East Asia Program sponsored the hiring of a specialist in Japanese, Eleanor Jorden, who had devoted her career to teaching Japanese and investigating language pedagogy, especially ways to develop more effective communicative competence.

Jorden's research and pedagogical materials had enormous influence on the kind of language instruction being done at Cornell, including in the languages of Southeast Asia. One example is the introduction of a full year of full-time instruction, in which students studied the target language exclusively for two semesters and a summer. This program, called FALCON (Full-Year Asian Language Concentration), was initially offered in Chinese and Japanese. After a year, it was tried for Thai, but that program lasted only one year. The following year, the Cornell administration approved a subsidy for a FALCON program in Indonesian, which endured for fifteen years and produced well over one hundred fluent speakers of Indonesian.

These developments in pedagogy changed the character and quality of the old Bloomfield method entirely. That method, in its original conception, assumed a supervising linguist directing an innocent native speaker who did not necessarily have much training or sophistication. But experience over the years and Jorden's Japanese program gave evidence that maximum effectiveness and optimal results required sophisticated instructors in all classroom activities. This meant that the native speakers who carried out the day-to-day activities had to have been thoroughly trained and know what they were doing when they were in class. They were able to make decisions regarding the curriculum and day-to-day classroom activities and procedures, and supervision from the professorial staff became superfluous, or the programs developed into team teaching, with cooperation between a linguist and the native speaker.

As the years went on, the linguistics faculty came to see themselves as less closely connected to language teaching than at the outset when the department was formed. By 1999, language teaching was moved from the Department of Linguistics to the Department of Asian Studies. As members of the faculty involved in teaching Southeast Asian languages retired, the language program was slowly turned over to the native speakers. I was the last linguist involved in a Southeast Asian language program, and after my retirement, the teaching was entirely in the hands of the native speakers.

The native speakers are now in charge of all aspects, including curriculum development, materials preparation, and supervision and training of teaching assistants if enrollment makes such personnel necessary. Cornell provides facilities and a specialist to help them keep abreast of the latest developments in teaching methodology and incorporate those developments into their teaching. There is no requirement that language teachers be holders of an advanced degree, although most do. They have the rank of lecturer or senior lecturer and are full faculty members of SEAP.

In this way, the teaching of the Southeast Asian languages continues to thrive and be effective, even though there is no longer input from a linguist. Being able to offer instruction with only one teacher has meant considerable financial savings, which, in the waves of belt-tightening periodically imposed on SEAP, has enabled us to offer the full range of instruction in all the major Southeast Asian languages, even though enrollment in many of them, especially at the upper levels, is limited and variable.

Team teaching had advantages that were lost when teaching was done by only one person, especially ensuring that the two aspects of language pedagogy would be kept apart. Speaking the language could be kept clearly separated from speaking about the language, and in particular, English could be categorically excluded from sessions devoted to speaking the language. Phasing out team teaching meant that positive features such as this became lost, but Cornell's programs of Chinese and Japanese, with their larger enrollments, have been able to continue to employ the team model.

Instruction in the Southeast Asian languages is possible at present through a partnership with the College of Arts and Sciences, with SEAP contributing a considerable amount of support through its endowment as well as through the US Department of Education Title VI funding with SEAP's designation as a National Resource Center. SEAP currently partners with Arts and Sciences to work on fundraising to support and protect these language programs into the future. Beyond funding, SEAP encourages and supports the study of Southeast Asian languages through events, scholarships, and outreach.

Notes

I would like to express my thanks to Professors Abby Cohn and John Whitman and to SEAP's associate director, Thamora Fishel, for their help in preparing this chapter.

1. The 1951 "Progress Report to the Rockefeller Foundation" states, "It is recognized that the program staff must include a mature scholar capable of taking charge of its work in linguistics and literature and of developing solutions to the problems involved in offering sound language training in an area with half a dozen major national languages," Box 10, Southeast Asia Program Archives at the Kahin Center, Cornell University.

2. SEAP's 1960 proposal for the National Defense and Education Act grant covered half of the salaries of Echols and Jones, one-quarter of C. F. Hockett's, and a new assistant

professor of linguistics position, as well as the cost of instructors (native speakers) for Burmese, Thai, Vietnamese, Indonesian, and Malay. Malay was dropped the following year, and the percentages of language faculty salaries covered under the NDEA grant were increased to two-thirds and three-quarters time.

3. For more about the Cornell University Library's Asia Collections, see chapter 41, Asia Collections in the Cornell University Library.

27. AFRICANA STUDIES AT CORNELL

An Insurgent Discipline with a Global Outlook

N'Dri T. Assié-Lumumba

The Africana Studies and Research Center (ASRC) has had an impact beyond the Cornell campus for many years, especially led by the efforts of James Turner as the initiator of a discipline and founding director of an academic unit. Turner's 2022 *Cornell Chronicle* obituary noted: "Turner . . . shaped generations of Black scholars and other diverse students over the last 50 years. His stewardship of the center, during an era of enormous civil turmoil, put Cornell at the forefront of Africana studies and provided a template for understanding and articulating Black experience that is now replicated in institutions throughout the world."[1] Turner's death reminds us about Africana's national and global reach during those extraordinary years.

Africana studies at Cornell consists of two intertwined components that are distinctly dynamic and intrinsic: the innovation of Africana studies as an academic discipline and the founding of the ASRC in 1969 as an academic unit at Cornell University. From its inception, the conceptualization, naming, design, and setting up of the center, as well as the definition and implementation of the discipline, have always embraced international dimensions. Indeed, both have as their focus the African continent and the worldwide African diaspora, centering the African American experience.

Neither one of these two major academic innovations emerged organically or was propelled by a simple administrative decision. Rather, both exemplified the cumulative processes of centuries-old struggles against the background of the transatlantic slave trade and institutionalized slavery following Africans' violent uprooting from the African continent, survival through the treacherous Middle Passage, and forced relocation throughout the Americas.[2] The two academic innovations are also linked to the tumultuous American and global contexts of the 1960s and 1970s.

Africans in the Americas steadfastly reclaimed their humanity and cultural roots, countering European narratives that portrayed them as having a blank

Figure 27.1 Professor James Turner, Africana Studies. (Photo by University Photography, provided by Division of Rare and Manuscript Collections, Cornell University Library)

slate with no prior history as a people. In the middle of the twentieth century, the epic, audacious, and opportune educational innovation of Africana studies constituted an important historical moment in the continuum of Africans' quest for recovery, agency, and complete history, affirming the international landscape, endeavors, and design in the academy.

The idea, accomplishments, and exciting promise of Africana studies as an academic discipline and the ASRC started and evolved in a tumultuous period globally. A commentary in the beginning of the documentary *Agents of Change* states, "From the well-publicized events at San Francisco State University in 1968 to the image of black students with guns emerging from the takeover of the student union at Cornell University in April 1969, the struggle for a more relevant and meaningful education, including demands for black and ethnic studies programs, became a clarion call across the country in the late 1960s."[3] While giving credence to the vision of Ezra Cornell's "Any person . . . any study" motto, the university—as a product of the American social fabric—manifested racialized imbedded ideologies and contradictions in its policies and practices in its evolution and ensuing struggles.[4]

As it has been articulated, the term "Africana" embodies naming and agency, capturing the vision of a dialectical relation between the African continent and

Figure 27.2 Exterior of the Africana Studies and Research Center, 2015. (Photo by University Photography)

the diaspora. It was chosen to reflect its philosophical and epistemological framework. Amid the growing demand for a systematic inclusion of Black or African studies, Cornell was identified as the first institution of higher learning to employ the overarching concept of "Africana studies" in contrast to "Black studies," "urban studies," "Afro-American studies," or "African studies," which all referenced limited socio-spatial realities. The concept included the African continent and the worldwide African diaspora. While the word "Africana" had been used previously by African American global scholars such as Carter G. Woodson and W. E. B. Du Bois, "Turner initiated the use of the term 'Africana' as a conceptual intervention in 'Black Studies: A Concept and Plan' in 1969; however, the article 'Africana Studies and Epistemology' provides the most insightful exploration of the notion."[5]

One of the most audacious aspects of Africana studies was the conceptualization of an interdisciplinary field that resonates with French sociologist Emile Durkheim's idea that sociologically a sum is not a simple addition of its parts, but rather a new and complex entity. The synthesized essence of interdisciplinarity of Africana studies was unique and intentional, and it aspired not to emulate the traditional disciplines, which tended to operate in silos and become mired in fierce competition.[6] The fundamental global essence of Africana studies was reflected in a curriculum that had an interdisciplinary component pertaining to specific courses, faculty, and academic events on the Cornell campus and their intrinsic connection to activism and outreach toward social transformation and community extending from the local to the global stage.

The accomplishments of Africana studies at Cornell and beyond the university are numerous. It turned out to be a prototype that advocated for inclusion of the study of people of African descent in totality, and in reference to intersectionality it incorporated in its program gender, sexuality, and other grounds of social differentiation. A vibrant undergraduate program was created, and its graduates moved on to pursue graduate and professional studies in other disciplines and a popular master's degree program.[7] Courses offered by the Africana faculty consistently enrolled students from across the Cornell campus and other institutions through course-sharing agreements with institutions such as Ithaca College and Wells College. Several Africana studies courses in the past had regular enrollment of hundreds of students.[8] The action-oriented engagements for a better world led to Africana's continued participation in community works and protests on campus, in the United States, and globally.

From its formative years with the contributions of Gloria Joseph from the US Virgin Islands, J. Congress Mbata of South Africa, and Rukudzo Murapa from Zimbabwe, throughout the decades the teaching faculty of Africana Studies has remained consistently international. The efforts to conceptualize, design, and implement the curriculum included the quest to offer African languages as one of the language options for the fulfillment of the College of Arts and Sciences language requirement. The argument was that African languages should be acknowledged for their intrinsic merit just like the other recognized languages on campus, dispelling the narrative that Africans have dialects, not languages. To achieve this, proponents worked on two fronts: the first was to secure the agreement of the university to treat African languages like any other, and the second was to make African languages a requirement for Africana undergraduate majors. Over the years, the first goal was achieved, and African languages are now accepted for the fulfillment of the language requirement.[9] The African language program was the basis for the 1991 successful joint bid, under the leadership of Africana Studies professor Robert Harris Jr., for the Africana Studies and Research Center, and the Institute for African Development in the Mario Einaudi Center for International Studies, to the US Department of Education Title VI program.[10]

Besides the residing faculty, several programs in Africana Studies or in partnership with other academic units or administrative programs at Cornell have made it possible for Africana Studies to receive distinguished scholars. For instance, iconic global scholars and political figures from Africa and the diaspora, especially the Caribbean, came to Africana Studies at Cornell or as key guests of other Cornell programs, including Walter Rodney of Guyana; Ali Mazrui and Micere Githae Mugo of Kenya; former prime minister of Jamaica Michael Manley; former president of Nigeria Olusegun Obasanjo; Archbishop Desmond Tutu of South Africa;

Adebayo Adedeji of Nigeria, who built the United Nations Economic Commission for Africa; Rex Nettleford of Jamaica; and Aklilu Habte, former president of Haile Selassie I University and former minister of Culture, Sports and Youth of Ethiopia.

Two major grants from the Rockefeller and Ford Foundations in the 1990s, also designed and managed by Africana Studies professor Robert Harris Jr. as principal investigator, enabled several cohorts of scholars from the African continent, the Caribbean, and Latin America (especially Brazil) to come to Cornell as visiting professors. The Rockefeller Foundation grant supported scholars for short visits that included participation in annual conferences in the United States affiliated with major professional Black studies associations such as the National Council for Black Studies (NCBS) and the Association for the Study of African American Life and History (ASALH). The Ford Foundation grant offered one-year visiting positions for scholars hosted by Africana Studies, providing the opportunity for the pursuit of their research and for shared experiences in seminars and public lectures.

Over the years, Cornell's ASRC has hosted several international conferences and global outreach programs as part of its engagement in the trajectory of social and global transformation. When the ASRC was founded, several African countries were still restrained by the shackles of colonialism, including those formerly colonized by Portugal, as well as Zimbabwe, Namibia, and, most notoriously, South Africa under apartheid. Africana Studies and other Cornell faculty led the struggle to convince Cornell to divest from South Africa, a process that led to the founding of the Institute for African Development. Subsequently, Africana faculty, especially James Turner and Locksley Edmondson, were involved in TransAfrica and the quest for reparations. They also kept pan-African engagements alive by attending numerous important meetings in different parts of the continent and the diaspora. For instance, Turner attended the Sixth Pan-African Congress in Tanzania. Other programs included organized trips to various parts of Africa, especially Egypt.

On campus, in the United States, and globally, the Africana Studies faculty have been involved in the international landscape through their courses, publications, speaking engagements, global conferences, and services as leaders of academic programs and as presenters or chairs of internationally focused professional organizations. Training of students constitutes the main raison d'être of any academic unit. Africana Studies has contributed to Cornell's global mission in training students from across the globe at the undergraduate, master's, and PhD levels.

Notes

1. David Nutt, "James Turner, a 'Giant' of Africana Studies, Dies at 82," *Cornell Chronicle*, August 12, 2022, https://news.cornell.edu/stories/2022/08/james-turner-giant-africana-studies-dies-82.

2. Marcus Rediker, *The Slave Ship: A Human History* (New York: Viking, 2007).

3. *Agents of Change* (Social Action Media, 2019), https://vimeo.com/ondemand/agentsofchange.

4. The burning of a cross on the lawn of a cooperative housing unit created for undergraduate students of African descent triggered the April 1969 Willard Straight Hall occupation. Ultimately, through negotiation, the students came out peacefully.

5. Jonathan Fenderson, "Introduction: Black Intellectual Insurgency—James Turner and the Discipline of Africana Studies," in *Discourse on Africana Studies: James Turner and Paradigms of Knowledge*, ed. Scot Brown (New York: Diasporic Africa Press, 2016), 106.

6. The interdisciplinary field of Africana studies encompasses social science and the humanities. Some use the term "transdisciplinary" to describe the field, which is seen as embracing and informing the traditional disciplines.

7. The Africana MPS was a rigorous academic program consisting of two years, with one full year of coursework and the second year focused on thesis writing and public defense.

8. Racism in American Society; African Cultures and Civilizations; and Kiswahili Language and Culture.

9. Besides the languages that have been taught at Cornell at different times—namely Swahili consistently, but also Bamanan and Yoruba—a resource-sharing arrangement with Columbia University and Yale University made it possible for Cornell students to learn other languages, specifically Wolof at Columbia and Zulu at Yale.

10. For more about the Institute for African Development, see chapter 8, Creating Connections with Africa: Cornell's Institute for African Development.

28. ENGINEERING SOLUTIONS TO WORLDWIDE WATER MANAGEMENT ISSUES

Daniel P. Loucks

Cornell's water systems program has taken faculty and students to projects at the far reaches of the globe. For many years, beginning in the mid-1960s, Cornell environmental systems engineers have been involved in assisting governments and international organizations in the planning and management of water systems in many different parts of the world. Typically, their involvement has been in the development and application of mathematical models designed to identify and evaluate alternative options for improving the management of the water resources in the region. They are used to estimate and compare the ecological, economic, environmental, physical, and social impacts of possible development or management decisions. The issues addressed by this kind of modeling have included conflicts over how water is shared over space and time, how to improve water quality, how to meet the demands for increased energy and agricultural production, how best to reduce the adverse impacts from floods and droughts or enhance river ship transport, and how to improve, and perhaps restore, the biodiversity of a region.

This international aspect has been an important part of the educational experience provided to Cornell engineering students involved in the water systems program. It is important not only for exposing them to real-world water management problems and for enhancing their modeling skills but perhaps more importantly for promoting the realization that to be successful, engineers must be able to work with and meet the needs of political institutions—the decision makers. This applies everywhere water is being managed. One might think that addressing water management issues and working with politicians and governing institutions in countries whose governments are democratic as opposed to those whose governments are more autocratic, socialistic, or communistic would be very different. But this is not always the case. In projects we have undertaken in various countries of Africa, Asia, Australia, Europe, the Middle East, and the Americas, the working conditions (such as access to data, affected stakeholders, and

Figure 28.1 Water: a valuable resource anywhere but especially in places like Yemen where there is not much. (Photo by author)

available computing resources) often differed, but the goals were the same (i.e., to satisfy the needs of those dependent on a safe and sufficient supply of water).

This brief chapter identifies some of the international water resource planning and management projects undertaken over the past five decades by Cornell postdoctoral and graduate students in the environmental and water resource systems group within the School of Civil and Environmental Engineering.[1] Some of these projects were completed in less than a year; others spanned many years. All involved working with, if not under the direction of, local professionals representing many disciplines. Many of these projects resulted in theses, and all required reports and presentations to our clients. All provided excellent opportunities for us to develop improved methods of modeling various water resource systems that addressed problems and issues that were of interest to governmental or international agencies. We all had to learn how to gain the trust of those who were asking for our analyses and advice. None of the projects were just academic exercises.

How did this happen? In the mid-1960s Cornell began offering graduate degrees in environmental systems engineering, a new field of study in the integration of engineering methods, economics, and government administration for addressing environmental and water resource development and management problems. Our work in this area was apparently noticed by others, who recommended us to lead a project that the United Nations was initiating in Poland. The project was called

Planning Comprehensive Development of the Vistula River System, and it focused on a major river flowing through much of Poland. The goal of the project was to formulate a water resource development investment program capable of meeting multiple demands for water in the Vistula basin up to the year 2000. Cornell was asked to contribute advice concerning the modeling aspects of this project. This involved visits to Warsaw to learn what they needed and the capabilities of their available computing resources. We were working mainly with two Polish institutions directly involved in the Vistula project: the engineering consulting firm Hydroprojekt and the Institute of Environmental Engineering of Warsaw University of Technology. Others participating in the project included the Polish Academy of Sciences and Resources for the Future, a nongovernmental organization focused on environmental economic issues and located in Washington, DC.

Perhaps based in part on our experience in Poland, we were invited to participate in other UN water resource planning projects in Eastern Europe, the Soviet Union, Africa, and South America. In the early 1970s, we were part of a group tasked with applying systems analysis methods to the planning of the redevelopment of the Upper Mures River Basin in the northern part of Romania. This basin had just experienced flooding and earthquakes, and the Romanian government asked the UN for assistance in planning its redevelopment. This project gave us new experiences in serving a government that did not want to share data. I recall the first meeting of our international group, sitting around a table and discussing with our Romanian colleagues just what development options we could, and should, consider. When we asked if we could look at a map of the river basin we were to model and study, they said no. I asked if I could buy a road map of the area. Again, the answer was no. I am not sure what we accomplished at that first meeting, but it motivated me to bring to our second meeting a large pile of US Air Force aviation maps showing detailed ground features. Those maps could be useful to our study. As soon as I put them on the table, they were taken away by our observers (and what we did and said to anyone was observed constantly). I asked them how many more they would like, and from whom they were keeping them secret. Eventually, they allowed us to work with maps. By the time the project was over, all but one of our Romanian counterparts had left their country. As beautiful as Romania was, and is, it did not seem to be a place where people, at least professional people, felt fulfilled.

From the late 1960s to the late 1970s, there was a thawing of the ongoing Cold War between the United States and the Soviet Union. This détente took several forms, such as visits of Soviet scientists to the United States, including Cornell, to observe how we model and evaluate alternative water resource development and management policies in river basins. On visits to the Soviet Union, we observed how they, the All-Union Scientific Research Institute for Water Protection, did the same tasks. I recall their engineers telling us, at the beginning of our visits, that they believed the reason why we capitalists could not implement cost-effective policies for controlling wastewater discharges and river water quality was that the municipalities, industries, and farms creating the polluting wastewaters were not under the control of one governmental agency that could impose such economically efficient policies. However, they declared, we in the Soviet Union can implement such policies because we are under a centrally planned and controlled economy whose goal, among many, is to maintain clean water. So why were their rivers polluted? After several exchanges over several years, our Soviet colleagues had to admit that they had the same problem as those of us living in capitalist societies. Even under a centrally planned economy, each minister of each agency overseeing the activities of its polluters had their own production objectives and budgets. Interagency coordination permitting cost-effective approaches to pollution control was not a prioritized part of their missions. Human behavior that results in externalities (i.e., pollution), unless constrained otherwise, seems to be the same, regardless of what economic or political system we live under.

In addition to those just mentioned, other international projects involving our environmental and water resource systems engineering graduate students over the past five decades included the following:

- analyzing reservoir development and engaging in conflict resolution on the Nile basin in Egypt, Ethiopia, and Sudan
- determining the capacity of Tsengwen Reservoir needed to meet water supply and irrigation demands in southern Taiwan
- planning the system of wells, pumps, pipes, and reservoirs of the Great Man-Made River in Libya, designed to bring water from aquifers in the Sahara Desert to where water is needed along the Mediterranean Sea coast, where most Libyans live and irrigate crops
- managing reoperation of the hydroelectric Akosombo Dam on the Volta River in southeastern Ghana to restore downstream aquatic ecosystems
- finding a politically and economically acceptable way of providing water security for Sanaa, the capital of Yemen
- identifying the sites, design capacities, and operating policies of infrastructure needed to capture, store, and deliver irrigation water to parts of the Sahara Desert for growing crops in Algeria
- identifying where to site and how to design and operate a series of dams to produce hydroelectric power without degrading the biodiversity of the Lower Mekong River
- developing operating policies for regulating the flows and water levels of the Great Lakes and St. Lawrence River that will better satisfy hydropower production, shipping, commercial fishing, recreational boating, shoreline protection, and ecosystem enhancement goals

- managing in real time the flows of the river Mosel waterway connecting France and Luxembourg to the river Rhine in Germany
- changing the culture of institutions involved in water resource planning and management in Portugal from one of dam building where technically feasible to one of more integrated planning that considered demands as well as supplies, benefits as well as costs, and environmental and social impacts
- planning multiple-purpose multiple-objective water resource infrastructure development for managing water in river basins in Cambodia, Chile, Egypt, Great Britain, Honduras, India, Iran, Malawi, Norway, and South Africa

The problems, modeling approaches, and results of many of these projects became the subject of theses of master of science students or design reports for professional master of engineering (civil) degrees. Most of our international projects successfully met the clients' goal of obtaining useful guidance on the design, development, and operation of infrastructure capable of successfully addressing their water-related problems. They also met our more academic goal of gaining knowledge on how to address interesting and often complex problems in politically acceptable ways. The few times I would say we partially failed were when the project funding agencies or project leaders wanted to impose ideas on what should be done that the implementing agencies in the country, or countries, considered unacceptable. Working with stakeholders (i.e., those who will implement decisions and those who may be affected by such decisions) is essential for gaining the level of cooperation and trust needed to successfully carry out any study, let alone see the results of such a study successfully implemented.

For all our projects involving modeling, Cornell graduate students developed and implemented the models needed to provide the information to complete the projects. This was often done in collaboration with the local project personnel. We depended on them for the data our models needed. For some projects, our students were able to travel to the countries involved to work and share knowledge with local project personnel. Similarly, some international project engineers and scientists were able to visit and spend time working with our students here at Cornell. It was not unusual to see Cornell students giving advice to and training project personnel in the operation of one or more computer programs used to solve models. The expertise we offered was in developing, applying, and solving models that addressed issues of concern. We considered it a sign of success when our advice and expertise were no longer needed.

It is reasonable to ask what Cornell has gained from all this international involvement in water resource planning and management. I will speak for myself when I admit to having learned more from those whom I have worked with on all these projects than they from me. I am sure these experiences have benefited not only my research but also my teaching by bringing to the classroom this wisdom and details of these adventures that are not usually found in textbooks. Surely students have benefited from this exposure to real problems in real places with different cultures and institutional decision-making environments. The students involved in these projects have not only learned a lot but, I am sure, also enjoyed working on real-world ongoing projects, knowing their work could potentially influence the decisions made by the institutions being served by the project. Experiencing different cultures, languages, and approaches to resource development planning, management, and use adds to the benefits all of us gain from participating in these international projects.

Note

1. For more details on some of the projects mentioned, see Daniel P. Loucks and Laurel Saito, eds., *Adventures in Managing Water: Real-World Engineering Experiences* (Reston, VA: ASCE, 2019).

29. GLOBAL HOSPITALITY

The Hotel School's International Legacy

Bill Summers

The Cornell Peter and Stephanie Nolan School of Hotel Administration has attracted international students since its inception in 1922—laying the basis for a global alumni base, in keeping with the industry's global focus. The program's first international student was H. Alexander MacLennan (class of 1926) from Great Britain, followed two years later by Kakumaro Kemmotsu (class of 1928) from Japan. For the program's first eighty years, overseas students accounted for, on average, 10 to 15 percent of its student body. In contrast, until the 1980s, students from overseas accounted for only 2 to 3 percent of Cornell's overall enrollment. In the fall of 2005, the Hotel School matriculated 175 freshmen and 49 transfers (131 women, or 58 percent), who came from a total of sixteen countries. There were twenty-four international students, or 11 percent.

Reflecting its commitment to hospitality, the school has worked to make every student feel welcome. A 1961 article in the Hotel School's student newspaper, the *Cornell Innkeeper*, advised students "not to feel sorry for your neighbor and fellow student from far across the seven oceans. Instead, try to understand his problems. Give him a hand without being asked for it. . . . Making the newly arrived and perhaps bewildered foreign student feel part of *all* phases of our school should be an easy task."[1]

Nami Thiyagaratnam (MPS 1985) from Sri Lanka remembered the warmth bestowed by Professor Vance A. Christian, the first African American member of the Hotel School faculty: "Who else would have thought of my family and driven to Hasbrouck Apartments, searched out my number, and collected my wife, two little children, and myself for our first American Thanksgiving dinner?" Thiyagaratnam asked. "When we reached his charming house, I found that Vance had collected twelve others for the same dinner who would otherwise have also been alone during this holiday."[2]

Figure 29.1 Students, faculty, and alumni attend a "Silk Road" dinner at the 2011 Hotel Ezra Cornell. (Photo by University Photography)

Alumni Bonds

Just as students come from points all over, as graduates they fan out across the globe. In 1955, for example, Ichiro Inumaru graduated and returned to Tokyo to run his family's business, the Imperial Hotel. Soon after, he joined with Kakumaro Kemmotsu and Frank A. Ready Jr. (class of 1936) to form the first overseas chapter of the school's alumni association, now the Cornell Hotel Society (CHS). In 1959, a Caribbean chapter was formed to serve alumni in Central America, and two years later Ready founded the first European chapter. By 1966, the alumni society reported that "the sun never sets on a Cornell Hotelman." Today, CHS has nearly sixty chapters in twelve regions representing more than thirty countries. With thousands of alumni and affiliated members, it is arguably among the most active and influential alumni associations in the world.

Many graduates have worked tirelessly to build strong alumni networks and promote the school. In Europe, for example, Rudolf W. "Rudy" Münster (class of 1962), former general manager of the Kempinski Hotel in Berlin, launched a fundraising campaign to help European hoteliers further their professional education. Under Münster's lead, from 1963 to 1988 the European chapter of CHS raised $360,000 that enabled 270 students to travel to Ithaca to attend the Hotel

School's summer professional development program. Münster would go on to become the second non-American president of CHS in 1996. The first president born outside the United States was Michael W. N. Chiu (class of 1966), who was born in China but resided in the United States when elected president in 1995. Deiv Salutskij (class of 1971) assumed fundraising responsibility from Münster in 1988 and has successfully drawn contributions from both corporate benefactors and school alumni. Leif R. Evensen (class of 1966), Ralph M. Starke (class of 1952 and former general manager of the Hilton Rotterdam), and Rudolphe W. "Ruedi" Schelbert (class of 1955 and former executive at Swiss Hotels) are among many others who have worked to build a thriving alumni network across Europe.

In the same way, real estate and hotel developer Chiu and hotel executives Liv Gussing Burgess (class of 1991) and Yuji A. Yamaguchi (class of 1961) have helped the school build a strong presence in Asia through the formation of CHS's Asia-Pacific Region, which held its first regional meeting in Hong Kong in 1995.[3]

Executive Education

Another way that the school diversifies its global reach is through its executive education programs. Much of the groundwork was laid in 1961 when Dean Robert Beck and Assistant Dean Gerald W. Lattin brought fresh thinking to this discipline. In 1962, 250 students from sixteen countries came to Ithaca to take summer session courses. By 1968, nearly half of the 350 summer students came from overseas.

The executive education programs, held primarily in the United States and Europe, continue to draw industry leaders from points across the globe. Each year more than a thousand professionals learn from Cornell faculty and apply that knowledge from Bangkok to Brussels. Over the years, the school has supplemented its core executive education programs by developing programs designed for corporate clients. In 2005 alone, the school delivered seventeen custom-designed programs for clients in fourteen countries.

Worldwide Academic Partners

In another move to expand its global imprint, the Hotel School has forged alliances with academic institutions around the world. In 1971, Dean Beck agreed to establish a two-year community college in Puerto Rico. Beck's boldest move may have come in 1981 when Cornell partnered with the École Supérieure des

Sciences Economiques et Commerciales Business School to create the Institut de Management Hotelier International. Beck recalls a cool reception from French journalists when the agreement was announced.

"They were saying, 'Why does France need Americans to come over and teach them about hotels?'" Beck remembers. "One man got up and said, 'This means the burgerization of France!'"[4]

Beck became inaugural director of the new two-year hospitality program located outside Paris, with Cornell developing the curriculum and providing faculty. Described by Beck as the first advanced school of hotel management in Europe, the program opened with forty-six students from seventeen countries, with about half from France.[5] The alliance with the École Supérieure des Sciences Economiques et Commerciales and Institut de Management Hotelier International was discontinued in 2004, as Hotel School leaders felt the program was being perceived as a joint degree, even though Cornell by then had little input in the curriculum and no financial interest in the program.

Several subsequent alliances have had less staying power. One that was formed in Australia in the 1990s with the Australia International Hotel School unraveled in the early 2000s. "A faculty committee's comprehensive review of the school's international strategy led to the decision that that particular alliance did not fully meet the school's strategic objectives for the future," according to David A. Butler, who served as dean of the Hotel School from 2000 to 2005.[6] In Australia, as well as in some of the Hotel School's other joint programs, Cornell had limited input. In some cases, the Cornell name was on the degree but the degree was not sanctioned by Cornell.

"We had little or no control over the quality of these programs," Butler recalls. "For these programs to work in the future, we decided that there needed to be an Ithaca experience to deliver programming that had meaningful contribution from the Hotel School."[7]

Even before Butler took the reins as dean, the school had been pursuing a partner to build a presence in Asia. After fourteen years of on-and-off negotiations, in the fall of 2004 Cornell and Nanyang Technological University announced the creation of a joint master of management in hospitality program, to be housed at Nanyang's campus in Singapore. The Cornell-Nanyang Institute of Hospitality Management (CNI) offered a graduate program beginning in 2006. The alliance created the first joint-degree program for both institutions and the first graduate hospitality program in Asia.

Cornell Hotel School professor Judy Siguaw, founding dean of CNI, described CNI as "an exciting opportunity to leverage the brand names of two prestigious institutions, while creating a renowned hospitality program for students seeking expertise in Asian markets."[8] With the CNI agreement, the school built on the good and bad experiences that came from developing and negotiating earlier agreements. Students would spend half their time in Singapore and half in Ithaca. The dean of the Cornell Hotel School appointed the dean of CNI, and members of a joint advisory board had equal representation from both schools. However, student enrollment ended up being lower than anticipated, and the program was discontinued in 2013.

The Cornell-Peking MMH/MBA was approved in 2021, partnering with the Guanghua School of Management at Peking University in Shanghai, China. The part-time two-year dual-degree program for executives provides the core MBA courses from Peking University faculty with the hospitality-focused curriculum taught by Cornell faculty. Residential sessions are divided between the Guanghua school's campus in Shanghai and Cornell's Ithaca and New York City campuses, with about 70 percent of the time spent in China.

Worldwide Research Partners

At Cornell, the Center for Hospitality Research (CHR) further extends the Hotel School's global reach. CHR's supporters include some of the industry's leading multinational companies and associations, including American International Group, ARAMARK, Cendant, Expedia, Four Seasons Hotels and Resorts, HVS International, the International Hotel and Restaurant Association, JohnsonDiversey, Kohinoor Group, KPMG International, Marriott, Marsh, Nestlé, PricewaterhouseCoopers, Smith Travel Research, Southern Wines and Spirits, SynXis, Taj Hotels and Resorts, the Thayer Group of Companies, Wimberly Allison Tong and Goo, and Wyndham International.

Faculty members work with CHR's industry advisory board to identify challenges, conduct research, and publish the results to help improve operating practices around the world. Tens of thousands of scholars and executives have access to original research reports through the center's website, which is supplemented by an active publicity campaign that promotes CHR's research through major media outlets worldwide. In 2005, that publicity program generated more than sixty-three million media impressions. Moreover, the *Cornell Hospitality Quarterly* (formerly the *Cornell Hotel and Restaurant Administration Quarterly*), the school's world-renowned academic journal first published in 1960, disseminates research to thousands of global subscribers.

The school has increasingly incorporated global content into its curriculum. Chekitan S. Dev is one of many faculty members who bring the world to the Ithaca campus. Dev travels one hundred thousand miles a year and has firsthand experience in thirty countries. He turns those experiences into case studies that he uses in the classroom. For example, students in his strategic marketing course study cases from Russia, France, and Hong Kong.

"I visit as many places as I can where interesting things are happening in hospitality," Dev says. "There is no better way to learn and understand than to work with executives as they take on challenges in the field. Reaching outside the United States provides context and makes the class that much richer."[9]

Dev also applies a global approach to his research. He has built a database of hotel managers in forty-six different countries, encompassing all classes and sizes of hotels in both developed and developing countries, giving him a rich resource to draw from as he builds global content into his coursework.

The Nolan School of Hotel Administration has long recognized the value of a global focus when it comes to hospitality, and it continues to adapt to an increasingly interconnected business world. In 2011, students selected "global hospitality" as the theme for that year's Hotel Ezra Cornell, an annual campus conference planned by students for industry leaders. Panels and discussions focused on topics like "Building Brands across Borders" and "Exploring Emerging Markets."[10] Cornellians became leaders in the hospitality industry around the world, with Cornell's global alumni network connecting them together and back to Ithaca.

Notes

This chapter is adapted from Bill Summers, *Hospitality Goes Global: The Cornell Hotel School* (Ithaca, NY: Cornell Hotel Society, 2007).

1. Quoted in Summers.

2. Summers.

3. See *60th Anniversary Book for Cornell Hotel Society: Europe, Middle East & Africa Region, 1961–2021* (2021), https://cornellhotelsociety.com/wp-content/uploads/2021/07/CHS-EMEA-60th-Ann-Book.pdf.

4. Summers.

5. "Prof. Beck Plants Hotel's Flag in France and It's Saluted," *Cornell Alumni News*, November 1982.

6. Summers.

7. Summers.

8. "Cornell Professor Judy Siguaw Named Founding Dean of Cornell-Nanyang Institute of Hospitality Management in Singapore," hospitalitynet, February 2, 2005, https://www.hospitalitynet.org/news/4022042.html.

9. Summers.

10. Ashlee McGandy, "Industry Leaders Examine Global Hospitality during Student-Run Hotel Ezra Cornell," *Cornell Chronicle*, April 12, 2011, https://news.cornell.edu/stories/2011/04/hotel-ezra-cornell-focuses-global-hospitality.

30. FLORA ROSE AND MARTHA VAN RENSSELAER

Relief Efforts in Belgium

Eileen Keating

Martha Van Rensselaer and Flora Rose, Cornell's first two women to achieve the rank of full professor, traveled to Belgium after World War I to research the aftereffects of the war on women and children and to share their skills as home economists. For their work, they were honored with one of the greatest honors of Belgium and began a tradition of international service at the College of Home Economics.[1]

Van Rensselaer came to Cornell in 1900 at the request of College of Agriculture professor Liberty Hyde Bailey to organize a reading course for farmers' wives. In 1907, she was joined by Rose, a scientist and nutritionist, who had recently received her MA in food and nutrition from Teachers College, Columbia University. They were named codirectors of the home economics program, which became a department in the College of Agriculture in 1909, a school in 1919, the College of Home Economics in 1925, and the New York State College of Human Ecology in 1969. The new progressive field of home economics emphasized science applied to the real world of the home, families, and their surrounding communities. It became a critical gateway for women to pursue higher educational opportunities.

Home economists at Cornell did research in housing design, clothing and textiles, home management, child development, consumer economics, nutrition, and health and hygiene practices. They used various means of communication to improve the lives of the people of New York State, in time expanding their message across the nation and then, in the 1920s, internationally.

In 1914, conditions in Europe were dire. After being invaded by Germany, Belgium suffered a severe food shortage. Britain had imposed an economic blockade hindering food imports, and the Germans requisitioned the limited food produced in the country. Under the leadership of Herbert Hoover (who would be elected the thirty-first US president in 1928), the Commission for Relief in Belgium (CRB), a massive international philanthropic effort, was organized in 1914 to respond

Figure 30.1 Martha Van Rensselaer (*right*) and Flora Rose (*left*) at a meeting of the League of Women Voters, held at the home of Franklin and Eleanor Roosevelt in Hyde Park, 1920s. (Provided by Division of Rare and Manuscript Collections, Cornell University Library)

to the humanitarian disaster. The CRB arranged for the delivery and distribution of five million tons of food to German-occupied Belgium. Described by a British official as "a piratical state organized by benevolence," the CRB "possessed some of the attributes of a government. It had its own flag, it negotiated 'treaties' with the warring European powers, and its leaders parlayed regularly with diplomats and cabinet ministers in several countries. It even had a 'pirate' leader in Hoover."[2] After the war, the CRB used its remaining money for child welfare work and education by founding the Child Health Section and the Belgian-American Educational Foundation.

During World War I, Rose served as director of the food conservation program in New York State, and Van Rensselaer directed the Home Conservation Division of the US Food Administration. Hoover, then US secretary of commerce, who had directed the US Food Administration, knew Rose and was familiar with her nutrition work at Cornell. He used CRB funds to pay for her trip to Belgium as a special investigator to gather information on the physical and nutritional status of Belgian schoolchildren and the relationship between these two conditions.[3]

In April 1923, Rose boarded the RMS *Majestic* and arrived in Southampton, England. After a few days of sightseeing, she drove to Brussels in her Model T Ford, which she lovingly called "Henri." To gather the information needed, Rose

Figure 30.2 Order of the Chevalier of the Crown, one of the medals presented to Van Rensselaer and Rose by the king and queen of Belgium. (Provided by author)

developed a quantitative and qualitative survey with over two hundred questions. It was unusual to conduct such a survey in the early 1920s, and it was an innovative way to do research on nutrition.

Interviews were conducted with 4,619 children born before, during, and after the war, from fifty different schools. A survey of this scale would not have been possible without the assistance of mayors, physicians, teachers, transcribers, translators (from Flemish to French), and statisticians. Physicians did physical examinations, and teachers were paid to conduct home visits during which the survey questions were asked. The questions asked about household income; number of siblings; number of rooms in the home; living conditions; whether they shared a bed with their siblings; how much coffee, milk, and beer were consumed; whether they played before or after school; how many days of school they missed; what clothing they wore; what a typical meal was; and many other topics.[4] The surveys collected a wealth of information describing daily life for Belgian children and revealed that food inequality still existed after the war. The Great War, in the words of Rose, "called the world's attention to the status of human affairs and aroused its conscience regarding the welfare of children."[5]

While Rose was busy collecting data in Belgium, in 1923 Van Rensselaer had been selected by the National League of Women Voters as one of the twelve greatest living women in America. That May, Edgar Rickard, joint director of the CRB, invited Van Rensselaer to Belgium to provide her "reaction on the possible direction of our work in that country [Belgium] particularly in child welfare problems."[6] While she did not have an official assignment in Belgium, she decided to venture to Europe on what would be her first and only trip to the continent. In June, she set sail for Europe on the RMS *Baltic*. Once in Belgium, Van Rensselaer visited home economics schools and housing projects, laying plans for a better homes campaign, modeled after the program in the United States, which encouraged people to own, build, remodel, and improve their homes after the devastation of the war. She visited the Louvain Library, which was destroyed early in the war and was being rebuilt with American money. She later donated personally selected home economics books to Louvain.

Van Rensselaer also visited dignitaries, including the head of the University of Brussels, a Catholic cardinal, and the American ambassador. Rose and Van Rensselaer met the Belgian queen Elisabeth at her palace in Laeken, near Brussels. She was interested in their work, even requesting a copy of Rose's report once it was finished. Van Rensselaer was impressed, writing in a letter home that the queen's "charm lies in her intelligence, simplicity, and beauty and her naïve manner which makes you forget she is a queen, although she carries herself with great dignity."[7] Today, the Cornell Fashion + Textile Collection houses the dress that Van Rensselaer wore, along with the gray beaded suede shoes that Rose bought her in Belgium to wear with the dress.

While in Europe, Van Rensselaer visited Nijkerk in Holland, the town of her paternal ancestors. In honor of her visit, a florist presented Van Rensselaer with dahlia bulbs named for her family. Once she returned to Ithaca, she gave the bulbs to Daisy Farrand, the wife of Cornell president Livingston Farrand, as well as to floriculture professor E. A. White and to a few friends.

While traveling in Europe, both Rose and Van Rensselaer kept in touch with their staff back home in Ithaca. The close-knit community of women that existed in the School of Home Economics was evident in the letters that Rose and Van Rensselaer wrote. One letter from Rose was signed, "Well, dear, old dears, again good night. Bless your hearts you very dear staff." There were letters from Van Rensselaer addressed to "my family" and "my dear and much neglected staff" and signed, "We think of you all the time."[8] They wrote often, some letters as long as four pages. These heartfelt letters paint a clear picture of both the devastation and the reconstruction efforts in post–World War I Europe. Van Rensselaer observed, "In America we know the story of maimed men but we do not realize the tragedy of century-old buildings, shelled and partly fallen and what is important to the family, of fields despoiled, houses and barns riddled with shells or whole villages abandoned by their original inhabitants who fled for safety. . . . The government has furnished brick for new houses and the farming country is dotted with new houses and barns made of bright red brick and bright red roofs, all offering a cheerful attitude."[9] Rose wrote to her staff before setting sail to return to Cornell, "I really love it here and I'm devoted to the Belgians."[10]

Rose and Van Rensselaer returned to the United States in September 1923. Van Rensselaer wrote her recommendations to the CRB. Belgian agencies, such as the Red Cross and Belgian Oeuvre National de l'Enfance (National Agency for Children), took up the hygiene and nutrition work that Rose had introduced to the Belgian children.

In 1924, the Belgian Oeuvre National de l'Enfance awarded Van Rensselaer and Rose six medals for their efforts in aiding the war-stricken nation. In August 1925, they were awarded the insignia of Chevalier of the Order of the Crown on behalf of King Albert in "recognition and appreciation of the good work they have done in child welfare during their stay in Belgium."[11] In December, they were invited to the Belgian embassy in Washington, DC, where the Belgian ambassador conferred the medals.

In 1926, upon request, the CRB Educational Foundation shipped the completed surveys to Cornell, of which eight hundred exist today. Rose used the data to write her dissertation for Teachers College.[12] The international influence of Flora Rose and Martha Van Rensselaer is evidenced in those surveys and their correspondence preserved in Cornell's Division of Rare and Manuscript Collections. These archival collections provide researchers with vital information on life in postwar Belgium and the impact the war had on its children. Today, the College of Human Ecology's historical commitment to and focus on human health and well-being can be traced back to the work of its early home economists.[13]

Notes

1. In 2019, Nel de Mûelenaere, a Belgian historian of nineteenth- and twentieth-century Europe in the Social and Cultural Food Studies research group at the Vrije Universiteit Brussel (Free University of Brussels), received the Dean's Fellowship in the History of Home Economics at Cornell. Her presentation "At Home in the World: Flora Rose and Martha Van Rensselaer in Belgium" for the Fellowship in the History of Home Economics in November 2019 provided much of the information presented here. The presentation is available online at https://www.youtube.com/watch?v=SOsncgig1LE. Nel de Mûelenaere, "Still Poor, Still Little, Still Hungry? The Diet and Health of Belgian Children after World War I," in *The Provisions of War*, ed. Justin Nordstrom (Fayetteville: University of Arkansas Press, 2021), also discusses their Belgian relief efforts.

2. George H. Nash, "An American Epic: Herbert Hoover and Belgian Relief in World War I," *Prologue*, Spring 1989, https://www.archives.gov/publications/prologue/1989/spring/hoover-belgium.html.

3. De Mûelenaere, "At Home in the World."

4. De Mûelenaere.

5. De Mûelenaere, “Still Poor?,” 216.

6. Edgar Rickard to Martha Van Rensselaer, May 7, 1923, Box 36, Folder 28, New York State College of Home Economics Records, #23-2-749, Division of Rare and Manuscript Collections, Cornell University Library.

7. Martha Van Rensselaer to staff, August 21, 1923, Box 36, Folder 27, New York State College of Home Economics Records, #23-2-749.

8. Flora Rose and Martha Van Rensselaer, letters to staff, 1923, Box 36, Folder 27, New York State College of Home Economics Records, #23-2-749.

9. Martha Van Rensselaer to staff, July 31, 1923, Box 36, Folder 27, New York State College of Home Economics Records, #23-2-749.

10. Flora Rose to staff, September 6, 1923, Box 36, Folder 27, New York State College of Home Economics Records, #23-1-749.

11. “Belgium Gives High Honor to Ithaca Women,” *Ithaca Journal-News*, August 14, 1925.

12. De Mûelenaere, “Still Poor?,” 210. Rose’s dissertation, titled “A Study of the Nutritional Status of Five Thousand Belgian School Children as Basic Material for Program in Health Education” (1932), was never published, and Rose never completed her doctorate.

13. New York State College of Home Economics Records, #23-2-749.

31. FEEDING THE WORLD

International Nutrition at Cornell

Malden C. Nesheim

The study of nutrition at Cornell has long addressed worldwide issues arising from the obvious importance of providing adequate food for the world's population. The study of nutrition at Cornell arose from two areas of interest: the proper feeding of animals in animal husbandry and the proper feeding of families in home economics.[1] Although early work in nutritional science dealt mostly with domestic issues, Cornell faculty soon became involved in international programs.

The first Cornell faculty member involved in international human nutrition programs was home economics professor Flora Rose, who after World War I led an extensive field survey relating to nutrition in Belgian children. Her international work developed during World War I when the German army occupied Belgium, causing major disruption of agriculture and food supplies. Herbert Hoover, then humanitarian and later president, led the Commission for Relief of Belgium to raise funds to send food to occupied Belgium. After the war, the commission continued to fund programs to help in the recovery of Belgium. To determine the part nutrition should play in such programs, Rose led an extensive field survey, involving some 4,619 Belgian school children, ages five to fifteen years. For these studies she was awarded the insignia of the Crown of King Albert of Belgium.[2]

In the 1950s, Hazel Hauck became another home economics faculty member to do research overseas. With the support of a Fulbright fellowship, she served as the nutrition specialist for a Cornell anthropology project in Thailand, studying the food habits of people living in Bang Chan, a rural Thai village, from 1952 to 1954. Later she served as a consultant for a program in eastern Nigeria under the auspices of the Unitarian Service Committee, working to introduce groundnuts into the diet of villagers to provide nutrients lacking in their usual diets.[3]

The leading figure in the development of nutrition programs at Cornell was Leonard A. Maynard, who joined the New York State College of Agriculture faculty in the Department of Animal Husbandry in 1915 after receiving his PhD from

Figure 31.1 Professor Michael C. Latham, director of the Program in International Nutrition. (Photo by University Photography, provided by Division of Rare and Manuscript Collections, Cornell University Library)

Cornell and was active in domestic and international nutrition until his retirement in 1956. His international involvement began in the 1930s. In 1934, he took a sabbatical leave to serve as a visiting professor at the University of Nanking in China, where he studied the nutrition of farm families. "Maynard commented on his return from the latter experience that he was pleasantly surprised on a visit to an orphanage outside the city to find a very modern dairy enterprise. However, he was really chagrined to learn that the orphans did not receive the milk. Instead, it was sold in the city for cash to maintain the orphanage."[4]

In 1939, the US Department of Agriculture's Agricultural Research Service established the US Plant, Soil and Nutrition Laboratory at Cornell, and Maynard became the first director, serving until 1945. In 1941, he became the founding director of the School of Nutrition. He also became the first head of the Department of Biochemistry in 1945. After World War II, Maynard participated in international efforts leading to the development of the Food and Agricultural Organization of the United Nations (FAO). He served on several FAO committees and was the US delegate to many international nutrition meetings after the war.[5]

Richard Barnes succeeded Maynard as director of the School of Nutrition in 1956. Under Barnes, it became the Graduate School of Nutrition, and Barnes was given the title of dean. Under Maynard, the Nutrition faculty had been largely made up of professors holding primary appointments in other Cornell departments, and Barnes added several members with international interests to the core faculty, particularly several biochemists. In 1960, the Graduate School of Nutrition signed a contract with the government of Peru for technical assistance, which supported faculty working with the National Institute of Nutrition in Lima. Charlotte Young taught a course in public health nutrition, and biochemists Lemuel Wright and James Gaylor taught a course in nutritional biochemistry.

But in 1962, Cornell made a major commitment to international nutrition with the appointment of André van Veen as professor of international nutrition, with responsibility for directing the Graduate School of Nutrition's new program in international nutrition. The announcement of the appointment stated explicitly that the program's purpose was to train US citizens interested in careers in international organizations dealing with nutrition problems, such as FAO, the World Health Organization, UNICEF, and the US Agency for International Development.

Born in the Netherlands, van Veen received his academic training at the University of Utrecht. In 1929, he was appointed to the Eijkman Institute in Batavia, Netherlands East Indies (now Jakarta, Indonesia). The Eijkman Institute was known for its role in the discovery of thiamine as the critical factor in preventing a nutritional deficiency disease, beriberi, studied in patients in Jakarta in the early 1900s. After the war, he helped to organize the Nutrition Division of FAO. He became a permanent staff member of the division in 1950, later serving as chief of the Food Science and Technology Branch until his retirement in 1962 and subsequent appointment at Cornell.

While at Cornell, van Veen began the practice of sending graduate students to carry out research in international settings, as opposed to sending them to the laboratory. He encouraged students to use methods from the social sciences to study nutrition problems in communities. Until his retirement from Cornell in 1968, van Veen directed programs for students who worked in Puerto Rico, Peru, Guatemala, Ghana, St. Vincent, and Mexico.

Following van Veen's retirement, Michael Latham was appointed to direct the international nutrition program. Latham was born and grew up in Tanzania, the son of a British medical officer of the British colonial administration. He attended Trinity College in Dublin, Ireland, where he was awarded both a bachelor's (1949) and a medical degree (1952). He returned to Tanzania, where he served as a medical officer and then director of nutrition in the Ministry of Health from 1955 to 1964. He later received a diploma in tropical medicine and hygiene from the University of London and an MPH from the Harvard School of Public Health. For his work in developing the nutrition program in Tanzania, Queen Elizabeth II honored him with the Order of the British Empire in 1965. Latham had an enormous impact on international nutrition at Cornell and internationally. For this work, he was named "a living legend" at the Nineteenth International Nutrition Congress in 2009, and his former students summarized his accomplishments in a book produced upon his retirement.[6] From 1968 to 1974, Latham was the primary faculty member advising students and carrying out research in an international context.

In 1974, the Division of Nutritional Sciences was formed, incorporating the faculty of the Graduate School of Nutrition and the Department of Human Nutrition and Food into a single large academic unit, comprising thirty-five faculty positions, with responsibility for undergraduate teaching, graduate programs, and public education in New York State through Cooperative Extension. The field of nutrition had been undergoing major changes since the late 1950s, with the emphasis moving away from the identification, isolation, and synthesis of individual nutrients to a study of populations, their food habits, and the effects of dietary patterns on chronic disease risk. Concern for global hunger and malnutrition grew with the recognition that large segments of the world population were undernourished and international efforts were needed to help relieve the burden of malnutrition in the developing world.

As the new division developed, it became clear that the field of nutrition needed to consider the world a laboratory to study and help relieve world problems of hunger and malnutrition, but also to study basic nutrition problems in populations and communities. The international nutrition activities in the division became increasingly important as several faculty members and their students carried out studies in settings in Latin America, Africa, and Asia with the aim of assisting those countries and obtaining basic information. My own research interests became more international as my students and I carried out studies on the relationship between parasitic infections and nutrition in Asia and Latin America.[7]

In 1980, the Division of Nutritional Sciences developed the Nutrition Surveillance Program, funded by the US Agency for International Development, to assist nations to "watch over nutrition in order to make decisions that will lead to improvements in nutrition in populations." The nation of Indonesia was one of the areas where the program was particularly active. John Mason and Jean-Pierre Habicht, leaders of the program, describe their work in a paper presented at the Twelfth International Congress of Nutrition.[8]

In 1988, Cornell established the Food and Nutrition Policy Program to conduct applied research and engage in technical cooperation and training on issues of poverty, human resource development, and food and nutrition policy in developing countries. Led by David Sahn and Per Pinstrup-Andersen, the program published extensively on international food and nutrition issues, especially in Africa.[9]

In 2015, I was able to identify 258 students from fifty-six different countries who received degrees based on international nutrition work since 1960. Of these students, 155 received PhDs, some received both MS and PhD degrees, while others completed MPS (master of professional studies in international development), MNS (master of nutritional science), or MPA (master of public affairs) degrees. Most conducted their thesis research outside the United States, although a few worked on international datasets while remaining in this country. A large proportion of the graduates worked in international organizations or governments dealing with food and nutrition issues.

Today, the formal Program in International Nutrition, led by Professor Saurabh Meta, continues to focus on research, policy, and action to improve nutrition and health in low- and middle-income countries. As the international program reaches its sixtieth birthday, faculty and students of the Division of Nutritional Sciences are working on projects in India, Ecuador, Mexico, Uganda, Ethiopia, Bangladesh, and Madagascar. Much international nutrition work remains to be done. Based on World Health Organization estimates, billions of people in the world suffer from problems of obesity or undernutrition and nearly half of the deaths of children under five years of age are caused by undernutrition.

Notes

1. Malden C. Nesheim, *The Division of Nutritional Science at Cornell University: A History and Personal Reflections* (Ithaca, NY: Internet First University Press, 2010), https://ecommons.cornell.edu/handle/1813/14711.

2. For more about Flora Rose, see chapter 30, Flora Rose and Martha Van Rensselaer: Relief Efforts in Belgium.

3. Helen H. Gifft, Esther H. Stocks, and Kathryn E. Walker, "Hazel Marie Hauck," Memorial Statements of the University Faculty, Office of the Dean of the University Faculty, Cornell University, 1964, https://ecommons.cornell.edu/handle/1813/18028. See also Hazel M. Hauck Papers, #23-14-730, Division of Rare and Manuscript Collections, Cornell University Library.

4. Kenneth L. Turk, Charlotte M. Young, and Harold H. Williams, "Leonard Amby Maynard," Memorial Statements of the University Faculty, Office of the Dean of the University Faculty, Cornell University, 1972, https://ecommons.cornell.edu/handle/1813/18182.

5. See Leonard A. Maynard Papers, #29-1-292, Division of Rare and Manuscript Collections, Cornell University Library.

6. Micheline Beaudry, Suzanne J. Gervais, and Michael C. Latham, eds., *Five Decades of International Research and Advocacy Conducted by Professor Michael Latham and His Cornell University Colleagues and Students* (Cornell University, 2009), http://www.wphna.org/htdocs/downloadsmay2011/Latham%20monograph%205%20decades%20of%20research.pdf. See also Michael C. Latham Papers, #29-2-3928, Division of Rare and Manuscript Collections, Cornell University Library.

7. David W. T. Crompton and Malden C. Nesheim, "Nutritional Impact of Intestinal Helminthiasis during the Human Life Cycle," *Annual Review of Nutrition* 22 (July 2002): 35–59.

8. John Mason and Jean-Pierre Habicht, "Nutritional Surveillance," paper presented at the Twelfth International Congress of Nutrition, August 17–21, 1981. See also Jean-Pierre Habicht Papers, #29-2-3679, Division of Rare and Manuscript Collections, Cornell University Library.

9. Cornell Food and Nutrition Policy Program, *Annual Report.* (1991), Box 3, Folder 4A, Division of Nutritional Sciences Records, #29-1-3247, Division of Rare and Manuscript Collections, Cornell University Library. See also Per Pinstrup-Andersen Papers, #29-2-4133, Division of Rare and Manuscript Collections, Cornell University Library.

32. JOHN P. WINDMULLER AND THE ILR SCHOOL'S GLOBAL EXPERIENCE

William J. Sonnenstuhl

Since its founding, the New York State School of Industrial and Labor Relations, which today is known as the ILR School, has had a deep commitment to the understanding of labor and management relations systems around the world. The founding faculty of the school, which was born in an era of labor-management and international conflict, were committed to resolving disagreements peacefully in the United States and globally. Professor John P. Windmuller played a key role in forging the field of international and comparative labor relations, which is now deeply integrated into the ILR School's mission and global focus.

In 1944, the New York State Legislature passed legislation establishing the school and its mission: "improving industrial and labor conditions in the State through provision for instruction on and off the campus, the conduct of research, and the dissemination of all aspects of industrial, labor, and public relations affecting employers and employees."[1]

In June 1945, Irving M. Ives, who was majority leader of the New York State Assembly and chairman of the New York State Joint Legislative Committee on Industrial and Labor Conditions and had championed creation of the school, was appointed dean and set about recruiting its first two faculty, Jean McKelvey and Maurice Neufeld, who wrote the curricula for an undergraduate and a graduate program. They were joined by Vernon "Pete" Jensen and Milton Konvitz to complete the founding faculty. On November 5, the school's first classes were held in Warren Hall. The inaugural cohort of students consisted of 107 students, including 67 World War II veterans and 11 graduate students.

Having lived through the turbulent 1930s and World War II, the ILR School's four founding faculty were steeped in both labor-management and international conflict and invested in their resolution. McKelvey wrote her dissertation about the American Federation of Labor; taught economics at Sarah Lawrence College, where she was chair of the Social Science Faculty; and was a member of the National War Labor Board. In 1947, she was the first woman admitted

Figure 32.1 Professor John P. Windmuller, the ILR School's "Mr. International." (Provided by the School of Industrial and Labor Relations)

to the National Academy of Arbitrators, becoming its first female president in 1970. Neufeld was well grounded in labor-management relations, serving as an organizer for the Amalgamated Clothing Workers in Philadelphia and education director of the International Ladies Garment Workers in Trenton. He was highly experienced in administration, serving as director of the Division of State Planning for New York State and, later, the state's deputy commissioner of commerce. In 1942, he enlisted in the US Army, serving most of his military career in Italy, where he helped rebuild the country after the Allied forces conquered it. In 1961, he published *Italy, School for Awakening Countries: The Italian Labor Movement in Its Political, Social, and Economic Setting from 1800 to 1960.* Jensen and Konvitz were also experienced in labor-management, civil rights, and dispute resolution on the national and international stages. In this context, the school took an early interest in studying labor and management relations in other countries and how to achieve peaceful and productive working relationships between employers and employees. In the summer of 1947, the school held its first international conference on teaching labor and management relations, giving birth to the Industrial Relations Research Association. In 1950, sixty-six leaders of German industry, unions, and governmental agencies visited the school for a six-week series of conferences sponsored by the US Department of Labor and studied topics such as collective bargaining, production and trade, labor law and legislation, and handling labor-management differences.

John P. Windmuller, the ILR School's "Mr. International," jokingly referred to himself as a one-person department of international and comparative labor relations. He was no stranger to conflict and its resolution. He was born in Dortmund, Germany, where his family became victims of Nazi persecution. To avoid even worse treatment by the Nazis, he and his family sought to escape Europe aboard the ill-fated *St. Louis*. When the passengers of the *St. Louis* were denied the right of entry by both Cuba and the United States, the Windmullers were forced to return to Europe, with the parents interned in France and John and his younger brother sent to a boarding school in France for refugee children. Eventually, the Windmullers made their way to the United States, where John enlisted in the army, spending his military service at Fort Dix, screening German prisoners of war. After the war, he enrolled in the University of Illinois, where he completed his BA in two years. His military experience and studies at the University of Illinois sparked his lifelong interest in international and comparative labor relations. In 1948, he enrolled in the ILR School's PhD program, completing, in 1951, his dissertation on American labor unions and their influence on foreign policy.

Upon graduation, Windmuller joined the ILR School faculty, creating the school's first course in international and comparative relations in 1951, which he almost single-handedly made a central feature of students' education. He taught the course throughout his career at the school until his retirement in 1987, inspiring generations of students to think globally and study abroad. Eileen Barkas Hoffman of the class of 1969 wrote in *The ILR School at Fifty: Voices of the Faculty, Alumni & Friends*, "ILR also looked to a more global economy before it was fashionable. The areas of comparative labor relations, so well taught by John P. Windmuller, excited me, and I decided to spend my junior year at the London School of Economics, looking at British and comparative labor relations, economics, and politics."[2]

In 1951, when the ILR School established the International Institute of Industrial and Labor Relations, Dean Martin P. Catherwood appointed Windmuller as its director. The institute had three objectives: improving labor-management relations in New York State and the nation by studying the experiences of other countries; helping other countries to improve their labor-management relations by becoming familiar with the American experience; and training professionals for employment in the field of international industrial and labor relations.

Within a few years, under Windmuller's direction, the school had achieved these objectives and set the pattern for international and comparative studies within the ILR School. In those years, many faculty members undertook research in other countries and taught courses and seminars related to that research. For example, Neufeld and Gardner Clark undertook work on Italy; Mark Perlman on Australia; Konvitz on Liberia; Henry Lansberger on Latin America; Robert Aronson on Ghana and Jamaica; Walter Galenson on Latin America, Africa, and Asia; and Alice Cook on Japan. The school welcomed many international visitors and students to study labor relations and how they might be applied in their countries. The German project, mentioned earlier, continued into the 1960s. The ILR School also developed programs with Chile and Turkey. Another important achievement was the ILR School library's decision to give substantial importance to the acquisition of books and documentary materials relating to foreign and international labor problems and to establish exchange agreements with institutions abroad. This policy helped to raise the standing of the library from being just one more well-equipped and competently administered institution to being an unrivaled leader in the entire world.

In his scholarly career, Windmuller became the world's leading expert on comparative labor relations. His many books include *American Labor and the International Labor Movement, 1940 to 1953*; *The International Trade Union Movement*; *Labor Relations in the Netherlands*; and *International Trade Secretariats: The International Trade Union Internationals*. His work shaped the field, and he received many accolades, including a silver medal from the government of the Netherlands for his work in that country.

Windmuller also forged a lasting relationship between the ILR School and the International Labor Organization (ILO), producing several important books: *Antecedents of the International Labor Organization*, *Collective Bargaining in Industrialized Marketing Economies*, and *Soviet Employers in the ILO: The Experience of the 1930s*. Today, ILR School faculty and students continue working with the ILO. Each year, many ILR School undergraduates complete internships at the ILO, studying and writing about current labor issues.

Windmuller also played an important role in expanding international work across the university, having been a member of the first executive committee of the Cornell Center for International Studies, headed by Mario Einaudi and now known as the Einaudi Center. In acknowledgment of his distinguished scholarship, he was awarded the first Martin P. Catherwood Professorship in the ILR School in 1983. In 2008, the ILR School established the John P. Windmuller Chair in International and Comparative Labor, awarding the honor to Professor Gary Fields.

In the 1990s, recognizing the importance of a global perspective, the ILR School created the Department of International and Comparative Labor, required all ILR School undergraduates to take a course in international and comparative labor, and created many more opportunities for students—undergraduate and graduate—to have an international experience. Since then, an international perspective has become more embedded in the ILR School curriculum. Today, undergraduates are required to take an advanced international and comparative labor course in addition to the introductory course. At the same time, the international focus has become embedded across the school and the faculty has voted to combine the Department of Labor Relations, Law, and History and the Department of International Comparative Labor into a new one: the Department of Global Labor and Work. The new department highlights that faculty who study labor relations no longer think of the United States as a separate area of study; rather, they view it as part of the broader topic of international labor relations, with the United States as one important national example.

ILR School faculty from across the school currently offer a broad range of international and comparative labor relations courses on such topics as globalization, development economics, union revitalization, international labor rights, comparative industrial relations, international migration, cross-cultural organizational behavior, comparative social policy and social movements, and strategic human resource management, as well as courses on specific countries and world regions. A few examples of the department's current international breadth include Dina Bishara, who studies Egypt and the Middle East; Alex Colvin and Virginia Doellgast, who do comparative research on European and North American labor relations; Gary Fields, who has expertise on Africa and Latin America; Eli Friedman, who specializes in China; Tristan Ivory, who researches sub-Saharan Africa; Sarosh Kuruvilla, who specializes in Southeast Asia; and Lowell Turner, who specializes in Europe. In 2022, the ILR School established the Global Labor Institute, which is dedicated to independent quantitative research and action on a new generation of strategies that the evidence says measurably improve labor conditions for large numbers of workers in global production.

The ILR School encourages all its undergraduates to have an international experience and provides them with many opportunities to do so. In addition to the Cornell Study Abroad Program, the ILR School's International Program provides students opportunities to engage in global service learning, which helps them understand the problems that plague a local community through collaborative work and solution-based efforts. For example, students may choose to work with communities in India, Vietnam, or Zambia on solving local problems. They may also choose to participate in one of the ILR School Exchange Programs. These include opportunities to study at the University College Dublin, the Bocconi University, the Universitat Rovira i Virgili, Queen Mary University of London, the University of Warwick, and Cardiff University. Students also have an opportunity to become ILR Global Scholars by incorporating the following components into their undergraduate experience: significant international experience while at the ILR School; foreign language study at the 2000 level at Cornell; completion of four international and comparative courses on different regions of the world (in addition to distribution requirements); and completion of the Global Scholars Capstone ILRIC 4940. Almost half of ILR School students graduate with some international experience, and 5 percent graduate with the distinction of being ILR Global Scholars.

At its founding, the ILR School's founders envisioned a culture that valued the peaceful resolution of labor-management conflicts both nationally and internationally. In today's global economy, that vision is as important as it has ever been, and the ILR School's faculty remains committed to its international and comparative labor agenda and providing all ILR School students with an international experience and global perspective. The school's founders and Professor Windmuller's legacy connect the school's past, present, and future and its vision for the United States and the world.

Notes

1. *Report of the Dean of the New York State School of Industrial and Labor Relations, 1945–1946* (1946, p. 1) quoted in *The ILR School at Fifty: Voices of the Faculty, Alumni & Friends*, ed. Elaine F. Gruenfeld (Cornell University, 1996), 15.
2. Gruenfeld, *ILR School at Fifty*, 89–90.

33. CORNELL ENGAGES EMERGING MARKETS AROUND THE WORLD

Lourdes Casanova and Royal D. Colle

In 2010, Cornell's Samuel Curtis Johnson Graduate School of Management founded the Emerging Markets Institute (EMI) "as a vehicle to bring together preeminent practitioners and academics from around the world to develop the next generation of global business leaders and to create the premier research center on the role of emerging markets in the global economy."[1] Defined by Andrew Karolyi, Charles Field Knight Dean of the Cornell SC Johnson College of Business, as "an underfunded growth opportunity with problems," emerging markets represent challenges that require problem-solving skills. "That's what these special types of people relish in becoming business leaders—challenging themselves, the basic business principles they have learned, in settings that are super complex and ever changing."[2]

Launching EMI was the culmination of the school's decision to enhance global programming, curriculum, and presence as a key priority in its 2008 strategic plan. Cornell recruited two senior faculty members with exceptional international expertise in research and teaching who wanted to help shape a new international institute. In fall 2009, Karolyi and Ya-Ru Chen joined Cornell—Karolyi as professor of finance and global business and Chen as professor of management and global business. Together, after gathering input and information from the college's students, faculty, alumni, and staff, as well as twenty top business schools, they developed the proposal to create EMI, the first of its kind at any leading business school.[3]

EMI offers a fellows program that gives MBA students the opportunity to pursue globally oriented coursework, projects, and experiences. In 2022, sixty-nine MBA students graduated as EMI fellows. Fellows are typically required to take an international study trip or semester abroad, and many participate in student treks organized by the college. In 2014–2015, more than two hundred Johnson students participated in study trips to South Africa, Israel, Colombia, Dubai, Japan and Korea, and western Europe.[4] The importance of traveling as part of the Johnson

Figure 33.1 Emerging Markets Institute team 2022 with director Professor Lourdes Casanova (*front left*). (Provided by Emerging Markets Institute)

School's graduate studies is captured by Miwa Takaki, a 2015 MBA graduate who went to the Middle East:

> Armed with a group of 32 close friends, we stormed the country in pursuit of exploring the country's rich and thriving startup culture. Day to day, we worked intimately with local startups as well as innovation centers on projects ranging from developing go-to-market strategies to creating PR campaigns for new users. We learned about the cultural, political, and social complexities of the region from captivating discussions about Arab-Jew relations, public media in current day, and the way of life for many religious groups in the area. We also had fun discovering the world of underground street art tour of Tel Aviv, camping in Bedouin tents in the desert, riding camels, waking up at dawn for a sunrise hike and yoga overseeing the Dead Sea, and of course, eating and dancing our way through Tel Aviv and Jerusalem.[5]

In 2019 and 2021, after years of supporting opportunities for EMI students, including participation in case competitions and experiences abroad in emerging markets, Roberto Cañizares (class of 1971, MBA 1974) and his wife, Gail, made

Figure 33.2 Emerging Markets Society president Andrew H. Lim, 2022. (Provided by Emerging Markets Institute)

gifts to Cornell to create an endowment for the academic and administrative directors of EMI. Additionally, they funded a pilot program to develop new case studies for EMI. "They will actually live a case. You go. You do a project in a developing country or an emerging economy, and then you come back and write about it," said Cañizares. "It allows students to learn experientially, while it also creates new, fresh, practical material from which other students can learn going forward. This will build a library of case studies that add to the teaching materials for engaging, teaching, and training new and future EMI students."[6]

The couple's gift also created the Cañizares Award for Distinguished Alumni in International Business and Emerging Markets. It recognizes people, Cañizares says, "who have for many years devoted their careers to developing and building businesses in and around the world. This enables EMI to reach back beyond the institute's ten years of existence and recognize people who more than ten years ago launched their business careers in emerging markets and are outstanding examples to inspire younger generations." Cañizares himself successfully built and transformed businesses around the world for more than two decades, including MSA International and air conditioning company Trane International Group. The inaugural award went to Paul Kavuma, founder and CEO of Catalyst Principal Partners in Kenya.

Reflecting on EMI History

International programs are not new to Johnson students. A 2003 issue of *Cornell Enterprise* described "vicarious globe-trotting." In addition to international classes at Johnson, Jan Katz, the Suter-Staley Director of Global Business, described how the school had "significantly ramped up a range of internationally-oriented events *outside* the classroom."[7] For example, WorldSmarts dinners featured the cuisine of a different country each month, helping students appreciate the finer points of a culture. Another monthly event was Art and Culture, which took students to the Johnson Museum of Art to visit exhibits from different countries to expose them to the wider cultural issues of a country. There was also International Education Week each November, which provided students with cultural "snapshots" from around the globe through guest speakers such as Jeffrey Lam Kin-fung, managing director of Hong Kong–based Forward Winsome Industries, one of the largest toy manufacturers in Asia, and Ma Xuezheng, senior vice president and chief financial officer of Legend Group (now Lenovo), whom *Fortune* named among the most powerful women in global business.

The launching of EMI was the next step in expanding Johnson's international focus. On EMI's tenth anniversary in 2020, Karolyi reflected on its progress:

> When we formed the Emerging Markets Institute, we wanted to change the mindset of our faculty to foster a greater appreciation of the importance of the global dimension of business. The stakeholders—Roberto Cañizares '71, MBA '74, Nell Cady-Kruse '84, MBA '85, and Bob Staley '58, MBA '59—understood the importance of what we were trying to do. We had a blueprint with a focus on co-curricular programming for what would become the EMI student fellows program with emphasis on immersion trips, job treks, and EM-intensive joint projects for the Institute. But I never thought that it would take off and have the success that it did. There was a great response among students because there was a fundamental demand: a good number of our MBA students wanted to immerse themselves in these complex markets. We affectionately referred to them as the "Navy SEALs of emerging markets"—specially-trained future business leaders who could be put into the most difficult of business environments, always changing, uncertain, volatile.[8]

Ya-Ru Chen also observes a change: "I certainly think the Johnson School has moved up in stature and become more globalized. We have EMI, the Cornell-Tsinghua Finance MBA program, a presence in India, and we helped to set up a new university in Vietnam, VinUniversity in Hanoi. Our colleagues on the faculty have become a lot more globalized: They travel the world to conduct research, to give talks, and to teach. Faculty who go to China to teach come back and point to their experience with a sense of pride, like, 'look at this cool thing that I just did.' Now, we're thinking about doing more internationally."[9] This global recognition is reflected in the *Financial Times* college rankings, which placed Cornell's two-year MBA program in the top ten worldwide for the first time (fifth in the United States and eighth globally).[10]

Global EMI Activities

EMI hosts a major annual conference in November that attracts a host of stakeholders from near and far, including international business leaders, government officials, academics, students, and Cornell alumni. Chen believes that the conference is a great way to consolidate EMI's achievements. Internally, she says, "a great conference brings people together to celebrate; it brings a lot of pride to alumni and students. Externally, it's a great way to engage alumni and key stakeholders, including existing supporters and new supporters." But it goes further than this. Karolyi insists, "Every scholar has some obligation to be able to translate their work for an external community that we care about. It's got to mean something to people beyond, those in industry, in financial services, in government; that's a Cornell value. What the annual EMI conference does every year in November is reinforce the Cornell value system on the importance of translating the research for its impactfulness. This conference is a manifestation of that in a beautiful way."[11]

EMI carries out several more events annually, including one aimed at young entrepreneurs around the world. In collaboration with business schools in emerging markets, the Cornell EMI Mark Mobius Pitch Competition is for early-stage ventures operating, or being launched, in emerging economies. It is open to undergraduates, graduates, and recent alumni, regardless of the college or university. Finalists will have networking opportunities in New York City, mentorship by fellows and global investors, media exposure, and the opportunity to compete for a cash prize of $10,000. It is an opportunity also for student entrepreneurs and recent graduates operating start-ups in emerging markets to network with fellow students, speak with expert mentors, and pitch their start-ups to investors in the emerging markets. The 2022 winner was a start-up from the Indian Institute of Technology in Kanpur.

Another annual event is the Cornell EMI Corning Case Competition, whose results appear during the annual EMI international conference. It boosts collaboration among universities and strengthens Johnson's ties with other academic institutions. It speaks to EMI's focus on international and interinstitutional collaboration. The goal of the case competition is for student teams from around the world to identify and answer challenges faced by an emerging markets multinational that real businesses and managers are posing today in relation to emerging markets. The growing role of emerging multinationals in the business world continues to evolve, and this case competition seeks to challenge people and organizations to come up with win-win solutions for expanding stakeholders.

Authored by Lourdes Casanova, EMI Gail and Rob Cañizares director since 2015, and EMI faculty fellow Anne Miroux, the Emerging Markets Multinationals Report series, now in its seventh edition, is a comprehensive exploration of the rise of emerging market multinationals. For example, in an early report, Casanova and Miroux examined the resilience of emerging economies in today's challenging global environment and their growing importance as foreign investors across all regions of the world.[12] Under the title *Reinventing Global Value Chains*, the 2022 report was written in collaboration with the Emerging Markets Network of the Development Centre at the Organisation for Economic Co-operation and Development, the International Financial Corporation of the World Bank, the United Nations Conference on Trade and Development, the Inter American Development Bank, and a network of partner universities like the Universidad de los Andes in Colombia, Tecnológico de Monterrey in Mexico, and Wuhan University in China, among others.

Since its beginning early in the twenty-first century, EMI has touched a wide range of people and important global issues. The institute leads the Emerging Multinationals Research Network with universities from all over the world, and in 2022 it also took over leadership of the Emerging Markets Global Players from Columbia University. EMI has brought experts to Cornell from emerging market countries, such as Veneta Andonova, dean of the Universidad de los Andes School of Management in Colombia; Humberto Ribeiro, former secretary of trade and services in Brazil; and PhD students from Tsinghua University and the University of São Paulo. EMI has sent Cornell graduate students for exposure to many of those countries, and it has built relationships via joint webinars with business schools such as those at the Universidad de los Andes in Colombia, Tecnológico de Monterrey in Mexico, the Universidad de San Andrés in Argentina, and the Universidad de São Paulo in Brazil. EMI's research has more recently included a focus on efforts of emerging markets to deal with environmental, social, and governance issues. These issues are a challenge for the future of emerging markets because of the poor availability and quality of data on them, "which limits investment firms' ability to identify investment opportunities as well as their willingness to take a risk by pouring money into emerging markets."[13] It is an issue that EMI students, faculty, and constituents will face in the future, and it is on the EMI agenda.[14]

Notes

1. Kaitlyn Ruhf, "$1.8M Gift Supports the Emerging Markets Institute," *Cornell Chronicle*, November 5, 2021, https://news.cornell.edu/stories/2021/11/18m-gift-supports-emerging-markets-institute.

2. Janice Endresen, "Celebrating the Emerging Markets Institute on Its 10th Anniversary," *Cornell Enterprise*, October 22, 2020, https://business.cornell.edu/hub/2020/10/22/celebrating-emerging-markets-institute-on-its-10th-anniversary.

3. Endresen.

4. Endresen.

5. Miwa Takaki, quoted in "A World of Possibilities," *Cornell Enterprise*, Spring 2015.

6. Ruhf, "$1.8M Gift."

7. "Seeing the World," *Cornell Enterprise*, Spring 2003.

8. Endresen, "Celebrating the Emerging Markets Institute."

9. Endresen.

10. Sarah Magnus-Sharpe, "The Financial Times Ranks Cornell University's Johnson School among World's Top 10 MBA Programs," Johnson BusinessFeed, February 13, 2023, https://business.cornell.edu/hub/2023/02/13/ft-ranks-cornell-johnson-top-mba-program.

11. Endresen, "Celebrating the Emerging Markets Institute."

12. These reports are available on Cornell's eCommons website: "Emerging Markets Institute Annual Reports," eCommons, Cornell University, accessed October 27, 2023, https://www.johnson.cornell.edu/emerging-markets-institute/.

13. Maria Minkser, "ESG Pressure Takes Center Stage at the 2021 Emerging Markets Institute Conference," *Cornell Chronicle*, December 8, 2021, https://news.cornell.edu/stories/2021/12/esg-pressure-takes-center-stage-2021-emerging-markets-institute-conference.

14. That challenge is spelled out in more detail by Lourdes Casanova and Anne Miroux in their opening comments to the 2021 Emerging Markets Institute conference. See Lourdes Casanova and Anne Miroux, "ESG and Emerging Market Multinationals," in *Emerging Market Multinationals Report (EMR) 2021: Building the Future on ESG Excellence* (Emerging Markets Institute, Cornell University, 2021), 25–56, https://ecommons.cornell.edu/handle/1813/110935.

34. GLOBAL AWARENESS AND COMMITMENTS OF CORNELL'S LAW SCHOOL

Mitchel Lasser

From its inception, Cornell Law School has been defined by its global awareness and commitments. Each generation has renewed and revitalized these international values in its own way, leaving a deep international imprint on the Law School's curriculum, students, faculty, research, and operations.

Myron Taylor Hall offers the most tangible manifestation of the Law School's foundational and enduring commitment to international ideals. During the period between the two world wars, the faculty decided that the theme of the new building should be "World Peace through Law." The structure was built in 1932, and this theme was carved into the stone spandrels of its great tower arch. Its eastern side demonstrates faith in domestic law, depicting Henry II of England sending itinerant judges to bring the king's peace to all parts of the realm. Its western side demonstrates a concomitant faith in international law, depicting a conference of international dignitaries striving to reach international accord.

The Law School's belief in the importance of international and comparative law took programmatic shape in the immediate postwar period. The faculty took several interrelated measures that have molded the Law School ever since. First, it hired a professor who would soon become one of the world's preeminent comparative law scholars: Rudi Schlesinger. Born in Munich to a Jewish family, Schlesinger was forced to emigrate in the 1930s, shortly after having completed his doctorate. He came to the United States and enrolled in Columbia Law School, where he was elected editor in chief of the *Columbia Law Review*, a remarkable feat for a German-born student during World War II. Rigorously trained in both the civil law and common law traditions, he would rapidly become the dean of the discipline of comparative law in the United States. Hired at Cornell in 1948, he first published his immensely influential textbook *Comparative Law—Cases, Text and Materials* in 1950. Still published over seventy years later, this textbook (now in its seventh edition) has introduced generations of law students to the study and comparison of the world's major legal systems. Schlesinger then spent

Figure 34.1 Professor Rudi Schlesinger in the Myron Taylor Hall Library. (Provided by Cornell Law School Communications)

some ten years engaged in an ambitious international effort to compare and theorize how contracts were formed in jurisdictions all over the world. Adopting an innovative fact- and problem-based method, he brought together a vast international team of scholars to examine the actual practices of contracting in different countries, leading eventually to the 1968 publication of the landmark *Study of the Common Core of Legal Systems*. As with his famous casebook, his methodological innovations endure over fifty years later: to this day, a large international team of scholars meets annually (usually in Italy) to study "the common core of European private law," adding new installments to an ongoing series of edited volumes published by Cambridge University Press.

The Law School's second important postwar achievement was to design and institute a targeted program of study for JD students especially interested in the study of foreign and international law. In a groundbreaking move, Cornell became the first American law school to establish a special degree program oriented toward international and comparative law: the Specialization in International Legal Affairs. This specialization degree program continues to this day, with eight to ten students a year choosing to shoulder the added curricular burden required to earn the degree and to attend regularly a lecture series (first established in the same postwar period) dedicated to international legal issues.

Figure 34.2 The exterior of Cornell Law School Myron Taylor Hall Library. (Provided by Cornell Law School Communications)

The fall of the Berlin Wall and the end of the Cold War ushered in the next great era of international developments at the Law School. In the early 1990s, Cornell Law School's International Legal Studies Program, now endowed by Leo and Arvilla Berger, got its second wind under the vigorous leadership of Jack Barceló, inaugural Elizabeth and Arthur Reich Director of the program. A series of major developments ensued. Professor Barceló designed and founded the Cornell–University of Paris I Summer Institute of International and Comparative Law. This pioneering monthlong summer program brought Cornell Law School professors to the traditional buildings of the law faculty of the University of Paris (in the shadow of the Panthéon), where they would teach a range of internationally and comparatively oriented courses to law students from Cornell and other US law schools as well as from abroad. This program, which also continues to this day, has periodically seen enrollments top one hundred per year, thus bringing Cornell Law School professors before thousands of students from all over the world.

The demand for cross-border legal education exploded during this period, and Cornell took the lead in developing innovative models for preparing students for the challenges and opportunities presented by an increasingly interconnected world. The university instituted a series of exchange programs that brought students from, and sent Cornell students to, a wide range of law faculties abroad. These exchange agreements now join Cornell Law School to some twenty-five law faculties situated on every continent but Antarctica. They range, for example, from the University of Amsterdam, King's College London, and the Catholic University of Portugal in Europe, to the University of Hong Kong and Waseda University in Asia, to the University of Chile and University of Buenos Aires in South America, to the University of Johannesburg and University of Pretoria in Africa, to the University of Sidney in Oceania. As a result, about one-third of all Cornell Law School students came to spend a full semester studying in a law faculty abroad, dramatically improving their capacity to practice effectively in a transnational environment. For those students even more committed to cross-border work, Cornell Law School also established innovative dual-degree programs with sister institutions with which it had developed particularly close contacts. Chief among them were the University of Paris I (now the Sorbonne Law School), which also houses the Summer Program in Paris, and the University of Heidelberg.

The 1990s also saw the beginnings of what would eventually become the exponential growth of the Law School's international student body. The Law School had already established its one-year LLM Program for foreign students wishing to pursue master's-level work and its JSD Program for those intent on performing doctoral-level research (usually with the goal of becoming law professors). But in this period, the size of the LLM class began to grow steadily, eventually reaching its current size of over 130 students in the 2022–2023 academic year. This gradually transformed the experience of legal education at Cornell: the presence of such a large contingent of foreign law students in the Ithaca classrooms has turned the Cornell Law School into a thoroughly international educational environment. This is only amplified by the number of more senior academics who come to the Law School every year under Cornell's Visiting Scholar and Visiting Researcher programs, which invite doctoral and postdoctoral scholars to come to Ithaca to advance their research in the Law School's outstanding library under the supervision of Cornell professors with expertise in their particular fields of research.

The Law School's current international projects have been amplified and supported through a number of vibrant research institutes, centers, and programs. The central figure in the design and funding of these institutions was undoubtedly alumnus Jack C. Clarke, who endowed the Clarke Program in East Asian Law and Culture, the Clarke Center for International and Comparative Legal Studies, and the Clarke Initiative for Law Development in the Middle East and Africa. To these one must add the Center on the Death Penalty Worldwide, the International Human Rights Clinic, the Center for Global Economic Justice, the Migration and Human Rights Program, and more.

The international commitments of the Law School have been motivated above all by the tremendous thirst of its faculty to engage in internationally oriented research and projects. This orientation dates back to the school's founding in 1887. One of its original faculty members was Herbert Tuttle, who was professor of the history of political and municipal institutions and international law. A student from Japan traveled to Ithaca to be a member of the inaugural entering class. Professor Tuttle and his colleagues were joined on the faculty by Charles Evans Hughes, who went on to become not only governor of New York and chief justice of the US Supreme Court but also a judge on the Permanent Court of International Justice. One of Hughes's students was Myron C. Taylor (class of 1894), who served as the personal envoy to the Vatican under Presidents Franklin D. Roosevelt and Harry S. Truman, and whose generosity led to the building of the Law School's Myron Taylor Hall and the funding of a lecture series on international legal affairs that continues to this day. Finally, Herbert W. Briggs served as the key figure who bridged the founding generation of Tuttle and Hughes to the postwar period personified by Schlesinger. Briggs taught international law and international politics as a professor in both the Law School and the Department of Government from 1929 to 1969 and served as president of the American Society of International Law and editor in chief of the *American Journal of International Law.* To this day, the Law School's student-led international law organization is named the Briggs Society of International Law.

The faculty's international orientation remains a hallmark of the Law School. Remarkably, some two-thirds of the current faculty have published comparative or international legal research. It is only fitting, therefore, that in 2021 the Law School appointed Jens Ohlin, a noted scholar of international criminal law and procedure, public international law, and the law of war, as its dean.

35. "DON'T FORGET THE HORSE-DOCTOR"

Veterinary Medicine's International Legacy

Royal D. Colle

The Cornell University College of Veterinary Medicine (CVM) has played an extraordinary role in Cornell's global history. Cornell's first veterinary professor, James Law, was educated at the Edinburgh Veterinary College. He also attended the University of Edinburgh Medical School, where he studied human anatomy and the principles and practice of surgery, later expanding his education with study at veterinary schools in Lyons and Alfort in France. He began building a powerful professional reputation at several institutions, serving on the faculty at the Edinburgh New Veterinary College in 1860 and publishing important veterinary-related papers. John Gamgee, founder of the New Veterinary College and an accomplished veterinarian and educator, greatly encouraged him. It was Gamgee who persuaded Cornell's president Andrew Dickson White to interview Law for a faculty position while White was in Europe in 1868, since, according to a likely apocryphal story, Ezra Cornell is reported to have bid White farewell by shouting, "Don't forget the horse-doctor."[1]

Law came to Cornell as a professor of veterinary medicine and surgery in 1868. White also returned with a variety of veterinary teaching materials that Law helped him gather in Europe. The *Ithaca Journal* reported that this included "a paper mâché figure of a horse (that can be) taken apart in 97 pieces, showing almost every muscle in the system of the animal: also enlarged specimens of the interior of the human ear two feet in length from which he remarked students can learn more in a single lesson than from the textbooks in a month."[2] In 1870, Law published his first textbook, *Farmer's Veterinary Advisor*, which—with its European influence—reached fifteen editions, not only supporting a modern veterinary practice but also promoting scientific methods in agriculture. The campus building James Law Hall, named after him in 1914, opened in 1896 to house Cornell's veterinary college. Law's influence on veterinary medicine, education, and public health was significant and should not be underestimated. As one biographer suggested, "Law was the most important veterinarian in the United States before the end of World War I."[3]

Figure 35.1 James Law Hall, Cornell University, circa 1908. (Provided by Cornell University Communications)

William A. Hagan became dean of CVM in 1932 and served for twenty-seven years, until 1959. He pushed the borders and influence of CVM well beyond Ithaca and the United States. He had studied as a European Fellow in the Robert Koch Institute for Infectious Diseases in Berlin, Germany. While dean, he returned to veterinary affairs in Germany in 1945, serving as a veterinary consultant for the US Control Council, where he was instrumental in the postwar rehabilitations of veterinary schools in Germany. Later he served for many years as the US member of the Permanent Committee for the International Veterinary Congresses. He served as US delegate to the Fifteenth International Veterinary Congress at Stockholm in 1953 and chairman of the US Committee to the Sixteenth Congress in Madrid in 1959. After he retired from his post as dean, Hagan headed a delegation of six veterinarians to study livestock in the Soviet Union. In his post-Cornell life, he was elected vice president of the World Veterinary Association. His leadership and contributions to veterinary medicine (including more than 120 scientific articles) earned him honorary membership in veterinary organizations in Great Britain, France, Sweden, and Greece.[4]

In 2018, CVM highlighted the extent of its reach abroad in *'Scopes: Making a World of Difference*, the college's 2018 annual report, noting recent partnerships with the Jockey Club College of Veterinary Medicine and Life Sciences at City

Figure 35.2 Bettina Wagner, professor in the Department of Population Medicine and Diagnostic Sciences, traveled to Iceland to work with the native Icelandic horse populations, 2016. (Photo by Lauren Cahoon Roberts)

University of Hong Kong (including a joint interdisciplinary PhD program); the Tata Trust Animal Medical Center in Mumbai, India; and Obihiro University of Agriculture and Veterinary Medicine in Japan. Many CVM faculty and alumni now work internationally. "When it comes to international efforts, CVM faculty are the fulcrum between energized students and engaged graduates. As they teach the importance of planetary health in the college's clinics, classrooms, and labs, they're also leading by example—forging new relationships with global partners and gathering invaluable data from fieldwork across continents. It is thanks to their efforts and inspiration that CVM continues to keep its finger on the pulse of the planet."[5]

The article went on to identify more than thirty countries where CVM faculty members have become involved. Some projects are national, such as the Quality Milk Production Service that services dairy producers in New York State and the rest of the country, but others engage with countries all over the world, with longstanding partnerships in Mexico, Italy, Turkey, Chile, China, Russia, and Brazil. CVM also conducts trainings and consulting in Canada, Uruguay, Denmark, Argentina, South Africa, the Netherlands, the United Kingdom, Spain, and Portugal.

We can observe two international projects more closely. Bettina Wagner, professor and former chair of the Department of Population Medicine and Diagnostic

Sciences, studies equine immunology. She has worked with native Icelandic horses to determine why their immune systems are more vulnerable to allergic diseases when they leave Iceland but their expat foals have far hardier systems. In 2012, she brought a breeding herd of Icelandic horses to Ithaca. Working with colleagues at the Institute for Experimental Pathology at Keldur, University of Iceland, in Reykjavik, she has gained key insights into how environmental factors affect immune development. Wagner and her Icelandic colleagues are currently developing an oral immunotherapy to treat allergies in imported Icelandic horses.

While tigers typically are not found on CVM's Ithaca campus, they are also part of the CVM international environment. Martin Gilbert, senior research associate in the Department of Population Medicine and Diagnostic Sciences and Wildlife Health, is Cornell's wild carnivore specialist. With support from Cornell's Feline Health Center, he has been investigating the prevalence of canine distemper virus infection in endangered wild tiger populations, especially in the Russian Far East. He has also examined the previously unstudied tiger populations of Indonesia, Thailand, India, and Nepal as the first step in characterizing the potential risk of canine distemper virus to these vulnerable groups. In 2018, Gilbert assisted local conservationists in Bhutan to help diagnose a wild tiger that had succumbed to an illness caused by a human tapeworm. Cornell's Animal Health Diagnostic Center in Ithaca analyzed tissues to determine what factors contributed to the condition and whether it was a rare anomaly or the first sign of a wider problem. The visit led to relationships that will increase the capacity of Bhutan's veterinarians by providing them with the tools and skills for managing the health of their wildlife. As a direct result, later that year, government veterinarian Yoenten Phuentshok joined Gilbert in Bangkok for specialized training to assess whether canine distemper may be a threat to tigers in Bhutan.[6] Gilbert, with support from the Cornell Atkinson Center for Sustainability, also has worked with a community-led initiative in the Pamir Mountains of Tajikistan and Kyrgyzstan to identify the most important health threats to wild and domestic goats and sheep and their effect on top predators like the snow leopard.

Additional faculty efforts include those of Robin Radcliffe, associate professor of practice in wildlife and conservation medicine, who has partnered with the World Wildlife Fund to help preserve the Javan and Sumatran rhinoceroses in Indonesia, and with the Jane Goodall Institute in the Republic of Congo and Uganda to protect great apes. Doug Antczak, the Dorothy Havemeyer McConville Professor of Equine Medicine, led a research project on Arabian horse genetics in Saudi Arabia. Jarra Jagne, associate professor of practice in the Department of Public and Ecosystem Health, has trained farmers in Southeast Asia, central Asia, and Africa on the fundamentals of good poultry management and trained local veterinarians in avian influenza outbreak response. David Russell, William

Kaplan Professor of Infection Biology, partnered with researchers in South Africa and Malawi to develop new drug treatments for tuberculosis and HIV.[7]

Cornell's major international program for students is Expanding Horizons, founded in the 1980s.[8] More recently, many Cornell veterinary students have gained overseas experience working with FARVets (Field, Abroad, Reaching-Out Veterinarians) International, a nonprofit organization that "promotes animal welfare domestically and abroad through sterilization, wellness and education."[9] Working alongside animal welfare partners in needy places abroad and in the United States, FARVets addresses overpopulation issues, educates about pet health and wellness and the human/animal bond, and provides a meaningful international experience for veterinary students. The program assists local animal welfare organizations abroad to increase animal welfare awareness via pet education, vaccination programs, medical treatments, and sterilization surgery clinics to address overpopulation. It provides students with an international service-learning experience in different languages, cultures, and socioeconomic circumstances. The students' typical weeklong program includes wellness procedures such as physical examinations, vaccinations, parasite control, and other medical procedures as necessary and possible. Cornell veterinary students have traveled to Mexico, Belize, Grenada, Costa Rica, Nicaragua, and Bulgaria as part of the program.

Before attending CVM, FARVets board member Jami Landry (DVM 2017) spent five years as the senior animal cruelty investigator for the Dutchess County SPCA in New York. While there, she developed a deeper appreciation of pet overpopulation and the need for low-cost veterinary services to serve low-income pet owners. Landry first joined FARVets on a trip to Chetumal, Mexico, as a licensed veterinary technician. In that and subsequent trips to Playa del Carmen, Puerto Morelos, Chetumal in Nicaragua, and Bulgaria, she has redesigned and modernized anesthetic and surgical protocols. She worked to make FARVets a contributor to research that would benefit international aid groups. Public health graduate student Mariacamila Garcia Estrella "visited Honduras with FARVets to help out in a sterilization clinic for dogs and cats and provided educational outreach in schools to teach about responsible pet ownership, illegal pet trade and rabies prevention."[10]

Veterinary faculty members George Kollias Jr. and Jamie Morrisey organized Techniques in International Wildlife, a CVM program that provides veterinary students the opportunity to learn about various nonnative species and gain hands-on experience working with these animals in wildlife sanctuaries, refuges, and bioparks in developing nations, currently Honduras and Belize, during winter and summer breaks. Coursework at the Tropical Education Center complements fieldwork. A student group, Veterinarians Internationally Developing Animal Health, furthers the interest of students through presentations by other students returning from abroad and speakers from national organizations involved in international veterinary medicine.

Lorin D. Warnick, Austin O. Hooey Dean of CVM, highlighted the importance of the internationalization of the college in a 2018 message: "Global events can now quickly impact us here at home—whether it be economic effects, movement of animals and people, transmission of disease or distribution and production of food. Our faculty and students must be involved internationally to work successfully in this highly linked world. Finally, our experience can benefit many around the world, and we are in turn enriched by the knowledge of international colleagues who work and study here in Ithaca. I believe it is essential that we preserve these international connections."[11]

Notes

1. Ellis Leonard, *A Cornell Heritage: Veterinary Medicine, 1868–1908* (Ithaca: New York State College of Veterinary Medicine, 1979), 31.

2. Leonard, 13.

3. Philip M. Teigen, "Law, James (1838–1921), Veterinarian, Educator, and Public Health Advocate," in *American National Biography* (New York: Oxford University Press, 1999).

4. Donald W. Baker, Myron G. Fincher, and Dorsey W. Bruner, "William Arthur Hagan," Memorial Statements of the University Faculty, Office of the Dean of the University Faculty, Cornell University, 1963, https://hdl.handle.net/1813/18636.

5. Lauren Cahoon Roberts and Melanie Greaver Cordova, "Faculty around the Globe," *'Scopes: Making a World of Difference, 2018 Annual Report*, Fall 2018, https://www.vet.cornell.edu/scopes/issues/2018-fall/faculty-around-globe/.

6. For more about Cornell in Bhutan, see chapter 18, Asia's Last Shangri La: Cornell's Engagement with Bhutan.

7. Roberts and Cordova, "Faculty around the Globe."

8. For more about the Expanding Horizons program, see chapter 53, Expanding Horizons: Veterinary Students Explore Their Profession and the World.

9. "Welcome to FARVets," Field, Abroad, Reaching-Out Veterinarians homepage, accessed October 28, 2023, https://www.farvets.org/.

10. "M.P.H. Student Makes Global Impact with FARVets," College of Veterinary Medicine, Cornell University, January 31, 2019, https://www.vet.cornell.edu/news/20190131/mph-student-makes-global-impact-farvets/.

11. Lorin D. Warnick, "Dean's Message," *'Scopes: Making a World of Difference, 2018 Annual Report*, Fall 2018, https://www.vet.cornell.edu/scopes/issues/2018-fall/deans-message/.

36. WEILL CORNELL MEDICINE
A Medical Campus Reaching across the World

Royal D. Colle

Over the past century, Weill Cornell Medicine (WCM)[1] has built a robust global health program, spanning a wide range of educational, clinical, and research initiatives. Early WCM faculty members and medical students embarked on projects in various parts of the world without the formal structure of an international program, and students from abroad were able to participate in clinical electives ranging from four to six weeks. Throughout its existence, the medical college's international initiatives have been multifaceted, including research and institution building, technical assistance, patient care, and medical training. As Antonio M. Gotto Jr., former dean of WCM, said, "We know that all the world is our hospital, our laboratory, and our classroom."[2]

In 1979, to formalize its commitment to global health, and supported by a gift from Stavros S. Niarchos, the Greek shipping tycoon, WCM established the Division of International Medicine. In 1995, the division incorporated infectious diseases and the college's AIDS program in its mandate and was renamed the Division of International Medicine and Infectious Diseases. Dean Gotto established WCM's Office of Global Health Education in 2004 to oversee the college's international educational programs for students, since renamed the Office of International Medical Student Education. The university-wide Global Health Program was announced in 2007, led by WCM and the Division of Nutritional Sciences at Ithaca, but also connecting with faculty in Cornell's Colleges of Arts and Sciences, Agriculture and Life Sciences, Human Ecology, and Veterinary Medicine.

Major International Programs

International programs have involved monumental research and institution-building activities in developing countries such as Brazil, Haiti, and Tanzania.

Figure 36.1 New York Hospital-Cornell Medical Center in the 1930s. (Provided by Medical Center Archives of New York-Presbyterian/Weill Cornell Medicine)

These represent the earliest formal attempts in WCM's history to build health and medical capacity abroad. In 1964 in Brazil, physicians Benjamin H. Kean, E. Hugh Luckey, and Edward W. Hook established a relationship with Brazil's Federal University of Bahia that reflects the approach characterizing many of WCM's programs abroad—an exchange in which partners each benefit from and contribute to the programs. Professor of tropical medicine Warren D. Johnson Jr. has noted that the Cornell-Bahia collaboration may be the longest collaboration of its type in the world today and a model for WCM's commitment to the education of medical personnel in the developing world. Bahia has the facilities and patient population for the training and research in infectious diseases, and WCM provides the training in clinical and basic sciences needed by Bahia's School of Medicine. More than 350 Cornell students, residents, fellows, and faculty members have participated in Cornell-Bahia programs, and more than 250 peer-reviewed journal publications have emerged from the research.[3] Supported by the Commonwealth Fund, this long-lasting collaboration opened the way for the establishment of Cornell's Tropical Medicine Research Center.

One of the first projects of the Division of International Medicine was the Cornell-Thailand Program under the leadership of founding director Thomas C. Jones. At the suggestion of medical resident Theodore C. Li (MD 1977), Cornell responded to the massive medical crisis on Thailand's border that included

Figure 36.2 Salzburg Cornell seminar participants in 1995. (Provided by Medical Center Archives of New York-Presbyterian/Weill Cornell Medicine)

malnutrition, malaria, and infectious diseases of all kinds. Political unrest and violence in Cambodia had sent refugees streaming into refugee camps across the border. An eighteen-member WCM team, consisting of eight nurses, five medical students, three residents, and two faculty members, was posted to Khao-I-Dang refugee camp under the overall administration of the International Rescue Committee, a New York–based nongovernmental organization mostly funded by the US government. Using a rotation system, ultimately fifty medical students, fifty nurses, forty medical residents, and ten faculty members from WCM and other universities contributed.

In addition to helping provide twenty-four-hour emergency service covering a wide range of critical medical problems for the refugees, the WCM team initiated a camp-wide education program for health workers, including key medical problems such as vitamin deficiencies, unusual manifestations of infection, and tropical diseases. The WCM team also provided a series of lectures to the Cambodian assistants on all aspects of health care epidemiology and intervention treatment. Patient care, education of local health people, and experiential medical school learning were all part of the experience.

In 1993, WCM launched the Salzburg-Cornell Seminars in collaboration with the American Austrian Foundation, primarily as a way to bring medical knowledge to physicians from central and eastern Europe. The training allows doctors to update their skills on an ongoing basis without having to emigrate from their countries, thus preventing *brain drain* and promoting *brain gain*. Since the first seminar in cardiology in 1993, WCM faculty members affiliated with the New York-Presbyterian Hospital, Memorial Sloan Kettering Cancer Center, and the Hospital for Special Surgery have volunteered their time to teach these intensive one-week seminars. In 2005, the Open Medical Institute was established to oversee the Salzburg seminars and additional medical programs developed by the American Austrian Foundation.

WCM's Office of International Medical Student Education, initially led by inaugural director Madelon Finkel, greatly expanded the number of international programs available to WCM medical students. Clinical, educational, and research opportunities enabled WCM medical students to experience firsthand how medicine is delivered in low- and middle-income country settings. Formal memos of understanding were signed with many countries to create a bilateral medical student exchange program. The United States–European Union Medical Educational Exchange program was the first to be established, providing bilateral student exchanges with WCM and Harvard Medical School in the United States and medical schools in Denmark, Germany, and England. Over the years, the medical student clinical exchange program that WCM administered has expanded to include more than ten medical schools around the world.

The Max Kade Foundation program, based in Vienna, Austria, enables WCM medical students to participate in clinical electives as well as to learn about the Austrian health care system. An exchange program with the University of Sydney in Australia allows students to obtain both an urban and a rural clinical experience, with students being placed in rural hospitals in Broken Hill and Dubbo in the Australian Outback. The Klinikum rechts der Isar/Technischen Universität program in Germany encompasses both student and faculty exchanges. In addition, WCM has international affiliation agreements with several institutions around the world, including the American Hospital of Paris (France), the American Hospital in Istanbul (Turkey), the Hallym University Medical Center (South Korea), and the Weill Bugando School of Medicine (Tanzania).

Creating a Medical School in East Africa

In 2001, WCM undertook the challenge of building the capacity of a medical school in Tanzania. The WCM board of overseers (now known as the board of fellows) decided to become part of the founding team of the fifth fully accredited medical school in Tanzania's Bugando University College of Health Sciences (BUCHS), which was a joint venture of the Roman Catholic Church and the Tanzanian Ministry of Health. It was based at the Bugando Medical Center (BMC) site. It was reported that "with significant financial contributions from Weill Cornell, Joan and Sanford Weill, and the Citigroup Foundation among others, the Bugando medical school opened in September 2003. . . . The Weills were honored in Mwanza with a lively celebration of songs, dances, speeches, and the unveiling of a new sign bearing their name. Several Weill Cornell faculty members attended, along with government officials and hundreds of staff and students from Bugando."[4]

Support from the TOUCH (Training Our Underdeveloped Countries' Healers) Foundation, established in 2004 with the support of the Citigroup Foundation and the Weills' private foundation, enabled WCM to address the educational needs of BUCHS. In February 2004, Sanford Weill, Citigroup chairman and WCM board member, and his wife, Joan, led a delegation of key US institutional supporters to observe the progress at BUCHS, and, partly as a result, in early 2006 WCM established a formal affiliation with BMC in Mwanza, Tanzania. A Weill BUCHS and BMC project involved improving and organizing the existing surgical curriculum for undergraduate medical students, emphasizing scheduled bedside teaching, and providing training in basic surgical procedures and surgical subspecialty techniques for residents and attending surgeons in neurosurgery.

When Sanford Weill retired from Citigroup leadership in 2006, Citigroup gave $5 million to TOUCH for its efforts at Bugando. In honor of the Weills' support, the Tanzanian Episcopal Conference named the Mwanza complex the Weill Bugando School of Medicine, which includes Weill Bugando University of Health Sciences and Weill Bugando Medical Center. The collaboration between WCM and Weill Bugando goes beyond the common name they share. It not only provides training for the next generation of Tanzanian physicians and scientists but also experiences for WCM faculty members and medical students from New York.[5]

WCM Faculty Outreach

Some international activities have been largely the result of individual efforts rather than a systematic institutional attempt. For example, Henry Murray, professor of medicine, established his own lab at WCM in the 1990s to do research on visceral leishmaniasis, a fatal disease transmitted by sand flies that is endemic in sixty-two countries and especially prevalent in the rural communities of India, Bangladesh, and Nepal. With the exception of malaria, visceral leishmaniasis kills more people than any other parasitic disease. A medical researcher from India offered Murray the opportunity to extend his research into a remote spot in Bihar, India, a geographic area where visceral leishmaniasis was prevalent. Through years of collaboration and with relatively few resources, by 2008 the modest initiative had resulted in a major Indian tropical medical research enterprise where Cornell medical students now complete internships.

Global Health Electives

The Office of Global Health Education formalized the involvement of Cornell medical students in activities abroad, offering students in their first and fourth years the opportunity to take a clinical elective abroad. Thanks to generous donors, fellowships were established to pay for students' international travel. Students spend six to eight weeks in a clinical or community health setting, or in a research project under the mentorship of the host researcher. Not only do participating students broaden their perspectives on health, illness, and health care delivery in other countries, they also gain an appreciation of cultural diversity and a greater understanding of local and epidemiological consequences of disease and the determinants of health and disease. After her first year at WCM, Anastasia Grivoyannis, in the WCM class of 2011, spent an international elective in the obstetrics ward of the Kilimanjaro Christian Medical University College in Tanzania, where she conducted research on HIV transmission from mother to child. She was challenged by electricity shortages, delivering babies by flashlight, and the difficulties the facility had in maintaining donated state-of-the-art equipment such as CT scanners.[6]

The Fogarty International Clinical Research Scholars Program, with WCM sites in Haiti and Brazil, helps students at WCM and other medical schools incorporate an international experience in their medical training. Ashita Batavia, WCM class of 2009 and the first Cornellian to receive a Fogarty Fellowship, took a year off from medical studies to do research at a tertiary-care HIV hospital in Chennai, India. In addition, Cornell's decade-old United States–European Union Medical Education Exchange enables WCM students annually to learn about the host country's health care system. The program now includes medical schools in Edinburgh, London, Munich, Stockholm, and Madrid. This is a bilateral program, as medical students from those countries take clinical electives at WCM and learn about the US health care system. Students in the exchange prepare a final report, describing the medical conditions of the patients assigned to them at the beginning of the elective and the health insurance policies that the patients have.

A Medical Campus Reaches across the World

WCM has been a global force in the health field for decades, ranging from the formation of Weill Cornell Medicine–Qatar[7] to its role in AIDS research in Haiti and in the formation of the Haitian Study Group on Kaposi's Sarcoma and Opportunistic Infections—a nongovernmental institution whose mission is to provide service, training, and research that has the potential to improve health care in Haiti.

WCM was also among the founding members of the International Health Medical Education Consortium, a group of medical colleges committed to global health education, research, and service. In 1991, a small group of faculty and administrators interested in international health formed the consortium with the goal of sharing information about appropriate sites, curriculum, and evaluation for student experiences abroad. In 2005, the International Health Medical Education Consortium changed its name to the Global Health Education Consortium to reflect the consortium's desire to include other health professions besides medicine and a preference for the more inclusive term "global" over the traditional "international," expressing an approach to health issues that transcend national borders, class, race, ethnicity, and culture.

WCM has reached out across the globe from its Manhattan home to strengthen the health infrastructures of many nations, train health professionals, address diseases prevalent in the host countries, build medical knowledge, and work with the host colleagues to provide health care for innumerable people from Brazil to Tanzania. "Reaching out," as various WCM faculty members have suggested, has a new meaning in the age of globalization: there is increasing emphasis on learning from colleagues abroad and exchanging knowledge with health professionals from across the world.

Notes

This chapter is an adaptation of a longer piece on Cornell's eCommons, titled "The Weill Cornell Medical College," in *Cornell University—The Global Dimension* (2008), https://ecommons.cornell.edu/handle/1813/11117. Joan May and faculty and staff at Weill Cornell Medicine were major contributors to the original document. Madelon Finkel, retired professor of population health sciences at Weill Cornell Medicine, contributed to this version.

1. Weill Cornell Medicine was formerly known as the Cornell University Medical College and Weill Cornell Medical College.

2. Antonio M. Gotto Jr., "All the World," *Weill Cornell Medicine*, Winter 2007, 2, https://news.weill.cornell.edu/sites/default/files/publications/winter_2007.pdf.

3. Warren D. Johnson Jr. is the B. H. Kean Professor of Tropical Medicine and director of the Division of International Medicine and Infectious Diseases.

4. Tobin Levy, "25,000:1," *Weill Cornell Medicine*, Winter 2007, 36, https://news.weill.cornell.edu/sites/default/files/publications/winter_2007.pdf.

5. Weill Bugando Medical Center, Weill Cornell Medicine International Affairs, accessed November 4, 2023, https://internationalaffairs.weill.cornell.edu/global-impact/key-initiatives/weill-bugando-medical-center%E2%80%8B.

6. Beth Saulnier, "Mother's Helper," *Weill Cornell Medicine*, Winter 2007, 15–16, https://news.weill.cornell.edu/sites/default/files/publications/winter_2007.pdf.

7. For more about Cornell in Qatar, see chapter 37, Weill Cornell Medicine–Qatar: Excellence Grown from the Sands.

37. WEILL CORNELL MEDICINE–QATAR

Excellence Grown from the Sands

Marco Ameduri

I remember us bumping over desert ground in our rented SUVs in spring of 2003, wearing hard hats and yellow vests, from our Weill Cornell Medical College–Qatar rooms in the high school, Qatar Academy, glancing across at the shell of our future campus, which we were visiting for the first time. We all had hope that we were building something that would make a difference, but I don't think any of us had an idea how much impact we could make in less than twenty years.

Emerging from the Sands

In March 2003, construction was progressing at a fantastic pace on one of the first campus buildings in Qatar's new Education City. This would be the home of the first overseas campus of Weill Cornell Medicine (WCM, then Weill Cornell Medical College), an initiative that had started just four years earlier and that would ultimately revolutionize medical education and research in the Middle East and shape global health care knowledge during the COVID-19 pandemic within a couple of decades. Ameduri was one of a small number of faculty and staff tasked with establishing the new medical school.

In 1999, Her Highness Sheikha Moza bint Nasser, consort of His Highness Sheikh Hamad bin Khalifa Al Thani, then emir of the State of Qatar, was advocating for increased investment in education in Qatar and across the world. She had founded the Qatar Foundation for Education, Science and Community Development with the aim of growing and modernizing Qatar through education and research. At the time, Qatar did not have a medical school; Qataris who wished to study medicine had to travel overseas. Sheikha Moza aimed to change this.

In March that year, US congresswomen Carolyn Maloney and Sue Kelly were in Doha, Qatar, to witness the first elections in a Gulf nation in which women were fully participating. During their visit, they met Sheikha Moza, who shared her vision for Qatar and asked the congresswomen whether they could

Figure 37.1 Her Highness Sheikha Moza bint Nasser with the first graduating class of Weill Cornell Medicine–Qatar in 2008. (Provided by Weill Cornell Medicine–Qatar)

recommend a US medical school that would be interested in establishing a campus in Doha's new Education City. They recommended WCM. Discussions with Cornell began almost immediately, and by January 2001 the Cornell University board of trustees and the WCM board of overseers approved the final contract with Qatar Foundation, founding what was initially called Weill Cornell Medical College in Qatar, now Weill Cornell Medicine–Qatar (WCM-Q).

Speaking at the time, WCM dean Antonio M. Gotto Jr. noted, "Thirty years from now, I hope that this will be looked back upon as a legacy for Cornell University and Weill Cornell Medicine—that we have made a positive impact in medicine and education in partnership with Qatar Foundation."[1]

The opening of the new medical school might have been threatened by the terrorist attacks of September 11, 2001. However, the chairman of the WCM board of overseers, Sanford Weill, was determined to overcome these challenges. He believed that the September 11 attacks highlighted the value of education and health care outreach offered by the new medical school. Weill said, "It's perhaps more important that we do this now than ever before."[2]

Testament to the determination of the Qatari and US teams to ensure the realization of this new collaboration, the first students started in WCM-Q in September 2002, less than two years after the agreement was signed. The foundations for the new medical school campus in Education City were just being laid, so its students and faculty had to use rooms in the nearby high school, Qatar Academy, while they waited for construction to be completed.

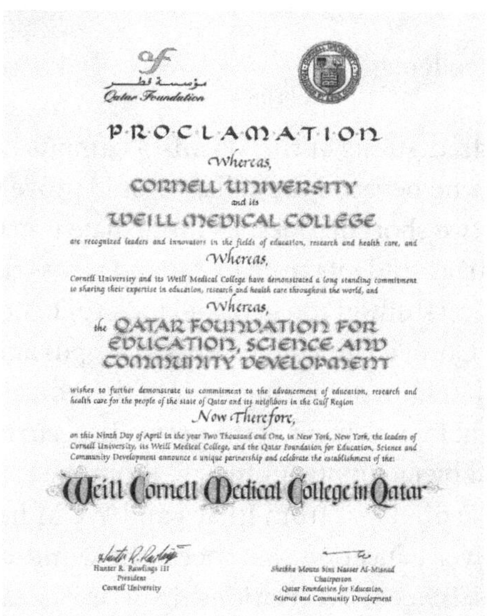
مؤسسة قطر
Qatar Foundation

PROCLAMATION

Whereas,

CORNELL UNIVERSITY
and its
WEILL MEDICAL COLLEGE

are recognized leaders and innovators in the fields of education, research and health care, and

Whereas,

Cornell University and its Weill Medical College have demonstrated a long standing commitment to sharing their expertise in education, research and health care throughout the world, and

Whereas,

the QATAR FOUNDATION FOR EDUCATION, SCIENCE AND COMMUNITY DEVELOPMENT

wishes to further demonstrate its commitment to the advancement of education, research and health care for the people of the state of Qatar and its neighbors in the Gulf Region

Now Therefore,

on this Ninth Day of April in the year Two Thousand and One, in New York, New York, the leaders of Cornell University, its Weill Medical College, and the Qatar Foundation for Education, Science and Community Development announce a unique partnership and celebrate the establishment of the:

Weill Cornell Medical College in Qatar

Hunter R. Rawlings III
President
Cornell University

Sheikha Mouza bint Nasser Al-Misnad
Chairperson
Qatar Foundation for Education, Science and Community Development

Figure 37.2 Proclamation establishing Weill Cornell Medical College in Qatar, signed by Hunter R. Rawlings III, Cornell University president, and Her Highness Sheikha Moza bint Nasser, chairperson, Qatar Foundation for Education, Science and Community Development. (Provided by Weill Cornell Medicine–Qatar)

Khalid Alkhelaifi (MD 2008) recalled the atmosphere as a student in the new medical school: "I remember the first day when we went in. There were a lot of high school and primary school students walking around. It was on the second floor, a small area for Weill Cornell Medical College, three or four rooms, classes, and a lab. There were a few laptops there, computers, and that was the end of it. I remember a few of our colleagues withdrew because they didn't feel like there was a future for this project. But me and the rest of my classmates who finished, we believed in this project."[3] Alkhelaifi is now a sports orthopedic surgeon at Aspetar in Qatar and assistant professor at WCM-Q.

Those early days of WCM-Q were focused on completing the new campus and establishing the premedical and medical programs. The new campus, designed by world-renowned Japanese architect Arata Isozaki, was emerging from the desert sands, combining Islamic architectural features and state-of-the-art medical school facilities in a landmark building.

The new WCM-Q campus was officially inaugurated on October 13, 2003, at an event presided over by the emir and Sheikha Moza. "Usually, when we celebrate the opening of a new project in Qatar, people tend to think that it is related to energy or industry," said Sheikh Hamad bin Khalifa Al Thani at the inauguration. "Today, however, we are celebrating an event that surpasses in its significance any economic or industrial project, however large it may be."[4]

Proving Enduring Excellence

Among the five hundred guests at the WCM-Q campus inauguration in 2003, there were likely few who believed the college would prove its global impact and resilience within just two short decades. Its immediate impact on medical education in Qatar was clear, as students from Qatar and across the region were admitted to its program, successfully graduated, and took residencies around the world.

Faculty from both Cornell University's Ithaca campus and WCM were integral to the success of WCM-Q in achieving its initial medical education mandate. For instance, the psychology element of the premedical curriculum was, and continues to be, delivered by faculty from Ithaca. From the earliest days of the new medical school, course directors from Ithaca and WCM have worked alongside peers in Qatar to deliver education that meets the world-class standards set by the home institutions. Indeed, the relationship between leadership at Qatar and the School of Continuing Education in Ithaca, under the leadership of Charles W. Jermy Jr., was vital to the establishment and ongoing evolution of the important premedical and foundation curricula in WCM-Q.

Once the medical education program was established, the college had another vital remit to fulfill: the delivery of world-class medical research. Sheikha Moza had clearly identified the importance of research in her earliest discussions with WCM administrators, noting, "We want to generate new knowledge."[5] This position clearly aligned with WCM's own ethos, which placed research at the heart of its medical school activities.

WCM-Q appointed Javaid Sheikh as vice-dean of research in early 2006, and he worked with colleagues in WCM to create a plan for initiating research at the Qatar campus, which was generously funded by Qatar Foundation in 2007. These pivotal moments saw the college embrace research within its activities and had an immediate impact on the provision of health care in Qatar and the region. Within a few short years, a research project to map the Qatari genome was completed by a team from WCM-Q, WCM, and Hamad Medical Corporation in Doha led by Ronald Crystal, informing population health care delivery in Qatar. Other research initiatives led to new insights in infectious diseases, cholesterol metabolism, children's health, and clinical epidemiology for cancer and diabetes.

The first dean of WCM-Q, Daniel Alonso, having formed successful partnerships in education and clinical training across Qatar, decided to retire after the graduation in 2008 of WCM-Q's first medical school class. Javaid Sheikh was subsequently appointed acting dean of WCM-Q in January 2009 and as permanent dean in January 2010. At his appointment, Sheikh said, "We are participating in a renaissance of science and education in the Middle East that will make a great contribution to the health and well-being of the people of Qatar, the Gulf region and the world."[6]

And so it proved. A decade later, in March 2020, the World Health Organization (WHO) declared the COVID-19 outbreak a pandemic. Facing a challenge unlike anything in its less than two-decade-long history, WCM-Q thrived. Its staff and faculty, and many of its returned alumni, played an immediate role in shaping Qatar's response to the pandemic under the leadership of Her Excellency Hanan Mohamed Al Kuwari, minister of public health. This science-driven response led to recognition from the WHO.

WCM-Q continued to fully operate, albeit remotely, during the pandemic. Faculty and staff rapidly and seamlessly transitioned their activities online, professional development opportunities for health care professionals in the region grew in number, and consistent informative health messages under the aegis of WCM-Q's Institute for Population Health were developed and delivered for the local community.

However, it was in its research activities that the college truly shone during the pandemic. From a college that had not existed twenty years earlier, more than fifty COVID-19 WCM-Q studies were published. Among those, two were in the *Journal of the American Medical Association*, two in *Nature Medicine*, and eight in the *New England Journal of Medicine*, ranking among the most-viewed publications on their website. These publications informed guidelines from the WHO and the US Centers for Disease Control, among others.

WCM-Q's Infectious Disease Epidemiology Group (IDEG), led by WCM-Q professor of infectious disease epidemiology Laith Abu-Raddad, was designated a WHO Collaborating Center in July 2020, in recognition of a decade of high-profile studies on the epidemiology of infectious diseases on the national, regional, and international levels, including COVID-19. The WHO Collaborating Center was inaugurated by Sheikha Moza and Minister Al Kuwari, with the latter saying, "The members of the IDEG are doing fantastic work with senior experts and officials in the Ministry of Public Health and at HMC [Hamad Medical Corporation] to ensure we minimize the spread of the coronavirus in the State of Qatar. Being awarded World Health Organization Collaborating Centre status on WCM-Q is a huge achievement, and further strengthens Qatar's ability to fight infectious diseases that affect communities all over the [eastern Mediterranean region] and beyond."[7]

In our earliest days, we knew we were doing something important. We believed in the ambitions of Qatar and Cornell. But I don't think any of us truly realized how far the reach of WCM-Q could extend. We have now graduated more than five hundred doctors, many of whom have gone on to shape healthcare delivery in Qatar and the region, and we have demonstrated our ability to build a deep and meaningful relationship with the local community, while conducting world-class research with immediate impact. If we can do this when we've only just begun, when those days driving past a shell of a building still seem like yesterday, then I can't even begin to think what we can, and will, do in the future.

With twenty years now passed since its first students entered Qatar Academy, WCM-Q is still a relatively young and ambitious institution. Javaid Sheikh, the longest-serving dean in Education City, commented, "COVID-19 provided a timely test of the strength of our foundations and structure. Our school has proven that our reputation as a contributor to the education and health of local and regional populations is deserved and that our contribution to science has tangible impact. We know we can continue to build the reputation of the Cornell campus in Qatar toward becoming an iconic institution."[8]

Notes

1. Scott McMurray, *Weill Cornell Medicine-Qatar: Global Pioneers in Healthcare* (Washington, DC: History Factory, 2018).
2. McMurray.
3. Khalid Alkhelaifi, personal interview with author, April 12, 2022.
4. McMurray, *Weill Cornell Medicine-Qatar.*
5. McMurray.
6. McMurray.
7. "WCM-Q to Support WHO," *Qatar Chronicle*, Winter 2020, 28–29.
8. Javaid Sheikh, personal interview with author, April 25, 2023.

38. CORNELL INTERNATIONAL EDUCATION NETWORK

A Home for International Educators

Heike Michelsen

By the early 1990s, more and more faculty and students across the university were engaged internationally, and the university was welcoming more and more international students and scholars. Yet Cornell lacked a central space to exchange information and experiences. Staff in international education emerged as a driving force to connect staff and faculty in diverse units engaged in international efforts.

The Mario Einaudi Center for International Studies, led at that time by Davydd J. Greenwood, oversaw the International Students and Scholars Office and Cornell Abroad, as well as the faculty-led Area Studies and Thematic Studies programs. Jerry Wilcox, the director of the office, borrowed the idea of forming an information-sharing network of international education from the University of Maryland, College Park. "My goal was to make sure disparate providers throughout campus outside of the student affairs silo could meet and share."[1] He developed a list of potential participants and invited them to attend meetings to share information. This was the launch of the Cornell International Education Network (CIEN).

CIEN's mandate was, and remains today, to promote resource sharing and professional development among staff and faculty working in international education. Any staff or faculty members with an interest in international education can join the network. Today, CIEN has more than two hundred members, mostly professional staff representing a broad cross section of the university.

"What makes CIEN unique is that it focuses on giving Cornell staff a meaningful way to learn from and support each other's [international education] work across all colleges of the university," reflects Lani Peck, former associate director of the Einaudi Center. "I don't know of any other networking group like it on campus. Faculty and students have numerous opportunities for sharing ideas and collaborating on projects, but in my many years at Cornell, I rarely found staff being encouraged to network across departments, let alone colleges, in the way CIEN afforded."[2]

Figure 38.1 Cornell International Education Network meeting with Einaudi Center director Nicolas van de Walle (*center right*) and David Wippman (*center left*), vice provost for International Relations, 2007. (Photo by author)

Beginning in 1991, between twenty and forty network members met in person once a month during the semester. While the monthly meetings created strong personal connections and collaborations, those who were not working on the Ithaca campus or were not able to attend the meetings could not reap these benefits.

In spring 2020, when COVID-19 forced the university to move online, CIEN followed suit. The online meetings brought a new dimension and widened the network significantly. Since then, participation has tripled, with more than sixty members attending each meeting. Most online meetings incorporate networking by including both small and large group discussions. Small breakout groups of three to six people toward the end of the meeting enable anybody interested to connect over topics sometimes related to the meeting and sometimes informal.[3]

Leaders

CIEN is a member-run network. Members volunteer to be appointed as one of two cochairs every year. The current cochairs decide who will serve the following year. Cochairs must have been network members for at least two years, and it is recommended that the chairs are from two different Cornell units, with one cochair coming from Global Cornell units.[4]

Leaders of CIEN have represented the diversity of its active members. For more than thirty years, forty-eight professionals have cochaired CIEN, representing twenty-four different units and colleges across campus. About half of those were part of Global Cornell. About 20 percent were from six colleges (Agriculture and Life Sciences, Arts and Sciences, Industrial and Labor Relations, the SC Johnson College of Business, the Law School, and the Graduate School). About a third were from campus-wide units, including the Intensive English Program, the Center for Teaching Innovation, the Cornell University Library, Engaged Cornell, the Language Resource Center, Career Services, and Cornell Health.[5]

Topics

Cochairs organize between six and nine meetings with different focuses and guest speakers during each academic year. CIEN has held more than two hundred meetings since it launched in 1991. Recognizing the changes at Cornell and in the world, topics and speakers have varied from year to year. While there were some topics and speakers of continued relevance, a review identified more than 120 topics related to international studies, learning, and engagement that were featured at CIEN meetings.[6]

"Staying abreast of the changing needs of the international student and scholar population at Cornell, of the needs to support the teaching and research of this world university is quite a challenge," asserted Beatrice B. Szekely, former associate director of Cornell Abroad. "Taking a lead in providing information and circulating has been a great achievement of CIEN and one that will surely be taken forward."[7]

The first meeting of the academic year typically focuses on networking, sharing information among members, and introducing and welcoming new members. Members give detailed updates about what happened over the summer in their units, such as orientation programs, events, and summer courses and programs; updates on enrollments; and plans for the coming year, such as special events, projects, initiatives, publications, and new strategic directions.

There are clusters of teaching, research, and service activities on campus for which CIEN has provided a much-needed forum, including

- general policies on international travel and risk management, international agreements and memoranda of understanding, and residential initiatives
- services for international students and scholars, including immigration and visa updates, orientation programs, financial aid, academic assistance, and career advising

- services for students going abroad, such as advising, predeparture programs, specific teaching and learning programs, and opportunities abroad
- health- and safety-related policies and insurance for traveling faculty and students
- international and global research, teaching, and outreach programs and initiatives, including exchange programs, foreign language programs, and service and community-based learning programs

Other sessions focused on updates on the international dimensions of admissions, student organizations, government affairs, athletics and physical education, crisis management, religious life, libraries, performing and media arts, and new communication and technology tools. There have also been sessions on professional development for CIEN members, notably on improving intercultural learning and communications. All these topics and many more were areas of shared interest and have been addressed at CIEN meetings. Finally, CIEN provides a forum for updates from professional organizations, particularly the National Association of Foreign Student Advisers: Association of International Educators and the Association of International Education Administrators.

Topics have been presented by faculty and staff directors and other professionals from different units, sometimes complemented by panels of students reflecting on their experiences. Meetings with Cornell's administrative leaders as guest speakers were particularly well attended. After the creation of the Office of the Vice Provost for International Relations in 2004 (now the Office of the Vice Provost for International Affairs), the vice provost became a regular guest speaker. Together with the director of the Einaudi Center, the provost addressed strategic plans and changes affecting the internationalization of Cornell. Several times, leaders from other local higher education institutions, including Ithaca College, the State University of New York at Cortland, Tompkins Cortland Community College, and Wells College, were invited to discuss international programs and initiatives at their respective institutions.

Despite the relevance of these presentations, many would argue that the networking opportunity at the beginning or end of each CIEN meeting, talking over coffee and comparing notes on current news and other issues, has added significantly to the value of the meetings.

"The presentations were always very well done, we learned a lot about various topics or programs at Cornell, but the discussions which the presentations generated were most valuable," said Brendan O'Brien, former director of the International Students and Scholars Office. "It was perhaps the only meeting that I hated to see come to an end. . . . Frequently people would linger, and much was accomplished during the informal meetings after the meetings."[8]

Key Reasons for Success

CIEN remains a rather informal network. Its complex web of social ties formed as colleagues communicated, and these ties have solidified over time into a surprisingly stable network. CIEN represents (a) a communication web across units and hierarchies; (b) an expertise network, as its members can be tapped for advice; (c) a trust network to which members turn with problems, challenges, and opportunities; and (d) a professional development network where members can learn from each other and guest speakers.

CIEN remains a member-run organization. While supported by the Einaudi Center and other units on campus, it never became part of Cornell's institutional structure. Instead, it remains open to all professionals linked to the international dimensions of Cornell, it selects its own leadership, and it sets its own agenda.

According to Davydd Greenwood, many universities, including Cornell, adopted "Taylorism," the dominant industrial organizational model, which divided the universe into disciplines and organized them into colleges, a segmented system of hierarchical power and authority. "CIEN is one of the few examples of a kind of network that is not channeled through the hierarchical structure of universities," he explains. "It permits sharing of information and experiences that otherwise the Tayloristic system cannot access. The amount of energy and knowledge liberated is impressive. Realistically CIEN also works because it meets a real need, and it does not have to raise resources or threaten any of the current power structures."[9]

CIEN remains a learning organization based on participatory approaches. At the end of each year and over the summer, its members reflect on the successes and challenges of the past year, discussing new directions, topics, relevant changes in the university and the world and adjusting the network's strategic direction. Challenges posed by COVID-19 were taken as an opportunity to open CIEN to much broader membership beyond the Ithaca campus.

"We talk a lot about finding a sense of belonging, and the first place I found it at Cornell was with our group of international educators," said Melina Ivanchikova, associate director for inclusive teaching at the Center for Teaching Innovation. "This was a place where people could be proud of their multilingual heritages and commitments, where intercultural skills in action were visible and delightful, where we could engage with each other and learn about each other's backgrounds, interests, and roles."[10]

Assessing Impact

During my sixteen-year tenure at the Einaudi Center, it was through CIEN that I became aware of the many dimensions of international education and engagement at Cornell. The network facilitated many collaborations across campus and was essential in developing, launching, and implementing initiatives such as the international fair, international education week, internationalization symposiums, and many other initiatives.

A CIEN meeting in 2008 featured a discussion about service learning from a range of perspectives, among them ongoing service-learning opportunities for students and service learning from a participant perspective and from an administrative perspective. The discussion inspired a CIEN subgroup who met regularly to advance the university's service-learning activities.

Today, Cornell's internationalization efforts have reached a new peak. Under the leadership of the vice provost for international affairs, a significant expansion of Global Cornell is centrally addressing many of the information needs and providing a wide range of services for staff and faculty linked to the international endeavors of the university. This leads to new thematic foci and directions for CIEN. It seems likely, however, that CIEN will continue to make a significant contribution to resource sharing, to developing professionalism, and to providing a home for international educators.

Notes

I thank the current and former cochairs of the Cornell International Education Network for their comments, insights, and reflections, particularly Davydd J. Greenwood, Melina Ivanchikova, Brendan O'Brien, Lani Peck, Beatrice B. Szekely, Nina Trautmann Chaopricha, and Jerry Wilcox.

1. Jerry Wilcox, former director of the International Students and Scholars Office and inaugural CIEN chair from 1991 to 1992, email correspondence with the author, May 16, 2022.

2. Lani Peck, former associate director of the Einaudi Center and CIEN cochair from 2007 to 2008, email correspondence with the author, April 25, 2022.

3. Nina Trautmann Chaopricha, Ithaca campus manager of the Cornell China Center and CIEN cochair from 2021 to 2022, email correspondence with the author, June 22, 2022.

4. Global Cornell units include the Einaudi Center, Area and Thematic Studies International Programs, the former International Students and Scholars Office, Cornell Abroad, and the Office of the Vice Provost for International Affairs.

5. See Cornell International Education Network, "The CIEN Binder: A Summary of Network Meetings from 1991 to 2019," internal collection of papers, 2022.

6. For a categorization of CIEN topics, see Beatrice B. Szekely, "History of CIEN," unpublished memo prepared for planning and review meeting, May 15, 1997; and Beatrice B. Szekely, "Cornell International Education Network (CIEN): A 13-Year Retrospective," unpublished memo prepared for the April 22, 2004, meeting, both in Cornell International Education Network, "CIEN Binder."

7. Beatrice B. Szekely, former associate director of Cornell Abroad and CIEN cochair from 1992 to 1993, interview with the author, April 27, 2022.

8. Brendan O'Brien, former director of International Students and Scholars Office and CIEN cochair from 1999 to 2000 and 2017 to 2018, email correspondence with the author, April 14, 2022.

9. Davydd J. Greenwood, former director of the Einaudi Center, email correspondence with the author, May 9, 2022.

10. Melina Ivanchikova, associate director for inclusive teaching and CIEN cochair from 2016 to 2017, email correspondence with the author, April 25, 2022.

39. EXPLORING OUR WORLD

Cornell Expeditions

Elaine D. Engst and Blaine Friedlander

Not long after Cornell University opened its doors, professors organized expeditions—and included students in those adventurous research sojourns. Since the very beginning, faculty and students have traveled to each continent and collected insects, plants, artifacts, and photographs.

Exploring Brazil

Charles Frederick Hartt—a student of Harvard's Louis Agassiz and Cornell's first professor of geology—participated in expeditions to Brazil between 1865 and 1878, falling in love with the country. In 1870, accompanied by eleven Cornell students, Hartt organized his own expedition to the Amazon, investigating the geology and animals of the area and the pottery in ancient Indigenous mounds. He later returned to study dialects of the Tupí language, compiling a "large volume on the grammar, vocabulary, and stories, which remains unpublished."[1] In his expeditions, he collected information and specimens primarily relating to geology but including the fossils, flora, fauna, linguistics, and ethnography of Brazil for Cornell and for the National Museum in Rio de Janeiro, and he encouraged Brazilian students to attend Cornell. Hartt gave popular lectures on Brazil, illustrated by large cloth posters. He died of yellow fever in Brazil at the age of thirty-eight and is commemorated at Cornell by a plaque in Sage Chapel. Hartt's collections can be viewed in the Cornell Anthropology Collections, and the Division of Rare and Manuscript Collections holds a collection of his papers and posters.[2]

Greenland Glaciers

Another Cornell geologist, Ralph Stockman Tarr, led an 1896 Arctic expedition around Greenland with then-lieutenant Robert Peary to study glaciers. The Cornell

Figure 39.1 Ethel Zoe Bailey and Liberty Hyde Bailey on the Orinoco River in Venezuela, 1921. (Liberty Hyde Bailey Hortorium Collection, provided by Division of Rare and Manuscript Collections, Cornell University Library)

party included A. C. Gill, professor of mineralogy, and students Thomas Leonard Watson (PhD 1897), Edward Martin Kindle (MS 1896), Jay Allen Bonsteel (class of 1896), and James Otis Martin (class of 1899, MA 1903). While geology was the focus of the expedition, collections of plants, insects, marine invertebrates, and birds were also made.

In August 1896, the *New York Times* reported that on the Cornell portion of the trip—the Peary party and the Cornell party had split up—the steamship *Hope* had hung up on an ice floe along the Greenland coast. But "Prof. Tarr . . . does not intimate that the vessel is in any immediate danger," said the *Times*. The professors and the students continued their exploration, and all aboard made it home safely in September.

In 1906, Tarr accompanied Peary to the Arctic, naming a glacier in Greenland for Cornell, and undertook four expeditions to study glaciers in Alaska. His student and eventual colleague O. D. von Engeln (class of 1908, PhD 1911) joined him on these expeditions in 1906 and 1909. The Cornell Library has digitized about two thousand of Tarr's photographs of glaciated areas in Greenland and Alaska and they are available online. Tarr died in 1912 and is commemorated at Cornell by a portrait plaque on a boulder seat at the southwest corner of McGraw Hall[3] and a stained-glass window in Sage Chapel.[4]

Figure 39.2 As part of her research on funerary culture in Sardis, Professor Annetta Alexandridis reassembles a marble sarcophagus from the third century AD, 2012. (Photo by Nicholas Cahill)

Early Travels in Asia Minor

In the early years of the twentieth century, Cornellians were also active in archaeological expeditions. In 1907, professor of Greek John Robert Sitlington Sterrett organized the fourteenth-month Cornell Expedition to Asia Minor and the Assyro-Babylonian Orient, led by four Cornell alumni: Albert Ten Eyck Olmstead (class of 1902, MA 1903, PhD 1906), fellow in the American School of Classical Studies in Athens; Benson Brush Charles (class of 1906), assistant in Semitics at Cornell; Jesse Erwin Wrench (class of 1906); and Clarence Owen Harris (class of 1898, PhD 1906). According to the *Cornell Alumni News*, "The journey is primarily one of education. . . . They will visit and study ancient sites, take photographs, measure and draw plans of ancient monuments, study the ancient topography and geography of the country, copy inscriptions, locate ancient cities and reconstruct the map of antiquity as far as they can."[5]

The expedition resulted in a collection of photographs, pottery, and, especially, copies of hieroglyphic Luwian (called Hittite at the time) inscriptions, made as "squeezes" by pounding wet paper onto the stone surfaces and allowing it to dry. They initially worked in Ankara at the Roman-era Temple of Augustus to secure a "new squeeze of the famous *Monumentum Ancyranum*, the inscription in which

Augustus gives an account of the main events of his reign."[6] The group then went on to cross the Taurus Mountains, as the expedition's journal describes, "through a fall of snow so thick that one could see only a rod or two in any direction." Once they arrived, the squeeze "froze as soon as it was on and refused to dry although we built a fire just in front. Finally darkness began to come on, and we were obliged to remove the squeeze in order to dry it over the fire. Then, in the darkness . . . we descended the mountain." The group never published the narrative of their journey, but the squeezes have been preserved and digitized and are now available through the Cornell Collections of Antiquities.[7]

Botanical Taxonomy of Palms and More

After his retirement, Liberty Hyde Bailey, dean of Cornell's College of Agriculture, devoted himself to extensive and frequently arduous travel for scientific purposes, observation, and collecting plants. During his first trip to China in 1917, he traveled around the country collecting specimens of trees, ornamental plants, and garden crops, especially *Brassica* (kales, mustards, cabbages, broccoli, cauliflower, etc.). He then went to Trinidad and Venezuela in 1921, to Cuba in 1929, to Hispaniola in 1931, to Guadeloupe and Martinique in 1938, to Mexico in 1940, and to Brazil in 1947. He collected *Brassica* along the coasts of Great Britain and western Europe, from eastern and central China, and from the marketplaces of four continents. Similarly, he collected *Cucurbita* (pumpkins and squash) from the backlands of Mexico, from isolated tribal plots of the Seminole Indians in Florida, and from Panama and northern South America.

But palms were Bailey's particular specialty, and their taxonomy was in disarray. He set out to correct that situation by collecting specimens in Mexico, Panama, Venezuela, Brazil, Colombia, Cuba, and many islands in the West Indies. His work increased the known palm species from seven hundred in 1914 to several thousand by the late 1940s. He spent his nineteenth birthday collecting palms in Grenada and his ninety-first in the West Indies.[8]

Bailey collected numerous specimens and books for his own research, and his more than two hundred thousand specimens represented a unique repository of cultivated plants, along with notes and photographs, to create a permanent record, which he called his "card index of the vegetable world." In 1935, he gave his herbarium and library to Cornell. Currently part of the School of Integrative Plant Science, it now includes the L. H. Bailey Hortorium Herbarium, the Cornell University Plant Anatomy Collection, the Ethel Z. Bailey Horticultural Catalogue Collection, the L. H. Bailey Hortorium Library, and the L. H. Bailey Conservatory.[9]

Continuing Exploration at Sardis

In 1958, with the support of the Turkish government, A. Henry Detweiler, Cornell professor of architecture and associate dean of the College of Architecture, Art, and Planning, joined George M. A. Hanfmann of Harvard in organizing the Archaeological Exploration of Sardis, a new expedition to excavate, research, conserve, and restore buildings at the site of Sardis in what is now western Türkiye, a city that had been the capital of the Iron Age empire of Lydia (seventh and sixth centuries BC) and remained an important city through late antiquity. This multidisciplinary project, with experts in disciplines including archaeology, art history, architecture, anthropology, conservation, numismatics, epigraphy, illustration, photography, geophysics, and history, continues to the present, directed since 2008 by Professor Nicholas Cahill of the University of Wisconsin–Madison.

Longtime associate director and Cornell history of art and archaeology professor emeritus Andrew Ramage made important discoveries in the art and architecture of the Lydians, especially a site for gold refinement and recycling, contemporary with the famous King Croesus.[10] The project also excavated and restored a bath-gymnasium complex, the largest synagogue in the ancient world, and Byzantine shops, as well as Lydian mudbrick fortifications sixty-five feet thick and forty feet high in places, the largest outside Mesopotamia. Excavators have also found what they think were the palaces of the Lydian kings and the largest monumental arch known from the Roman world, which collapsed in the earthquake in 17 AD that brought an end to two millennia of urban settlement at Sardis.[11]

A new biennial Sardis Lecture series, sponsored by the Department of Classics, began in 2020 with an inaugural lecture by Cahill. Introducing the lecture, history of art professor Annetta Alexandridis said, "Situated at the crossroads between the Mediterranean in the west and the Anatolian plateau in the east, the Lydian City of Sardis was a meeting place—a site of conflict and of fruitful exchange—between many different peoples, languages, cultural traditions and religions over centuries. . . . Given the importance of the site and the long-term archaeological engagement with it, I felt that Sardis did not have the prominence within the Cornell population it deserved."[12] Alexandridis continues to work at Sardis, along with Cornell history of art and classics professor Benjamin Anderson, Frances Gallart Marqués (PhD 2014), and, most recently, Hannah Master (class of 2023), as well as other faculty and graduate students from Cornell and around the world, continuing Cornell's tradition of global exploration.

Notes

A version of this chapter appeared as "Cornell Rewind: Exploring Our World and Beyond," by Elaine Engst and Blaine Friedlander, in the *Cornell Chronicle*, September 16, 2015, https://news.cornell.edu/stories/2015/09/cornell-rewind-exploring-our-world-and-beyond.

1. Richard Rathbun, "Sketch of the Life and Scientific Work of Prof. Charles Fred Hartt," *Proceedings of the Boston Society of Natural History* 19 (April 17, 1878): 347.

2. See Charles Frederick Hartt Papers, #14-15-511, Division of Rare and Manuscript Collections, Cornell University Library. Hartt's Amazonian ceramics can be seen in "Collection: Selections from the Cornell Anthropology Collections," Digital Collections, Cornell University Library, accessed October 3, 2023, https://digital.library.cornell.edu/?f%5Barchival_collection_tesim%5D%5B%5D=Amazonian+ceramics&f%5Bcollection_tesim%5D%5B%5D=Selections+from+the+Cornell+Anthropology+Collections.

3. The Ralph Stockman Tarr portrait plaque and boulder seat can be seen at "Ralph Stockman Tarr Portrait Plaque," Digital Collections, Cornell University Library, accessed October 3, 2023, https://digital.library.cornell.edu/catalog/ss:31877545.

4. The Ralph Stockman Tarr memorial window in Sage Chapel can be seen at "Ralph S. Tarr Window," Digital Collections, Cornell University Library, accessed October 3, 2023, https://digital.library.cornell.edu/catalog/ss:31876902. Tarr's glacier photographs are available online in "Historic Glacial Images of Alaska and Greenland," Digital Collections, Cornell University Library, accessed October 3, 2023, https://digital.library.cornell.edu/collections/tarr. See also Ralph Stockman Tarr Papers, #14-15-92, Division of Rare and Manuscript Collections, Cornell University Library; and "Guide to Ralph Stockman Tarr Papers, 1883–1961, 1883–1912 (Bulk), Collection Number: 14-15-92," Division of Rare and Manuscript Collections, Cornell University Library, accessed October 3, 2023, https://rmc.library.cornell.edu/EAD/htmldocs/RMA00092.html.

5. *Cornell Alumni News*, February 27, 1907.

6. The squeezes from the Cornell expedition can be viewed in "Cornell Expedition," Cornell Collections of Antiquities, accessed October 3, 2023, https://antiquities.library.cornell.edu/squeezes/cornell-expedition.

7. "Cornell Expedition." See also J. R. Sitlington Sterrett Papers, #3903, Division of Rare and Manuscript Collections, Cornell University Library.

8. See the online exhibition *Liberty Hyde Bailey: A Man for All Seasons*, Division of Rare and Manuscript Collections, Cornell University Library, 2004, https://rmc.library.cornell.edu/bailey. See also the Liberty Hyde Bailey Papers, #21-2-3342, Division of Rare and Manuscript Collections, Cornell University Library; as well as "BH: North America's Largest Palm Herbarium," L. H. Bailey Hortorium Herbarium, accessed October 3, 2023, http://www.plantsystematics.org/palms/palms.html.

9. For more information about the Bailey Hortorium, see "Bailey Hortorium," School of Integrative Plant Science, Cornell University, accessed October 3, 2023, https://cals.cornell.edu/school-integrative-plant-science/school-sections/plant-biology-section/bailey-hortorium.

10. Franklin Crawford, "Archaeologist Andrew Ramage Strikes Gold Again with New Book," *Cornell Chronicle*, May 11, 2000, https://news.cornell.edu/stories/2000/05/archaeologist-andrew-ramage-strikes-gold-again-new-book.

11. For more information on the Archaeological Exploration of Sardis, see "Digital Resource Center," Archaeological Exploration of Sardis, accessed October 3, 2023, https://sardisexpedition.org/en; "The Palace of Croesus Shines Again," Harvard Art Museums, May 17, 2017, https://harvardartmuseums.org/article/the-palace-of-croesus-shines-again; and Sardis Expedition, "Drone Flight over Sardis: The Roman Arch, Lydian Gate, Bath-Gymnasium Complex, and Synagogue," YouTube video, 7:21, posted October 15, 2015, https://www.youtube.com/watch?v=8x0ipdPFK14.

12. Kate Blackwood, "New Lecture Series Introduces Research at Ancient Sardis," *Cornell Chronicle*, April 1, 2020, https://news.cornell.edu/stories/2020/04/new-lecture-series-introduces-research-ancient-sardis. The second biennial lecture was held on November 2, 2022. "Second Biennial Sardis Lecture," Cornell University Events, accessed October 3, 2023, https://events.cornell.edu/event/second_biennial_sardis_lecture.

40. GLOBAL CONNECTIONS BRING ASIAN ART TO THE HERBERT F. JOHNSON MUSEUM OF ART

Ellen Avril

In 2023, the Herbert F. Johnson Museum of Art celebrates the fiftieth anniversary of the opening of its building, designed by internationally acclaimed Chinese American architect Ieoh Ming Pei, which replaced the A. D. White Museum of Art. Pei's elegant brutalist-style building provides a spectacular setting for exhibiting art from around the world.[1] The success of Pei's ingenious concept and siting of the Johnson Museum is perhaps best experienced from the Asian art galleries, where visitors enjoy highlights of this important strength of the museum's global collection. The framing of the views of Cayuga Lake, Ithaca, and the Cornell campus with long horizontal windows simulates the experience of viewing a landscape in the East Asian handscroll format. On misty days, the views of the lake and surrounding hills call to mind classic ink paintings of famous Chinese landscapes such as West Lake or the Xiao and Xiang Rivers.

Highlights of the Asian Art Collection

Today, the Asian art collection, one of the top university collections of Asian art in the United States, forms about one-fourth of the museum's global collection of over forty thousand works of art. This is due in large part to the vision of Martie Wing Young, Cornell professor in history of art and Johnson Museum curator of Asian art until 1998, who focused on building the Asian art collection to enrich classroom learning by providing direct experiences of original works of Asian art. Young found the ideal partner for supporting this endeavor in Mary Rockwell, wife of Cornell University trustee George Rockwell (class of 1913). Mary's deep interest in Asian art, stemming from her childhood years in China, led to numerous donations, the bequest of the Rockwells' personal collection, and an endowment that continues to support acquisitions of Asian art. More than 1,200 artworks, ancient to contemporary, from across Asian cultures, have been acquired through

Figure 40.1 Ma Quan (Chinese, active eighteenth century), *One Hundred Butterflies*, 1723. Handscroll, ink and colors on silk. Collection of the Herbert F. Johnson Museum of Art, Cornell University. Gift of Daisy Yen Wu in memory of Yen Hsiao-fang and Yen Tse-king, 79.060.004. (Image courtesy of the Johnson Museum)

the Rockwells' philanthropy. Their financial legacy led to a complete renovation of the galleries for Asian art, supported by the National Endowment for the Arts, in conjunction with the museum's 2011 expansion, designed by Pei Cobb Freed Partners.

Over the decades, the collection has grown to encompass the arts of almost every Asian culture. Ranging in date from the most ancient times to the present day, the collection serves as a vital resource, along with the museum's works of art from Europe, the Americas, and Africa, to connect to Cornell's curriculum across disciplines. Each year, approximately eighty-five thousand visitors come to the museum to engage with the world through works of art.

Many donations of Asian art came from alumni, faculty, and friends of Cornell with deep connections to Asia, only a few of whose fascinating stories can be mentioned here. Daisy Yen Wu and her son Ray Wu, Liberty Hyde Bailey Professor of Molecular Genetics and Biology at Cornell, donated important Chinese paintings and calligraphy that they inherited from the distinguished collection formed by Daisy's grandfather, Yan Xinhou. Scion of a family of successful businessmen and research scientists, Yan Xinhou played an important role in the art market and collecting at the end of the Qing dynasty.[2]

Japanese sword furniture and other art of Japan came from Kisaburo Konoshima, who immigrated to the United States in the early twentieth century. After he and his family were released from the Heart Mountain internment camp at the end of World War II, they became naturalized citizens. Konoshima collected Japanese and Chinese antiques and wrote tanka poems poignantly reflecting on his Japanese heritage and life in America.[3]

Donations from Elzie Liddell, wife of Cornell professor of psychology Howard Liddell, and others form a large and distinguished collection of 1,500 nineteenth-century photographs of China, Japan, India, and Southeast Asia by European and Asian photographers. In partnership with the Cornell University Library, a

Figure 40.2 Rina Banerjee (American, born 1963 in India), *Clouds of women, who remained in their villages, in empty homes, empty lands, empty kin, and people's migration*, 2017. Mixed media on paper. Collection of the Herbert F. Johnson Museum of Art, Cornell University. Acquired through the George and Mary Rockwell Fund, 2018.025. (Courtesy of the artist)

recent exhibition of nineteenth-century photographs by Lai Fong was the first to focus on the work of one Qing dynasty Chinese photographer.[4] Loans to the exhibition came largely from the collection of Cornell Law School alumnus Stephan Loewentheil, a major donor of historic photographs to the library, who gave a group of photographs by Lai Fong to the museum.

Class of 1955 alumna Joanna Haab Schoff's collecting of fine *surimono* had its roots in her experience living in Japan while her classmate and husband, James Stanley Schoff, served in the American military occupation. A 2006 exhibition of the Schoff collection revealed the literary wit of these exquisite prints. Later, the Schoffs donated a portion of their collection to the museum.

Southeast Asian art is a particular strength of the museum, owing to the research and travels of Southeast Asia Program faculty.[5] Indonesian dance masks, shadow puppets, and *golek* puppets, many that had been collected by dancer and art historian Claire Holt, were donated to the museum by her student, professor of government and international studies Benedict R. O'G. Anderson.[6] Through the contacts of history of art professor Stanley J. O'Connor, visiting scholar Alexander Griswold donated Thai Buddhist sculpture and paintings.[7] The museum's holdings of Southeast Asian ceramics, comprising donations from businessmen Dean

Frasché and Jennis R. Galloway, were further enhanced by Ruth Sharp, wife of Cornell anthropology professor Lauriston Sharp, who had been collecting ceramics from antique markets in Thailand while her husband was conducting field research.[8]

The museum prioritized building its collection of Indonesian, Burmese, and Thai textiles through purchase and through important gifts.[9] An exhibition of nuclear physicist John R. Menke's Vietnamese ceramics led to museum purchases, supported by funds provided by alumna Judith Stoikov and by a bequest from professor emerita of human development and Asian American studies Lee C. Lee. Professor Lee's endowment also made possible purchases of Chinese and Japanese paintings and ceramics, as well as contemporary Chinese photography. Her personal collection of Chinese art, formed largely while she was a visiting professor in Hong Kong, was a gift of her estate.

Collecting and exhibiting South Asian art at the Johnson Museum has involved significant local collaborations. Five exhibitions of exquisite Indian textiles from the extensive collection of Cornell physics professor Jeevak Parpia and Banoo Parpia have been presented over the last two decades, including most recently *Traded Treasure: Indian Textiles for Global Markets* in 2019.[10] The museum has long partnered with the local Tibetan community and Namgyal monastery to exhibit the living art of sand mandala creation[11] and commissioned paintings and sculptures by local Tibetan artists for the collection.

Collecting and Exhibiting Contemporary Asian Art

The A. D. White Museum of Art collected contemporary Asian art early on, as exemplified by a seminal group of prints and paintings by Chinese French artist Zao Wou-ki, donated in the 1950s. The Johnson Museum was among the earliest American museums to form a collection of contemporary Japanese ceramics. Distinguished among art museums in the United States is the Johnson's collection of modern Malaysian and Singaporean paintings, formed by Dolores Wharton and her agricultural economist husband, Clifton, while they were living in Kuala Lumpur in the 1960s.[12]

The Johnson Museum also organized a series of international loan exhibitions of contemporary Asian art beginning in the 2000s, guest curated by Cornell faculty and graduate students. History of art professor An-yi Pan, for example, guest curated several exhibitions of contemporary art borrowed from museums and artists in Taiwan, including Tong Yang-Tze's monumental calligraphy *Immortal at the River*. Indonesian art has been represented by exhibitions like *Taboo and Transgression in Contemporary Indonesian Art* (2005) and *Identity Crisis: Public and Private Life in Contemporary Javanese Photography* (2017), the first survey of contemporary Indonesian photography in the United States.

In 2002, the museum presented Xu Bing's installation work *Living Word 2*, which began a decades-long relationship between the Beijing- and New York–based artist and Cornell. After Xu Bing was named an A. D. White Professor-at-Large, the museum presented two more exhibitions of his work: *The Character of Characters* (2018), which was shown along with traditional Chinese paintings and calligraphy drawn from the museum's collection, and *Background Story: Cornell* (2022), based on the museum's original Ming dynasty painting by Yang Xun, which the museum has acquired.

Lines of Control: Partition as a Productive Space expanded on the significance of partition in South Asia by also addressing physical and psychological borders, trauma, and the reconfiguration of memory in other partitioned areas—North and South Korea, Sudan and South Sudan, Israel and Palestine, Ireland and Northern Ireland, and Armenia and its diaspora—as well as questions of Indigenous sovereignty in the United States.[13] The museum acquired works by several artists included in the exhibition, and these were featured along with photographs by alumna Margaret Bourke-White (class of 1927) in a 2022 exhibition curated by students from Cornell's South Asian Council to commemorate the seventy-fifth anniversary of Partition.[14]

In recent years, the museum has organized exhibitions that present the works of international contemporary artists and art collectives, including many from Asia, who call attention to global issues such as migration and climate change. In 2019, *how the light gets in*, one of the largest exhibitions the museum has ever organized, addressed themes of migration, immigration, displacement, and exile by artists from twenty-nine countries.[15] The exhibition's presentation coincided with the announcement of Cornell University's Global Grand Challenge on migration. *Art and Environmental Struggle* featured contemporary works by Indigenous and other artists speaking to their own communities' lived experiences with environmental degradation and climate change.[16] The exhibition was presented in conjunction with an international conference, *Rhythms of the Land: Indigenous Knowledge, Science, and Thriving Together in a Changing Climate*, held at Cornell in 2021.[17] The museum acquired significant artworks from both exhibitions for the permanent collection.

Over the last fifty years, the Johnson Museum's collection has expanded in ways that deepen the story of artistic creation across Asia and support the Cornell curriculum, attracting hundreds of class visits to the museum each academic year to engage directly with original works of art. The connections of Cornell faculty and alumni to Asia, whether through their own heritage or through their research or professional endeavors, greatly influenced the growth of the museum's holdings either directly through donations of their own collections or indirectly through their global contacts with collectors and colleagues. In addition, the museum's program of temporary exhibitions of modern and contemporary Asian art enhances visitors' access to the vibrancy of Asian art today.

Notes

1. For more about the museum's building, see John Sullivan III, "The Design of the Johnson Museum of Art: A Recollection," in *A Handbook of the Collection: Herbert F. Johnson Museum of Art*, ed. Sarah D. Benson et al. (Ithaca, NY: Cornell University, 1998), 28–40.

2. Yuhua Ding, "From Merchant to Elite Artist and Collector: Yan Xinhou, His Family and a Collection's Journey to the Herbert F. Johnson Museum of Art," *Journal of the History of Collections* 34, no. 1 (March 2022): 71–84, https://doi.org/10.1093/jhc/fhab008.

3. Robert D. Wilson, "Kisaburo Konoshima: An Interview with David Callner," *Simply Haiku* 3, no. 3 (August 2005), https://simplyhaiku.com/SHv3n3/features/david_callner_intrvw.html.

4. The exhibition was curated by Kate Addleman-Frankel and Stacey Lambrow, with the assistance of Yuhua Ding. "Lai Fong (ca. 1839–1890): Photographer of China," exhibition at Herbert F. Johnson Museum of Art, Cornell University, February 7–March 15, 2020, https://museum.cornell.edu/exhibition/lai-fong-ca-1839-1890-photographer-of-china/.

5. For more about Cornell's Southeast Asia Program, see chapter 4, The Southeast Asia Program: Global Cornell from the Beginning.

6. Benedict R. O'G. Anderson, "A Language Learned in Java: A Collector's View of His Masks," *Southeast Asia Program Bulletin*, Spring 1999, 6–8.

7. Alexandra Dalferro, Astara Light, and Anissa Rahadiningtyas, "Recollecting . . . Celebrating the 70th Anniversary of SEAP at the Johnson Museum," *Southeast Asia Program Bulletin*, Spring 2021, 9–12, https://ecommons.cornell.edu/handle/1813/103534.

8. Nora Taylor and Jennifer Foley, "A Sharp Eye: The Ruth B. Sharp Collection of Southeast Asian Ceramics at the Herbert F Johnson Museum of Art," *Southeast Asia Program Bulletin*, Spring 1999, 2–5.

9. Donors included anthropologists and authors Michael Gaworski and Wanda Warming, who spent years in Indonesia documenting the makers' processes, and the family of Heng Liong Thung (class of 1959, MS 1960, PhD 1972).

10. Ellen B. Avril, ed., *Traded Treasure: Indian Textiles for Global Markets* (Ithaca, NY: Herbert F. Johnson Museum of Art, 2019).

11. George Lowry, "The Dalai Lama Blesses an Exhibit of Evanescent Beauty," *Cornell Chronicle*, October 8, 2007, https://news.cornell.edu/stories/2007/10/dalai-lama-blesses-mandala-exhibition-johnson-museum.

12. Dolores organized the first exhibition of modern Malaysian art in the United States. See Dolores D. Wharton, *Contemporary Artists of Malaysia* (New York: Asia Society, 1971); and Amanda Rath, "Cultural Infusion: Modern Paintings of Malaysia and Singapore," in *Southeast Asian Art: Recent Gifts to the Collection* (Ithaca, NY: Herbert F. Johnson Museum of Art, 1999), exhibition brochure.

13. Iftikhar Dadi and Hammad Nasar, eds., *Lines of Control: Partition as a Productive Space* (London: Green Cardamom; Ithaca, NY: Herbert F. Johnson Museum of Art, 2012).

14. See exhibit information at "75 Years of Consequence: The Partition of India," exhibition at Herbert F. Johnson Museum of Art, Cornell University, August 13, 2022–January 22, 2023, https://museum.cornell.edu/exhibition/75-years-of-consequence-the-partition-of-india.

15. The exhibition was curated by Andrea Inselmann. "How the Light Gets In," exhibition at Herbert F. Johnson Museum of Art, Cornell University, September 7–December 8, 2019, https://museum.cornell.edu/exhibition/how-the-light-gets-in/.

16. The exhibition was cocurated by Andrew Weislogel, Kate Addleman-Frankel, and Ellen Avril. "Art and Environmental Struggle," exhibition at Herbert F. Johnson Museum of Art, Cornell University, August 26–December 19, 2021, https://museum.cornell.edu/exhibition/art-and-environmental-struggle/; Ellen Avril et al., "Art and Environmental Struggle: Curating an Exhibition about Place-Rooted Ecological Knowledge," *GeoHealth* 6, no. 12 (December 2022), https://doi.org/10.1029/2022GH000625.

17. The conference was organized by natural resources professor Karim Aly-Kassam. See "Rhythms of the Earth: Ecological Calendars and Anticipating the Anthropogenic Climate Crisis," special issue, *GeoHealth* 7, no. 4 (April 2023), https://agupubs.onlinelibrary.wiley.com/doi/toc/10.1002/(ISSN)2471-1403.ECOCAL2021.

41. ASIA COLLECTIONS IN THE CORNELL UNIVERSITY LIBRARY

Elaine D. Engst

The Cornell University Library's Asia Collections date back to the earliest years of the university, when founding president Andrew Dickson White acquired the collection of one of the founders of historical linguistics, Franz Bopp. One-third of the collection related to the Sanskrit language and to the Indian subcontinent.[1] The library then began acquiring journals of the Asiatic Society, Bibliotheca Indica, and the Royal Asiatic Society.

Today, Cornell's Carl A. Kroch Library houses Cornell's distinguished Asia Collections, one of the largest and most significant collections of Asian historical and literary materials in North America. The Severinghaus Asia Reading Room, named for Leslie Severinghaus (class of 1922), who taught at Peking Union Medical College, provides a welcoming study and reference space. To promote cross-regional research, the book stacks integrate all Asian material by subject matter, not language. Asia-related DVDs and microfilm can be found in Uris and Olin Libraries, and numerous electronic resources are available online. Rare books and manuscripts are housed in the Division of Rare and Manuscript Collections.[2]

Wason Collection on East Asia

While special appropriations were provided to the library for books on the "Far East" between 1902 and 1909, those titles were all in English. In 1911, undergraduate Hu Shih (class of 1914) wrote to George W. Harris, university librarian, on behalf of a group of Chinese students who were offering to give the library Chinese books that they had brought with them:

> I am often of the opinion that, though the lack of a department of Chinese books would scarcely diminish the value of an American library, yet a collection of such books would surely add something to the completeness of the library itself. . . .

Figure 41.1 Carl A. Kroch Library interior detail, 2000. (Photo by University Photography)

> To help the growth of the Library, to furnish our American friends materials for their study of the language in the future, and perhaps to originate an establishment of the Chinese language in this University in time to come, we now offer ourselves to make a collection of Chinese books for the Cornell University Library on the only condition that the Library will accept it.
>
> For their own use, the Chinese students in this University have brought with them over three hundred volumes of Chinese books. Of this number are about two hundred volumes of sacred writings, classics, and literature. The rest are histories of all the ages. These we intend to offer to the Library.[3]

Harris accepted enthusiastically and the books became part of the library. The library's Asia holdings grew further in 1914, when William Elliot Griffis, minister of Ithaca's Congregational Church, donated a collection of about five hundred Japanese books, periodicals, and maps on a wide variety of subjects that he had accumulated while teaching science in Japan in 1870.[4]

In 1918, Charles W. Wason (class of 1876) bequeathed his library on China and the Chinese to Cornell. Wason, an engineer and businessman, had traveled to China and Japan in 1903. In 1910, he began collecting books, seeking to obtain everything about China published in English. Working with a Cleveland

Figure 41.2 Asia Collections poster, 2014. (Designed by Carla DeMello, provided by Cornell University Library)

bookdealer, Wason acquired over 9,000 volumes, including some 500 manuscripts, 750 pamphlets, files of 37 English-language periodicals, volumes of 62,000 articles, maps, drawings, and photograph albums. The collection also included sixteenth- and seventeenth-century books in Portuguese and Spanish; manuscripts from Lord Macartney's mission to China from 1792 to 1794; and five volumes from the *Yongle Dadian*, the famous Chinese "encyclopedia," originally compiled in 1408 and reproduced in 1568. Wason also bought standard works on Japan, Korea, the Russian Far East, the Philippines, Burma, Indochina, Malaya, and the East Indies to provide a more comprehensive view of the region.

With the collection, Wason provided a $50,000 endowment fund to supplement the holdings after his death. When Gussie E. Gaskill became curator in 1927, she expanded the holdings in Western languages and planned for the development of a Chinese-language collection. Japanese holdings were merged with the Wason Collection. A 1938 grant from the Rockefeller Foundation, which also brought to Cornell its first full-time professor of Chinese history in Knight Biggerstaff, added funds to the library.

During the 1950s and 1960s, the Wason Collection focused on acquiring contemporary publications on all subjects regarding post-1949 mainland China. When materials became unavailable during the Cultural Revolution, attention shifted to closing gaps in materials for the earlier period. More recently, priorities returned to contemporary China, and the Wason Collection now holds an extensive array of historical and modern material on China in all formats.

In 1997, the library significantly enhanced its Japanese holdings with acquisition of the more than ten-thousand-volume personal library of the Japanese literary scholar and critic Maeda Ai. The collection includes titles on a wide variety of subjects, which form a well-rounded picture of the types of woodblock-printed publications available in late nineteenth-century Japan. The Wason Collection continues to add to its Japanese holdings in modern and premodern Japanese literature, classic theater, modern poetry, popular culture, and ethnic studies related to Japan's minorities. In recent years, efforts to enlarge the library's Korean holdings also have increased.

The Division of Rare and Manuscript Collections holds numerous manuscript collections, photographs, and graphics documenting the history and cultures of East Asia and describing life in China, Japan, and Korea during the last hundred years. Many resulted from the experiences of Cornell students, faculty, and staff living and working in China, including agricultural economist Gerow D. Brill at the Hupeh Agricultural College and Experimental Farm; journalist, diplomat, and investment banker Willard D. Straight in China, Korea, and Manchuria; Harry Houser Love, professor of plant breeding and special consultant at the University of Nanking; oilman Floyd R. Newman in Shanghai; Hu Shih, Chinese scholar, educator, and diplomat; and Cornell University president Jacob Gould Schurman, who served as minister to China in the 1920s.[5]

The John M. Echols Collection on Southeast Asia

While East Asia continued to be the library's primary focus in the first half of the century, a 1950 grant from the Rockefeller Foundation funded a five-year project to develop a Southeast Asia program at Cornell.[6] From the beginning, the program emphasized the importance of "building up a library collection adequate for teaching and research and, if possible, of a sufficiently high quality to make Cornell a world center for scholarship on Southeast Asia."[7] In 1958, Cornell became a National Resource Center for Southeast Asian Studies, agreeing to acquire a copy of every publication of research value produced in Southeast Asia. In 1977, the Southeast Asia Collection was named in honor of John M. Echols, professor of linguistics and literature in the Southeast Asia Program. Echols worked closely with Giok Po Oey, the collection's first curator, to develop the collection.[8] Funding for library staff and acquisitions continued to be provided by endowments from the Rockefeller, Ford, and Mellon Foundations.

The Echols Collection has collaborated with Southeast Asian countries, including in a 1970s partnership between Cornell and the Royal Netherlands Institute of Southeast Asian and Caribbean Studies to film Cornell's Indonesian holdings for Indonesia. In the 1980s, Cornell undertook another project to film all its holdings of publications from Cambodia to rebuild the national collection there after years of devastation under the Khmer Rouge regime. Cornell conservators also traveled to Cambodia to assist in efforts to conserve and microfilm endangered palm leaf manuscripts.

The collection currently includes many thousands of volumes in Indonesian, Thai, Vietnamese, Burmese, Malaysian, Filipino, Khmer, and Lao, as well as additional volumes in Chinese and Japanese about Southeast Asia. Holdings in Western languages exceed one hundred thousand volumes. Students and researchers also have access to more than eighty newspapers published throughout Southeast Asia and more than four thousand periodicals ranging from research journals to news and popular culture magazines.

Supplementing the holdings of the Echols Collection on Southeast Asia, the Division of Rare and Manuscript Collections contains significant manuscript collections, photographs, and maps relating to Indonesia, the Philippines, Thailand, Vietnam, Laos, and Burma. The papers of Jacob Gould Schurman, third president of Cornell and head of the first Philippine Commission in 1898, include extensive correspondence about the Philippines and document his continuing advocacy of Philippine independence. The Cornell Los Baños Records, Department of Plant Breeding Records, and records of deans of the College of Agriculture William I. Myers and Charles E. Palm document Cornell's participation in agricultural research and education at the Colleges of Agriculture and Forestry of the University of the Philippines after World War II.

Anthropologist Lauriston Sharp's papers include records from the Cornell-in-Thailand project, one of the Cross-Cultural Methodology projects conducted by the Department of Anthropology during the 1950s and 1960s. The papers of François-Jules Harmand, a French physician, natural scientist, and diplomat, contain extensive diplomatic, archaeological, botanical, and ethnographic information about French Indochina. The photographs by Niels Douwes Dekker, a Dutch photographer, document Indonesia during the 1940s and 1950s and are complemented by other photograph albums documenting Dutch colonial life in Indonesia. The division also holds the papers of Professor John M. Echols on linguistics and Indonesian languages and literature.

South Asia Collections

While the Bopp Collection formed the initial basis for the library's South Asia holdings, the library supported the formation of a collection on India in 1946, initially funded by an anonymous gift. In 1949, members of the Cornell

Hindustani Association and friends in the United States and India developed the Gandhi Memorial Library of books by and about Gandhi. Today, with material from India, Pakistan, Sri Lanka, Bangladesh, and Nepal, the South Asia Collection is the fourth largest in the United States.

As a US Department of Education National Resource Center, Cornell maintains a specialized library collection, with a particular interest in Sri Lanka and the Himalayas.[9] Along with books, magazines, and newspapers, collections of videos, films, maps, and sound recordings cover a broad range of subject areas, with the most comprehensive holdings in the country on language, literature, and linguistics. About half of the South Asia Collection is in English, with the remainder in one of the eleven languages taught at Cornell—Bengali, Hindi, Nepali, Pali, Persian, Punjabi, Sanskrit, Sinhala, Tamil, Tibetan, and Urdu—as well as additional materials in Marathi, Oriya, and Malayalam. Numerous eighteenth- and nineteenth-century German, Dutch, and French volumes document the history of India and surrounding regions.

Two extensive archival collections document the multidisciplinary Cornell India Project, which began in 1950 in conjunction with Lucknow University to study two communities in North India, Senapur and Rankhandi. The papers of Morris E. Opler relate to his research in India, especially at Senapur. The Rankhandi project is documented by extensive records, photographs, films, and audiotapes. Correspondence, diaries, and visual materials document the career of the Reverend Henri R. Ferger, a missionary and educator with the Presbyterian Board of Foreign Missions in India. The Rudyard Kipling Collection includes correspondence about British foreign affairs, especially the question of home rule for India. The library also holds emerging archival collections of visual materials including colonial trade labels and Indian political posters.

The bilingual (Marathi and English) Bombay Poets Archive, a recent acquisition, illuminates the Bombay literary scene of the 1970s, comprising the personal papers of several eminent Indian poets, including Arvind Krishna Mehrotra, Adil Jussawalla, and Dilip Purushottam Chitre, as well as magazines and clippings documenting the Clearing House poetry cooperative.[10]

Digital Resources

The Kroch Asia Rare Materials Archive is a digital collection that provides images online from various Asia collections. The Klaus Ebeling Ragamala research collection, a collection of more than 3,500 slides of South Asian art, is freely available online. Other digital collections include Knowledge of the World in Early Modern Japan, Theater Prints and Books from Early Modern Japan, Southeast Asia Visions, and Depicting the Sri Lankan Vernacular.[11]

From Andrew Dickson White's acquisition of the Franz Bopp collection to the digital resources of today, the Cornell Library's Asia Collections help provide students, researchers, and visitors an appreciation of the diverse cultures that make up this significant part of our global arena.

Notes

1. Franz Bopp, *Catalog der aus dem Nachlass des in Berlin verstorbenen Professor Franz Bopp zum Verkauf stehenden Bibliothek* (Berlin: Druck von F. Zschiesche, 1868).

2. Read more about the history of the Carl A. Kroch Library Asia Collections in "History of Kroch Library," Cornell University Library, accessed October 4, 2023, https://asia.library.cornell.edu/history-of-kroch-library/#collectionshistory.

3. Hu Shih to Cornell University Library, October 11, 1911, Cornell University Library Miscellaneous Correspondence Collection, #13-1-501, Division of Rare and Manuscript Collections, Cornell University Library.

4. Alan Wolfe, "The William Elliot Griffis Collection of Old and Rare Japanese Books, Olin Library, Cornell University," *Journal of East Asian Libraries* 1980, no. 63 (October 1980): 40–47, https://scholarsarchive.byu.edu/cgi/viewcontent.cgi?article=1185&context=jeal.

5. For more about Cornell's East Asia Program, see chapter 3, Building the Foundations of a Campus-Wide Interdisciplinary East Asia Program.

6. For more about Cornell's Southeast Asia Program, see chapter 4, The Southeast Asia Program: Global Cornell from the Beginning.

7. Audrey Kahin, "A Historical Overview of Cornell's Southeast Asia Program" (unpublished manuscript, n.d.).

8. "Building a Collection: Giok Po Oey and the John M. Echols Collection," Online Exhibitions, Cornell University Library, accessed October 4, 2023, https://exhibits.library.cornell.edu/giok-po-oey.

9. For more about Cornell's South Asia Program, see chapter 5, A Center of the Periphery: The South Asia Program.

10. "Films, Mills, and Poets: Mid-century Bombay," Online Exhibitions, Cornell University Library, accessed October 4, 2023, https://exhibits.library.cornell.edu/films-mills-and-poets.

11. Digital collections available online include the Kroch Asia Rare Materials Archive (https://digital.library.cornell.edu/?f%5Bcollection_tesim%5D%5B%5D=Kroch+Asia+Rare+Materials+Archive), the Ragamala Paintings (https://digital.library.cornell.edu/?f%5Bcollection_tesim%5D%5B%5D=Ragamala+Paintings), Knowledge of the World in Early Modern Japan (https://digital.library.cornell.edu/collections/japaneseworld), Theatre Prints and Books from Early Modern Japan (https://digital.library.cornell.edu/collections/japanesetheater/), Southeast Asia Visions (http://seasiavisions.library.cornell.edu/), and Depicting the Sri Lankan Vernacular (https://digital.library.cornell.edu/collections/srilanka).

42. THE FISKE ICELANDIC COLLECTION

Facets of an Enduring Literary Gem

Patrick J. Stevens

In November 2014, Iceland's president, Ólafur Ragnar Grímsson, visited the Fiske Icelandic Collection and conferred with Cornell researchers collaborating with Icelandic counterparts in sustainable energy initiatives and equine medical studies. The president awarded an Icelandic knighthood, the Order of the Falcon, to Patrick J. Stevens, the collection's curator, on behalf of the people of Iceland, in recognition of Cornell's "leadership in preserving the Icelandic literary and history collection, and also for making it new every year by adding new books."[1]

Origins

The origins of the Fiske Icelandic Collection antedate the founding of Cornell University by approximately a decade. Daniel Willard Fiske, a native of New York State possessing restless intellectual curiosity and uncommon linguistic aptitude, dropped out of Hamilton College after two years and was sojourning in Copenhagen by 1850. Already fluent in German and Danish, and having had lessons in Old Icelandic, he studied at the University of Uppsala until he returned to New York in 1852 with Swedish added to his repertoire of languages, and with the first books of his Icelandic collection. This private collection achieved renown in America even before the US Civil War.

Pursuing librarianship, journalism (including publication of a chess magazine), and even diplomatic service over the next decade and a half, Fiske received in 1868 an invitation to become the first university librarian and professor of Nordic languages at Cornell.

In the summer of 1879, Fiske, on leave from Cornell and accompanied by two younger Americans sharing his fascination with the lands, language, and literature of Norse civilization, finally set foot in Iceland. Traveling on horseback from Húsavík on the north coast to Reykjavík in the southwest, the party pursued a

Figure 42.1 Daniel Willard Fiske in April 1904. (Provided by Division of Rare and Manuscript Collections, Cornell University Library)

course calculated to take in as many of the natural and cultural sites of the island as possible. This three-month sojourn would prove to be Fiske's only personal visit, but many of the friendships he made there were to endure for life.

In 1880, he married the wealthy Jennie McGraw, daughter of the late John McGraw, a trustee and major contributor to the university. Already ill with tuberculosis, she died a year later. As a now wealthy widower, Fiske lived comfortably in retirement in Florence, Italy, from 1883, acquiring and organizing spectacular book collections that would all make their way to the Cornell University Library. He traveled constantly, and above all maintained contact with booksellers and literati throughout Europe and also in Egypt, where he studied Arabic and developed a romanization scheme for Egyptian Arabic.

Before his death in September 1904, Fiske had employed two young Icelanders to assist him in Florence with the growth and cataloging of his Icelandic collection. One stayed for a year and the other, Halldór Hermannsson, stayed with the collection for a lifetime.[2]

The First Curator

The transition of a book collection from the private domain of an educated and wealthy citizen to a university setting can involve a sea change. However, Fiske's

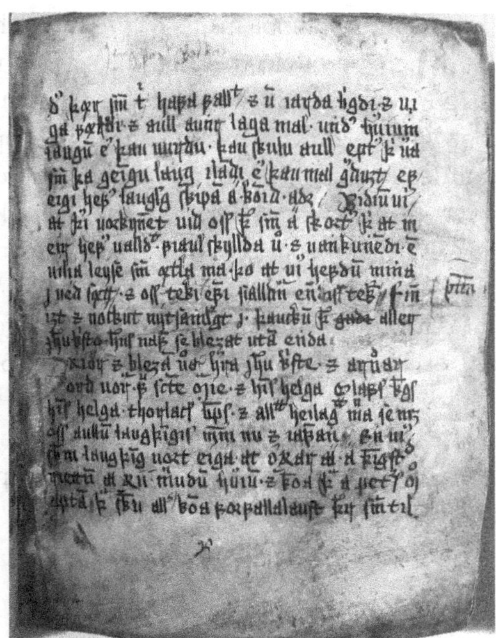

Figure 42.2 Leaf from a manuscript copy (ca. 1550) of *Jónsbók*, a major Icelandic law code promulgated in 1281. (Provided by Division of Rare and Manuscript Collections, Cornell University Library)

collections of Rhaeto-Romanic literature on Dante, on Petrarch, and on the Old Norse and Icelandic world were the work of an experienced professional librarian as well as astute collector and included remarkable arrays of manuscripts, printed editions, and literary criticism uniquely suited to scholarly study. The Icelandic collection left virtually no stone unturned in adding to its shelves "all the annals, travels, natural histories, government documents, ecclesiastical writings, biographies, and bibliographies, which can, in any way, throw light on the history, topography, indigenous products, commerce, language, and letters of Iceland."[3]

The collection indeed experienced a sea change in 1905, traversing the Atlantic to find its home in Ithaca. Halldór Hermannsson, named at Fiske's recommendation as the first curator of the Fiske Icelandic Collection, immediately went to work on two major projects that would occupy most of his forty-three-year career, during which the collection experienced phenomenal growth: compiling a catalog of the Icelandic Collection and inaugurating (in 1908) the Islandica series of scholarly monographs, including comprehensive bibliographies of medieval saga literature, on Norse and Icelandic culture and literature.

The 1914 *Catalogue of the Icelandic Collection Bequeathed by Willard Fiske* is a major work of bibliography, remarkably accurate in transcriptions, abounding in indices, supplying a classification scheme for shelf marks, and providing useful information in notes. It comprehends the broad range Fiske envisioned for the collection, and two printed supplements would follow in 1927 and 1943.

Taken together, the catalog and supplements record through about 1930 virtually the entire output of printed books in Icelandic—along with thousands of titles in other languages, chiefly Danish, English, German, Norwegian, and Swedish—that focus on Old Icelandic literature, much of it copied and transmitted in medieval Icelandic manuscripts, and on nearly all other aspects of life in Iceland. The catalog remains a reference for antiquarian booksellers.

The legacy of Halldór Hermannsson, aside from his unflagging efforts to acquire virtually all books published in Icelandic, not to mention scores of periodicals and a hefty corpus of critical literature in all major languages, lies not only in his capacity for organization but also in his ability to convey bibliographical and historical information to scholarly readership in generous but not overwhelming quantity and format. In so doing, he made the Icelandic Collection accessible through the media then available. His catalogs and bibliographies are thorough in scholarship without being intimidating.

The Fiske Icelandic Collection Transformed

The history of the Fiske Icelandic Collection after the retirement of Halldór Hermannsson in 1948 reflects the many major transformations in academic libraries, in Cornell University, in Iceland, and indeed in information as a foundational element of civilization. The three curators who served in succession after Halldór Hermannsson until 1983 were all born and educated in Iceland and thus immersed in the Icelandic literary tradition and native speakers of the language. The next two curators were American scholars who enjoyed and employed a postgraduate knowledge of Old Norse literature. The present curator, also American, is a librarian with a reading knowledge of Icelandic and Old Norse.

From the early 1970s onward, the Cornell University Library gradually transformed its catalogs into online resources in consonance with the transformation of information access wrought by computer systems. The Icelandic Collection benefited from this epochal change, evolving from an accumulation of books sequestered in a cage into a resource attracting scholarly attention from afar as well as near. Two major grant-funded projects in the last quarter of the twentieth century made progress toward representing the collection comprehensively in the online catalog. Both, however, encountered difficulties intrinsic to working with relatively esoteric languages.

Meanwhile, the prominence, which is not to say the importance, of the Icelandic Collection had receded since the early twentieth century as the Cornell Library almost literally grew up around it and proliferated across campus, leaving several early constituent collections in relative obscurity. For all its linguistic and cultural significance, publication in Icelandic and about Old

Norse was infinitesimal by contrast with, for example, the veritable explosion of English-language literature in the social, biological, and physical sciences.

Iceland itself changed with astonishing rapidity. Computerization progressed swiftly in Icelandic private homes and public institutions after around 1985. In the cultural sphere, arguably few recent projects in Iceland have been as instrumental as the amalgamation of the national and university libraries into one National and University Library of Iceland (NULI), or Landsbókasafn Íslands–Háskólabókasafn. More subtle, yet even more significant, are Icelandic bibliographical resources online, from the national catalog, which records individual book copies extant in every branch library, to digitization of hundreds of Icelandic journals and newspapers in historical depth.

The fascination and increasing feasibility of digitization for the humanities motivated NULI, in the person of Þorsteinn Hallgrímsson, to reach out to the Fiske Icelandic Collection in 1995 to propose an online initiative called Saganet (known in Icelandic as Sagnanet). This online resource was the fruit of "a cooperative project by NULI and Cornell University with the association of the Árni Magnússon Institute [in Iceland] to give access via the Internet to digital images" from thousands of manuscript leaves and printed pages, according to the description still registered in the online Digital Library Directory. Although superseded by a new Icelandic-Danish site and no longer accessible, the project offered access to vast manuscript holdings in Iceland and much of the early corpus of scholarly editions and literary criticism that define so significantly the holdings of the Fiske Icelandic Collection. Saganet was not only a successful early digitization initiative but also emblematic of the enduring relationship between Iceland and Cornell University.[4]

In 2000, to commemorate in part the Norse exploration of the North American coastline a millennium ago, Cornell University collaborated with NULI, the Library of Congress, and the University of Manitoba Libraries on a traveling exhibition. "Living and Reliving the Icelandic Sagas" chronicled the history of Old Icelandic saga literature, including Icelandic manuscripts and books never seen before in North America and printed books from Cornell and the Library of Congress.

What does the future hold for the Fiske Icelandic Collection? In multiple dimensions, the future of the collection is already here. Pragmatic considerations led to the intershelving of circulating books from the collection among the books in Olin Library early in the twenty-first century. Nonetheless, this component, now available for circulation to all, retains its distinct identity in the online catalog. The rare portion of the Icelandic Collection resides in the vault of the library's Division of Rare and Manuscript Collections and is available for research in the reading room. Work on this portion of the collection has continued in recent years to add fully articulated records of books to our online catalog.

Digital technology has been vitally important for facilitating access, through the Cornell University Library Digital Collections portal, to the image compilations embedded in the Icelandic Collection. These include the Icelandic and Faroese Photographs of Frederick W. W. Howell and Icelandic Stereoscopes (photographic prints from Iceland), with more opportunities for digitization contemplated. Both early and modern photographs from Iceland contribute importantly to understanding changes in the land- and seascapes of the island as well as the evolution of Icelandic society into thoroughgoing modernity.[5]

The rare books of the Fiske Icelandic Collection offer not only a record of intellectual history and expression in the Nordic world, from sagas to theology to poetry, but also insight into literate Icelandic society, in particular through the paratextual evidence preserved in these works. This evidence includes bindings, typeface quality, origin of paper, and marks of provenance, such as the names of women inscribed in several antiquarian books. Textual loss in rare Icelandic books and its subsequent compensation through exact manuscript reproduction of missing text suggest both a reverent regard for the personal library and the impetus of textual preservation in penury.

Two attributes of the Fiske Icelandic Collection in the twenty-first century are worth noting in closing. One is the endurance across the last century of the aforementioned Islandica series, which Daniel Willard Fiske envisioned in his bequest as a publication treating the culture of Iceland and the Norse world. More than sixty volumes have appeared over the decades, with more volumes in preparation. Recent volumes are also available online.[6]

The second attribute is the continuing acquisition of Icelandic literature in all genres in the Cornell University Library. One genre in particular, the Icelandic crime novel, has lent itself in copious measure to translation, and to our acquisition of these translations along with the original Icelandic editions. Iceland, like virtually all of Scandinavia, produces more crime novels than crime statistics, but if fiction is a creative window with a view on reality, perhaps the language, the portrayals, and the intrigues in the Icelandic crime novel are informing us about something in modern Icelandic society.

In November 2022, Guðni Thorlacius Jóhannesson, president of Iceland since 2016, honored Cornell with a visit of his own and enjoyed an exhibition of rare volumes and archival manuscripts from the Icelandic Collection. Sustainable energy and the College of Veterinary Medicine's herd of Icelandic horses were once again major features of the agenda for this presidential visit, and justifiably so, foretelling a long future of collaborative research projects between our famed university and the academic and industrial communities of this remarkable island nation.

Notes

1. Krishna Ramanujan, "Iceland President Honors Fiske Collection Curator," *Cornell Chronicle*, November 24, 2014, https://news.cornell.edu/stories/2014/11/iceland-president-honors-fiske-collection-curator.

2. See *The Passionate Collector: Willard Fiske and His Libraries*, Division of Rare and Manuscript Collections, Cornell University Library, 2005, https://rmc.library.cornell.edu/collector/index.html. See also Kristín Bragadóttir, *Willard Fiske: Friend and Benefactor of Iceland*, trans. from Icelandic by Patrick J. Stevens, Islandica 61 (Ithaca, NY: Cornell University Library, 2020).

3. Halldór Hermannsson, *Catalogue of the Icelandic Collection Bequeathed by Willard Fiske* (Ithaca, NY: Cornell University, 1914).

4. Handrit.is homepage, accessed October 4, 2023, https://handrit.is/.

5. "Icelandic and Faroese Photographs of Frederick W. W. Howell," Division of Rare and Manuscript Collections, Cornell University Library, accessed October 4, 2023, https://rmc.library.cornell.edu/howell/.

6. See Islandica vols. 53–60, eCommons, Cornell University Library, accessed October 4, 2023, https://ecommons.cornell.edu/handle/1813/55752.

43. TEEAL

Mann Library Providing Global Access to Scholarly Information

Jim Morris-Knower

In January 2001, Gracian Chimwaza was flying to Addis Ababa from a business trip at Mekelle University in Tigray, a remote area of northern Ethiopia. He struck up a conversation with the man seated next to him, who introduced himself as Dr. Mitiku Hailu, dean of Mekelle University's agricultural school. When Chimwaza asked him where he was traveling to, Dean Hailu said, "Switzerland. I'm writing a paper on harvesting water in micro-dams in Tigray and I'm going to Geneva to do a literature review for this paper." It was the nearest place he knew of with full access to the journals he needed.

The irony of this was not lost on Chimwaza, the head of the Information Training and Outreach Centre for Africa (ITOCA), a capacity-building organization aimed at enhancing information and communications technology throughout sub-Saharan Africa.[1] He had been in Ethiopia as a sort of information evangelist, visiting universities to spread the word about the Essential Electronic Agricultural Library (TEEAL).

Nicknamed the "library in a box," TEEAL had been launched a few years earlier in the fall of 1999 by Cornell's Albert R. Mann Library. It weighed in at forty-four pounds and consisted of 172 compact disks packaged in two large towers, offering researchers in over one hundred low- and middle-income countries access to the full text of articles from 130 agriculture and life science journals.[2] Chimwaza pointed out to Hailu that if Mekelle University got its own TEEAL set, he would be able to carry out such research from his office. "He was quite excited and impressed," said the ITOCA director, "and wished he could have secured funding to acquire TEEAL sooner."[3]

Cornell's development and support of TEEAL represents one story of the university's commitment to its land-grant mission of disseminating knowledge and enhancing the lives and livelihoods of people around the world. It also represents an answer to one simple but long-standing and vexing question: How is it possible to efficiently and affordably get the most important (and current) scholarly

Figure 43.1 Mann Library provides electronic access to the Essential Electronic Agricultural Library (TEEAL) and Access to Global Online Research in Agriculture (AGORA), 2005. (Photo by Kevin Stearns, University Photography)

information into the hands of researchers whose institutions could not afford them? And for twenty years, from 1999 to 2019, it kept answering that question.[4]

When the first library in a box was delivered to the University of Zimbabwe in August 1999, the initial sets cost $10,000, and annual updates were $5,000. This seems like a lot even today, especially for developing countries, but that was just a fraction of the $375,000 it would normally have cost to subscribe to those same journals. With the support of development agencies like the Rockefeller Foundation and the Bill and Melinda Gates Foundation, as well as leading publishers and the directors of Mann Library, many countries were able to acquire TEEAL sets over the twenty years of its existence as a continually updated and expanded library.

But we are getting ahead of ourselves; we will start by acknowledging that most of us probably do not own a CD player these days, and depending on your age, it is challenging to fully appreciate the impact of this collection of journals when it debuted almost twenty-five years ago. In the late 1990s, the technology of storing information digitally on round plastic discs was still relatively new. Can you remember life before Google and the World Wide Web, let alone YouTube? When Cornell researchers wanted to read the latest published studies in their field, they walked from their offices to Olin Library or Mann Library's current periodical reading rooms.

Figure 43.2 TEEAL "a library in a box." (Provided by Mann Library)

To truly appreciate TEEAL and its legacy and impact, you have to go back even further to the 1980s. There you can find the project's genesis as an idea shared by a couple—librarians Wally and Jan Olsen.

Wally Olsen was TEEAL's first project director, and Jan Olsen was Mann Library's director from 1982 to 1999. For many years before coming to Ithaca, they had traveled throughout the developing world in various roles. What they witnessed over and over again in their work for organizations like the World Bank and the National Agricultural Library was a strong but largely unmet need of scientists in low-income areas of the world to access the latest scholarly literature in their fields. The problem then (as it is still today) was that subscription prices for the leading scientific journals put them well outside the budgets of struggling academic libraries in these countries. Again, it is important to keep in mind the pre-internet context—there was no digital information really, and certainly no open-access journals or repositories providing free and easy access to data and studies.[5] The Olsens witnessed scholars in poor countries put at a disadvantage because many of their libraries had stopped subscribing to expensive Western journals. Often the newest material in these libraries was years or decades old, and their existing print collections were deteriorating rapidly due to hot and wet climate conditions.

Fast-forward to the 1990s; the Olsens were in Ithaca, where Jan was running Mann Library, one of the premier academic agricultural libraries in the world, and Wally had started work on what would become the Cornell University Press–published multivolume *Literature of Agricultural Sciences*. Published in eight volumes between 1991 and 1996, the series used input from agricultural scholars and extensive citation analysis to identify the core books and journals in the fields of agricultural economics, agricultural engineering, animal science, soil science, crop science, food science, and forestry. It was this massive undertaking, which won the American Library Association's 1997 Oberly Award for best bibliography in the field of agriculture, that would identify the list of 130 journals to be included in the first TEEAL sets.

The Olsens were not the only piece of the puzzle that came together at this time and led to the birth of TEEAL. Other key ingredients were the development of CD-ROM technology; the support of scholarly publishers; donor funding; and the support of the library. The advent of the CD made it possible for the first time to package and distribute the agricultural library in countries where a stable internet infrastructure was many years off and print was both expensive and difficult to preserve. The Olsens recognized immediately how it would make TEEAL a possibility.

They were much more centrally involved in the second piece: securing the cooperation of major scientific publishers like Elsevier, Kluwer, Wiley, and Springer, as well as major scholarly societies, to all agree to waive their subscription and royalty fees and offer affordable copies of their selected titles to eligible countries.[6] This was indeed central, as without their participation there would have been no way to offer the content.

The third piece was the generous financial support of the Rockefeller Foundation, which underwrote the creation of TEEAL.[7] There is a Cornell connection here as well: the director of agricultural sciences at the foundation at the time of TEEAL's launch was Robert Herdt, Cornell class of 1961, who later returned to Ithaca as a professor in the College of Agriculture and Life Sciences. "This was an essential thing for scientific education all over the world," says Herdt, describing his initial support for TEEAL and extended work on the boards of both TEEAL and Access to Global Online Research on Agriculture (AGORA), a fully web-based, second-generation agricultural journal library supported by the Food and Agriculture Organization of the United Nations offering free online access to over fifteen thousand agricultural journals.[8]

Finally, Mann Library's support was also crucial. TEEAL was stewarded over its two decades by dedicated project staff under the leadership of Mann Library directors—Jan Olsen, then Janet McCue, and finally Mary Ochs.

Ochs was also for many years the TEEAL project director, and today, despite being retired from Cornell, she remains actively involved with Research4Life, the umbrella organization that continues the TEEAL mission of providing scholars in low- and middle-income countries with online access to academic and professional peer-reviewed content from leading health, agricultural, and legal journals.

"TEEAL proved wonderfully effective in using a self-contained digital library to connect agricultural researchers at our partner institutions to the highest quality life sciences information and data available," she said in 2019 when it was announced that it would no longer be updated. "As the past two decades have seen more robust internet infrastructures established in many countries of the developing world, we are happy to now be moving forward with our partners into the even more promising future of accessible information made possible by fully online resources like AGORA."[9]

By then, it was clear that internet capacity in the developing world was finally reaching a stage where TEEAL could be retired, something that had been expected from the very beginning. In 2003, Mann Library was instrumental in the development of AGORA, again with the support of the Rockefeller Foundation, and in partnership with the UN Food and Agriculture Organization, knowing that the future was online. Surveys and correspondence with TEEAL users confirmed that more and more subscribers were able to make successful use of online resources, thanks to increasingly reliable internet capabilities at their home institutions. The 2019 sunsetting of TEEAL represents the completion of this long-anticipated transition to online access through AGORA.

TEEAL's transformative impact on the scholarly lives of countless researchers across the world, and Cornell's many roles in its development and success, stands as one of many examples of Cornell's positive impact across the globe. From one university in Zimbabwe in 1999, its presence would grow to about 230 institutions across the world. TEEAL's legacy is captured beautifully by Ugandan agricultural librarian Onan Mulumba, who witnessed its evolution from forty-four-pound CD set to palm-sized mini-computer while working at the College of Agricultural and Environmental Sciences of Makerere University: "We shall always be grateful to Cornell University's Albert R. Mann Library (and the entire staff), to ITOCA, and the Bill and Melinda Gates Foundation," said Mulumba when TEEAL's retirement was announced. "The TEEAL project has really contributed a lot to academic and research triumph at Makerere University. . . . I will always remember TEEAL every time I look at [the] current database."[10]

Notes

1. At the time, Chimwaza was more or less a one-man shop, with headquarters in Zimbabwe. Today, ITOCA—headquartered in Pretoria, South Africa, with a considerably larger staff—offers training throughout the continent for the six major programs that compose Research4Life: Access to Global Online Research on Agriculture (AGORA), Hinari, Online Access to Research in the Environment, Access to Research for Development and Innovation, Research for Global Justice, and the Essential Electronic Agricultural Library (TEEAL).

2. This behemoth would grow and shrink—the CDs and their tower were eventually replaced by a palm-sized Mini-ITX computer weighing less than a pound and running Ubuntu, providing access to a fully searchable collection of six hundred thousand articles in more than five hundred journals.

3. Gracian Chimwaza, personal interview with author, November 2021. See also "Gracian Chimwaza Concerning the Information Training and Outreach Center for Africa: An Oral History Interview at Cornell's Mann Library by Royal D. Colle, July 2013," https://ecommons.cornell.edu/items/a41165f3-e9e3-4438-9655-b49853b551cc.

4. As of 2019, TEEAL is no longer being updated. It continues as a legacy platform and remains a vital conduit to the core agricultural journals it offers. At some point in the future, it will exist more as an archive of the history of agricultural science and the history of information technology.

5. The oldest and best-known preprint archive—arXiv.org—provides this free and immediate access for physics and computer science scholars. arXiv was started at about the same time as TEAAL, by physicist Paul Ginsparg, who would come to Cornell in 2001. For a fascinating history, see "Of Historical Note: When arXiv Was Born," Institute for Advanced Study, 2019, https://www.ias.edu/ideas/historical-note-when-arxiv-was-born.

6. Eligibility for TEEAL was limited to countries identified by per capita income in the World Bank's *World Development Report*.

7. The Bill and Melinda Gates Foundation would also be a key financial supporter of TEEAL during its active run.

8. For more information about AGORA and Mann Library's other international outreach efforts, see "International Community," Mann Library, Cornell University, accessed October 4, 2023, https://mann.library.cornell.edu/international-community. AGORA is available at https://www.fao.org/agora.

9. "TEEAL Wraps Up," Mann Library, Cornell University, December 6, 2019, https://mann.library.cornell.edu/teealwrapsup.

10. "TEEAL Wraps Up."

44. RETURNING MUSHROOMS TO CHINA
Seventy Years of Safekeeping

Royal D. Colle

It was a coast-to-coast story in 2009: Cornell, China, and mushrooms. You could read it in the *Seattle Times* on November 8 and hear it on National Public Radio on November 14. And who would ever believe that mushrooms would be the star? The *Times* story was headlined "Mushroom Trove Returns to China after 7 Decades." The story reported, "At ceremonies at the Chinese Academy of Sciences, Cornell University President David Skorton handed over the collection that had been meticulously gathered by scholar Shu Chun Teng."[1]

The mushroom story began in the 1920s when Teng left Cornell with "a knowledge of fungi unequaled in China."[2] He completed his master's degree in mycology in 1926 and continued into a PhD program but did not finish before returning to China in 1928, where he had been awarded a professorship. He spent his post-Cornell days, sometimes with Cornellian Fang-Lan Tai (class of 1918), traveling around China for a decade on horseback gathering molds, lichens, yeasts, rusts, and morels in the forests, fields, and marshes of his country. According to the *Times*, "During these travels Teng made meticulous notes and drawings of the fungi he found—and frequently mailed duplicates to Cornell."[3] Many of his findings became part of the collection at the National Herbarium in Nanjing, which he once directed. In 1939, he also published a major English-language book related to his work: *A Contribution to Our Knowledge of the Higher Fungi of China*.[4]

In 1937, during the Japanese invasion of China and before the near destruction of Nanjing, Teng arranged for his best specimens to be removed from the institute to save them from possible damage during the war. Teng and C. C. Wang divided and packed precious specimens documenting the biodiversity of Chinese fungi. About two thousand fungi collections were smuggled to Chungking, and in 1940 they were smuggled by ox cart to Indochina and then to Washington, DC, by ship and land. Many of Teng's specimen packets came to Cornell for safekeeping by the Cornell Plant Pathology Herbarium. These became the Fungi of

Figure 44.1 S. C. Teng (*right*) at Taughannock Falls during his time as a graduate student at Cornell in 1926, with mycologists Julian C. Miller (*left*) and Arthur H. Chivers (*center*). (Photo by University Photography)

China Collection. After World War II, Teng returned to teaching and restored a national mycology laboratory in China.

According to the *Seattle Times* report, while the mushrooms were saved, Teng's fate was disastrous. During the Cultural Revolution in China from 1966 to 1976, he was discharged from his lab, jailed, and "subjected to daily beatings that ruined his health and career. He died in 1970 at 67." His daughter (Rosaline) Deng Yi explained further, "During that time my father was classified as a counterrevolutionary and labeled with many different crimes. The main crime he was blamed for was maintaining illicit relations with foreign countries [presumably including the United States and Cornell]—selling out our heritage. The reason was this [mushroom] collection."[5]

In 2009, Cornell divided up the Teng-initiated Fungi of China Collection to share those Chinese fungi specimens with the Chinese Academy of Sciences Institute of Microbiology in Beijing. In April 2009, a delegation came to Cornell from China to begin the repatriation of the fungi. According to an ABC News story, to observe the repatriation, Cornell president David Skorton presented a high-level Chinese delegation with a rare mushroom called *Lentinus tigrinus*, reaffirming the university's desire to share a collection he said Cornell "has held in safekeeping for the global scientific community since 1940."[6] The leader of the

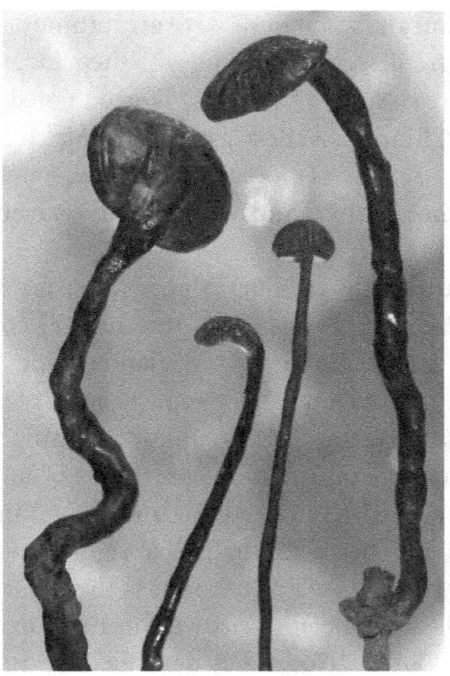

Figure 44.2 Reishi mushrooms, a medicinal mushroom with special cultural significance in China, collected by S. C. Teng. (Photo by Kent Loeffler, Plant Pathology and Plant-Microbe Biology, Cornell University)

Chinese delegation, Liu Yandong, said of the China collection that "examples of this kind almost do not exist in China which makes this collection invaluable (for) the study of the variety, distribution and evolution of Chinese fungi. . . . I would like to say a big thank you to Cornell University."[7] At the time, Yandong was the highest-ranking female official in China. Also attending the ceremony at Cornell was Ji Zhou, the minister of education; Wenzhong Zhou, the Chinese ambassador to the United States; and many other high-ranking Chinese officials.[8]

In November 2009, President Skorton traveled to China to return the priceless fungi—some 2,278 specimens—to the Chinese Academy of Sciences after almost seventy years of safekeeping. About one hundred Chinese scientists and officials attended the event, including Jiayang Li, vice president of the Chinese Academy of Sciences; Ping Hao, vice minister of China's Ministry of Education; two of Teng's children; and Wenying Zhuang, who studied under Richard Korf, Cornell professor emeritus of mycology, and was elected to the Chinese Academy of Sciences two days before the repatriation ceremony.[9]

The *Seattle Times* reported that at the ceremony Teng's daughter Deng Yi commented, "So now that these specimens have returned to their home country, my father up in heaven would feel a great happiness in his heart." She also noted,

"I think his motivation and his actions were great things, because he saved this treasure so that we can still see and research with them today. Some of the samples do not exist anywhere else."[10] At the event, Skorton noted, "The important and impressive Fungi of China Collection, gathered by Mr. Teng and fellow Cornell alumnus Fang Lan Tai, contains more than 2,000 specimens that document the biodiversity of Chinese fungi, and includes fifty-seven irreplaceable type specimens."[11]

How significant are the fungi from China? Professor Kathie Hodge, director of the Cornell Plant Pathology Herbarium, a research collection of preserved fungi and plant pathogens, said regarding the repatriation event, "The fungi are invariably tiny—just dried up leaves, most of them, or pieces of wood with a little dot on them. To an average person they look like something you would sweep off your kitchen floor. But under the microscope, they're beautiful and exciting and incredibly diverse. I think it's important to understand the diversity of life on Earth and we are far from being able to do that right now. And fungi are one of the last great frontiers of biology."[12] Later, parts of the China collection were photographed by Cornell's Kent Loeffler and were featured in a twenty-photograph exhibition in Mann Library. Hodge has described the fungi in the exhibit as "scrumptiously, vibrantly beautiful."[13]

Teng's manuscripts related to his work with fungi were confiscated during the Cultural Revolution. Years after Teng's death, the manuscripts were recovered by his family. His daughter worked with Richard Korf to complete and publish in 1996 the book *The Fungi of China*, which was an expanded edition of Teng's 1939 book. Korf "has been instrumental also in collecting fungi from Japan, making the Cornell collection of several thousand Japanese fungi almost certainly the largest collection outside of Japan." Korf sent all the divisible specimens to the National Science Museum in Japan in 2009, the same year that the Teng collection returned to China.[14]

Notes

1. David Wivell, "Mushroom Trove Returns to China after 7 Decades," *Seattle Times*, November 8, 2009.
2. Ben Dobbin, "An Ivy League School Is Giving China Back Its Treasured Mushrooms," *San Diego Union-Tribune*, April 13, 2009.
3. Wivell, "Mushroom Trove Returns."
4. Kathie Hodge, "Celebrating the 10th Anniversary of Cornell's Repatriation of Precious Fungi Collection to China," *Cornell China Center*, 2019, https://chinacenter.cornell.edu/celebrating-10th-anniversary-cornells-repatriation-precious-fungi-collection-china/.
5. Wivell, "Mushroom Trove Returns."
6. Dobbin, "Ivy League School."

7. Dobbin.

8. Kathie Hodge, "Homeward Bound: Fungi of China," *Cornell Mushroom Blog*, April 14, 2009, https://blog.mycology.cornell.edu/2009/04/14/homeward-bound-fungi-of-china/.

9. Krishna Ramanujan, "Cornell Returns Collection of Rare Fungi to China," *Cornell Chronicle*, November 12, 2009, https://news.cornell.edu/stories/2009/11/prized-fungi-collection-returns-china.

10. Wivell, "Mushroom Trove Returns."

11. Ramanujan, "Cornell Returns Collection."

12. Dobbin, "Ivy League School."

13. Kathie Hodge, "Cornell's Fungi of China Collection Has Had an Interesting Journey . . . ," *Department of Plant Pathology 2005 Alumni Newsletter* (2005), http://www.plantpath.cornell.edu/newsletter/20080111ddo1-alum05.pdf.

14. *East Asia Program (2010): East Asia Program Cornell University Celebrating 60 Years (1950–2010)*, anniversary booklet.

PART II

STUDENT AND ALUMNI EXPERIENCES

45. THE STRONG FOUNDATIONS OF CORNELL-CHINA RELATIONSHIPS

Jeff MacCorkle and Liren Zheng

Cornell and China

The historical relations between Cornell and China can be traced back to the university's early days. In 1870, only two years after the university's official inauguration, Cornell began to offer Chinese language courses taught by Professor Frederick L. O. Roehrig. In comparison to its peers, Cornell was one of the first universities in the United States to offer Chinese language classes.[1]

In 1897 the first Chinese student, Sao-ke Sze (who called himself Alfred), enrolled at Cornell in the class of 1901. Sze had come to the United States as an attaché of the Chinese Legation in the United States and graduated from high school in Washington, DC. In an 1897 interview in the *Ithaca Journal*, he noted, "I came to Cornell instead of going to Harvard or any of the other Eastern universities, because I had friends who were coming here, and also because I heard that the climate of Ithaca is healthy. I heard that they had this new elective system also, and that was an inducement. . . . I have taken up the arts course, with French, German, history, political economy."[2]

After he graduated in 1901 and received a master's degree in 1902, Sze returned to China and played a very active role in Sino-American relations. He served as the longest-term Chinese minister (1911–1912, 1920–1929, 1932–1934) as well as the first Chinese ambassador to the United States (1935–1937) when the diplomatic relationship between the two countries was upgraded.

In 1897, Zhang Zhidong, the governor general of Hubei and Hunan, contacted Cornell to seek an American expert to direct the construction and operation of an agricultural school and model farm. Gerow D. Brill, who had graduated from Cornell's College of Agriculture in 1888 and lectured in agriculture at Cornell, was offered the position. He developed the Hubei Agricultural College and Experimental Farm in Wuchang, which evolved into Huazhong Agricultural University.[3] While Brill had no formal Cornell connection during his time in China, Cornell

Figure 45.1 Yuan Shan Djang (BA 1915), 1913. Lincoln E. Patterson, Foreign Students at Cornell University Scrapbooks, #37-6-334. (Provided by Division of Rare and Manuscript Collections, Cornell University Library)

would begin its first international cooperation program in the 1920s with the University of Nanking in China.[4]

Encouraged by the spirit of this partnership, numerous Chinese students and faculty came to Cornell's College of Agriculture and many American students went abroad to research Chinese agriculture. When you visit the Nanjing Agricultural University today, you can see many preeminent Chinese professors' pictures hanging in the library reading room—and many are Cornell alumni!

In 1906, the Chinese government sent an imperial commission to investigate the political, judicial, and educational systems in the United States in order to carry out reforms in China. The commission, led by Dai Hongci (Tai Hung Chi), China's vice finance minister, and Duan Fan (Tuan Fang), the governor of Hunan Province, included twenty-five members, with Cornell alumnus Sze serving as secretary and chief interpreter. At Sze's recommendation, they selected Stanford, UC Berkeley, Lincoln University, Columbia, Cornell, Yale, and Harvard for observation.[5] They arrived in Ithaca on February 9, 1906, to a warm welcome from the Cornell community. After a student welcome ceremony, Cornell president Jacob Gould Schurman expressed Cornellians' admiration of China and Chinese culture. Then Tai Hung Chi addressed Cornell students. He expressed his admiration

Figure 45.2 Shield celebrating Cornell's semicentennial, presented by the Alumni Clubs in China, 1919. Chinese Cornell Alumni of North China, Proclamation and Plaque, #41-6-3607. (Photo by Heike Michelsen, provided by Division of Rare and Manuscript Collections, Cornell University Library)

for Cornell, which he considered one of the greatest universities in the United States. He also shared the progress of the Chinese educational system as he spoke of the need for "Western learning" felt throughout China, which had resulted in the commission's visit.[6]

As early as the 1900s, Cornell University had encouraged Chinese students with financial aid, but in 1906, as a result of the visit of the Chinese government mission, the Cornell board of trustees authorized six scholarships a year for Chinese students. In 1908, the US Congress passed a bill creating a scholarship program using the Boxer Indemnity funds imposed on China for American losses during the Boxer Rebellion of 1900. These two initiatives led to an increasing number of Chinese students studying in Ithaca.

In 1914, Chinese students at Cornell inaugurated an organization called the Science Society of China and published a magazine, *Ke Xue* (Science), the first modern scientific organization and the first modern scientific magazine in China. In this sense, Cornell is the birthplace of modern China's science organization and science magazine. In 1918, the Science Society of China moved to China, where it played a significant role in the development of China's modern science and technology.[7]

Led by Hu Shih (class of 1914), Chinese students donated approximately 350 Chinese-language books to the Cornell University Library, expanding its collection of Chinese language materials. In 1918, Charles W. Wason realized Hu Shih's ideal of establishing a Chinese collection at the Cornell University Library with the bequest of his private collection of over nine thousand volumes of materials and a generous endowment to Cornell. The collection has since become one of the nation's finest Western-language libraries devoted to China.[8]

From 1901, when the first Chinese student, Sze, graduated from Cornell, to 1920, Cornell awarded a total of 177 academic degrees to Chinese students: 121 bachelor's degrees, 52 master's degrees, and 4 doctorates. Among these early Chinese Cornellians were such notable individuals as Sze; Hu Shih; Zhao Yuanren (Chao Yuen Ren, class of 1914), father of modern Chinese linguistics; Bing Zhi (Ping Chih, PhD 1918), founder of modern biology in China; Mao Yisheng (Thomas Eason Mao, MCE 1917), pioneer of China's modern bridge-building industry; Lu Yanzhi (Lu Yen Chih, class of 1918), pioneer of Chinese modern architecture; Zhou Ren (Chow Jen, class of 1918), pioneer of China's modern metallurgy; Guo Tanxian (Kuo Tan Shin, MS 1915), founder of China's Agriculture Society; Ren Hongjun (Zen Hoong Chiung, class of 1916), founder of the China Science Society and publisher of *Ke Xue*; Zhang Yuanshan (Djang Yuan Shan, class of 1915), president of the Western Returned Scholars Association; and Jin Bangzheng (King Pang Cheng, MS 1915), Tsinghua University president.

Cornell Alumni in China

When Cornell celebrated 150 years of history and groundbreaking achievements in 2015, the university and its alumni reconnected with its historical context internationally. For the Cornell Alumni Clubs in China, the greatest discovery of the sesquicentennial year was a beautiful cloisonné reproduction of the Cornell seal. Created by the Cornell Alumni Association of North China to commemorate Cornell's semicentennial in 1914, it was accompanied by congratulatory proclamations calligraphed in Chinese and English. When that group decided to prepare a semicentennial gift to express their passion for Cornell, they never imagined they were laying the groundwork for one hundred years of cooperation between China and Cornell and the foundation for what would become the largest Cornell alumni group outside North America.

The shield and proclamations now reside in the University Archives, but their journey there took nearly a hundred years. It seems the items were entrusted to Alumni Affairs sometime during the 1920s when the first director of Alumni Affairs was hired. In the early 2000s, Mary Berens, former director of Alumni Affairs, found the items in the Alumni House at 626 Thurston Avenue. She explains, "I was searching through old alumni records and artifacts that were set apart from the current active records and found the shield among the old files. I immediately knew it was something special relating to the early years of China-Cornell University relations."[9] In 2013, Hongnan Ma, director of international alumni affairs at the time, became aware of the North China gift. Ma shared this information with the Cornell Clubs in China, where alumni were keen to learn more about the earlier group.

The effort to design and deliver the semicentennial offering had been led by Zhang Yuanshan (Djang Yuan Shan), secretary of the Cornell Alumni Association of North China in 1914. The gift is particularly interesting given the historical context within which the North China alumni found time to share their love of Cornell. Many of the members of the association were busy with the process of building the New China and reshaping China's position in the world when they embarked on the production of these commemorative items.[10]

The proclamations were easier to complete and were sent to Cornell rolled into a cylindrical shipping container, entrusted to an unknown student traveling to Cornell in 1914. The cloisonné shield, on the other hand, required intricate craftsmanship to complete and was delayed. University archivist Evan Fay Earle noted that the North China alumni appear to have "used a standard plaque and shield available for purchase at the time that was mounted on wood and then added additional beautiful decoration."[11] Part of the delay in presenting the shield was likely due to the fact that the standard base had to be sent from Cornell to China, where the elaborate cloisonné was added and the plaque affixed to the shield.

We know from the packaging that once the shield was complete, it was shipped in a wooden crate, leaving Beijing during a particularly frigid December in 1918 amid light snow, often indicating good fortune in Chinese culture. The crate traveled by the Jingshan rail through Beijing and Hebei Province, via Langfang, to Tianjin, where it was loaded onto the steamer *Taigu*, bound for New York through the newly completed Panama Canal.

Once the ship arrived in New York, the crates were transferred to the Lehigh Valley Railroad and delivered to Ithaca, where, on a spring day in 1919, they arrived in Cornell president Jacob Gould Schurman's office.

Although there is no record of the North China shield or proclamation as part of the semicentennial celebration, they may have made it in time.[12] An October 18, 1919, *Cornell Daily Sun* article titled "Chinese Alumni Give Shield to University" is the only mention of the arrival of the shield. After a brief description, it notes, "the shield is on exhibition in the lobby of the University library."[13]

In China, the North China Alumni Association remained active until the 1940s and 1950s when internal strife scattered many of North China's early Cornellians across China and the world. Sino-US confrontation further curtailed the relationship between Chinese alumni and their alma mater. By the mid-1950s, communications between Cornell and Chinese alumni had largely stopped. In China and the United States, the North China Alumni Association faded into history for decades.

In the 1980s, the Cornell Club in Beijing was resurrected and overseen by Li Pei, a prominent scholar in Beijing. The club was largely made up of academics at Beijing universities and academies of science who were influenced by the first wave of Cornellians to China and remembered them fondly. Professor Li Pei and her husband, Cornell engineering professor and leader in the fields of mechanics and applied mathematics Guo Yonghuai, joined with other Cornell Club members to preserve the foundation laid by the North China Alumni Association earlier in the century.

In the twenty-first century, Cornell alumni activity in China has flourished. By 2000 there were about two hundred alumni on Cornell Club rolls in China. By 2010, there were five hundred active members, and in 2023 there are four thousand. Today there are four official Cornell Clubs—in Beijing, Shanghai, Shenzhen, and Hong Kong—and several affiliate groups across China.

One hundred years after the North China Alumni Association presented their cloisonné shield and the commemorative calligraphies in honor of Cornell's semicentennial celebration, they would be pleased but perhaps slightly surprised that China is home to the largest group of Cornellians outside North America.

Notes

1. Yale began offering Chinese classes in 1877, Harvard in 1879, Berkeley in 1896, and Columbia in 1903.

2. *Ithaca Journal*, November 18, 1897.

3. For more information about Gerow D. Brill and the Cornell-Nanking project, see Randall E. Stross, *The Stubborn Earth: American Agriculturists on Chinese Soil* (Berkeley: University of California Press, 1986), 156–157.

4. For more about the Cornell-Nanking project, see chapter 1, A Pioneering International Program: The Cornell-Nanking Story.

5. There are various ways (Pinyin, Wade-Giles, dialect pronunciations, etc.) to romanize Chinese names, although the name will be the same in Chinese characters. The Cornell alumni directories usually used the Wade-Giles system, with individual variations. We have used the standard Hanyu Pinyin, with the Cornell version in parentheses.

6. "Commission Entertained," *Cornell Daily Sun*, February 10, 1906.

7. A documentary by the Shanghai Publication Museum and Shanghai TV Station titled *Huozhong: Zhongguo Kexueshe* (Kindling: The Science Society of China) recognizes the achievement. The opening ceremony of its launch in China in 2008 was attended by US consul general in Shanghai Kenneth Jarrett, Cornell University class of 1975.

8. For more about the Cornell University Library's Asia Collections, see chapter 41, Asia Collections in the Cornell University Library.

9. Mary F. Berens, email correspondence with author, October 26, 2022.

10. Alfred Sao-ke Sze (class of 1901, MA 1902), Cornell's first graduate from China, and his brother S. C. Thomas Sze (class of 1905), a railroad administrator in China, were certainly aware of the project, as were other noted Cornellians, which likely included Yih Koliang (class of 1908, MS 1909), the editor of the *Peking Daily News*, and Fung Hing Kwai (class of 1908, MS 1910, PhD 1911), a leading agricultural economist.

11. Evan Fay Earle, email correspondence with author, October 25, 2022.

12. While Cornell's semicentennial should have been celebrated in October 1918, it was deferred for a year because of World War I.

13. "Chinese Alumni Give Shield to University," *Cornell Daily Sun*, October 18, 1919, https://cdsun.library.cornell.edu/?a=d&d=CDS19191018.2.17.

46. A GREAT SCHOOL FACES THE GREAT WAR

Elaine D. Engst and Blaine Friedlander

In early 1917, fighting raged in Europe. German submarines prowled the Atlantic shipping lanes, and Germany secretly had tendered to Mexico a partnership offer to wrest Texas, Arizona, and New Mexico back from the United States. US president Woodrow Wilson, Congress, and the American people could no longer avoid joining the Great War, the conflict that would become known as World War I.

Wilson signed the congressional declaration of war on April 6, 1917, and scarcely a week later about 575 male Cornell undergraduates registered for military service.

In fact, Cornellians already were participating in the war effort. Edward Tinkham left Cornell in February 1916, amid his final undergraduate semester, to drive an ambulance in France. For his extraordinary heroism at Verdun, he was awarded the Croix de Guerre. Tinkham returned to Cornell in 1917 to organize a Cornell unit in the American Ambulance Field Service (and successfully petitioned the faculty to confer his degree retroactively for June 1916). When the unit arrived in France on April 14, 1917, the United States had joined the war, and the group eventually transferred to an American Motor Transport Unit. Commanded by Tinkham, this was the first American fighting unit to carry the American flag to the front.

The Aviation Ground School Takes Flight

Back on campus, students, faculty, and administrators had signed a petition asking the US War Department to establish an aviation ground school at Cornell. The petition was granted—and the US Army School of Military Aeronautics at Cornell University was born. Cornell became one of six universities to host a ground school.

Figure 46.1 Cornell provided 4,598 commissioned officers in World War I, more than any other institution, including West Point. Cornell suffered 264 casualties, and they are remembered at the War Memorial on West Campus. (Photo by University Photography)

Cornell's first class of soon-to-be pilots arrived May 17, 1917. Buzzers for wireless (radio) practice were installed in the basement of Schoellkopf Hall. The pilots received engine class training in Rand Hall, and physics professor Ernest Blaker held classes on flight theory, meteorology, and radio work. Applicants to the ground schools—one merely needed to show up to gain admittance—grew beyond the originally allocated twenty-five students to about two hundred at any given time.

Schoellkopf Hall, adjacent to Alumni Field, served as a barracks. James Edwin "Ted" Meredith, a gold medalist at the 1912 Olympic Games in Stockholm and the University of Pennsylvania's quarter-mile and half-mile intercollegiate champion, "now hangs his clothes in a locker and sleeps on a bunk in the track dressing room of Schoellkopf Hall—war is full of surprises," declared the *Cornell Alumni News*.[1] Meredith flew combat missions over Germany and returned home after the war.

With bulging enrollment, the aeronautics school outgrew Schoellkopf. Future flyboys—hundreds of them—had quarters at the newly opened New York State Armory and Drill Hall, built for $350,000. In 1940, the building was named Barton Hall in honor of alumnus Colonel Frank A. Barton, who returned to Cornell in 1917 to serve as commandant of the Cornell Cadet Corps for the second time.

Figure 46.2 Pilots examine airplanes in the airplane laboratory in Drill Hall (now Barton Hall) during ground school at the United States Army School of Military Aeronautics at Cornell. Photographs, #33-2-188. (Photo by John P. Troy, university photographer, provided by Division of Rare and Manuscript Collections, Cornell University Library)

"One of the Most Beautiful Spots"

For the pilots, final exams required comprehensive and skillful answers. In the engines class, students saw questions like, "What are the advantages of [a] double ignition system for airplane motors?" or "How many times per second does the interrupter break the primary current of a magneto which is furnishing the ignition for an eight-cylinder engine running 1400 rpm?" or "Make a sketch of a two-gear oil pump, showing path of oil and direction of rotation of gears."

To achieve superior field intelligence, the army needed aerial photography. Alongside the pilots, photographers trained at Cornell for reconnaissance missions, providing important images of revealed camouflage, decoy trenches, barbed wire, and hidden batteries.

Lewis Lupton Kaylor was among the many aerial photographers. In a March 1918 letter to Ruth Smeltzer, he wrote of Ithaca's natural splendor: "I stood out this evening at sunset, with all its glory, and I could hardly hold myself, for thinking of you. . . . This morning, six of us went on a hike. . . . This is one of the most beautiful spots in the world, Ruth, with so many waterfalls."[2]

In August 1918, the US War Department created the Student Army Training Corps to provide special academic and military training on campuses. The Reserve Officers' Training Corps had been created by the federal government two years earlier, but it was a university program that operated in conjunction with the federal government, while the Student Army Training Corps was under the complete jurisdiction of the US War Department and had an expedited training timeline. At the end of the war, the Student Army Training Corps would be disbanded and the Reserve Officers' Training Corps returned.

Armistice and Cornell's Contributions

On November 11, 1918, the war ended when armistice was achieved.

During World War I, Cornell provided 4,598 commissioned officers to the war effort, more than any other higher education institution, including West Point. Cornellians earned at least 526 decorations and citations during the war, including several special distinctions.

Five pilots became aces—with more than five victories each. Lawrence Kingsley Callahan (class of 1916) and John Owen Willson Donaldson (class of 1921) flew for England's Royal Air Force. Jesse Orin Creech (class of 1920), James Armand Meissner (class of 1918), and Leslie Jacob Rummell (class of 1916) flew for the United States. Alan Louis Eggers (class of 1919) became the only Cornellian in the war to win the Medal of Honor, recognizing his bravery for rescuing several wounded men amid enemy fire.

Cornell women physicians also served, although the US Army would not commission women doctors. As "contract surgeons," they were not officers and earned less than their male counterparts. Two Cornell College of Medicine graduates, Caroline Sanford Finley (MD 1901) and Anna Irene von Sholly (MD 1902), were awarded the Croix de Guerre by the French government and received lieutenants' commissions in the French Army, making them among the first American women to attain army rank. Alumna Mary Merritt Crawford (class of 1904, MD 1907) went to France in October 1914 to serve as a "house surgeon" in the American Ambulance Hospital at Neuilly-sur-Seine. Others included Anne Tjomsland (class of 1911, MD 1914), an anesthesiologist working at Bellevue Hospital in New York City who served overseas; and Anna Kleegman (class of 1913, MD 1916) and Gertrude Guild Fisher McCann (MD 1915), who worked stateside. Jean Harwood Pattison (MD 1919) volunteered at various hospitals including the French Hospital at Meaux and the American field hospital at Chateau Thierry.

Nurses were a different story. An all-female US Army Nurse Corps had been founded in 1901; nurses could serve officially, and more than ten thousand were sent overseas during the war. Julia Catherine Stimson, who graduated from the

New York Hospital Training School for Nurses (a predecessor of the Cornell University–New York Hospital School of Nursing), became director of nursing for the American Expeditionary Force. She was awarded the Distinguished Service Medal, and after the war she became superintendent of the Army Nurse Corps and the first woman to attain the rank of major in the US Army.

Today, there are no barracks in Barton Hall, and pilot and aerial photography classes vanished close to a century ago. But as an everlasting tribute to the brave souls who walked these grounds, the War Memorial on west campus commemorates Cornell's World War I casualties.[3] The building, which doubles as a residence hall, was dedicated by US president Herbert Hoover in a nationally broadcast radio address in 1931. A year earlier, Cornell published *Military Record of Cornell University in the World War*, with a "roll of the fallen"—short biographies of those who died in the war—and a service roster with basic information on all who served, based on a survey the university sent to all alumni.[4]

Notes

A version of this chapter appeared as "Cornell Rewind: A Great School Faces the Great War," by Elaine Engst and Blaine Friedlander, in the *Cornell Chronicle*, January 22, 2015, https://news.cornell.edu/stories/2015/01/cornell-rewind-great-school-faces-great-war.

1. "Cornell's School of Military Aeronautics," *Cornell Alumni News*, June 14, 1917.

2. Paul W. Krieg, ed., *The Glass Negative, Cornell University: The Personal Notebook of Lupton Kaylor Made during Study at the U.S. Army School of Military Aeronautics, Aerial Photography Program, Cornell University, January 1918* (privately published, 2011), 140–141.

3. The War Memorial includes the names of 264 Cornellians who lost their lives in service, but it excludes the name of Hans Wagner, who died fighting for the German military.

4. Martin W. Sampson, ed., *Military Record of Cornell University in the World War* (Ithaca, NY: Cornell University, 1930). The book is available online through HathiTrust. The original survey sheets are available in Alumni Records in the Division of Rare and Manuscript Collections, Cornell University Library.

47. HU SHIH

Forging a US-China Alliance

Moying Li

Hu Shih (胡适), also known as Hu Shi or Hu Suh, was a Chinese diplomat, scholar, philosopher, and educator.[1] He is recognized today as a seminal contributor to Chinese language reform in his advocacy for the use of written vernacular Chinese. He is also remembered as an advocate for women's rights and education, as well as the Chinese ambassador to the United States from 1938 to 1942.

Hu Shih came to Cornell as a recipient of a Boxer Indemnity Scholarship given by the United States to Chinese students.[2] Initially studying agriculture, he soon changed his major to philosophy. When he graduated in 1914, he had already made a name for himself. He was elected to Phi Beta Kappa and became president of Cornell's Cosmopolitan Club. He met with US president Woodrow Wilson at the White House and was the first Asian student to win Cornell's Corson Browning Prize, awarded for essays on Robert Browning. An instant celebrity, he was in demand as a public speaker and sought after by leading citizens of Ithaca. After graduating from Cornell, he went on to get a PhD from Columbia University.[3]

Hu Shih returned to China in 1917 to become one of the youngest professors at Peking University, the first public institution of higher learning in China, where he started many groundbreaking initiatives, including women's education. During the 1920s and 1930s, he traveled and lectured in the United States, visiting Ithaca, before returning to resume teaching in China. In the fall of 1931, Japanese troops marched into the three resource-rich provinces of Northeast China, igniting a combat that, in 1937, became an all-out war across the country. Hu Shih hoped for peaceful solutions to the situation since, at the time, he did not think China was sufficiently equipped to defeat the Japanese. If, however, war with Japan did become inevitable, he thought China would have to defend itself at all costs. He expected the insanity of Japan would eventually provoke the United States into a war in the Pacific.

On the night of July 7, 1937, shots were fired at Lugou Qiao—known to the West as Marco Polo Bridge. Japanese troops had laid siege to the town of

Figure 47.1 "Photo of Hu Shih, 1914. Taken by old friend Fred Robinson." (Provided by the Hu Shih Memorial Hall, the Institute of Modern History, Academia Sinica)

Wanping—about twenty kilometers from Beiping[4]—claiming one of their soldiers had disappeared and demanding to march into town for a search. The Chinese army fought back. The shots ignited a full-scale war between Japan and China.

A year later, in July 1938, Chiang Kai-shek appointed Hu Shih as the Chinese ambassador to the United States. At first Hu Shih was unwilling to accept Chiang's offer, having turned down numerous political appointments in order to maintain his independent voice, but he knew China now needed him. For the first time in his life and at a grim moment in Chinese history, Hu Shih became a reluctant government official.

The United States that Hu Shih returned to in 1938 was entrenched in isolationism in both the administration and the public psyche. Between 1935 and 1937, Congress passed three Neutrality Acts to try to keep the country out of any foreign war. The Chinese government, however, was anxious for Hu Shih to win American support, financial and military. As a diligent student and keen observer of the country, Hu Shih knew America would never act on another nation's timeline. To turn a regional conflict imposed by Japan into an international engagement, China would have had to make the ultimate sacrifice and hope that, after three or four years of fierce resistance, a financial and military crisis would force Japan to negotiate. In the meantime, the United States and Great Britain would likely

Figure 47.2 Ambassador Hu Shih (*center*) showing President Franklin D. Roosevelt (*left*) a document with over ten thousand signatures condemning the Japanese invasion of China, 1941. (Provided by author from Wikimedia Commons)

also recognize an impending war with Japan in the Pacific. By then China would be in ruin, Hu Shih understood, but Japan would be depleted as well.[5] The true strength of China's diplomacy, Hu Shih believed, would come from the courage and sacrifice of its citizens. If the Chinese people could show the world how they had risked everything, sacrificed everything, and fought to their deaths, international help would come, and America would surely step in to shoulder its moral responsibility and contribute to the survival of humanity.

For this to happen, Hu Shih knew he had much to do. To win American public support for China, Hu Shih launched a nonstop speaking campaign across the United States, addressing the media, schools, churches, and government agencies, sometimes giving three speeches a day in different cities. On December 4, 1938, he was invited to New York City to deliver a talk titled "Japan's War in China" at the Harmonie Club. He stated, "If I were asked to sum up in one sentence the present conditions in my country, I would not hesitate to say that China is literally bleeding to death. . . . We have suffered one million casualties. . . . We have lost all the important cities on the coast and along the Yangtze River. . . . Sixty million civilian sufferers . . . have been driven from their destroyed homes, farms, shops, and villages. . . . China is now at Valley Forge. . . . How did the fathers of this Republic ever get out of Valley Forge and march on to the final victory of Yorktown?"[6]

China did not expect any other nation, however friendly and sympathetic, to take up arms and fight at its side, Hu Shih told his audience, but China did expect, and had a right to expect, that a sense of justice and the feeling of a common humanity might yet be strong enough to move the men and women of the democratic and peace-loving countries to put a stop to the inhuman traffic of supplying weapons of war and essential raw materials to a nation unanimously condemned by over fifty nations as the violator of solemnly pledged treaties and as a breaker of world peace.[7]

Hu Shih's dynamic voice and forceful message were hailed by the American public and media but caused serious alarm in Japan. The *New York Times* reported that Ambassador Hu Shih's speaking tour had prompted the anger of the *Japan Times*, which saw the US State Department behind "this discreditable show." "How can the president," remarked the *Japan Times*, "carry out his pledge to keep America out of the war when a foreign ambassador goes about stumping the country for war?" The article accused Hu Shih of misusing his diplomatic office on a tour "designed to arouse the masses to hate Japan and bring America into war with this country."[8]

Hu Shih and his colleagues worked tirelessly with President Franklin D. Roosevelt and his cabinet to secure two loans for China while the United States tried to stay neutral in appearance. Having a warm rapport with the president, Hu Shih knew that Roosevelt had a nostalgic view of China through his family's history in the China trade. Even with the Neutrality Acts in place, the president had promised the ambassador that he would do his best and more. What happened next surprised Hu Shih.

On October 18, 1941, General Hideki Tojo replaced the moderate Prince Konoe Tadahiro to form a new Japanese cabinet. The following month he sent special envoy Saburo Kurusu and Ambassador Kichisaburo Nomura to the US State Department with their latest demands. Japan would reduce its troops stationed in French Indochina to twenty-five thousand, they claimed, provided that the United States agreed to allow Japan access to oil, to restore American trade with Japan, and not to offer China any moral or military support.

The following day US Secretary of State Cordell Hull met with Hu Shih. During their meeting Hull shocked the ambassador by telling him that the United States was considering a provisional acceptance of Japan's offer. Hu Shih was infuriated but controlled himself. "If you allow Japan to keep 25,000 troops in Indochina," he argued, "they would take control of the Burma Road"—China's vital transportation link for military supplies from her allies. "Will your three-month temporary acceptance stop Japan from attacking China?"[9] On the same day, Hull also convened with ambassadors from Great Britain, Holland, and Australia to seek their response. None of them objected to Hull's solution.

Hu Shih dispatched an urgent telegram to Chiang Kai-shek. "The Chinese resistance will collapse if the US, in any way, relaxes its economic sanction of Japan," an alarmed Chiang immediately cabled back. "Even if America offers China support in the future, it would serve no purpose, and China will never expect any assistance from the country. And [America] will not recover from the loss of international trust and moral principle."[10] Secretary Hull asked for another meeting with the four ambassadors on November 24, during which he presented them with a draft acceptance proposal. Hu Shih was the only one who opposed it.

The next day Hu Shih issued a formal protest and requested an appointment with the president. An unusual tension seemed to permeate the Oval Office as he sat down with Roosevelt. Hu Shih could not believe his ears as the president tried to convince him of the merit of reconciliation with Japan. For the first time in his diplomatic career, the soft-spoken scholar lost his temper in front of the president of the United States. He objected to any move that would capitulate to the Japanese position and reminded the president of his many freely given pledges to China.[11] In the meantime, Winston Churchill also cabled the president. If China collapsed, he wrote, this would intensify the crisis for England and America.

As he waited for Roosevelt to deliberate, Hu Shih sat in his study with his close friend and American legal adviser to the Chinese embassy in Washington, DC, his Cornell classmate Harold Riegelman. Worried, Riegelman suspected that it was possible the president could give in to Japan's demands. Hu Shih disagreed. A nation, like an individual, he remarked, possessed a character, and one could quite accurately predict that neither a nation nor an individual acted inconsistently with that character. The national character of the American people was at variance with yielding or forcing China to yield to the blackmail of surrender as the price for peace, and no responsible political leader would or could sanction it. This prophetic statement, Riegelman recalled, was made with simple and complete conviction, without any hesitancy or reservation. Riegelman cautioned his friend that this might involve America in a war with Japan. Hu Shih responded, "This would at least be more in keeping with the character of the United States."[12]

On December 6, 1941, Hu Shih was about to deliver a speech in New York City when he received an urgent telephone call from the White House asking him to meet with the president. He scheduled the appointment for the next morning and rushed back to Washington, DC. The president was in a totally different mood when Hu Shih entered the Oval Office. Roosevelt spoke as if to a friend instead of a foreign ambassador: "Those two fellows [Japanese envoys] have been here and I already refused their proposal. Please tell Generalissimo Chiang about this right away. But war in the Pacific can break out at any time now, possibly in the Philippines, Guam, or somewhere near there."[13] Hu Shih was the last foreign diplomat the president had met on that fateful morning of December 7, 1941.[14]

After leaving the president, Hu Shih stopped by the US State Department before rushing back to the embassy. Before he could catch his breath, the phone rang, "Hu Shih, I've just received reports that the Japanese air and naval forces have fiercely attacked Pearl Harbor," came the husky voice of President Roosevelt.[15] The president wanted Hu Shih to be among the first to know.

With a sigh of relief, Hu Shih put the receiver down. "Now my nation can breathe," he said. "The situation in the Pacific will change dramatically."[16] Two days after Pearl Harbor, Chiang Kai-shek sent President Roosevelt the following message: "To our now common battle we offer all we are and all we have to stand with you until the Pacific and the world are freed from the curse of brute force and endless perfidy."[17]

The Chinese ambassador had helped to keep China and the United States together and won the greatest triumph of his diplomatic career, declared *Life* magazine.[18]

Notes

1. Although the name would now be spelled as "Hu Shi" in Pinyin, the phonetic romanization system used in China since the 1950s, in this article I have used the spelling "Hu Shih," from the older Wade-Giles system, to be consistent with the way he spelled it during his lifetime. As a Cornell student, he used the form "Suh Hu" (using his surname last, as would have been done in the West). In 1923, he wrote to his Ithaca friend Edith Clifford Williams, "I now try to correct the transcription of my name and often sign myself thus: Hu Shih." Hu Shih to Edith Clifford Williams, March 12, 1923, Archive of the Research Institute of Modern History at the Chinese Academy of Social Sciences, Beijing, China.

2. The Boxer Indemnity Scholarship was an educational program for Chinese students to study in America. In 1908, the US Congress passed a bill to remit to China the surplus of the Boxer Indemnity. Despite opposition, US president Theodore Roosevelt endorsed it and established the Boxer Indemnity Scholarship to educate young Chinese as a chance, he believed, for American-directed reform in China in the future.

3. For the digital collection of Hu Shih's papers, see "Hu Shih and Cornell University Library," Division of Rare and Manuscript Collections, Cornell University Library, accessed October 4, 2023, https://rmc.library.cornell.edu/hushih.

4. Beijing (meaning "northern capital") was changed to Beiping (Peace in the north) when the nationalist government established its capital in Nanjing (Southern capital) in 1928. It was reverted back to Beijing in 1949 with the founding of the People's Republic of China.

5. Hu Shih to Wang Shijie, in *A Collection of Hu Shih's Correspondence* (Beijing: Zhonghua Shuju, 1979), 2:646.

6. Hu Shih, "Japan's War in China," in *English Writings of Hu Shih* (Beijing: Foreign Language Teaching and Research Press, 2012), 3:99–105.

7. Hu Shih, 3:99–105.

8. Hu Shih, diary entry of October 31, 1940, in *The Complete Works of Hu Shih*, (Hefei: Anhui Education Publishing House, 2007), 33:407.

9. Hu Songping, *The Expanded Chronology of Mr. Hu Shih* (Taipei: Lianjing Publishing Company, 1984), 5:1744.

10. Hu Songping, 5:1744–1745.

11. "Ambassador Hu Shih," *Life*, December 10, 1941.

12. Harold Riegelman to Paul Chih Meng of the China Institute in America, March 26, 1962, Harold Riegelman Recollections of Hu Shih, #41-5-m.1002, Hu Shih Papers, Cornell University, Hu_Shih_Papers_41-5-2578.PDF (53.81 MB), pp. 33–35.

13. Hu Songping, *Expanded Chronology of Mr. Hu Shih*, 5:1748.

14. Stenographer's Diary, December 7, 1941, in "Franklin D. Roosevelt Day by Day," Pare Lorentz Center at the FDR Presidential Library, http://www.fdrlibrary.marist.edu/daybyday/daylog/december-7th-1941/.

15. Hu Songping, *Expanded Chronology of Mr. Hu Shih*, 5:1748.

16. Hu Songping, 5:1748.

17. Hu Shih, "Our Honorable Enemy," speech at the China Society of America's twenty-eighth annual dinner on December 19, 1941, in *English Writings of Hu Shih*, 3:172.

18. "Ambassador Hu Shih."

48. BUILDING MEDICAL CAPACITY IN INDIA

The Legacy of Ida Scudder

Royal D. Colle

In 1898, Ida Scudder rode her bicycle from Philadelphia to New York to enroll in Cornell University's new medical college, one of the first coeducational medical schools in the United States. In much less time than it took her for that journey, faculty members of the college today travel the 6,700 miles from New York to Doha to teach classes in the Qatar branch of Weill Cornell Medicine.[1] Of course, there are differences between these journeys, yet a thread joins these extraordinary trips, and it reflects the impacts Cornell has had beyond New York in the field of medicine. That thread is the tradition of reaching out beyond the facilities at 1300 York Avenue on the east side of New York City to far-off places such as Haiti, Brazil, India, Tanzania, and Qatar to share health resources wherever they are needed.

Ida Sophia Scudder was born in 1870, the daughter of John Scudder, a second-generation medical missionary in India and one of seven brothers who were all missionaries, and his wife, Sophia. One brother—perhaps a model for Ida—was Dr. Silas Downer Scudder, who had established the Scudder Memorial Hospital, which was heavily committed to serving poor people, in Ranipet, India, in 1866.[2] He was also instrumental in establishing medical missions in South India, which became a support for Ida Scudder's work there.[3]

After graduating from Northfield Seminary in Massachusetts, Ida Scudder returned to the family home in Vellore, India, where she had grown up. Biographer Dorothy Clarke Wilson tells of meeting Scudder during a missionary conference at Northfield in 1922 where Scudder declared that, early on, she had had "just one idea in her mind, that she was never, *never* going to be one of those missionary Scudders." But life changed. Wilson writes about a story Scudder told—the story of the "three knocks in the night" that happened during a visit to her parents in 1894.[4]

Scudder had been at home that night writing letters, when she was interrupted three times by men: a Brahmin, a Muslim, and a high-caste Hindu. Each requested

Figure 48.1 Ida Scudder (*center*) gathering with staff and friends at her hospital in Vellore, India, ca. 1960. (Provided by Scudder Association Foundation)

her urgent assistance to save the life of his very young wife who was dying in childbirth. As she had no medical training, she recommended her father, who was a doctor, and offered to accompany him to their homes. But each of these men refused. Their religion did not allow men outside the family to enter the women's quarters of their homes. They preferred to allow their wives to die rather than to break the laws governing the salvation of their souls. The three visits left Scudder very distressed, and she could not sleep that night. The following morning, she asked a servant to inquire about the three young women, but the sound of funeral tom-toms accompanying processions to the riverbank gave her the answer. Each of these women had died because there was no woman doctor to help them. As Wilson writes, "That was her call. All other ambitions were swept aside."[5]

Witnessing the death of women due to lack of a female doctor convinced Scudder that God wanted her to become a physician to help the women of India.[6] Scudder returned to the United States and enrolled in the Woman's Medical College of Pennsylvania. She later transferred to the newly established Cornell Medical College to take advantage of Cornell's "exceptional" clinical training.[7] From the beginning, the Cornell Medical College accepted women students, and in 1899 Scudder became one of twelve women in the school's first graduating class.

Figure 48.2 Doctors Rita Isaac (*left*) and Madelon Finkel (*right*) on a trip to one of the rural clinics run by the Rural Unit for Health and Social Affairs. (Provided by Madelon Finkel)

After graduation, the new *Doctor* Scudder returned to India to start a one-room dispensary and clinic in her father's bungalow in Vellore, where she handed out medicines from a window to a long line of female patients. She soon added her mother's guest room to her dispensary with three beds for patients. It was the start of a lifelong medical career in India guided by her early primary concern for the health of women, the poor, and other marginalized people. She was intent on "taking medical care to the doorstep of those lacking access to health care" and to many who had never seen a real doctor or nurse.[8] It was a theme that was to appear frequently in Weill Cornell Medicine's global activities throughout that century and into the twenty-first century.

In 1902, after small expansions of her bungalow dispensary, Scudder opened a forty-bed hospital for women and children. She had raised money for it in the United States, including a $10,000 donation from banker Robert Schell to develop the Schell Memorial Hospital in Vellore in memory of his wife, Mary Taber Schell. At first, Scudder was the entire medical staff, but the hospital expanded rapidly, later becoming the Christian Medical College (CMC Vellore).[9]

In 1909 Scudder—traveling by donkey cart—started to treat patients in the countryside who could not make the trip to Vellore. Her weekly trips offered public health services and education for people in remote areas and developed into a system of roadside clinics. By 1916 this led to the launch of CMC's "roadside" dispensary. Transformed into Vellore's Rural Unit for Health and Social Affairs, these roadside dispensaries received much recognition in international health services and were praised as a model for offering public health services to large rural areas.[10]

Scudder also started to offer medical training for Indian women at CMC. In 1909, she began a program to train women to become nurses and in 1918 to train seventeen young women to become medical doctors. With support from Christian denominations, CMC significantly expanded over the years by adding new buildings in a beautiful valley. In 1918, CMC founded a nursing school, the first college of nursing in India. In 1924, it added a new 267-bed hospital, becoming the Christian Medical College and Hospital. The Reformed Church in America became the main supporter for the school and, after Scudder agreed to offer coeducational training, it also received support from forty missions. Over the years, thousands of Indian students, primarily women, graduated as doctors. Today, the school has 242 students and over 60 percent are women.[11]

CMC Vellore brought many significant achievements to India. Wilson notes that during Scudder's lifetime, she "saw her medical center become one of the largest in all Asia, and the number of departments multiply to include radiation-oncology[,] . . . thoracic surgery, nephrology, leprosy surgery and rehabilitation[,] . . . microbiology, rural work, mental health, ophthalmology, and many others—a list of 'firsts' in India commensurate with [Scudder's] abounding energy, indomitable will, and consecrated purpose."[12]

The Christian Medical College and Hospital's list of "firsts" also includes the first reconstructive surgery for leprosy in the world (1948), first successful open-heart surgery in India (1961), first kidney transplant in India (1971), first bone marrow transplant (1986), and first successful ABO-incompatible kidney transplant (2009).[13] A 2021 guide to the Christian Medical College reported that there has been significant growth in health care services in the one-hundred-plus years since Scudder opened the first small clinic: CMC serves more than 2,300 inpatients and 7,500 outpatients daily.[14]

In 2006, Madelon Finkel, professor of health care policy and director of the Office of Global Health Education at Weill Cornell Medicine, was invited to visit CMC in Vellore and "immediately fell in love with the place." Finkel established a successful screening program for cervical cancer at CMC and sent numerous students.

> I tell them, "I can't explain in words what you're going to experience, but you will be transformed. You'll become a more compassionate individual and a more compassionate physician. You'll see diseases that people shouldn't necessarily get or die of, but they do. You'll see things that may be upsetting—but

> you'll also see the dedication of physicians who literally come back after dinner every night to continue seeing patients. The city of Vellore is chaotic—there are people, traffic and animals in the streets at the same time—yet when you enter the medical center, it's an oasis of calm."[15]

Finkel returned annually to continue her cervical cancer work and has served as a member of the CMC Vellore Foundation Board.[16] Second-year students have spent summers in Vellore doing public health research; fourth-year students have gone on four-to-six-week clinical rotations. The Scudder Association Foundation offers a scholarship, known as the Ida S. Scudder 1899 Fellowship, each year to a graduating Weill Cornell Medicine student to spend four weeks in Vellore. In 2017, Weill Cornell Medicine hosted the annual Dr. Ida S. Scudder Humanitarian Oration, cosponsored by the Office of Global Health Education and the CMC Vellore Foundation.

Scudder, known by many in her time as Aunt Ida, has been recognized in many ways during and after her lifetime. In 1920, she received the Kaisar-i-Hind Medal for Public Service in India, which was awarded between 1900 and 1947 by the British monarch (as emperor or empress of India).[17]

At the sixtieth anniversary of its first graduating class (1899), the Cornell Medical College presented Scudder with its annual Award of Distinction. On the occasion, S. Lawrence Samuels commented, "[Our recipient] is not only an outstanding physician and teacher, and the founder of a hospital, a medical college and nursing school, but one of the best goodwill ambassadors ever sent from these shores to foreign lands."[18]

Scudder died at her bungalow in India on May 23, 1960, age eighty-nine. The Ida Scudder School in Kalinjur, Vellore, is named in her honor. There is also a road in Vellore named after her. Biographer Dorothy Clarke Wilson wrote, "Dr. Ida lighted a small candle. In her hands it became a blazing torch. Her successors have taken up that torch of life, passed it from hand to hand, multiplied it by thousands until its light illuminates not only the land of India but many other countries of the world."[19]

Notes

1. For more about Cornell in Qatar, see chapter 37, Weill Cornell Medicine–Qatar: Excellence Grown from the Sands.

2. The history of the Scudder family in missionary and medical work is told in Dorothy Jealous Scudder, *A Thousand Years in Thy Sight: The Story of the Scudder Missionaries of India* (New York: Vantage, 1984).

3. "The Origin and Growth of Scudder Memorial Hospital," *Journal of Emerging Technologies and Innovative Research* 6, no. 6 (June 2019): 237–240.

4. Dorothy Clarke Wilson, "The Legacy of Ida S. Scudder," *International Bulletin of Missionary Research* 11, no. 1 (January 1987): 26–30.

5. Wilson.

6. "Dr. Ida S Scudder," *Missionaries of the World* (blog), March 12, 2012, https://www.missionariesoftheworld.org/2012/03/dr-ida-s-scudder.html.

7. "Dr. Ida Sophia Scudder," Changing the Face of Medicine: Celebrating America's Women Physicians, last updated June 3, 2015, https://cfmedicine.nlm.nih.gov/physicians/biography_290.html.

8. "Dr. Ida Scudder Given Annual Award of Distinction by Cornell University Medical College," *Scudder Association Bulletin*, Bulletin 19 (October 1959): 10.

9. "Scudder, Ida Sophia (1870–1960), Medical Missionary in India," History of Missiology, School of Theology, Boston University, accessed October 4, 2023, https://www.bu.edu/missiology/missionary-biography/r-s/scudder-ida-sophia-1870-1960/.

10. "Scudder, Ida Sophia (1870–1960)."

11. "Ida S. Scudder," Scudder Association Foundation, accessed October 4, 2023, https://scudder.org/about/history/india-medical-missions/ida-scudder-story.

12. Dorothy Clarke Wilson, "Scudder, Ida Sophia," in *Biographical Dictionary of Christian Missions*, ed. Gerald H. Anderson (New York: Macmillan Reference USA, 1998), 609–610.

13. "Medical Missions," Scudder Association Foundation, accessed October 4, 2023, https://scudder.org/philanthropy/medical-missions. This is reported on the Scudder Association Foundation web page, which also describes the foundation's focus: "The Scudder Association Foundation is dedicated to the perpetuation of a two-century tradition of 'Service to Others,' support for the Scudder family founded hospitals in southern India, the promotion of education in the social / religious arts & medical sciences and the preservation of Scudder family history." Scudder Association Foundation homepage, accessed October 4, 2023, https://scudder.org.

14. *A Guide to Christian Medical College Vellore India*, 56th ed. (Christian Medical College), 2013, https://web.archive.org/web/20131020002858/http://www.cmch-vellore.edu/pdf/guide.pdf.

15. "Dr. Scudder's Legacy," *Weill Cornell Medicine*, October 12, 2017, https://news.weill.cornell.edu/news/2017/10/dr-scudder%E2%80%99s-legacy.

16. Vellore Christian Medical College Foundation homepage, accessed October 4, 2023, https://vellorecmc.org.

17. The name Kaisar-i-Hind means "Emperor of India" in the Hindustani language. See Kaisar-I-Hind Medal—for Public Service in India, Coll-1500, University of Edinburgh Library Heritage Collections, accessed March 23, 2023, http://lac-archivesspace-live1.is.ed.ac.uk:8081/repositories/2/resources/83644.

18. "Scudder Given Annual Award," 10.

19. Wilson, "Legacy of Ida S. Scudder," 30.

49. SENDING STUDENTS OVERSEAS

The History of Cornell Abroad

Kristen A. Grace and Davydd J. Greenwood

Founding and Development

A university education abroad office did not need to exist for the first intrepid Cornell students to engage in study abroad as part of their undergraduate degree. Students had to research what opportunities existed and what might be a good fit for them, and then propose that to the relevant office in their college. Cornell president Jeffrey Lehman, who graduated with the class of 1977, did just that in order to study math and French in Paris during his four years on the Hill (or three, if we are counting literally). Getting permission to study abroad took different paths depending on the major and college. There was no standard way to make sure that students received credit or financial aid, and thus study abroad was limited to students not dependent on financial aid.

In the early 1980s that all changed. Comparison with peer institutions revealed that Cornell was behind in sending students abroad. In 1982, Cornell sent 1.1 percent of undergraduates or 4.3 percent of the junior class, while Columbia sent 17 percent and Brown sent 23 percent. The Cornell University Council tasked President Frank Rhodes and Provost W. Keith Kennedy to coordinate and improve all of Cornell's international programs. The Mario Einaudi Center for International Studies, led by new director Davydd Greenwood, was given responsibility for this coordination campus-wide, and the center reported directly to the provost. As a result, all the foreign language and area studies programs, the international topical programs, and the Office of International Students and Scholars were brought together under the umbrella of the Einaudi Center. Among the key priorities set by the administration and the Cornell University Council was the creation of a university-wide study abroad program. Greenwood appointed Ann Roscoe as associate director with the responsibility to design and implement a set of Cornell-wide study abroad programs available to all students regardless of their financial aid status. Key faculty leaders, including Arch Dotson and Mary Katzenstein of the

Figure 49.1 Justin Alicea (*left*), psychology major, on the Cornell Global Program, CASA-Sevilla, 2017. (Provided by Consortium for Advanced Studies Abroad Sevilla)

Department of Government, helped shape the future direction, and Dotson ensured the initial transition.

Christened "Cornell Abroad" in 1983, the new office was to create a set of "gold standard" study abroad programs and make them accessible to all students. The golden aspect was to have programs run by Cornell with Cornell faculty supervisors, for students to directly enroll in the overseas universities, and for students not to live in "island" programs separate from local students. In short order, programs were created in Spain, France, Germany, Switzerland, Israel, and Egypt, and a "circuit rider" faculty member was appointed to coordinate various study abroad agreements with UK universities. Because of the decentralized nature of college administrations, Cornell Abroad was set up as the one-stop point of entry for all Cornell students. The Cornell Abroad office put study abroad on the map for Cornell students and provided a seamless connection with the university and college registrar, bursar, and financial aid office. Academically and administratively, studying in another country became an integrated part of the Cornell undergraduate experience.

In the year before the creation of the Cornell Abroad programs, Cornell had only 88 students abroad. In the 1985–1986 academic year, the first year of Cornell Abroad's formal existence, 259 students studied abroad for a semester or year. Sixty-four percent were female and 69 percent were from the endowed colleges

Figure 49.2 Serena Lotreck, Biological Sciences, during her semester on the Cornell Global Program, CASA-Sevilla. (Provided by Consortium for Advanced Studies Abroad Sevilla)

(Architecture, Art, and Planning; Arts and Sciences; Engineering; and Hotel Administration). In its second year, Cornell Abroad started tracking race and ethnicity. In that year, 73 percent of the participants identified as Caucasian. These statistics were relatively stable through the first ten years.

One of Cornell Abroad's inaugural programs was in partnership with the University of Michigan at the University of Seville, Spain. The Cornell-Michigan (and later Penn) and now Consortium for Advanced Studies Abroad Sevilla (CASA-Sevilla) program in Seville offered a unique opportunity: to study in a Spanish-speaking university alongside degree-seeking students, live with local families, receive academic and cultural programming and administrative support for relations with the University of Seville, and receive intensive language support provided by a small local program staff. Urbain "Ben" DeWinter, assistant professor of Spanish and subsequently the first permanent director of Cornell Abroad, led the program. Cornell and Michigan faculty rotated teaching and administrative responsibilities, working with a local staff who arranged homestays, orientation, and other academic classes and tutorials for our students. With a Spanish-only policy at the center for all classes and activities, students were given a full-immersion experience with the hope that they would improve not only their language skills but their cross-cultural understanding.

This model seemed to hold for the first twenty-five years until businesses like Ryanair, and more importantly the internet and smartphones, coupled with cultural changes among the student body, threatened the immersion experience. The story of the Seville program captures how one program addressed these challenges head on to create new ways to achieve the original immersion goals. To help students become independent in the culture, the program would have to be more proactive in providing a pedagogical structure and support.

The CASA-Sevilla Program and Reform toward "Active Pedagogy"

While the goals of the program had not changed, the technological conditions and student habits had. When Greenwood became the faculty member teaching in the program in 2014, he was surprised by the behavior of many (but not all) of the students. Not only was the Spanish-only agreement not being followed, but many of the students left Seville on Thursday for flights to various parts of Europe and North Africa, returning late on Monday. They competed to post their exploits on Facebook, interacted little with their host families, and built few relationships with Spanish students.

Greenwood confirmed this impression with the Seville program staff and reported his evaluation to Cornell Abroad director Marina Markot. As luck would have it, the University of Michigan wanted to leave the program and Cornell saw an opportunity to take it over as the administrative leader. Markot executed this and then invested significant resources and Cornell staff time in a process led by Greenwood together with the local Seville staff to restructure and recalibrate the program.

The goal remained cultural and linguistic immersion, but the methods changed. Reconceptualizing students not as recipients of services but as the necessary protagonists in their own study abroad experience, we restructured the program in various ways. We shifted the language-training strategy to the Common Framework of the European Union, in which goal setting and self-reporting by the student in consultation with the language faculty were the mechanisms. The homestays and excursions were reconceptualized explicitly as ethnographic learning opportunities with specific learning goals and required reporting. To engage the students with life in Seville and help them engage with local life "beyond the stereotypes," brief cultural placements in a variety of municipal agencies and organizations were created in which the students worked side by side with Sevillanos for the semester. Students established learning contracts, with on-site staff mentoring them on their goals and progress. Many of the excursions focused on learning about Seville and its sociocultural systems from direct engagement. The whole focus was to teach the students how to learn their way productively into new cultural and linguistic situations.

Overall, this new model, which is in continual evaluation and development, has borne significant fruit. The staff note major changes in student attitudes and learning styles in the local environment; the homestay families have noticed the increased curiosity and connection and have become real partners in the students' learning trajectory. Significant improvements in language acquisition compared with earlier times have been documented. The local staff have shifted from being only administrators and facilitators to being cultural mentors as well. And word of mouth about the program drives students to consider the Seville program over programs in more "popular" cities such as Barcelona. Here are some reflections of students:

- "The CASA-Sevilla program makes it impossible to drift through your five months in Spain without fully experiencing Seville, with its rich history, its proud Andalusian people, its incredible food, and its quintessentially Spanish culture."—Elizabeth Marks, CASA-Sevilla, Spring 2016[1]
- "The vocabulary I picked up from working with Mujeres Supervivientes helped me become the empathetic, passionate activist that I always strive to be—in Spanish. . . . By the end of my time in Sevilla, . . . I had learned the language of agriculture, but I had also learned the language of activism, collaboration, sisterhood, and self-care."—Aleson Laird, CASA-Sevilla, Spring 2017[2]

While no pedagogical design succeeds with all students, Cornell is certain that this design represents a significant improvement in study abroad programming. The Seville program is now part of a larger consortium of Ivy Plus peer institutions (CASA), where the program shines as a leader and model for engaged learning. Greenwood and the staff have published articles and book chapters about this experience and presented the results at various international congresses devoted to international education where audiences have shown intense interest in this emerging model.

Study abroad program options today still emphasize direct enrollment in a partner university (including Cornell's new "Global Hub" partners around the world) and "golden" programs like Seville and other Cornell consortium partners (Barcelona, Berlin, Bologna, Dublin, Granada, Havana, Kyoto, Paris, and Santiago), where Cornell faculty and staff help oversee the academics and student services offered by the program, now administered through the Office of Global Learning, the successor to Cornell Abroad.

In 2019–2020, 755 undergraduates studied abroad for a semester or year with the support of the Office of Global Learning or their home college for college-specific programs and exchanges. The majority of students studying abroad are still female (67 percent)—no doubt dissertations have been written on that topic, as it is not unique to Cornell. But Cornell now attracts and sends abroad a greater diversity of students (only 48 percent identified as white), giving the opportunity to enhance disciplinary knowledge and cultural understanding to more students who will take that experience with them as Cornellians, wherever they go.[3]

Notes

1. Linda Copman, "Beyond Stereotypes: CASA-Seville," Global Cornell, August 4, 2016, https://global.cornell.edu/news/beyond-stereotypes-casa-seville.

2. Aleson Laird, "Urban Gardening for Survivors," Education Abroad, accessed October 25, 2023, https://web.archive.org/web/20230329054725/https://abroad.globallearning.cornell.edu/story/urban-gardening-survivors.

3. Other sources for this chapter include Mary F. Katzenstein and Anne F. Roscoe, "Proposed Direction for Study Abroad at Cornell" (internal report for Mario Einaudi Center for International Studies, Cornell University, 1983); Kathy Lynch, interview with author, May 4, 2022; Beatrice Szekely, interview with y the author, May 20, 2022; Luisa Álvarez-Ossorio et al., "A New Model of Linguistic-Cultural Immersion: The Pedagogical Reform in the CASA-Seville Program," *Revista de Humanidades* 31 (2017): 39–56; Uttiyo Raychaudhuri et al., "Incorporating Engaged Learning Pieces into Curriculum," *Forum Focus* 5, no 3 (June 2019): 11–13; Melina Ivanchikova, Eva Infante Mora, and Davydd J. Greenwood, "Active Pedagogy and Ethnographic Research: CASA-Sevilla's Perspective," in *Undergraduate Research Abroad: Approaches, Models, Challenges*, ed. Kate Patch and Louis Berends (New York: NAFSA, 2020), 102–108; and Eva Infante Mora, Davydd J. Greenwood, and Melina Ivanchikova, "Action Research for University Reform: The CASA-Sevilla Study Abroad Programme in Spain," *Learning and Teaching* 12, no. 3 (December 2019).

50. SUPPORTING THE GLOBAL COMMUNITY

International Student and Scholar Services

Jerry Wilcox

Cornell has enlisted many different people and organizations to address the needs of students from abroad, including community volunteers; cultural, religious, and country organizations; faculty and academic departmental staff; and professional staff. These communities have all worked to assist international students and scholars with a variety of matters, including adjustment to life in Ithaca and the United States, financial challenges, medical concerns, crises with their home countries and families, and legal status.

In 1933, Cornell became the first US higher education institution to dedicate a staff member to work with international students. The *New York Times* reported, "Cornell is unique among colleges in the United States in having a member of the faculty whose sole responsibility is the care and counsel of the foreign students. John L. Mott, son of John R. Mott, was appointed last year as assistant to the dean of the university faculty in charge of foreign students, in addition to holding the post of secretary of the International Association."[1] At the time, Cornell had approximately 175 international students enrolled.[2] The International Association of Ithaca had been founded that year by several faculty and local leaders to purchase and manage the student-run Cosmopolitan Club's international student residence in Collegetown.

John L. Mott was the son of John R. Mott (class of 1888), who had founded the nationwide Committee on Friendly Relations among Foreign Students in 1911. For several years, the committee conducted a nationwide census of international students, published as *Unofficial Ambassadors*.[3] He also played a role in the founding of the World Student Christian Federation in 1895 and the World Council of Churches in 1948. In 1946, while serving as chairman of the International Missionary Council and president of the World Alliance of Young Men's Christian Associations, Mott won the Nobel Peace Prize "for his contribution to the creation of a peace-promoting religious brotherhood across national boundaries."[4]

Figure 50.1 US Exchange students from Malaysia meet in front of Goldwin Smith Hall. (Photo by University Photography, provided by Division of Rare and Manuscript Collections, Cornell University Library)

John L. Mott left Cornell in January 1935 to serve as director of the International House in New York City. In 1936, alumnus Donald C. Kerr (class of 1912) was hired as Mott's successor to counsel international students, once again under the aegis of the dean of the faculty. Like Mott, Kerr was also appointed executive secretary of the International Association and served as director of the Cosmopolitan Club. Kerr's work with international students became a full-time university appointment in 1939, moving under the newly created Office of the Counselor of Students. Kerr remained in the role until his death in Indonesia in 1956 while on a traveling fellowship.

One of the guiding principles of Cornell's international office staff throughout the years has been to share knowledge and innovate. Kerr, like every subsequent leader of international student advising at Cornell, was very involved with supporting the improvement of services to international students at Cornell and nationally. He was a founding member of the National Association of Foreign Student Affairs (NAFSA), which had been created in 1948 "to promote the professional development of U.S. college and university officials responsible for assisting and advising the 25,000 foreign students who had come to study in the United States after World War II. The academic institutions, government agencies, and private organizations that combined to form NAFSA knew that meeting the needs

Figure 50.2 An international student adviser greets students arriving in Ithaca from Liberia, India, and the Philippines. (Photo by University Photography, provided by Division of Rare and Manuscript Collections, Cornell University Library)

of diverse students required special knowledge and competencies."[5] In the early years, Kerr wrote a widely cited publication called *Immigration without Tears*, which emphasized the "need to organize in order to have an effective voice in dealing with the Immigration Service and the Department of State about policy changes that needed to be made."[6]

This publication was among the first efforts to advise and educate those working with international students about the laws, rules, and regulations that not only came to govern the lives of international students and their accompanying families but also regulated the postsecondary institutions enrolling these students. Making international students and scholars feel welcome as they maneuver the regulatory demands from the federal level remains a balancing act for international student and scholar advisers nationwide.

By 1955, international student enrollment in the United States had grown to 36,500, with Cornell's international student enrollment numbering over 525. David B. Williams, who succeeded Kerr as counselor to foreign students in 1956, became the first director of the newly created Foreign Student Office in 1959 (renamed the International Student Office in 1962). He worked for more than thirty years at Cornell with international students and alumni. Williams was also active in NAFSA and chaired the NAFSA Field Service Steering Committee. This initiative was funded by the US State Department to improve the professionalism of the foreign student advisers nationwide. Thus it continued Cornell's outreach commitment to the field of international student advising.

Support nationwide for international students—including financial, language acquisition, settling in, and housing—has been quite varied. After World War II, as international students flocked to the United States for postsecondary education, a large number of graduate students especially gravitated toward US research universities that often offered financial support via federal research grants. The creation of the federally funded Fulbright Program in 1946 supported incoming international students and outgoing US students with the goal to improve intercultural relations, cultural diplomacy, and intercultural competence between the people of the United States and those of other countries through the exchange of people, knowledge, and skills.

For many years, international graduate students at Cornell gathered in university housing in Sage Hall, Cascadilla Hall, and apartments for families. In addition, these students sought inexpensive off-campus apartments. In the spirit of Mott's work in New York City, Cornell established an international residence in 1970 and the International Student Office cosupervised its resident director. The International Living Center was renamed the Holland International Living Center in 1985 for Cornell trustee Jerome H. Holland (class of 1939, MS 1941). When the university-wide student residence system changed, the International Student Office's role in supervising the resident director of the center was no longer needed. The Holland International Living Center's early success helped it survive to this day.[7]

In 1964, the International Student Office supported the creation of the Cornell International Friendship Program. For over fifty years, the program matched local volunteers with international students to create a personal connection to make them feel at home and become better immersed in American culture. "I call it 'promoting world peace one friend at a time,'" said Stu Berg, who, with his wife, has volunteered to be a friendship partner for about thirty years.[8] Many relationships with students extended past the first year, and some lasted for a lifetime. As recalled by Michaela Novakova (class of 2018) from the Czech Republic, "In my freshman year, I met a couple—a professor and his wife—through the International Friendship Program. Most of my favorite memories are with them. They are my family away from home, and together we explored Ithaca and its gorgeous surroundings. Going for a hike to Treman State Park and talking for hours about the world around us is one of my fondest memories."[9]

Upon its creation in 1959, the International Student Office became a standalone unit that reported to the vice president for student affairs. With the increase in popularity of a US education for international undergraduates and the subsequent increase in applications, the need for an international undergraduate admissions specialist became clear. Housed in the International Student Office, under Williams's leadership, the admissions specialist also served as the introductory foreign student adviser to incoming international undergraduates.

Additionally, although emergency short-term loan aid was available for both graduate and undergraduate international students, support for degree-seeking undergraduate international students was a more difficult challenge. The university assigned a budget that allowed a few international undergraduates with financial aid needs to enroll each year, depending on the number of those graduating. The International Student Office administered that aid, and the international admissions officer developed a specialized financial needs analysis system specific to international students. Acting in cooperation with the various college admissions offices, the admission and support of these international scholarship students became the hallmark of Cornell's commitment to ensuring the flow of needy and brilliant undergraduate students throughout the various colleges.

In 1979, Williams began work on what was to become the university's first International Alumni Affairs Office. "Cornell has more than 13,000 foreign alumni, many of whom have lost touch with the university. This program will be aimed at establishing better communications between the university and its foreign alumni," he said.[10] His efforts helped set in motion a more permanent commitment by the university to relate to its international graduates who live abroad. That effort eventually was taken over by Alumni Affairs and Development.

In 1980, Cornell's US State Department Exchange Visitor Program for visiting scholars was moved from the Provost's Office to the International Student Office. This program permitted universities and other approved entities to sponsor visiting scholars and researchers for a defined time period. Frances Helmstadter joined the International Student Office in 1980 as the first full-time adviser to international academic staff. She solidified previous contacts at each active department, established clear policies to clarify who is qualified to be invited using nonimmigrant visa status, and provided reassurance that faculty requests would be processed in a timely fashion. Her expertise with the H-1 temporary worker visa, US Labor Department requirements, and the immigrant visa application process became admired throughout the Ivy League. These international research and teaching faculty positions have played a key role in ensuring Cornell's superior academic reputation.

Given the added responsibility for international academic staff, the office name was changed to the International Students and Scholars Office (ISSO) in 1986. Being part of a larger unit allowed the ISSO staff to assist incoming international scholars and researchers, and hiring departments across the campus could get their questions answered and papers prepared in a timely fashion with the reassurance that the office staff member in charge was committed to meeting the needs of the international staff and the academic department.

ISSO arranged events to support international students and scholars and their accompanying family members such as the annual traditional American Thanksgiving feast and local trips to state parks and wineries. Although destinations have changed over the years, annual excursions have been offered since the mid-1960s. In the 1960s and 1970s, a US history–focused trip to the Gettysburg battlefields; Washington, DC; and Colonial Williamsburg, Virginia, was popular. A US State Department grant supported graduate students' trips to Washington, DC, to meet with officials from the US Chamber of Commerce, the US Department of Agriculture, and the World Bank.

Jerry Wilcox, director of the ISSO from 1981 to 1998, and Brendan O'Brien, director from 1998 to 2018, continued Williams's legacy. During their tenures, enrollment of international students grew from 1,283 in 1981 to 5,322 in 2018.[11] Wilcox held several offices in NAFSA, primarily involved with immigration matters. He eventually served as president and chair of the governing board. For many years, O'Brien was chair of the Ivy League group of international student and scholar services that met once a year.

In the early 1990s, the university's student affairs administration was revamped, and the ISSO was moved under the auspices of the Mario Einaudi Center for International Studies. Wilcox introduced the Cornell International Education Network to bring together staff across the campus who work with both incoming and outgoing students and scholars.[12]

During this time, ISSO created an undergraduate orientation program called Prepare, which is still offered today. It allows incoming international undergraduates to move into their on-campus residences early and participate in a specialized orientation program. Approximately 150 incoming international students participated in this orientation program. Four days of structured activities and experiences for new students were enhanced by the participation of approximately forty returning international student volunteers. "I think this extra bit of orientation is essential for international students as we have to familiarize ourselves with the culture, as well as the environment," said Aman Chawla, a student from India who participated in the summer of 2000.[13]

Subsequent administrative homes for serving the international student and scholar population have evolved. With the creation of the Office of Global Learning in 2018, ISSO and Cornell Abroad were brought together under one comprehensive administrative unit, with International Services and Education Abroad as the primary staff teams. The current sophisticated web presence of Global Learning is a sign of the remarkable commitment of the university to serving over 6,000 international graduate- and undergraduate-enrolled students and 1,500 international visiting faculty and researchers; many families accompany both enrolled international students and visiting faculty and researchers.

Notes

1. "Foreign Students Flock to Cornell," *New York Times*, May 20, 1934.

2. "Cosmopolitan Clubhouse Is in New Hands," *New York Times*, September 25, 1933. For more about the Cosmopolitan Club, see chapter 55, Above All Nations Is Humanity: The Cornell Cosmopolitan Club.

3. Ruth Haines Purkaple in "The Idea of NAFSA: Five Founders Discuss the Origins of NAFSA," *International Educator*, Spring 1998, https://www.nafsa.org/about/about-nafsa/idea-nafsa-five-founders-discuss-origins-nafsa.

4. "John R. Mott—Facts," Nobel Prize, accessed October 5, 2023, https://www.nobelprize.org/prizes/peace/1946/mott/facts.

5. "The History of NAFSA: Association of International Educators," NAFSA, accessed October 25, 2023, https://web.archive.org/web/20221204224137/https:/www.nafsa.org/about/about-nafsa/history-nafsa-association-international-educators.

6. Forrest Moore in "Idea of NAFSA."

7. For more about the Holland International Living Center, see chapter 56, Providing a Home for a Global Community: The Holland International Living Center.

8. Nancy Doolittle, "Program Promotes 'World Peace, One Friend at a Time,'" *Cornell Chronicle*, June 16, 2014, https://news.cornell.edu/stories/2014/06/program-promotes-world-peace-one-friend-time.

9. "Michaela Novakova: 'The Cornell Community Made Me Feel at Home,'" College of Arts and Sciences, Cornell University, May 1, 2018, https://as.cornell.edu/news/michaela-novakova-cornell-community-made-me-feel-home.

10. Franklin Crawford, "Scholarship Fund Is Memorial to David B. Williams, Who Led International Students Office," *Cornell Chronicle*, November 8, 2006, https://news.cornell.edu/stories/2006/11/gifts-being-accepted-scholarship-david-williams-memory.

11. "International Services Annual Statistics Reports," eCommons, Cornell University Library, accessed October 5, 2023, https://ecommons.cornell.edu/handle/1813/66731.

12. For more about the Cornell International Education Network, see chapter 38, Cornell International Education Network: A Home for International Educators.

13. Mario Einaudi Center for International Studies, *Annual Report 2000–2001* (Ithaca, NY: Mario Einaudi Center for International Studies, 2001), 77.

51. CORNELL AT THE PALAZZO

The Cornell in Rome Program

Roberto Einaudi

In 1986, the dean of the College of Architecture, Art, and Planning at Cornell, Bill McMinn, decided to open a program in Rome, Italy. He had arrived at Cornell in 1984 after having passed a year in Rome in 1982 with a fellowship at the American Academy, a time that had opened his eyes to the great teaching possibilities of the eternal city. I, on the other hand, after finishing my undergraduate studies at the College of Architecture, Art, and Planning at Cornell in 1961 (and a master's at MIT in 1962), had gone to live and work in Rome. After twenty-five years, my contacts with my past Cornell professors in Ithaca were limited. As fate would have it, I was interviewed on international TV regarding a restoration project for the Colosseum. My former Cornell art professor Jack Squier saw the program and immediately told Dean McMinn that I was probably the appropriate person to help set up the program in Rome. Bill McMinn contacted me without delay, also because he knew of my work as an architect for the restoration of the American Academy in Rome.

The first step was to try to find the appropriate location for the facilities. The plan to use the large apartment that had been previously identified as a possible place in the Parioli district, belonging to the Dalai Lama, was quickly abandoned when I proposed as a more appropriate location the Palazzo Massimo alle Colonne, a magnificent Renaissance palace designed by Baldassarre Peruzzi in the center of Rome. Dean McMinn knew the palazzo well, as all architects must, but he needed to visit it with me because the spaces available for rent needed to be restored and refurbished to make them suitable for classroom and teaching use.

As the director of the program, I had to work hard on all aspects, including restoring the palazzo for Cornell's use, finding the local faculty and staff, securing housing for the students, programming site trips, teaching classes, and so on. The restoration work had to be done immediately to allow the facilities to be ready for the fall semester of 1986. The problem was that obtaining the permission to do work in a historic building was and is a long process. After getting

Figure 51.1 View of Palazzo Massimo alle Colonne in Rome in a print by Giuseppe Vasi (1710–1782). (Provided by author)

preliminary approvals from the state and city authorities, we started only essential work. We managed to open in time for the arrival of approximately twenty new students, but much of the needed restoration work was done over the course of several years. We were fortunate enough to convince the Istituto Centrale del Restauro (the national restoration school) to do all the restoration work on the magnificent frescos and stucco at no cost to us, except for providing the scaffolding. One year, we had lessons under the scaffolding, and the students could view and learn from the restoration process.

The spaces had been furnished with suitable tables, chairs, equipment, and lighting. Local professors were chosen from an international base of scholars, critics, architects, and artists—experts in using Rome as a resource for instruction and inspiration. In addition, we established an intensive initial program to teach basic Italian to the students to allow them to interact better with the local community. Cornell faculty from the Departments of Architecture and Art in Ithaca, and subsequently from City and Regional Planning, came to live and teach in Rome during each semester. The two professors who arrived from Ithaca for the first semester were John Shaw in architecture and Jack Squier in art, both with their wives. It was a wonderful occasion to meet them again after twenty-five years, especially Jack and Jane, with whom I had remained in contact.

I found apartments for both Ithaca professors and a nearby pensione (guest house) for the students. Subsequently, after talking to the students, it was decided that the program would find apartments of varying sizes in the historic city center in characteristic buildings that gave students the opportunity to experience typical Italian neighborhoods, as well as the chance to discover different places to eat. The apartments were located within walking distance from the classes and studio spaces at the palazzo, but they frequently needed to be restored and furnished, and also required periodic cleaning and maintenance.

The program was formally dedicated on March 14, 1987, with the presence at the Palazzo Massimo of the president of Cornell University, Frank H. T. Rhodes. On that occasion he stated, "Cornell's presence in Rome is something much more than educational, as important as that is. We are, in a sense, engaged in a living partnership, celebrating all the strengths and variety of the past, committing us to an experience that spans the oceans and spans the centuries."[1]

One of the most important people responsible for supporting the program in Rome was Colin Rowe.[2] Rome, for Colin, well expressed his interest in both the complexity and unity of the urban texture and its individual monuments. In order to enjoy and study Rome, he had taught at the University of Notre Dame's Rome School of Architecture in the early 1980s because Cornell at that time had no Rome program. Colin became a strong supporter of the new program in Rome and of the Palazzo Massimo location, helping support it, first from Ithaca, then directly by teaching in Rome.

The program had a tough life initially. It was not supported by many of the Ithaca faculty, who thought it was inappropriate and too costly. Colin wrote a long memorandum to the faculty, strongly supporting the program and suggesting improvements and greater commitment and involvement. With his usual wit and sarcasm, he ended by saying, "There used to be a graffito in the New York subway: 'Jesus saves, but Moses invests.' So are we to emulate Jesus . . . or are we to emulate Moses and place reasonably conspicuous venture capital in Rome? The dividends are reliable, sometimes brilliant and, never, have they been less than good."[3]

I found an apartment for Colin, available for other Cornell faculty when he was not there, at the Palazzo Massimo di Pirro right next door. We could even talk to each other from adjacent windows, he from his apartment and I from my tiny office.

Colin loved the Palazzo Massimo. He loved its architect, Baldassarre Peruzzi, and he loved the architect Giulio Romano. He knew all about the many palazzi designed by each, but he was surprised when he learned about my discoveries during the restoration of the Palazzo Massimo. Peruzzi's palazzo was superimposed on an earlier Romano one, burned during the sack of Rome in 1527 but not destroyed. When Peruzzi rebuilt it, he had kept many of the spaces designed by Romano, including one with a magnificent fresco that had been burned during the sack of Rome and later white-washed to remove the soot. I discovered it by seeing the faint incisions made in the stucco as a guide to Romano for the painting of the fresco. We managed to partially restore the ceiling with funds from the Samuel H. Kress Foundation and the help of able restorers.

One of Colin's favorite buildings in Rome was Romano's Palazzo Maccarani, near the Senate, a few blocks away from Palazzo Massimo. I remember Colin's anguish when, on the day scheduled for his lecture on Palazzo Maccarani, his slides were not to be found. I suggested he could make the best of the situation by taking the students directly to the palazzo and give the lecture on site. Colin retorted with an avalanche of objections: the palazzo was badly restored, it had an addition on top, there was too much traffic and other distractions, he would not be able to show his diagrams, and so forth. Colin did manage to find his slides and I attended his lecture. His beautiful drawings illustrating rhythm, proportions, and details were essential for a complete understanding of the building.

The Rome program proceeded very well at the Palazzo Massimo location; the students were enthusiastic, but there was mounting opposition in Ithaca. During the first Iraq crisis of 1990, the college wanted to shut down the Rome program, but five students were already in Europe and one of the Ithaca faculty, Roger Trancik, was also committed. So we remained open with five students for the semester, but all the fixed costs remained, and the program lost more money than usual. When subsequently the dollar lost value and everything in Rome became relatively more expensive, the college decided to close the program, despite my objections. The students in Ithaca staged a sit-in, in front of the dean's office, until that decision was revoked.

Trancik returned to Rome several times to teach city and regional planning. During his stays in Rome, he developed *Layers of Rome*, a digital textbook that enabled students to study the physical transformations of Rome's Campus Martius from ancient to modern times. Extensive 3-D computer models and animations of buildings, streets, and public spaces were constructed to visualize the layers of the city, synthesized into a tool for interactive learning. Wrote Roger, "Rome embraces its physical and cultural past in unprecedented ways illustrating how different layers of history are grafted onto one another. Students can learn from the complexity of Rome's physical history about adaptive reuse and sustainable urban design to address today's widespread problem of lost space. We cannot continue to build cities around the automobile while ignoring the heritage of place."[4]

The Rome program has prospered and enrollment has increased; the Palazzo Massimo became too small and the program was first moved to Palazzo Lazzaroni, a few hundred meters from the Palazzo Massimo, and then, when dean of the college Kent Kleinman made it obligatory for all architectural students to attend a semester in Rome, it moved to even larger and better spaces in the Palazzo Santacroce, a spectacular seventeenth-century building with ample studio space, library, materials shop, and tech support, suitable for up to ninety students each semester, where it still is today.

I retired as director of the Rome program in 1993. After my very intensive and demanding term of six years, my responsibilities were split into three roles, with all directive decisions now made in Ithaca. The academic and field trip coordination in Rome was assigned to Jeffrey Blanchard, who had started teaching a course in Renaissance and Baroque architecture and art in the program in 1988, and the responsibility for the administration was assigned to Anna Rita Flati, who had worked with me since 1976. Anna Rita retired in 2019 after thirty-three years working for Cornell in Rome. Blanchard is still responsible for the academic and field trip coordination and teaching. He feels that today "this most ancient and complicated of cities is the ideal laboratory for the disciplines of architecture, art, and planning."[5] We have continued to work together in other cultural institutions such as the Keats-Shelley Memorial House museum.

In 2017, Kent Kleinman, dean of the College of Architecture, Art, and Planning, decided to celebrate the thirtieth anniversary of the formal founding of the Cornell in Rome program.[6] I have continued serving at times as visiting critic or lecturer for each of the three programs—architecture, art, and planning—and I gave a guest lecture at the anniversary celebrations. A 2017 student blog post on the Cornell in Rome program website described the event:

> The Cornell in Rome program continues to inspire and educate Cornell students in the heart of Rome. We had the pleasure of having Roberto Einaudi as our first architecture guest lecturer last Thursday. . . . It felt incredible to meet and learn about the man that gave us the opportunity to be here in Italy today.
>
> Einaudi's legacy to Cornell University stretched all the way to World War II when his father Mario taught at Cornell to U.S. officers who were going to the campaign in Italy. . . . Hearing him talk about his work, I was inspired by how he sought to preserve the past as well [as] his own family history.
>
> Since my experience so far studying in an ancient city has allowed me to further appreciate old traditions, I am therefore even more grateful for the goals Einaudi's worked towards in the past to achieve what we have today. Overall, it was a very inspirational lecture to understand the history of the program in a larger context.[7]

Notes

1. Frank H. T. Rhodes, "Rome Center Dedicated," Cornell Architecture Art and Planning, Summer 1987, "Cornell in Rome Program Dedication," Box 78, Folder 16, College of Architecture, Art, and Planning Records, #15-1-512, Division of Rare and Manuscript Collections, Cornell University Library.

2. Colin Rowe (1920–1999), architectural historian, critic, theoretician, and teacher, served as the Andrew Dickson White Professor of Architecture from 1962 to 1990. He is considered to have been a major influence on world architecture and urbanism in the second half of the twentieth century. In 1995, the Royal Institute of British Architects gave Rowe its highest honor, the Royal Gold Medal of Architecture, for being "perhaps the single most critical influence in architectural education of the mid-20th century." Michael Spens, "Obituary Colin Rowe," *The Guardian*, November 17, 1999, https://www.theguardian.com/news/1999/nov/18/guardianobituaries2; "Cornell Faculty Memorial Statement: Colin Frederick Rowe, March 27, 1920–November 5, 1999," eCommons, Cornell University, accessed October 27, 2023, https://ecommons.cornell.edu/server/api/core/bitstreams/6c58d1a0-843f-442b-8d79-325bbc150396/content.

3. Roberto Einaudi, "Colin Rowe, Rome, and Cornell," a talk given at the Palazzo Lazzaroni in Rome on the occasion of the Cornell CAAP Rome Program seminar "Urban Design and the Legacy of Colin Rowe," June 19, 2014, https://colinrowecentenary.wordpress.com/2020/03/21/colin-rowe-rome-cornell/#:~:text=Rome%20for%20Colin%20well%20expressed,to%20enjoy%20and%20study%20Rome.

4. Roger Trancik, "Layers of Rome: Architecture, History and Geography of Ancient and Modern Rome," CD-ROM (Ithaca, NY: Live & Learn, Inc., 2000).

5. Patti Witten, "AAP Mourns Former Dean and Cornell in Rome Founder Bill McMinn," Cornell Architecture Art Planning, August 28, 2020, https://aap.cornell.edu/news-events/announcements/aap-mourns-former-dean-and-cornell-rome-founder-bill-mcminn.

6. "30 Years of Cornell in Rome: An Anniversary Celebration," accessed October 26, 2023, https://events.cornell.edu/event/30_years_of_cornell_in_rome_an_anniversary_celebration; Daniel Aloi, "Cornell in Rome Program to Celebrate 30 Years in March," January 31, 2017, *Cornell Chronicle*, https://news.cornell.edu/stories/2017/01/cornell-rome-program-celebrate-30-years-march.

7. "Einaudi's Lecture," *Cornell in Rome* (blog), March 23, 2017, https://blogs.cornell.edu/cornellinrome/2017/03/23/einaudis-lecture/.

52. CORNELL IN THE HIMALAYAS

The Cornell-Nepal Study Program

Kathryn S. March

By the 1990s, Cornell had become a significant center for Nepal and Himalayan studies, and student interest in studying in Nepal was strong. We began to think about developing our own Cornell study abroad program. But what kind of program? With the help of Om Prasad Gurung, then head of sociology and anthropology at Tribhuvan University (TU), the oldest public university located in Kathmandu, and support from Cornell Abroad, I traveled to Nepal in 1992 for a series of meetings.

Mutual Benefit

As we explored possible collaborations, mutual benefit emerged as the most important concept for everyone at the table. It was not acceptable to TU colleagues that they and their students receive no benefit from the presence of students and scholars from premier global educational institutions, who largely lived separately, who did largely unsupervised research, and who did not share their research or facilities. It was unacceptable to me that Cornell students be thrown into inadequate and unsanitary housing or be left to fend for themselves in a course of study taught in lectures geared toward rote examinations, by largely absentee faculty, without books or facilities.

TU had recently instituted a thesis requirement for master's students, so Nepalese students whose entire experience of education had been rote-exam-driven learning were suddenly told to choose an original topic, research it, and submit a written thesis—in English. The effect was dramatic: of the six-hundred-odd students who were officially enrolled in the MA program in sociology and anthropology, fewer than a dozen managed to finish in the ensuing years.

Here was our opportunity. The US students who chose to study abroad in Nepal wanted to see and learn about the country, to do research on a wide variety of

Figure 52.1 *Left to right:* Amy Johnson, Nhanu Dimdung Tamang, and Mona Aditya during the Cornell-Nepal Study Program village study tour in Mhanégang, Nuwakot, spring 2008. (Photo provided by Mona Aditya and Amy Johnson)

topics relevant both to their own field of study and to Nepal, and to develop meaningful relationships with the people there. The Cornell faculty wanted students to learn about Nepal from a wide variety of perspectives but especially those of the Nepalese themselves; to do intellectually challenging, methodologically appropriate, and ethically responsible research; and to have sustained interactions not just with host families and villagers but with their academic peers. The TU students wanted help navigating their thesis research and writing, improving their English, and getting access to research materials; but they also wanted to get to know Americans and to make friends. The TU faculty wanted to be fairly compensated for time devoted to supervising and teaching, and they wanted access to Cornell scholarly resources.

In 1992, we embarked on the collaborative Cornell-Nepal Study Program (CNSP), in which faculty and students from both institutions would benefit. From the beginning of the program in 1992 until its suspension following the 2015 earthquakes, we agreed that Tribhuvan would allow their faculty and students to participate in the CNSP and would assist in obtaining Nepalese visas for the non-Nepalese students and staff. Cornell would cancel all the tuition usually paid by international students (minus a modest administrative cost). Over the years,

Figure 52.2 *Clockwise from lower left:* Rabindra Parajuli (in light-colored headband), Kath March, Suren Himdung Tamang, David Holmberg, and Paul Josephson (pointing), at the pilgrimage site on Phyukhri Ridge, with Cornell-Nepal Study Program and Cornell Outdoor Education, winter 2010. (Photo by Katie Walker)

we refined the ways in which the CNSP could be mutually beneficial to the students, the faculty and their institutions, and the wider communities in Nepal.

Students

In Nepal, CNSP students were involved in the residential program house, research preparation, and research itself. Graduate students, ideally one from Cornell and one from TU, were employed as residential coordinators (RAs) and academic coordinators (TAs). Selected TU faculty worked with Cornell faculty to develop curricula and materials for field-based instruction and provided individual research guidance. The CNSP flourished under the extraordinarily capable and insightful direction of Banu Oja, who had taught Nepali for the Peace Corps and at Cornell.

In the program house, Nepalese and non-Nepalese students lived as roommates. They ate and took part in both academic and extracurricular activities together. Residential programming included orientation discussions about living with each other's differences, weekly "Culture Nights" where alternating Nepalese and non-Nepalese students would organize a group event, and space for each group to develop different specific activities.

While there were cultural differences in cuisine and many students had deeply held ideas about food, dining was the focus of life. Since gas, electricity, and water were unreliable at best, food had to be purchased and prepared daily on propane or kerosene cooktops by household staff. Under Banu Oja's adept guidance, the routine was set to accommodate these needs, desires, and constraints.

Following the practices of many large extended households in many of the varied caste and ethnic communities in Nepal, a simple breakfast was delivered to each resident's room early in the morning. For the non-Nepalese residents, this was like breakfast in bed. And it kept them out of the kitchen, where preparation of the morning meal was underway.

Morning meal was Nepalese, served at or before 10:00 a.m., the traditional time when school and work began: rice, lentils, vegetables, chutney, and, for those who ate it, meat, all prepared deliciously. To the Nepalese students, this was the only thing you could legitimately call "food." For the non-Nepalese students, this was part of why they had come to Nepal, and some came to love and devour it; others tried it and ate it but were happier with either the afternoon "snack" or "dinner."

Afternoon snack was eaten at around 4:00 p.m., whether in agricultural fields or in offices. To a non-Nepalese it looked like a meal—noodles and vegetables, vegetable fried rice, flatbreads and yogurt or curry, fried soybeans with onions—it just did not include the all-defining rice. Dinner was typically later than in the United States, at 7:30–8:00 p.m. Entrées were Western—spaghetti, pizza, or fried chicken and French fries—although anyone who wanted rice or lentils could always have some of the morning's leftovers.

The CNSP was not all residential fun and feasting, however. There were classes. There was research. There were readings and papers. Language teachers taught both spoken and written Nepali to the non-Nepali-speaking participants and English to the non-English-speaking ones.

To accommodate all students, two different pathways through the course of study were developed. For the non-Nepalese participants, the CNSP operated like a stand-alone study abroad program: students studied language; did coursework, including an omnibus lecture series on Nepalese culture, history, politics, religion, society, and development, as well as a class on research design and proposal writing; and completed a field research project. Two short and one longer group field study tours took students to visit, trek, and stay in all three of Nepal's major ecological zones—the lowland Terai, the Himalayan mountains, and the intensely agricultural Mid Hills. After their research proposals were approved, students received funding for three to four weeks of independent field research (including a translator or peer assistant) on topics ranging from monastic musical instruments to women's contraceptive choices to botanical responses to climate change, at locales across the country.

Although the Nepalese students took part in all aspects of the CNSP, their experience was divided into three different fellowships: (1) residential fellows received room and board at the program houses, shared a room with a non-Nepalese CNSP student, and participated in the residential activities and study tour field trips; (2) research fellows participated in the research design and proposal writing course, then prepared an approved field research proposal, for which they received CNSP funding for three to four months; and (3) thesis writers received support for the actual thesis production and submitted approved copies both to TU and the CNSP.

While Cornell students had to complete coursework, field research, and a paper within the term or year of their residency, TU students were allowed to take longer, often being in residence one year, preparing their research the next, and only completing their thesis after that.

Working out ways to support both Cornell and TU students equally and equitably was a complex process. Eventually more TU students completed their master's theses with CNSP support than the total number of participating Cornell students. Moreover, although the CNSP did not directly support any TU students for further study in the United States, many managed to get admitted with funding to US graduate programs, often with the informal help of their non-Nepalese CNSP roommates and friends. One of the very first Nepalese CNSP students, Dambar Chemjong, continued to complete a PhD in anthropology at Cornell and later headed the Central Department of Anthropology at TU.

Faculty and Institutions

Creating mutual benefit for TU faculty posed its own challenges. It became a fundamental commitment of the CNSP to pay Nepalese and non-Nepalese employees at the same rates with comparable benefits. For TU faculty, participation in CNSP roughly doubled their salaries and they had office space at the program house and access to the CNSP library. They also received the help of the academic coordinator, who provided logistical support, as well as running discussion sections and assisting students on a more daily basis. In exchange, CNSP working faculty allocated a commensurate amount of their time to teaching and advising at the program houses and to accompanying students on study tours. They were welcome to dine with the students. The CNSP soon had a very dedicated cadre of faculty and staff.

The decision was made to focus initially on two departments: Botany (which also taught ecology and environmental science) and Sociology/Anthropology.

Every year, small grants of at least $1,000 were made to both departments, as well as to the library. These grants could be used for anything—the departments did not have to write a proposal, but they did have to submit a final accounting. Showing how scarce resources were at TU at the time, Sociology/Anthropology built a bathroom with its first grant. Subsequent grants established an audiovisual collection, built bookshelves and other furniture, and bought computer equipment.

TU faculty and administrators were eager to visit Cornell. Given budget constraints, only one to three TU faculty and administrators who were teaching at the CNSP could visit Cornell for two to three weeks, but numerous research collaborations grew, and the CNSP financed an annual university-wide lecture series.

Communities

TU was the main community within which the CNSP operated and to which it provided as much support as its resources and the principle of mutual benefit would allow. But the CNSP affected at least two other communities: Kirtipur, the ancient town where TU is located, and Mhanégang, the Tamang ethnic community where many CNSP students lived with families while they got field training. These living experiences, like those of the independent research period, profoundly shaped student learning—of both the Nepalese and the international students—and, once again, creativity was necessary to identify ways for mutual benefit. Each year CNSP students did community service projects, one in Kirtipur and one in Mhanégang. In addition, the CNSP made annual cash grants directly to the village committees managing the school, the temple, or the health post.

Factors of Success and Impact

The CNSP involved students and faculty from both Cornell and TU from 1992 to 2015. It developed a collaborative program for training and research that was committed to long-term mutual benefit, each year assisting up to twenty advanced undergraduate or beginning graduate or professional students coming to Nepal and as many as double that number of Nepalese students, along with modest TU faculty exchange visits to Cornell, social and scholarly exchange activities, and direct grants to TU departments, as well as small service projects in the host communities.

The funds for the CNSP came exclusively from the tuition or program participation fees that Cornell Abroad charged non-Nepalese students. Nepalese students were entirely funded by the CNSP. The financial cutoff point, below which not even fixed costs like rent and skeleton staff could be met, required at least seven to ten paying students per year. Ten years of civil war and ensuing years of political unrest in Nepal, as well as an overall decline in student interest in long-term study abroad, sometimes made it tough to meet that threshold. But there were also years when the numbers were high enough to contemplate expanding activities.

While the program budget was unpredictable, the CNSP always tried to foster a long-term, mutually beneficial, and collaborative program, in a spirit of transparency and genuine scholarly exchange. It required considerable ongoing nurture to balance competing needs, interests, and understandings. I continue to believe that any ethical format for so-called study abroad programs should embrace its underlying principles. I am grateful and proud to have been a part of it.

53. EXPANDING HORIZONS

Veterinary Students Explore Their Profession and the World

Olivia M. Hall

In the mid-1980s, Samuel Gordon Campbell, associate dean for academic affairs at the College of Veterinary Medicine (CVM), mulled over ideas on how to open students' eyes to the wider world—and the result was the Expanding Horizons program.[1] A Scotsman who had studied in Canada and been posted in Malaya as part of his British military service before earning his doctorate in microbiology from Cornell, Campbell had an international outlook and would later become director of international programs for CVM.[2]

The foundations of the program have stayed largely the same over the past four decades. Students may participate any time during their four years in veterinary school, though—given the demands of the curriculum and the academic calendar—most do so during the summer of their first or second year. While in the past they could also choose to work stateside, Expanding Horizons currently focuses on developing countries, where students identify their own projects and contacts.[3] About one to two dozen individuals respond to a call for proposals every fall and, in a typical year, as many as twenty of them receive approval in the spring.[4] Financial support is provided by annual gifts from the Lincoln Ellsworth Foundation and a variety of funds, including an endowment by Karel (Ton) Schat, professor emeritus in the Department of Microbiology and Immunology, whose own international experiences had a powerful impact on his research on poultry diseases.[5]

"It's an incredible program," said Jai Sweet, assistant dean of student services and admissions. "There are some very innovative projects—a couple of PhD theses have even grown out of them—and some partnerships are sustained, with different students going there year after year." Upon returning, students write a report and give a presentation through a student-run club called Veterinarians Interested in Developing Areas, often accompanied by food from their host country. "It truly is a window into an experience many students would otherwise never have gotten; for some it's even their first visit to a developing country," Sweet said. "Whether

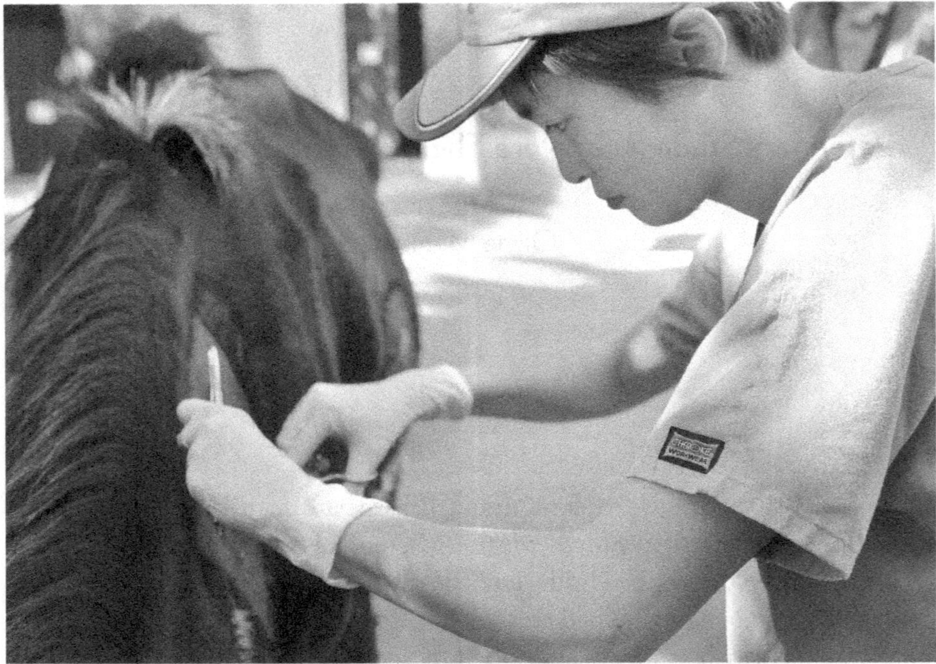

Figure 53.1 Through the Expanding Horizons program, Gabrielle Woo spent five weeks at the American Fondouk, a charitable veterinary hospital for working equids in Fez, Morocco, 2016. (Photo by Jennet Chan, provided by College of Veterinary Medicine)

or not a student chooses to pursue International Medicine after they graduate, I think these projects have had a lifelong impact."[6]

One of those students, Ilana Schafer (DVM 2008), is not where she expected to be when she was a student at CVM envisioning her future career.[7] "If you had told me I was going to specialize in infectious diseases—one of the hardest parts of vet school—I would have probably laughed," she said. Today she not only is a veterinarian board-certified in preventive medicine but also has a decade of service as an award-winning veterinary epidemiologist at the US Centers for Disease Control and Prevention (CDC) under her belt.

Her career is partly thanks to Schafer's two formative summers with CVM's Expanding Horizons international education program. Traveling to Brazil and Senegal, she became one of hundreds of Cornell veterinary students funded by the program over the past four decades. Recipients spend six to ten weeks in developing countries engaging in research or other veterinary experiences from wildlife rehabilitation to disease surveillance and—true to the program's name—stepping outside their comfort zones to gain valuable new perspectives on their chosen field and the world. "My Expanding Horizons experiences definitely played a big role in how I ended up doing what I'm doing," Schafer said.

Figure 53.2 Daniel Jackson studied brucellosis in domestic yak and their herders in Nepal as part of his Expanding Horizons project, 2012. (Provided by College of Veterinary Medicine)

When Schafer came to Cornell in 2004, Expanding Horizons was already on her to-do list. Alfonso Torres, who served as a professor and associate dean for public policy at CVM, and Alexander Travis, then an assistant professor of reproductive biology at the Baker Institute for Animal Health, connected her to colleagues at the Smithsonian National Zoo to work on a maned wolf conservation project in Brazil for five weeks, funded by Expanding Horizons. "It was like living a dream," Schafer said about sleeping at the foot of a national park and going out every day in a truck to track the animals. Still, she realized that her interests were broader. "The park was surrounded by farms, and I thought it would be really interesting to look into potential infectious diseases spread between the wolves and the dogs or even the people," she explained. "That's just where my brain went."

Torres helped Schafer set up her second Expanding Horizons experience a year later, which finally brought her to Africa. Thanks to Cheryl French of the USDA's Animal and Plant Health Inspection Service, she gained broad insights into livestock infectious diseases in Senegal and what the country was doing to control them. Whether helping with a livestock vaccination campaign in traditional villages, shadowing a slaughterhouse inspector, or documenting poultry farms as avian influenza threatened to reach the country, Schafer thoroughly enjoyed herself. "I fell in love with the country, and I loved the work," she said.

After graduating from Cornell, Schafer enrolled at George Washington University in a public health program with a heavy focus on infectious and tropical diseases. Her decision to complete an MSPH degree and apply her veterinary background to human health as well was driven in part by her interest in the Epidemic Intelligence Service at the CDC. She was accepted into the service on her first attempt. As an officer in the Commissioned Corps of the US Public Health Service, a nonmilitarized uniformed service that is deployed to respond to emergencies, she was thrown right into the deep end of the pool. In the first four months, Schafer worked on four different Ebola and Marburg outbreaks in Africa, setting the tone for two busy years with the CDC's Viral Special Pathogens Branch.

One of the accomplishments Schafer is most proud of is developing an application with the CDC's software group to better manage data and contact tracing for viral hemorrhagic fevers in an international database. Named Epi Info, it was quickly put to the test during the Ebola epidemic in West Africa in 2014 and 2015, with data being combined at an international level. Schafer next worked with the CDC's Bacterial Special Pathogens Branch as the epidemiology subject-matter expert on leptospirosis, a bacterial disease that affects humans and animals. For six years, her work focused on everything from dealing with a canine outbreak of the bacterium in Arizona to using her clinical skills as a phlebotomist for a human serological survey—a test for previous exposure to the bacteria—in the US Virgin Islands. Schafer's contributions on both the viral and bacterial pathogen fronts were recognized by the CDC in 2017 with the prestigious James H. Steele Veterinary Public Health Award. Most recently, Schafer has been applying her expertise in epidemiology, surveillance, and outbreak response in the CDC's National Public Health Institute program, helping other countries set up CDC-like organizations of their own.

Steve Osofsky (DVM 1989), a former student of Samuel Gordon Campbell and now the Jay Hyman Professor of Wildlife Health and Health Policy at CVM as well as the director of the Cornell Wildlife Health Center, was one of the first recipients of Expanding Horizons funding. "It was life-changing," he confirmed. Over the course of three summers, he learned many of the lessons that students following in his footsteps would also encounter—about cultural competence, resilience, flexibility, and the career paths that stood open to them.[8]

Osofsky's first Expanding Horizons trip, in the summer of 1986, was to Kenya to assist a researcher running an elephant project. "I saw firsthand what happens when an expatriate researcher disregards local knowledge and sensibilities," he said. "From a failed research protocol to most of the foreign research team being hospitalized for malaria, that summer was an unforgettable lesson in what not to do." Cultural competence will serve veterinarians well, whether they are active internationally or in a US practice, Caroline Yancey, director of CVM international programs and chair of the Expanding Horizons program committee, agreed.

"Veterinarians typically work with a diverse mix of clients and staff in their daily work; fostering veterinary students' cultural sensitivity supports effective communication and other interpersonal skills critical to professional success," she said. Expanding Horizons presents a perfect classroom.[9]

The following summer with the Florida Panther Project showed Osofsky what deep sensitivity to both people and animals could look like in practice. "My mentor saw every opportunity to handle a panther as an honor, never forgetting that our patients never visit us by choice," Osofsky remembered. "The lessons I learned that summer have stayed with me throughout my career."[10]

Testing out ideas for potential careers in the field is a key benefit of Expanding Horizons. "You just can't get that in your academic program," Osofsky said. Nearly three decades after his influential encounter with the panthers, he watched Zachary Dvornicky-Raymond (class of 2015, DVM 2019) receive the same affirmation for his vocation from an eight-week experience with cheetah conservation in Otjiwarongo, Namibia, in 2016. "It blew the lid off of anything I'd ever expected from myself and from a career," Dvornicky-Raymond said. "It's hard to express how much my world view changed when I went on that trip. . . . When I came back from that, I finally knew what I wanted to do."[11] He has pursued a path in One Health and conservation ever since.[12]

But figuring out what you *do not* want to do can be just as valuable. Osofsky's third Expanding Horizons summer, at a major US zoo, was a fun, hands-on experience—and taught him that it was not the right work for him. "There are some students who, for example, try fieldwork and realize they don't like not having access to the internet or they don't like cold showers," he said. "I think it's important for them to figure that out now."

Four decades in, Expanding Horizons continues to be a treasured opportunity for students to explore their professional options and themselves.[13] "We've really tried to develop it as a signature program that we can promote," Sweet said. The plan has worked. "A lot of incoming accepted students we talk to choose Cornell in part because of Expanding Horizons; it's a big draw and, I think, critically important," Osofsky said.

"In envisioning Expanding Horizons, Dean Campbell wanted to foster students' internal reflection and self-awareness in the context of being global citizens," Osofsky said. "He wanted Cornell students to consider the full range of opportunities our training represents, and to understand the importance of using veterinary medicine to really help people, animals, and the environment that sustains us all. I remain forever grateful to Dr. Campbell for his clearly 'One Health' vision, although there was no such term at the time."

Notes

1. Steve Osofsky, interview by the author, June 2022.

2. “Samuel Gordon Campbell, December 10, 1933–September 29, 1997,” eCommons, Cornell University, accessed November 7, 2023, https://ecommons.cornell.edu/server/api/core/bitstreams/1542b0e1-fbd7-4eef-8d52-8bf9e61e16ea/content.

3. “Expanding Horizons,” College of Veterinary Medicine, Cornell University, accessed October 5, 2023, https://www.vet.cornell.edu/education/other-educational-opportunities/expanding-horizons.

4. Steve Osofsky, interview by the author, June 2022.

5. Cecilia Madsen, “Expanding Horizons: International Program for DVM Students,” Public *Health @ Cornell* (blog), June 17, 2016, https://blogs.cornell.edu/onehealth/2016/06/17/expanding-horizons-international-program-for-dvm-students.

6. Jai Sweet, interview by the author, June 2022.

7. Ilana Schafer, interview by the author, May 2022.

8. Steve Osofsky, interview by the author, June 2022.

9. Caroline Yancey, interview by the author, June 2022.

10. Carly Hodes, “Expanding Horizons Builds Foundation for a One Health Career,” *’Scopes*, October 2014, https://cpb-us-e1.wpmucdn.com/blogs.cornell.edu/dist/2/7450/files/2017/02/2014-Scopes-EH-article-25skakz.pdf.

11. “The Student Experience: Helping to Change Lives,” video, Cornell Wildlife Health Center, accessed October 5, 2023, https://wildlife.cornell.edu/resources/student-experience.

12. Zachary Dvornicky-Raymond, LinkedIn profile, accessed November 8, 2023, https://www.linkedin.com/in/zachary-dvornicky-raymond-875027224/.

13. “Celebrating the Achievements of Recent Cornell Veterinary Medicine Alumni: Saving the World Is a Growth Industry!,” Cornell Wildlife Health Center, accessed October 26, 2023, https://wildlife.cornell.edu/news/celebrating-achievements-recent-cornell-veterinary-medicine-alumni-saving-world-growth.

54. CORNELL AND THE PEACE CORPS

A Valuable Partnership

James E. Haldeman

Leprosy is one of the oldest diseases known to humans. Throughout its history, it has been much feared and misunderstood, and it has often led to exclusion from society. Following special training in the Virgin Islands and at the leprosarium in Carville, Louisiana, my wife, Janet, and I volunteered to work from 1967 to 1969 for the Peace Corps at the Masanga Leprosarium in Sierra Leone. It was founded in 1964 and provided free leprosy treatment and general treatment. I became the farm manager and developed a farm to make the three-hundred-patient hospital self-sufficient. We introduced poultry, developed land, and introduced new crops to improve the patients' diet. Janet initiated an occupational therapy department where she worked with leprosy patients, teaching various trades that used local materials. Our experiences were life changing, defined our careers, and continued engagement with the Peace Corps.

Cornell University began its involvement with the Peace Corps over sixty years ago. On March 1, 1961, US president John F. Kennedy launched the Peace Corps with a vision to foster cooperation and connections across cultures worldwide. The mission of the Peace Corps is to help people of interested countries meet the need for trained men and women, help people from host countries have a better understanding of people from the United States, and help people from the United States have a better understanding of other peoples. Cornell alumnus Richard Ottinger (class of 1950) was a founding member of the Peace Corps and played a major role in the organization's success. He served as director of programs for the west coast of South America in the early 1960s. Cornellian Glenn W. Ferguson became the first Peace Corps director in Thailand, served as associate Peace Corps director in Washington, and was special assistant to director Sargent Shriver from 1962 to 1964.

Over these sixty-plus years, the Peace Corps has offered Cornell a wide variety of opportunities for collaboration, and Cornell students have been the beneficiaries. In 1961, the Peace Corps approached the College of Agriculture (later the

Figure 54.1 Preschool activities for village children in Sierra Leone, 1968. (Photo provided by author)

College of Agriculture and Life Sciences, CALS) to organize and carry out training programs for new volunteers. The first cohort of Peace Corps volunteers from Cornell included eighteen graduates from CALS. In 1962, on-campus training for rural community development was initiated. One hundred three Peace Corps trainees reported for the Cornell-Peru Project.[1] In 1963, training was conducted for sixty-nine volunteers headed to Sierra Leone. That year, CALS established the International Agriculture Program with the objectives of educating and training students to work in international agricultural development, conducting research, and establishing cooperation with universities and exchange of students. From 1968 to 1972, the Peace Corps offered an internship program in Colombia to provide food production and nutrition programs with skilled graduates in these fields. The interns served as technical leaders in agriculture and nutrition, working with Colombian officials and Peace Corps volunteers with more general undergraduate training. From 1974 to 1976, CALS cooperated with the Peace Corps in the Future Agricultural Research Manpower Program in the Philippines. The college assisted in identifying needs for volunteers and then made information about specific opportunities available to faculty and interested students.

In 1976, International Programs in CALS established an on-campus Peace Corps student representative position to build a stronger link between land-grant

Figure 54.2 Leprosy patients harvest a new variety of lowland/swamp rice in Sierra Leone, 1968. (Photo provided by author)

colleges and the Peace Corps. According to Larry Zuidema, former associate and acting director of International Programs in CALS, the idea was to put former Peace Corps volunteers on land-grant campuses as Peace Corps representatives in order to communicate to agricultural students about Peace Corps opportunities and to provide opportunities for graduating undergrads and completing Master of Professional Studies in International Agriculture and Rural Development (MPS-IARD) students to gain experience abroad before seeking a career in development.[2]

Cornellian Robert Stavins (MS 1979), who had served as a Peace Corps volunteer in Sierra Leone, was selected to be the first on-campus Peace Corps representative. "The origins of my affinity for the natural environment and my interest in resource issues are to be found in the four years I spent in a small, remote village in Sierra Leone, West Africa, as a Peace Corps Volunteer, working in agricultural extension (in particular, paddy rice development)," said Stavins. "It was there that I was first exposed both to the qualities of a pristine natural environment and the trade-offs associated with economic development."[3] Stavins became the A. J. Meyer Professor of Energy and Economic Development at Harvard University.

More recently, in 1998, Cornell established a Master's International program as a partnership between the Peace Corps and Cornell. The program combined two semesters of Cornell coursework with a twenty-seven-month Peace Corps field experience and completion of a master of professional studies project paper.

In 2001, Cornell Law School professor Muna Ndulo, director of the Institute for African Development, along with law professor Robert Kent and city and regional planning professor David B. Lewis, organized the Lawyers in Africa Program with the Peace Corps. The program aimed to send recent graduates of the Cornell Law School to understaffed African law schools as Peace Corps volunteers, which has proved to be an immensely beneficial program for the young lawyers as well as for their host countries.

In 2010, Peace Corps director Aaron Williams visited the Cornell campus. "Cornell has had a long and distinguished record and partnership with Peace Corps, from the very beginning," he remarked. "Cornell was a place where we trained many Peace Corps volunteers in the early years, it's a place where we recruited their faculty to serve as staff, and Cornell was a principal university that return Peace Corps volunteers came back to, to pursue graduate education."[4] Three years later, International Programs in CALS celebrated its fifty-year collaboration with the Peace Corps with a major symposium. Cornell and the US Peace Corps signed a memorandum of understanding to establish the Paul D. Coverdell Fellowship, a graduate fellowship program that offers significant financial assistance to returned Peace Corps volunteers (RPCVs). RPCVs attend graduate school to pursue a master of professional studies followed by an internship in an underserved New York community. Cornell recruits RPCVs from all seventy-plus Peace Corps countries around the world.

"RPCVs make great graduate students," affirms Mildred E. Warner, professor in city and regional planning and herself a Peace Corps volunteer in Ecuador from 1979 to 1981. "The RPCVs come to Cornell and receive special support or summer internships in underserved US communities as part of their program." RPCVs bring valuable lessons learned from their Peace Corps service not just to the classroom but also to a local community. In addition to its affiliation with the Department of Global Development in CALS, the program is offered in the Department of City and Regional Planning in the College of Architecture, Art, and Planning, as well as with the Master of Public Administration Program in the Brooks School (formerly the Cornell Institute for Public Affairs in the College of Human Ecology).

Testimonies of Impact

Combining a Cornell learning experience with hands-on Peace Corps service had a profound impact on the volunteers and the communities they serviced. Theodore Endreny (class of 1990) served as a Peace Corps volunteer in Honduras from 1990 to 1992 and is now a professor of environmental resources engineering at the State University of New York College of Environmental Science and Forestry. His mother had been an enthusiastic Peace Corps volunteer in the 1960s, influencing his goal to pursue a career in international development. "Cornell University, by which I mean its people, courses, programs, and networks, educated me to address the global crisis of sustainability. [Being a] Peace Corps Volunteer was my dream job while a Cornell student from 1986 to 1990, pursuing a BS in Natural Resources Management," he said. "Cornell has had a transformative impact on my international service, which now extends to my students serving as Peace Corps Volunteers, and those who have returned and work with the international community toward global sustainability."[5]

Anne Bousquet (MPS 1993) was a Peace Corps volunteer in Botswana and Equatorial Guinea from 1986 to 1991 before joining the Catholic Relief Services. "My Peace Corps experiences were life changing and solidified my desire to serve overseas and try to make the world a better place," she said. "I have dedicated my life to serving and being an ambassador of the US for nearly thirty-five years. Anyone wanting to pursue a career in international development should consider Peace Corps as a steppingstone to a lifelong career in international development and contributing to building a more peaceful world of understanding."[6]

Gemma Kite (MEng 2011), a Peace Corps Master's International program/master of engineering student in the CALS Department of Biological and Environmental Engineering from 2007 to 2011, served in Mali as a Peace Corps Water and Sanitation volunteer from 2008 to 2010. The project included educating farmers on how to make several natural pesticides with locally sourced materials (e.g., neem, chili peppers, and soap) and how to use the natural pesticides to maximize plant growth and reduce pests. She stated, "The real value I brought as a volunteer was being able to connect trained and experienced Malians with my community to be able to carry out projects that met a specific need."[7] After graduating from Cornell in 2011, she worked for a French nongovernmental organization in Kamakwie, Sierra Leone, where one of her main projects was to implement a grassroots pump maintenance and repair program for the district.

Jeffrey Wall (MPS 2012, MS 2014, PhD 2018) was a Peace Corps volunteer from 2009 to 2011 in Azerbaijan before coming to Cornell for graduate school. After learning that there were problems with the chestnut tree population, he contacted Cornell plant pathology professor Michael Milgroom. Together they worked to build a research program that could not only verify the presence of this disease in Azerbaijan but also characterize the genetic variation of the fungus in the country. Milgroom also put Wall in touch with Swiss scientists working on chestnut blight in the Caucasus, and the ensuing partnerships led to the development of a biological control for the disease. "It all began with the empowerment and wisdom I received through my Masters of Professional Studies Degree in International Agriculture and Rural Development at Cornell's International Programs and the College of Agriculture and Life Sciences," he said.[8]

Parker Filer (MPS 2011) was a Peace Corps volunteer in Honduras from 2009 to 2011. "The hybrid experience of academic study at Cornell, combined with two years of legitimate field experience in rural development with the Peace Corps, was a unique opportunity that continues to influence me personally and professionally," he reflected on the program. "As both a graduate student and a Peace Corps volunteer at once, my service was a stimulating mix of theory and practice that can't be duplicated."[9]

Lorraine Perricone-Dazzo (MPS 2014) served as a Peace Corps volunteer in Senegal from 2009 to 2011 and as a Peace Corps volunteer leader from 2011 to 2013. The following year, she was a contractor with the Peace Corps supporting the Food Security program in Senegal and West Africa more broadly. "Living and working in Senegal has shaped my worldview and informed my long-term career and personal life goals like no other experience I've ever had," she reflected. "The knowledge and connections I established at Cornell before beginning my service increased the potential impact of my work by training me to think like a community organizer and agricultural extension agent."[10]

The Partnership Endures

The relationship between Cornell and the Peace Corps that started more than sixty years ago remains very strong.[11] Nearly two thousand Cornell alumni have served as Peace Corps volunteers. Cornell consistently ranks in the top five medium-size colleges and universities in terms of numbers of volunteers recruited each year. In 2009, Ithaca and Tompkins County led the nation in per capita Peace Corps volunteers (12.85 volunteers per 100,000 residents).

The Cornell–Peace Corps collaboration is a proven and mutually beneficial partnership that benefits local communities around the world, Peace Corps volunteers, the United States, and the university community. It provides graduates with skills that are highly sought by employers in the nonprofit, governmental, and private sectors. Through the Master's International program, volunteers are better prepared to contribute to their assigned community. The RPCV program represents a win-win-win situation, as it enriches the classroom environment and a local community by bringing the new knowledge and experience gained by volunteers.

Notes

1. For more about the Cornell-Peru Project, see chapter 25, Applied Anthropology in the Andes: The Cornell-Peru Project.

2. Larry W. Zuidema, *Cornell University Meets the Challenge of World Agriculture* (Ithaca, NY: International Programs, College of Agriculture and Life Sciences, Cornell University, 2014), https://hdl.handle.net/1813/112751.

3. Robert Stavins, "Environmental Economics—a Personal Perspective," *HuffPost*, August 1, 2017, https://www.huffpost.com/entry/environmental-economics-a-personal-perspective_b_5980ef14e4b0b35d274c5e5a.

4. Krishna Ramanujan, "Peace Corps Experience Is 'Transformative,' Says Director," *Cornell Chronicle*, September 3, 2010, https://news.cornell.edu/stories/2010/09/peace-corps-director-says-experience-transformative.

5. Theodore Endreny (class of 1990), email correspondence with the author, May 23, 2022.

6. Anne Bousquet (MPS 1993), email correspondence with the author, April 2, 2022.

7. Gemma Kite (MEng 2011), email correspondence with the author, March 20, 2022.

8. Jeffrey Wall (MPS 2012, MS 2014, PhD 2018), email correspondence with the author, April 1, 2022.

9. Parker Filer (MPS 2011), email correspondence with the author, April 6, 2022.

10. Lorraine Perricone-Dazzo (MPS 2014), email correspondence with the author, April 4, 2022.

11. "Peace Corps and Cornell: A Proven Partnership," Cornell University, accessed October 27, 2023, http://www.peacecorps.cornell.edu/index.cfm.

55. ABOVE ALL NATIONS IS HUMANITY

The Cornell Cosmopolitan Club

Elaine D. Engst and Blaine Friedlander

Sitting next to Modesto Quiroga at an Ithaca boarding house supper table, a young woman heard his difficulties with the English language. Her own brothers had just returned from the Spanish-American War.

"You are a Spaniard," she said.

"I, a Spaniard? No," said Quiroga. "I am an American."

Quiroga—a Cornell graduate student from Argentina who would receive his MS in 1905—considered himself a world citizen. "His vision took in the whole world," wrote Thomas F. Hunt, a Cornell professor of agronomy who left Cornell to become Pennsylvania State University's dean of agriculture. He said, "[Quiroga's] philosophy was not circumscribed by any school. He not only had knowledge of world movements and ideas, but understanding, and with it that sympathy that grows out of acquaintance and understanding." The idealistic Quiroga embraced national diversity in the highest sense. "Modesto Quiroga is one of those rare spirits who see things in true perspective without local color or prejudice," explained Hunt.[1]

International students had come to Cornell from the beginning of the university, and some students—graduate and undergraduate—and faculty created social organizations for themselves. In 1873, the Brazilian students published *Aurora Brasileira*, a monthly newsletter written in Portuguese, and established Club Brasileiro. In fall 1889, Latin American students from Nicaragua, Puerto Rico, Honduras, and Brazil created Alpha Zeta, a short-lived so-called foreigner's fraternity officially founded over the winter break on January 1, 1890. In 1894, the Canadian Club appeared, and the Club Latino-Americano flourished for a time. The Chinese Students Association was founded in 1904; a Filipino Cornellians group began in 1924.

Figure 55.1 The Cosmopolitan Club's soccer team, which became the 1925 Cornell Inter-Fraternity soccer champions, pose for posterity. Cosmopolitan Club Records, #37-4-441. (Provided by Division of Rare and Manuscript Collections, Cornell University Library)

Origins of the Cosmopolitan Club

Organized by Quiroga, Cornell's Cosmopolitan Club, a group intended to include all international students, as well as interested American students, first met on November 10, 1904, in Barnes Hall, with sixty students attending. Quiroga—along with faculty members Vladimir Karapetoff, engineering professor; George Prentice Bristol, professor of Greek; and Liberty Hyde Bailey, the renowned dean of the newly established New York State College of Agriculture—led the meeting. At the next meeting, weeks later, more than one hundred people crammed into tight quarters at the law school in Boardman Hall (now the site of the Olin Library). The *Cornell Daily Sun* reported, "The object of the new club will be to unite in social and intellectual intercourse Cornell students of all nationalities, and to extend the influence of Cornell abroad."[2]

The group initially rented rooms at 313 Eddy Street. Many Cornell faculty became members. Townspeople were eligible for "associate membership"; Ithaca Unitarian minister Cyrus Heizer joined as a charter member, and the *Ithaca Journal* reported on the group's activities. Cornell president Jacob Gould Schurman and former president Andrew Dickson White were frequent visitors and honorary members of the organization. Countries represented in the early years included

Figure 55.2 Cosmopolitan Club building, ca. 1930. Cosmopolitan Club Records, #37-4-441. (Provided by Division of Rare and Manuscript Collections, Cornell University Library)

Argentina, Australia, Brazil, Bulgaria, China, England, Germany, India, Ireland, Japan, Mexico, the Netherlands, Peru, the Philippines, Romania, Russia, Scotland, South African, Sweden, and Turkey.

"They Might Find the Best in One Another"

In 1911, the club moved into its newly built residence at 301 Bryant Avenue, with rooms for thirty to forty men, a dining room for one hundred, and an auditorium seating four hundred to five hundred. The building was dedicated on November 11, 1911, with a speech by President White titled "The Hague Conference and the Maintenance of Peace."[3] While the Cosmopolitan Club ceased operations in 1954, the building remains in Collegetown as a private apartment house.

For five decades, the Cosmopolitan Club would meld international students and elevate peaceful thoughts. Christian Bües, a German undergraduate student, concisely explained the existence of Cornell's Cosmopolitan Club: "It was founded to bring intelligent thinking men of different nations in such contact that they might find the best in one another; that they might learn to love, to live on common bases side by side; it was founded to make men understand the spirit of nations so that in difficult international conflicts they might have a clear judgment and correct reasoning."[4]

The club—with the motto "Above all nations is humanity"—became a machine of continuous activity. It was an opportunity for students and professors to illuminate other students about the world. It participated in university activities and held informal summer programs, important for international students who could not travel home for the summer. One of its objects was also "to promote the organization of chapters in other universities in the United States of America and in other countries."[5] As early as 1907, there were chapters in Michigan, Wisconsin, and Illinois, and the national Association of Cosmopolitan Clubs was founded.

National Nights

The group met to discuss "various forms of government now flourishing in the world" or free trade and protection.[6] In 1905 Professor Nathaniel Schmidt gave a talk titled "Travelling Experiences in Palestine." When the 1906 San Francisco earthquake occurred, geological sciences professor Ralph Stockman Tarr addressed the club. Jeremiah Jenks, professor of history and political science, spoke to the group on the hot topics of immigration and the Chinese boycott of American goods. The club held national nights for China, Japan, Argentina, the Netherlands, Brazil, Britain, and South Africa.

At the club's first annual banquet, on June 3, 1905, the members dined on little-neck clams, consommé royal, baked bluefish à la creole, veal croquettes, and Cosmopolitan Punch, all the while listening to a program of Edvard Grieg's "Solveig's Song," mixed with more music by the Cosmopolitan Club Orchestra, and a lecture, "The Present Political Situation in Sweden and Norway," by professor of history Ralph Catterall. He explained the ongoing civil war following Norway's breakaway from Sweden. "The quarrel between Norway and Sweden was quietly discussed in the peaceful atmosphere of tobacco smoke," reminisced Abraham Abbey Freedlander in his "Retrospect," for the *Cornell Cosmopolitan Club Annual* in 1907.[7]

Initially, women were not included in the club, probably reflecting the relatively few women students from other countries, as well as cultural sensitivities. Events including women were held as early as 1906, and the Women's Cosmopolitan Club was founded in 1921. Thirty years after the men's club formed, the group's constitution was amended to include female students.

"A More Human Place"

In 1920, Leonard Elmhirst (class of 1921) became president of the Cosmopolitan Club. Elmhirst, an English student and Cambridge graduate who had become a disciple of the Indian philosopher Rabindranath Tagore, had come to Cornell to study agriculture so that he could go back to India to teach farming. The club was in serious debt, and Elmhirst approached Dorothy Straight, widow of Willard D. Straight (class of 1901). She was sympathetic and particularly interested in fulfilling the request in Willard Straight's will to make Cornell "a more human place."[8]

Along with planning for what would eventually become Willard Straight Hall, Dorothy Straight provided an amount equal to 70 percent of the debt and $5,000 to renovate the house. Eventually she married Elmhirst and moved to England to begin a progressive school, Dartington Hall.

"Peace and Security in the Near Future and Forever"

At the club's annual Initiation Banquet on Saturday, December 6, 1941, the group dined on vegetable soup and lamb chops. Ornithologist George M. Sutton, recently back from an expedition to Mexico, gave an address, and Shigeo Kondo (class of 1943) gave the night's welcoming remarks. The next day their lives changed.

While America was swept into the throes of World War II, Kondo ascended to the presidency of the Cosmopolitan Club. For the club's annual senior farewell banquet, on May 10, 1942, he served as toastmaster. Kondo's family had been classified as "enemy aliens," and in June 1942, after Kondo's father had quickly sold off the family's personal belongings, Kondo and his family boarded a ship, the *Gripsholm*, and sailed to Japan. Kondo was conscripted into the Japanese Army despite only speaking English, having grown up in New Jersey.

Although he never finished his Cornell degree, Kondo returned to the United States in 1952 and had a career as a physician. He remained engaged with the university and was honored in January 2014 at the Cornell Alumni Leadership Conference in Boston with the William "Bill" Vanneman '31 Outstanding Class Leader Award for his more than fifty years of service as an officer of the class of 1943.

Members of Cornell's Cosmopolitan Club acknowledged the war, all the while keeping their own international spirits alive. Handwritten on a program from the club's initiation banquet on December 12, 1942, was a benediction that encompassed the sincerity of all of its members: "We who are gathered here tonight from all over the world pray that the Great Spirit who rules the Universe will guide us to the accomplishment of the finest that is in us, to the end that all nations and all peoples will be able to live in peace and security in the near future and forever."[9]

Notes

A version of this chapter appeared as "Cornell Rewind: 'Above All Nations Is Humanity,'" by Elaine Engst and Blaine Friedlander, *Cornell Chronicle*, November 20, 2014, https://news.cornell.edu/stories/2014/11/cornell-rewind-above-all-nations-humanity.

1. Thomas F. Hunt, "Modesto Quiroga," *Cornell Cosmopolitan Club Annual*, June 1907.

2. "Cosmopolitan Club Formed," *Cornell Daily Sun*, November 11, 1904, 1–3, https://cdsun.library.cornell.edu/?a=d&d=CDS19041111.2.9.

3. Andrew Dickson White was president of the American delegation to The Hague Peace Conference in 1899. He would later lead the efforts to build the Peace Palace in The Hague, which houses the International Court of Justice, the Permanent Court of Arbitration, The Hague Academy of International Law, and the Peace Palace Library. The palace opened in 1913.

4. Christian Bües, "Lines from Far Away Peru," *Cornell Cosmopolitan Club Annual*, June 1907, 22–23.

5. "Constitution of the Cornell Cosmopolitan Club," *Cornell Cosmopolitan Club Annual*, June 1907, 72.

6. Abraham Abbey Freedlander, "Retrospect," *Cornell Cosmopolitan Club Annual*, June 1907, 11.

7. Banquet program/menu, 1905, Box 4, Folder 15, Cosmopolitan Club Records, #37-4-145, Division of Rare and Manuscript Collections, Cornell University Library. Abraham Abbey Freedlander, "Retrospect," *Cornell Cosmopolitan Club Annual*, June 1907, 5–17.

8. "Willard Straight Gift Enriches Cornell Life," *New York Times*, October 18, 1925.

9. Banquet program/menu, 1942, Box 4, Folder 25, Cosmopolitan Club Records, #37-4-145, Division of Rare and Manuscript Collections, Cornell University Library.

56. PROVIDING A HOME FOR A GLOBAL COMMUNITY

The Holland International Living Center

Jerry Wilcox

In response to increased international enrollment, Cornell opened the Holland International Living Center (HILC) in 1970 as a student living arrangement. The following statement from its website describes its role and function well:

> HILC is dedicated to creating a globally conscious community. Originally conceived as a space to matriculate international students into Cornell, HILC has grown to encompass more. Our residents are both international and domestic students, from multicultural families, and students with experience and interest in the international community. HILC encourages its residents to be active participants in an internationally focused community by educating others, sharing experiences, and appreciating all cultures represented. HILC strives to be a hub of international life and global engagement on the Cornell campus. International students and domestic students share rooms, stories, and their lives in HILC. You can walk down the hall and meet someone from the other side of the world. Undergraduate students of all class years live here and help one another learn about Cornell, Ithaca, and the US. We know you will come to love HILC as much as our current residents and alumni have![1]

HILC was originally planned to house 144 students—60 percent from abroad—in a North Campus residence hall. In a unique funding cooperative among three Cornell University departments—Housing, University Unions, and the International Student Office—each department contributed one-third toward the salary of a full-time live-in residence hall director starting in the summer of 1971. In its first academic year, a graduate student and his wife lived in HILC's new apartment for fall term 1970 and spring term 1971.

The idea that the center should operate year-round in serving international students was unique among the surrounding North campus dormitories and special

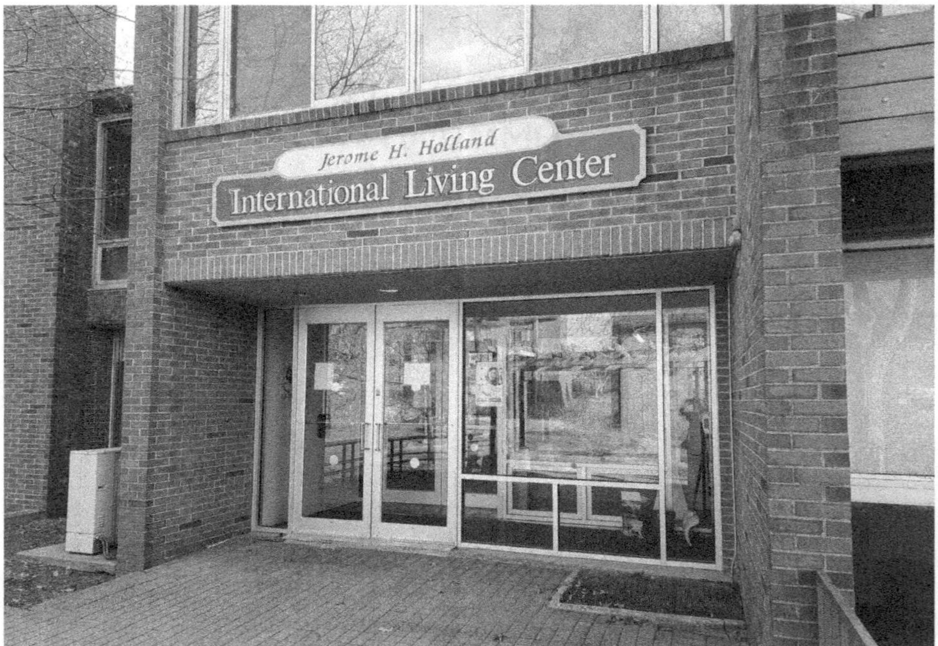

Figure 56.1 Entrance of the Holland International Living Center, 2023. (Photo by Heike Michelsen)

interest residence halls. In the early years of the HILC, newly arriving international students could request temporary housing there before the residence halls opened for fall term. This service ceased in late August to allow time for residence hall preparation and move-in of the incoming HILC residents. On occasion, some international students chose to stay permanently if space allowed.

HILC also recognized the importance of food in the internationalization process. Aside from a main kitchen, each of the four units had a small food preparation area. These kitchen areas grew far beyond the intent of their original design and became centers of intercultural exchange. Unit and all-house dinner groups developed, with food preparation shared among the members. Occasional Sunday brunches were held in the main hall. Each corner of the hall tested the building's electrical capacity by highlighting different regional foods, with residents inviting friends and favorite faculty to enjoy great food and conversation as they whipped up various dishes. One of the unit lounges became the site of the national flags of the residents, updated by the residents themselves.

In the early years, by design, a few graduate students also lived in HILC. This mixing of ages and experiences from first-year students to graduate students made for a mature atmosphere of discussion and friendship. Over time, as the university honed its in-house educational programs and developed more housing for international graduate students, this option was dropped.

Figure 56.2 The Holland International Living Center provides a home for undergraduate and graduate students from around the world, ca. 1996. (Photo by University Photography)

Over the history of HILC, the energy and creativity of its residents have been instrumental in its success. Capable residence hall directors, resident advisers, and enthusiastic residents all contributed to fulfilling the goals of this unique living center.

Just three years after the opening of HILC, the *Ithaca Journal* reported, "'The ILC provides a valuable experience for everyone, but I think it is particularly good for Americans,' said Renu Chahil, a graduate student from Delhi, India, 'because so many of them ordinarily don't have the opportunity to get to know students from other countries and cultures.' Another student, Firoz K. Shariff, a Kenyan of Indian descent, also noted: 'Though there are students here who come from conflicting countries, they usually play down these differences, at least on a personal level. I feel this creates a more congenial atmosphere for discussion on 'hot' political issues.'"[2] Resident directors contributed to increase intercultural communications within the HILC community over the years. Programming initiatives included intercultural orientation programs held off-campus in the early fall term as well as intercultural communication workshops during weekends.

Historically, it should be noted that the first counselor to international students at Cornell, John L. Mott, left Cornell to lead the International House in New York City from 1935 to 1954.[3] This accommodation on Riverside Drive has provided housing for international and US students at Columbia University for decades. International Houses at the University of Chicago and the University of California at Berkeley also are part of that effort to encourage intercultural living for people in higher education.

In January 1985, the International Living Center was named in honor of Jerome H. "Brud" Holland (class of 1939, MS 1941). Holland was an All-American football honoree and a university trustee. A former president of Delaware State University and the Hampton Institute, Holland was the first Black board member of the New York Stock Exchange and also chaired the American Red Cross and served as the US ambassador to Sweden from 1970 to 1972. He furthered international efforts that improved intercultural communication in line with the principles on which HILC was founded.

Since HILC has now been operating successfully for more than fifty years, its popularity and usefulness have been passed on to the next generation. Children of former residents have indeed enjoyed the HILC experience themselves during their Cornell study. Kudos to the Cornell originators of this unique North Campus living arrangement and the consistent support provided by the university that allows HILC to remain a popular residential option.

Notes

1. "About HILC," Cornell University Campus Groups, accessed March 19, 2023, https://cornell.campusgroups.com/hilc/about-hilc/.

2. "International Center 'More than Dormitory,'" *Ithaca Journal*, February 5, 1973, 4.

3. For more about John L. Mott's role, see chapter 50, Supporting the Global Community: International Student and Scholar Services.

57. PERFORMING AROUND THE WORLD

Cornell's Musical Ambassadors

Corey Ryan Earle

Although Cornell University would not form the official Department of Music until 1903, student musical ensembles have been performing since the very start of the university. Over the years, these vocal and instrumental organizations have toured across the United States and around the globe, bringing the Cornell name to alumni and nonalumni alike as global ambassadors for the university and the nation.

The Cornell University Glee Club, a tenor-bass choral ensemble that traces its origins back to the very earliest months of the university, is perhaps Cornell's most well-traveled student organization. Under the direction of Hollis E. Dann from 1889 to 1921, the choir began a tradition of annual concert tours, typically over the Christmas holiday, to major US cities. For over fifty years, these trips also included the university banjo and mandolin ensembles, under the collective umbrella of the Cornell Musical Clubs. Their traveling performances were popular with alumni, who relished the opportunity to host lavish postconcert receptions and relive their old college days. For the students, it was a chance to venture beyond Ithaca, bond with classmates over tour successes and failures, and bring their music to (hopefully) appreciative new audiences.

In 1895, the Musical Clubs undertook their first international voyage, traveling to England. The university crew had applied to compete at the Henley Royal Regatta, a prestigious rowing event hosted annually on the river Thames, and the Musical Clubs jumped at the opportunity to accompany the athletes. The musicians sailed for Europe on June 19 and were honored with a Fourth of July dinner by the American Club of London upon arrival. Their first concert, held at London's St. James Hall on July 5, received mixed reviews by English critics. While some praised the skill and humor of the Cornell performances, others were confused by the eclectic American style of light entertainment. Local audiences were also offended by the large group of American students in attendance, who waved an American flag and applauded enthusiastically. One particular critic

Figure 57.1 Departure of Glee Club members to Ceylon, Asia, in 1966. (Photo by Thomas Patrick Cullen)

described the concert as "rather depressing" and "prolonged to an altogether absurd length by the number of encores." The reviewer went on to note the "rather characterless instruments," song selections that merited "no special mention," and composers who were "quite unimportant." Hollis Dann, reflecting on the experience, noted that one of the problems was "the utter failure of the Britons to acknowledge the worth of anything new. . . . They were at a loss whether to treat it from a professional standpoint or as an amateur affair."[1]

Compounding the negative reception was the university crew's own performance several days later. On July 10, the Cornell rowers defeated the British Leander Club crew, who claimed they had not been ready to row when the umpire signaled to begin, barely leaving the starting line as the Cornellians rowed on. The Big Red team was defeated by the Trinity Hall Boat Club the next day, and the press vilified Cornell's unsportsmanlike behavior and unorthodox American rowing style. The crew's reception amplified the struggles for the performing ensembles. Although the Musical Clubs had expected to perform more than twenty concerts in England, Ireland, and Scotland, the tour was abandoned after only six concerts, with the tour manager claiming that many venues had canceled and that the musicians had "lost heart" as a result of the bad press for the Americans.

With the student performers left homeless and bankrupt without concert revenue, they were befriended by the Savage Club of London, a gentlemen's social club whose members entertained each other with music, storytelling, and other

Figure 57.2 Glee Club director Thomas Sokol (*left*) takes the lead performing a ritual Japanese dance at the Tea House of the August Moon in Okinawa during the group's historic tour of Asia, 1966. (Photo by Thomas Patrick Cullen)

talents. Upon returning to Ithaca, several of the Cornellians received permission to found the Savage Club of Ithaca, an offshoot of the London entertainers that is still performing over 125 years later. Despite the tour's abrupt end, it remains one of the first international concert tours by an American collegiate musical ensemble, perhaps predated only by the Amherst Glee Club's visit to England the previous year.

It would be nearly sixty years before the Glee Club traveled internationally again, giving a concert at the Palacio de Bellas Artes in Mexico City on a cross-country 1954 tour. The enthusiastic Mexican audience cheered wildly for performances of the folk song "Cielito Lindo" and the Mexican national anthem. The following decade would see the Glee Club venture beyond North America and Europe with two tours that made history for their ambition and scope.

In December 1960, the Glee Club departed for fourteen days in the Soviet Union—seven in Moscow and seven in Leningrad. Under the leadership of Thomas A. Sokol, professor of music and director from 1957 to 1995, the ensemble worked with the US Department of State, Council on Student Travel, Soviet Committee of Youth Organizations, and Bureau on International Youth Travel to make the necessary arrangements. Seventy-five students were selected for the trip and given lessons in Soviet culture and the Russian language. The tour is believed to have been the first by an American collegiate musical ensemble to the Soviet Union and consisted of eight concerts at venues like the Moscow State University, Moscow Power Engineering Institute, and Leningrad State University. It concluded with a brief visit to London, including a reunion with the Savage

Club. During the trip, performances were broadcast on Radio Leningrad and the BBC.

The Glee Club would return to England again in 1963, but its three-month spring 1966 tour of East Asia would bring the Cornell name to a wider audience than nearly any other student endeavor. As Michael Slon writes in *Songs from the Hill: A History of the Cornell University Glee Club*, "In so short a time no Cornell organization has ever touched so many people's lives as the Glee Club on its 1966 tour of the Far East. It was estimated more than 100 million people heard the group during those three months, and the bonds formed remained for lifetimes."[2] Funded and organized by the Cultural Presentations Office of the US Department of State, the goodwill tour was intended to bolster the American image abroad.

The eighty-six-day trip covered thirty-seven thousand miles and included forty-nine formal concerts, thirty-eight radio and television appearances, and over fifty informal and impromptu performances. Stops included Ceylon (now Sri Lanka), Singapore, Malaysia, Thailand, the Philippines, Hong Kong, Taiwan, Okinawa, South Korea, and Japan, and performances included the national anthems and folk songs in the native language of each country. Although the forty-one students were forced to take the semester off from Cornell, an arrangement was made for them to remain registered "in absentia" in order to maintain student immunity from the draft and conscription into the military.

The tour was a remarkable triumph of musical and cultural exchange, forever changing the lives of the Cornell participants. Many of the men later lived or worked in Asia, and one married a woman he met on the trip. Afterward, one Cornell alumnus in the Philippines wrote to the university president to note that the students were "the best ambassadors of goodwill that ever came to this country and they have not only sown good public relations but left good memories and a good image of the country where they come from."[3] The tour alumni have continued to reunite in Ithaca regularly, performing with the students of the Glee Club at a homecoming weekend concert on several occasions.

The Glee Club's tradition of annual tours continues today, with later international travels bringing them to Germany (1970, 1972), Czechoslovakia (1972), Austria (1972), England (1979, 1982, 2012), Singapore (1989), China (1989, 2008), Hong Kong (1989), France (1992), Spain (1992), Switzerland (1992), Canada (1993, 2012, 2020), Venezuela (2001), Brazil (2004), Wales (2012), Scotland (2012), Guatemala (2016), and Mexico (2016). Each trip forged new cross-country bonds and cultural awareness. Among the tangible outcomes of touring was the popularization of the song "Ave Maria" by Franz Biebl. The sheet music was shared with Professor Sokol by Biebl while the Glee Club recorded a program for the Frankfurt Radio Network in 1970. The Glee Club would premiere the piece in the United States later that year, and it would go on to become a mainstay of men's choral repertoire.

In recent decades, several other Cornell ensembles have also served as musical ambassadors worldwide. The treble-voice Cornell University Chorus would join with the Glee Club for the tours to Venezuela (2001), China (2008), Guatemala and Mexico (2016), and Canada (2020). The group took its first international trip in 1998 to Taiwan, where they performed for Lee Teng-hui (PhD 1968), president of Taiwan. Their other travels have brought them to Canada (2000, 2019) and Italy (2005). Several Cornell a cappella ensembles have also taken trips abroad, although typically at a much smaller scale and of a more informal nature.

In the twenty-first century, Cornell's instrumental ensembles have joined in international exchange efforts. In January 2006, the Cornell University Wind Symphony, under the direction of professor of music Cynthia Johnston Turner, traveled to Costa Rica for a concert tour that included performances for two former presidents of Costa Rica and a reception at the home of the US ambassador. The trip had been inspired by family members of Johnston Turner who worked in Costa Rica and had asked about obtaining instruments for students there. Of particular note, the ensemble donated fifty musical instruments to schoolchildren while on the trip. The tour was such a success that it was repeated in 2008, 2010, 2012, and 2014, with each visit including workshops, recitals, concerts, and donated instruments. According to Johnston Turner, "The relationships formed, through teaching, traveling and performing together, were true and deep."[4] More recently, under the direction of Professor James Spinazzola, the wind symphony has taken service-learning trips to Haiti and the Dominican Republic in 2017 and 2019.

The Cornell Symphony Orchestra, led by professor of music Chris Younghoon Kim, began its own tradition of touring in January 2007 with a performance of works by Brahms and Shostakovich in Berlin, Germany. Visits to Ireland (2012, 2015), Puerto Rico (2014), Argentina (2017), and Taiwan (2019) followed, each with its own opportunities for cultural exchange and appreciation.

Music has sometimes been described as the universal language of humankind, and Cornell University's performing ensembles have demonstrated time and again the value of shared song across international borders. The opportunity to collaborate with international ensembles and perform for global audiences has given generations of Cornellians a life-changing experience and a cultural education that can only be achieved beyond the classroom.

Notes

1. Quoted in Michael Slon, *Songs from the Hill: A History of the Cornell University Glee Club* (Ithaca, NY: Cornell University Glee Club, 1998), 183.
2. Slon, 211.
3. Quoted in Slon, 135.
4. Elisabeth Rosen, "Cornell Wind Ensemble's Fourth Costa Rica Tour a Success," *Cornell Chronicle*, February 1, 2012, https://news.cornell.edu/stories/2012/02/student-musicians-trip-costa-rica-success.

58. TRACK AND FIELD AND THE TRANSATLANTIC SERIES

Arthur C. Smith

In December 1920, when the Cornell cross country team boarded a ship and braved a wintry Atlantic Ocean to take its first overseas trip to the United Kingdom, the young athletes and their coaches who took part in this voyage did more than usher in a lasting track and field tradition on the Hill. More profoundly, they joined an extraordinary cultural, educational, and social exchange. With the Great War only recently completed and the world weary of war, efforts by universities on either side of the Atlantic to bridge differences were seen as a step forward for both the United States and Europe. Cornell became part of a larger effort to bring two cultures closer together through shared experiences.

Cornell's athletic involvement with Oxford and Cambridge did not begin with this trip. The Big Red's prowess in rowing had already brought the university renown in Great Britain and other parts of Europe. And Cornell was not the first Ivy League team to compete in track and field against Oxford and Cambridge. That tradition was already a quarter century old in 1920 as the combined forces of Harvard and Yale had been taking on the Oxford and Cambridge teams since 1894. Under the leadership of legendary head coach Jack Moakley, the Big Red had become a dominant force in intercollegiate track and field in the first decades of the twentieth century, retiring the trophy for the prestigious Intercollegiate Amateur Athletic Association of America (IC4A) track title due to a five-year winning streak and a record-setting low score in winning the 1918 IC4A cross country title. Given the esteem with which the Big Red was already held in rowing, the prospect of competing against the top-flight Cornell cross country teams helmed by Moakley was an attractive challenge for Oxford and Cambridge.

That first cross country competition in 1920, held over 7.5 miles outside London and won by Oxford and Cambridge by the close score of twenty-six to twenty-nine, is immortalized in a newsreel film that commemorated the day. The genuine enthusiasm of the cheering crowds when the first finisher, a Cambridge student, crossed the line is evident in the streaky black-and-white images. But what is more

Figure 58.1 Cornell's Lewis "Lou" Elmer (class of 1931) wins the 440-yard dash in fifty-one seconds at the 1930 Transatlantic Series meet at Stamford Bridge, London. Cornell University Track and Field Collection, #40-9-1820. (Provided by Division of Rare and Manuscript Collections, Cornell University Library)

profound is the final piece of the reel when the first Cornellian crosses the line in second place and is immediately met with a warm embrace by the race winner. The two are asked to stage a pose, shaking hands, but the smiles and warm feelings are real. The British won the day, but the overall theme of friendship and shared experience was the defining aspect of the competition. This remains the only competition over hill and dale between Cornell and its friends from Oxford and Cambridge, but that spirit continues to this day in the Transatlantic Series on the track. It was this cross country match that set the table for the track and field series that would follow.

During the cross country team's winter trip to Great Britain, a fortuitous meeting between longtime Cornell track coach John "Terry" McGovern (class of 1900) and Cambridge's Rex Salisbury Woods proved to be critical for Cornell's involvement in the series. Woods, twice an Olympian for Great Britain and already a decorated war hero by the time Cornell arrived in 1920, was deeply involved in Cambridge athletics. McGovern, a future vice president of the US Olympic Committee, had been a standout on Moakley's early Cornell teams and was still deeply involved in the Big Red program. While at Cambridge visiting with Woods after the cross country match, McGovern proposed that Cornell join the series of track

Figure 58.2 The Cornell and Princeton track teams in 1930, with Cornell track coach Jack Moakley (*far right*); Charlie Treman, class of 1930 (*second from left in front row*); and Carl Meinig, class of 1931 (*fourth from left in the second row*). Cornell University Track and Field Collection, #40-9-1820. (Provided by Division of Rare and Manuscript Collections, Cornell University Library)

competitions already underway between the combined teams of Harvard and Yale and their Oxbridge counterparts. McGovern recalls Woods "deploring the irregularity of the competition."[1] After all, Cambridge and Oxford had only enjoyed a handful of matches with Harvard and Yale in the quarter century since their series had begun, and this was Cornell's first entry. Not wanting the "fun of the day's" races to be a one-time-only event, the two set in motion the organization and rotation of the track and field series that continues to this day. McGovern wrote,

> The suggestion developed was to organize a group of six colleges, including Oxford and Cambridge, and four from America. Oxford and Cambridge would be, of course, permanent. The four-year rotation system was accomplished by a plan to have, on the year following the Olympics, Oxford and Cambridge visit the United States and compete in two meets here: one against Princeton and Cornell; the other against Yale and Harvard. In the second year, two of the American colleges would go to England; in the third year, the remaining two would go over; and the fourth year would again be bland to provide for the Olympic Games.[2]

The idea put into motion a series of track meets that would happen three times every Olympiad (twice for Cornell) over the next century, interrupted only by the resumption of hostilities on the Continent during World War II. Cornell joined forces with Princeton for a generation until financial difficulty kept the Princeton Tigers from continuing, with their final tour occurring in 1950. Beginning in 1953, the Big Red teamed up with the University of Pennsylvania, and that partnership continues to this day.

The 1920 cross country meet was a direct precursor to a track meet in 1921 on Travers Island, New York, that, fittingly enough, resulted in a tie between the combined Cornell-Princeton team and the athletes from Oxford and Cambridge. After another match stateside in 1925, the Cornell and Princeton teams crossed the Atlantic again in the summer of 1926 for the first track and field expedition to the British Isles. Nearly a century later, and after forty-five matches on both sides of the Atlantic, the series retains its timeless ability to bring teammates and foes closer together. And the plan hatched by McGovern and Woods, with three competitions in every four years of the Olympic cycle (the Olympic year being the only year in which the competition would lie fallow) still holds.

The athletic excellence that blossomed as a part of the quadrennial trips by Cornell to compete against its sister schools in England—and that continued in the reciprocal trips by Oxford and Cambridge (and later, the University of Birmingham) to visit Ithaca, Philadelphia, New Haven, and Boston—is a remarkable tradition in collegiate and international athletics. But the relationships and experiences forged through this series of athletic competitions and tours have produced an even richer story that has created friendships (and even marriages), deepened institutional and cultural bonds, and left lasting marks on the universities themselves even while providing those involved with life-changing memories.

Many of the experiences that students had while visiting Oxford and Cambridge in the roaring 1920s would not be distinguishable from what was encountered by those who took the trip in the bullish 1980s or, for that matter, in any of the intervening decades. The series has survived war, financial and economic crisis and downturn, a pandemic, and institutional changes. It has thrived because of a shared sense of responsibility between leaders at Cornell and its British peers. Beginning in 1982, women took part in the exchange for the first time, reflecting the increasing inclusivity that has transformed sport in both the United States and Great Britain.

The most exciting part of this history is learning how this series transformed generations of male and female scholar-athletes on both sides of the Atlantic—for example, the intersection of the historical and personal connections that have made travel abroad a coming-of-age passage for so many through the years. That this important milestone occurred amid a track and field excursion for Cornellians who were committed to the sport has undoubtedly contributed to the significance of these memories for so many. The means of travel has changed through the decades (from a weeklong trip by ship to a six-hour flight by jet), but the power of seeing a new country with different social norms and traditions and making connections across those dissimilarities has linked Cornell track athletes over nearly one hundred years.

Another defining highlight of the Transatlantic Series through the years has been the creation of meaningful and lifelong connections on both sides of the Atlantic. The softening of the walls of rivalry between Princeton and later Pennsylvania, the fortified and deepened friendships within the Cornell team, and the connections made with students and staff on both sides of the Atlantic have all been critical to the tour's legacy.

Track and field was the reason for the tour, but far from its heart and soul. The meaningfulness does not solely reside in the field of competition, but in the friendships forged, in the travel challenges overcome and conquered, and in the transformational nature of a trip abroad that has repeated itself, almost without fail, every four years. The transition into adulthood is no small thing; to be able to combine that important rite of passage with the shared love of track and field and within the bonds of friendship created by the Cornell track team is unique indeed.

Cornell track and field has a history full of many remarkable achievements: Olympic gold medalists, championship teams, and Hall of Fame coaches. But it is the Transatlantic Series that helps make the experience of our students truly special and worldly. It began with a winter cross country meet, evolved into a highly competitive and spirited series of track and field meets, and continues a century later as a means of planting the seeds of meaningful friendships that grow long after each tour is over.

Notes

1. John McGovern, "Historical note," in the International Track Meet program brochure for the Oxford-Cambridge vs. Cornell-Penn-Army-Yale track and field competition held at Franklin Field in Philadelphia, June 13, 1953, p. 5.

2. McGovern.

CONCLUSIONS

Characteristics and Achievements of Cornell's Global Dimensions

Heike Michelsen

Cornell's history is unique, and so is the history of its international engagements. Although repeated over and over, the fact that Cornell's founders laid the foundation for its international orientation cannot be overstated.

This collection of stories provides insights into fascinating and engaging international dimensions of learning, discovery, and creativity. The alumni, faculty, and administrative leaders who wrote these stories present different perspectives and cover very different time periods. Hundreds of other stories could be added that illustrate the international dimensions of Cornell's curriculum and co-curriculum, students and alumni, faculty and visiting scholars, research, outreach, and operations from the very beginnings to more recent years. The stories presented provide a sample of Cornell's global endeavors since 1865. From meaningful individual activities to massive institutional programs, they allow us to draw some conclusions about the characteristics of international engagements and their benefits, outputs, outcomes, and impact.

Characteristics of Cornell's Global Dimensions

Cornell addressed different global and international opportunities and threats over time: The two world wars, the Cold War, post–Cold War, and post-9/11: these time periods defined the external environment in which Cornell operated and defined its global awareness and commitments. Whether providing commissioned officers in World War I or promoting teaching and research on the moderation or avoidance of war during the Cold War period, each generation has renewed and revitalized these international values in its own way and left a deep imprint on the university.

Cornell's administrators, faculty, and staff played key roles in internationalizing the campus: The values of Cornell's founders, Andrew Dickson White and

Ezra Cornell, are well known. Maybe less known are the unique international careers of Jacob Gould Schurman, president from 1892 to 1920; Frank H. T. Rhodes, president from 1977 to 1995; and college deans such as William A. Hagan, dean of the College of Veterinary Medicine from 1932 to 1959. In addition, faculty and staff played a key role in establishing major institutional arrangements, supporting and catalyzing international teaching, research, and outreach interests.

Cornell embraced comprehensive internationalization: At Cornell, comprehensive internationalization initially was led by the College of Agriculture and Life Sciences, going back to 1960 when Dean Charles E. Palm and a faculty committee identified international agriculture as the College of Agriculture and Life Sciences' "fourth dimension." It was defined as a strategic, coordinated process that seeks to align and integrate policies, programs, and initiatives to position the college as more globally oriented and internationally connected. Consequently, international work would be equal to the functions of teaching, research, and extension. International Programs in the College of Agriculture and Life Sciences was the first unit of its kind in an American college of agriculture and was often cited as the model for others.

Interdisciplinary university-wide and cross-college units were important drivers: Problems in the real world usually do not correspond with the historical structures of universities, and solutions usually cannot be developed with the departmentalized knowledge of specific disciplines. Area studies programs, international thematic programs, and the Center for International Studies were important institutional arrangements that reinforced Cornell's global dimensions. Founded after World War II, they served as interdisciplinary hubs for students and faculty across departments and colleges, but also for community members and academic visitors. They provided a real and intellectual space in which students and faculty could learn from one another. For example, as Professor Thomas Pepinsky stated in his chapter, "SEAP's [the Southeast Asia Program's] comprehensive approach to Southeast Asian area studies, encompassing the social sciences and the humanities as well as the applied sciences, combined with the program's commitment to studying the entire region to produce an unusually rich and eclectic body of research on the region and its human and natural environment."

In addition, graduate study at Cornell is interdisciplinary by design. Graduate fields span departments and disciplines. Graduate students are admitted to fields of study, which are composed of faculty members who come together around shared intellectual interests and may draw from different colleges.

Cornell addressed a wide range of issues worldwide: This book presents the international engagements in medicine, veterinary medicine, agriculture, life sciences, arts, sciences, social sciences, business, labor relations, engineering, human ecology, law, and many more. While not limited to specific countries or regions, these included engagements in Europe, Asia, Africa, Australia, and the Americas. The breadth and depth of Cornell's international engagements reflect its institutional complexities of colleges, schools, and fields of studies. Cornell is an institution that combines the strength of an Ivy League university with the land-grant mission to disseminate knowledge and enhance the lives and livelihoods of people around the world.

Achievements of Cornell's Global Dimensions

International orientation and engagements educated generations of "global citizens": Cornell has offered a wide range of curricular and co-curricular activities on and off campus that increased awareness and understanding of global issues; developed intercultural competencies, cross-cultural understanding, and cultural sensitivity; and fostered a deeper engagement with these issues.

The many on-campus activities described here contributed to an increased understanding of global issues, societies, cultures, and economies by students, faculty, and staff. These included comprehensive academic programs of international courses and degree options within the colleges; diverse language programs; area studies programs and the Center for International Studies; an international education network; libraries, the museum, and other collections; international-oriented student organizations and living communities; and much more.

Off-campus activities, some of these offered over many decades, show how students gained relevant experiences and skills critical to professional success. Whether short- and long-term study abroad programs, expeditions, international music performances, faculty-led courses abroad, research, service, or internship opportunities, all of these exposed faculty and students to real-world challenges and actively engaged them abroad with local institutions, communities, students, and Cornell alumni. In many cases, they developed long-lasting, mutually beneficial partnerships and collaborations.

Different generations of a few selected students and faculty who were deeply engaged with global issues are featured throughout this book, including Ida Scudder (class of 1899, Medicine), Hu Shih (class of 1914, Philosophy), and Ilana Schafer (class of 2008, Veterinary Medicine), as well as Professors Allan Holmberg of anthropology, John P. Windmuller of industrial and labor relations, and John W. Mellor of agricultural economics.

International engagement attracted international students and professionals: Cornell's global orientation attracted international students and professionals from across the world from the beginning. When they came to campus, they brought their culture, skills, knowledge, and experiences. Cumulatively, their presence added international dimensions to Cornell's curriculum and co-curriculum available to all and contributed to Cornell's ever-expanding stature as a center for international scholarship.

Many graduate students from abroad had professional experience and were seeking advanced education before returning to their home countries to assume leadership positions in government agencies, nongovernmental organizations, academic institutions, or the private sector. The Institute for African Development's Tuition Fellowship Program, for example, facilitated advanced Cornell degrees in a wide range of disciplines for more than four hundred midcareer professionals from over twenty countries in sub-Saharan Africa.

The exemplary achievements of international students in their countries and in the world are well documented, including those of Modesto Quiroga from Argentina, who founded the Cosmopolitan Club with the motto "Above all nations is humanity"; Charles Kajimanga (LLM 1993), a judge on the Supreme Court of Zambia; Emil Javier (PhD 1969) and Gelia Castillo (PhD 1960), who became outstanding Filipino agricultural leaders; and Sonam Wangyel Wang (PhD 2008), who developed a national strategy for addressing Bhutan's human-wildlife conflicts.

Cornell faculty also welcomed and offered training programs for thousands of individuals and groups of international professionals. These included professionals from countries with developing, emerging, and postsocialist economies and leading hotel and food industry managers across the world. They received Cornell training to enhance their leadership and technical skills, and many became leaders and agents of change in their home countries.

International engagement strengthened Cornell's research and knowledge-production capacity: While it is nowadays widely accepted that faculty (and students) must be involved internationally to work successfully in this highly connected world, many Cornell faculty recognized the benefits of international engagements early on. When asked whether Cornell's first major technical cooperation project with the University of Nanking in the 1920s was only of benefit to China and not to Cornell, leading faculty strongly disagreed. They testified that they gained much from the experiences, which even led to new seed varieties for New York farmers.

In many other examples, faculty reflect on the significant implications of becoming internationally engaged and how it expanded their research and teaching horizons, leading to new ideas and innovative initiatives as well as to remarkable professional contributions both on and off campus. As summarized by Daniel P. Loucks in his chapter, "Experiencing different cultures, languages, and approaches to resource development planning, management, and use adds to the benefits all of us gain from participating in these international projects."

Cornell's international programs catalyzed the relationships among faculty with similar interests but from very different fields. These programs brought many international scholars to Cornell's community who taught classes, gave presentations, and worked with Cornell faculty and students on projects. The programs also attracted significant financial support for faculty's international-oriented teaching and research. Government agencies, alumni, and foundations such as Carnegie, Ford, Gates, MacArthur, Mellon, and Rockefeller created significant endowments and provided funding for these programs. Area studies programs were successful in receiving significant grants from the US government to address the need to better understand the world beyond our borders. The United States Agency for International Development also provided support to Cornell for institution building, technical assistance, and research projects abroad.

Increased individual competencies, collective capabilities, assets, and relationships increased Cornell's research and knowledge-production capacity. This book features many examples of faculty and student research, how they identified issues and produced new knowledge and policy recommendations to address issues across the globe. Examples include producing crop improvements in Asia, identifying children's nutrition deficits in Europe, addressing virus infections in Asian wild tigers, characterizing the transformation of an Indigenous civilization in Latin America, analyzing the effects of new technologies on the conduct of war, and, more recently, discovering knowledge about COVID-19, migration issues, and climate change. With its wide range of contributions, Cornell remains at the cutting edge of international scholarship and contemporary political, social, scientific, and literary areas of research, increasing its reputation and international rankings.

International engagement built institutional capacities around the world: Cornell has an impressive track record of institution-building projects that reaches back to the beginning of the twentieth century and encompasses technical assistance, training, and capacity-building programs. Numerous examples in this book from Asia, the Middle East, Europe, Latin America, and Africa show how Cornell made major contributions in developing research and education institutions across the globe with wide-ranging impacts. Specifically, Cornell

- introduced a more comprehensive program of cooperation between American colleges and their overseas counterparts as an important part of the US technical aid program
- influenced the post–World War II rehabilitation of veterinary schools in Germany
- transformed a community of people bound under an exploitative feudal-like hacienda system into a self-governing independent community in control of their own land in Peru
- helped the University of the Philippines College of Agriculture in Los Baños to become the premier agricultural education and research university in Southeast Asia

- changed the scholarly lives of countless researchers in developing nations by providing digital access to scientific journals
- brought new communication and information technologies to rural households in Guatemala and Vietnam, giving them access to information through telecenters and improving their livelihood and welfare
- strengthened teaching and research capacities of institutions in postsocialist Eastern and Central Europe
- revolutionized medical education and research in the Middle East

Formal international engagements were mutually beneficial: International engagements fostered meaningful connections and valuable collaborations across the world and often resulted in long-term collaborations. The motivating factors for engaging in these partnerships were diverse. For faculty, they included a better perspective and understanding of development or global issues, professional development, hands-on knowledge, and support for graduate programs and research. For partners, they included the need for specific experiences and expertise, access to information and resources, professional advancement, improved visibility and credibility, and increased legitimization and recognition.

Successful collaborations require that each partner benefits. Cornell's engagement in Eastern Europe and Nepal as well as its relationship with the International Labor Organization (ILO) demonstrate different types of benefits. Cornell faculty members modeled contemporary research and pedagogical methods and philosophies, while counterparts in Central and Eastern Europe provided deep knowledge of diverse national and cultural contexts relevant to the design and conduct of scholarship on social and economic transformations in the region. The ILR School has a lasting relationship with the ILO, which has resulted in several important books coauthored by Cornell faculty and ILO researchers. ILR School faculty and students continue working with the ILO, and many ILR School undergraduates are interns at the ILO, studying and writing about current labor issues.

And, as part of the Cornell-Nepal Study Program, Cornell students could learn about the country, do research on a wide variety of topics relevant both to their own field of study and to Nepal, and develop meaningful relationships with the people there. The Cornell faculty wanted students to learn about Nepal from many perspectives but especially those of the Nepalese themselves; to do intellectually challenging, methodologically appropriate, and ethically responsible research; and to have sustained interactions with not just host families and villagers but their academic peers. The Tribhuvan University students received help in navigating their thesis research and writing, improved their English, and got access to research materials; but they also got to know Americans and made friends.

The Tribhuvan University faculty was fairly compensated for time devoted to supervising.

The extent, depth, breadth, and impact of Cornell's international engagements over time are truly remarkable and unique. This is a story of an institution where education, research, and services were used to educate generations of global citizens, to create new understandings of the world, and to effect positive change in the world. This is the story of the impact of Cornell's global dimensions.

AFTERWORD
Cornell's Global Future

Wendy Wolford

As this collection illustrates, Cornell has been active and at home in the world since its founding in 1865. The university counted international students among its first class of students, and although academic outreach abroad was unusual in the early twentieth century, Cornell faculty and students worked on agricultural development in rural China in the 1920s.

Today, Cornell students and faculty work around the world, advising governments, collaborating with researchers, consulting on international law and human rights, developing new practices and treatments for AIDS prevention in Haiti and new wheat varieties in Africa and Asia, and helping to design cities of the future from Jakarta to São Paulo.

International students from 129 countries currently make up 24 percent of the student body—and our international students go on to become international alumni. About thirty thousand Cornell alumni live in 160 countries, carrying Cornell's mission and spirit to every corner of the globe. Our international alumni are the presidents of universities, CEOs, entrepreneurs, environmental activists, world-famous architects, and global leaders in every field. Cornell has produced not one but two presidents of Taiwan, as well as policymakers and advisers in governments around the world.

Cornell promotes "knowledge for the greater good," and our students are educated as global citizens so they can effect change on a worldwide scale. The goal of international work and mobility is not solely to learn *about*, it is to learn *from*—from other perspectives, different cultures and experiences, to build empathy and understanding.

In his travel memoir *The Innocents Abroad*, Mark Twain famously observed, "Travel is fatal to prejudice, bigotry, and narrow-mindedness." As soon as you go someplace new, you have learned something because you are seeing the world from a different vantage point. After experiencing the COVID-19 pandemic at Cornell, with our campus closing in March 2020, we and people around the world learned we do not have to leave home to be part of a global community: travel can be a state of mind, a way of seeing the world, rather than a physical journey.

This volume offers insight into the history and success of international activities across the university. Cornell's Office of the Vice Provost for International Affairs was created in the early 2000s to expand Cornell's border-crossing spirit of exploration, learning, and shared discovery in order to propel Cornell's global mission into its next 150 years.

Global Hubs, one of Cornell's most recent international initiatives, launched in fall 2022 as a network of world-class peer institutions partnering with Cornell to support faculty, students, and staff as they collaborate, teach, intern, and study internationally. Global Hubs are not physical centers. They are a relationship-based global extension of the Cornell community that lets us share resources, expertise, and infrastructure without investing in a brick-and-mortar presence. Hubs are reciprocal; both campuses benefit by exchanging people and ideas. These university-wide partnerships are the kind of sustained international engagement that can lead to meaningful change.

Launched in 2019, Cornell's first Global Grand Challenge, the Migrations initiative, continues to cultivate collaborations that advance science, scholarship, teaching, outreach, and engagement in ways that create new insights into critical world problems and prepare researchers, entrepreneurs, policymakers, communities, and future leaders like the students at Cornell to thrive in a world on the move.

In November 2022, President Martha E. Pollack noted that international cooperation across universities and borders is imperative in our rapidly changing world when she introduced Cornell's second Global Grand Challenges Symposium: Frontiers and the Future. This emphasized that by working together across disciplinary silos and national borders, we can make a real difference in solving global problems.

In the past year, Cornell has provided a safe refuge, a welcoming community, and a way forward for people from Afghanistan, Ukraine, Russia, Turkey, Myanmar, and other countries where freedom to speak, write, and learn is under attack. Since 2016, Global Cornell has led campus and community support for international scholars, students, and human-rights defenders whose work puts them at risk in their home countries.

Cornell's support for scholars under threat upholds academic freedom while preserving human dignity in the face of overwhelming adversity. The momentum of this initiative aligns with the 2023–2024 university-wide theme "The Indispensable Condition: Freedom of Expression at Cornell."

These are only a few ways we embrace the global future of our world-class university. Cornell's international outlook profoundly shapes how we teach, learn, conduct research, and solve contemporary challenges. If we want our students to be leaders, our science to be at the leading edge, and our teaching and research to be relevant, we must continue to plan and work in collaboration with partners around the world. Taking up these challenges is our responsibility as global citizens and our privilege as the only Ivy League "land-grant university to the world."

ABOUT THE EDITORIAL TEAM

Royal D. Colle is a professor emeritus of communication at Cornell University, where he taught development communication for forty years. He has worked on Cornell projects in India, Samoa, and Guatemala and has served as a consultant on development communication projects in Africa, Asia, and Latin America for many international organizations, including the World Health Organization, the World Bank, UNICEF, the Food and Agricultural Organization of the United Nations, and the Ford Foundation. He prepared two booklets for the UN on engaged learning that focus on teaching information and communication technologies for development. He received the International Communication Association Lifetime Achievement Award and is recognized on the Wall of Honor at the East-West Center in Honolulu, Hawaii, for his development work in Asia.

Heike Michelsen was responsible for programming, assessments, communications, and grant writing at Cornell's Mario Einaudi Center for International Studies during the sixteen years before her 2019 retirement. Before, she was a senior research officer at the International Service for Agricultural Research, which is a member of the Consultative Group of International Agricultural Research Centers with projects across sub-Saharan Africa focusing on higher education systems, institutional partnerships and collaboration, and institutional performance. She has also served as a consultant to the Social Science Research Council, the American Council on Education in support of Higher Education for Development, and the Network for Agricultural Research for Development. She holds a doctorate in economics from the University of Hohenheim (Germany).

Elaine D. Engst, Dr. Peter J. Thaler '56 Cornell University Archivist Emerita, began work in the Cornell University Library in 1979, serving in many roles, notably as Cornell University archivist from 1996 to her retirement in 2015 and as director of the Division of Rare and Manuscript Collections from 1999 to 2013.

She also served as assistant director of the New York Historical Resources Center at Cornell, managing the New York State Historical Documents Inventory. In 1996, for her professional accomplishments, she was named a Fellow of the Society of American Archivists. She holds an MA from Cornell and has given numerous presentations, curated exhibitions and websites, and written articles, reviews, exhibition catalogs, and books.

Corey Ryan Earle is a visiting lecturer in the American Studies Program at Cornell University, where he has taught thousands of students in a popular course on the history of Cornell since 2011. He is a frequent speaker and author on topics related to Cornell history and has served as a history resource for departments and organizations across campus while working in Alumni Affairs and Development since 2008. He previously worked in the Division of Rare and Manuscript Collections in the Cornell University Library and holds a BS from Cornell University and an MA from Teachers College, Columbia University.

ABOUT THE AUTHORS

Marco Ameduri is senior associate dean for premedical education and Education City collaborative curricular affairs at Weill Cornell Medicine–Qatar. He was born in Italy and received his undergraduate degree in physics from the University of Turin, Italy, and his PhD from Cornell University. After spending two years as a guest scientist at the Max Planck Institute for the Physics of Complex Systems in Dresden, Germany, he joined Weill Cornell Medicine–Qatar in 2002. His interests are in theoretical physics and in philosophy.

N'Dri T. Assié-Lumumba is a professor of Africana studies and was director of the Institute for African Development at Cornell University. She is currently president of the World Council of Comparative Education Societies, Distinguished Visiting Professor in the Ali Mazrui Centre for Higher Education Studies at the University of Johannesburg (South Africa), immediate past chair of the Scientific Advisory Committee of UNESCO's Intergovernmental Program for the Management of Social Transformations, and past president of the Comparative and International Education Society. She has published extensively. A fellow of the World Academy of Art and Science and recipient of numerous awards, she has held other distinguished visiting positions globally and has served in many UN agencies, African think tanks, and governmental panels in the world. She earned her PhD in comparative education (economics and sociology) from the University of Chicago.

Ellen Avril is chief curator and the Judith H. Stoikov Curator of Asian Art at the Herbert F. Johnson Museum of Art at Cornell University. A specialist in Chinese art, she has conducted curatorial work that broadly spans the field of Asian art, and she has organized numerous exhibitions and grown the Asian art collections across cultures over her twenty-five years at the Johnson, in addition to serving on the leadership team of the museum. She led the reinstallation of the museum's renovated and expanded Asian art galleries that opened in 2011 with support from the National Endowment for the Arts.

Daniel Bass is manager of the South Asia Program at Cornell University and adjunct assistant professor of anthropology and Asian studies. He received his PhD in anthropology and MA in South Asian studies from the University of Michigan. He is the author of *Everyday Ethnicity in Sri Lanka: Up-Country Tamil Identity Politics* and coeditor (with Amarnath Amarasingam) of *Sri Lanka: The Struggle for Peace in the Aftermath of War*, and (with Balasingham Skanthakumar) of *Up-Country Tamils in Sri Lanka: Charting a New Future.*

David L. Brown is International Professor Emeritus of development sociology in the Department of Global Development at Cornell University. Brown's research focuses on migration and urbanization, social and spatial inequality, and social and economic processes occurring in the rural-urban interface. He has published over sixty-five scholarly articles and is author or editor of twelve books. His latest book, *Rethinking Rural Studies*, will be published in 2024.

Lourdes Casanova is the Gail and Rob Cañizares Director of the Emerging Markets Institute and a senior lecturer at the Cornell SC Johnson College of Business, Cornell University. Formerly she was with INSEAD (Institut privé d'enseignement supérieur). Named one of the fifty most influential Iberoamerican intellectuals and one of the thirty most influential Iberoamerican women intellectuals by Esglobal, she was a Fulbright Scholar and is author and coauthor with Anne Miroux of the *Emerging Market Multinationals Report 2022, 2021, 2020, 2019, 2018, 2017* and *2016.*

Debra A. Castillo is Stephen H. Weiss Presidential Fellow, Emerson Hinchliff Professor of Hispanic Studies, and professor of comparative literature at Cornell University. She is past president of the international Latin American Studies Association. Her recent books include *South of the Future: Speculative Biotechnologies and Care Markets in South Asia and Latin America* (with Anindita Banerjee), *The Scholar as Human* (with Anna Sims Bartel) and *Scholars in COVID Times* (with Melissa Castillo-Planas).

Ronnie Coffman served as International Professor of plant breeding and genetics at Cornell University from 1981 to 2022, when he was named emeritus. He was director of International Programs in the College of Agriculture and Life Sciences from 2001 to 2022 and led many years of class trips to Costa Rica, Honduras, India, Mexico, Myanmar, and Thailand.

Iftikhar Dadi is the John H. Burris Professor in the Department of the History of Art and Visual Studies at Cornell University. He also served as the Binenkorb Director of the Cornell South Asia Program from 2018 to 2023. His publications include *Lahore Cinema: Between Realism and Fable* (2022), and *Modernism and the Art of Muslim South Asia* (2010). Other publications include the edited volumes *The Lahore Biennale Reader 01* (2022) and *Anwar Jalal Shemza* (2015); the coedited catalog *Lines of Control* (2012); and the coedited reader *Unpacking Europe* (2001).

Roberto Einaudi worked as an architect in Africa, the Middle and Far East, the United States, and Europe from 1962 to 1986 designing schools, hospitals, universities, and new cities. He founded the Cornell in Rome program in 1986, directing it until 1992. His architectural office in Rome, Studio Einaudi, specializes in museums, exhibitions, archeological sites, restoration of historical buildings, and urban sites. Einaudi received a BArch from Cornell University in 1961 and a MArch from MIT in 1962. He writes and draws about dreams, family history, the poet John Keats and the architect-engineer Pierluigi Nervi.

Blaine Friedlander is the senior science writer at the *Cornell Chronicle*, and he has been a science journalist and communicator for more than three decades. He graduated from Ohio University in 1983 with a bachelor's degree. Blaine wrote the "Sky Watch" astronomy column in the *Washington Post* from 1986 to 2023.

Gene A. German (d. 2023) was a professor emeritus at Cornell University, having spent his academic career on the faculty in the Dyson School of Applied Economics and Management (formerly the Department of Agricultural Economics) with a primary focus in the field of food distribution and marketing. Two of his sabbatical leaves were spent in Japan, where he developed close ties with executives in various food companies and established a strong relationship with Japanese professors who were conducting research in his field. During his time in Japan, he presented seminars for a wide range of Japanese food companies and established an annual seminar series between Cornell and the Japanese food industry. He received his BS degree from Michigan State University and his MS and PhD from Cornell University.

Kristen A. Grace is the senior education abroad adviser in the Office of Global Learning, formerly Cornell Abroad. Kristen studied in Senegal and lived and worked internationally before coming to Cornell University where she earned a PhD in Foundations of Education. Since 2003, Kristen has helped manage study abroad programs, including the Consortium for Advanced Studies Abroad Sevilla, and has advised undergraduate students on spending a semester or year abroad as a way to meet their academic, personal, and professional goals.

Davydd J. Greenwood is the Goldwin Smith Professor Emeritus of Anthropology, having taught at Cornell for forty-four years. He is the former director of the Mario Einaudi Center for International Studies and of the Cornell Institute for European Studies. His work has focused on action research, the anthropology of Spain, industrial democracy, and higher education reform.

Peter Gregory is an adjunct professor in the Department of Global Development at Cornell University and the former director of Cornell's Hubert H. Humphrey Fellowship Program, which he led for ten years. His career has spanned five decades, thirty-four of which have been at Cornell, where he gained experience in crop biochemistry research and teaching as well as in university research administration and global development projects. In addition, he has served in leadership positions at the International Potato Center in Lima, Peru; the World Bank; and the consulting firm Novigen Sciences (since integrated into Exponent).

James E. Haldeman is the former senior associate director of International Programs in the College of Agriculture and Life Sciences at Cornell University. He has served as rural development specialist and adviser to the Ethiopian Ministry of Agriculture, assistant director of planning for the Maine State Anti-poverty Program, and program leader for agriculture and community resource development for Cornell Cooperative Extension. He received a BS in agricultural economics from Cornell University in 1965 and an MS in resource economics from the University of Maine in 1967, and served in the Peace Corps in Sierra Leone from 1967 to 1969.

Olivia M. Hall is a writer, anthropologist, and travel blogger. After years of living and studying in three different countries and visiting more than thirty, she has made the Finger Lakes her home base for further explorations, near and far. She received her AB in psychology from Harvard University and her MA and PhD in anthropology from Cornell University.

Matt Hayes is director of communications for the Department of Global Development in the College of Agriculture and Life Sciences. A strategic communications expert and content strategist, he has experience across areas of international agriculture, food security, global development, and higher education. He manages communications and marketing efforts for the department and a portfolio of more than two dozen global programs that are engaged in efforts connected to well-being and inclusion, environmental sustainability, and food and nutritional security.

David Holmberg is a graduate professor of anthropology and professor emeritus at Cornell University, where he serves as the Fulbright/Fulbright-Hays adviser. His research focused on the Tamang of highland Nepal. Together with anthropologist Kathryn March, he received the 2021 Sir Edmund Hillary Mountain Legacy Medal for their many decades of friendship and assistance to Nepal, and for their leadership in educational exchange programs between Tribhuvan University and Cornell University.

Polly Endreny Holmberg, a conservation biologist, has extensive experience in organizing international exchange and education initiatives. Her work centers on collaborating with global groups of professionals in the fields of food systems, sustainable development, and natural resource management. Polly serves as the associate director of the Cornell Humphrey Fellowship Program and leads the World Food Prize New York Youth Institute. She has previously worked with organizations such as the Nature Conservancy, the National Oceanic and Atmospheric Administration, the Peace Corps (Madagascar), and the Cornell Alliance for Science.

Carol Kammen was a senior lecturer in history at Cornell University from 1983 to 2007 and is author of *Cornell: Glorious to View*; *Part & Apart: The Black Experience at Cornell University, 1865–1945*; *First-Person Cornell: Students' Diaries, Letters, Email, and Blogs*; and *On Doing Local History: Reflections on What Local Historians Do, Why, and What it Means*, as well as regular contributions to the *Ithaca Journal* and *History News*. She served as Tompkins County historian from 2000 until her retirement in 2023.

Eileen Keating has served as the university records manager and the College of Human Ecology archivist at Cornell University for over twenty-five years. She has written articles, lectured, and curated exhibits about the history of the College of Human Ecology.

Mitchel Lasser is the Jack G. Clarke Professor of Law, director of graduate studies, and codirector of the Cornell Summer Institute of International and Comparative Law in Paris. He teaches and writes in the areas of comparative law, law of the European Union, and comparative constitutional law. He has published three monographs with Oxford University Press: *Judicial Deliberations: A Comparative Analysis of Judicial Transparency and Legitimacy* (2004); *Judicial*

Transformations: The Rights Revolution in the Courts of Europe (2009); and *Judicial Dis-appointments: Judicial Appointments Reform and the Rise of European Judicial Independence* (2020).

James P. Lassoie is International Professor Emeritus in the Department of Natural Resources and the Environment, having joined Cornell in 1976 with an extension and research appointment in forest ecology and management. He began an international focus on agroforestry in the mid-1980s and has advised over one hundred graduate and undergraduate students studying conservation and sustainable development in Africa, Asia, Central and South America, Canada, and the United States. Lassoie has over 270 research and extension and outreach publications. He also developed several innovative courses focused on engaged learning and was widely recognized for his teaching and dedication to student mentoring.

Moying Li grew up in China during the tumultuous Cultural Revolution (1966–1976). During that period, Li was primarily self-taught, following the guided lessons and reading lists her father was able to send to her from a hard-labor farm. In 1980, thanks to a generous scholarship and a plane ticket from Swarthmore College, Li became one of the first private scholarship students from China since the Cultural Revolution to attend a US university. She earned an MA from Swarthmore College and an MBA and a PhD from Boston University. Hu Shih was a close friend of her grandfather's family and was also the topic of her PhD dissertation. Li was co-anchor of *English as a Second Language Program* on CCTV, the largest television network in China. Her memoir *Snow Falling in Spring: Coming of Age in China during the Cultural Revolution* won numerous awards, including the *New York Times*' Editor's Choice.

Daniel P. Loucks is an emeritus professor in the School of Civil and Environmental Engineering and the Brooks School of Public Policy at Cornell University. His research and teaching have focused on the development and application of ecology, economics, engineering, and systems analysis methods to the solution of environmental and regional water resources and various public policy problems. He has held positions in other universities and research institutes in the US, Australia, Europe, and North America, and in various US government and UN agencies, NATO, and the World Bank. He has participated in water development projects in Africa, Asia, the Americas, and Europe. He served as an aviator in the US Navy for twenty-six years and retired after commanding the navy's largest air transport squadron.

Jeff MacCorkle is managing director of Pacific Rim Resources, a Hong Kong–based energy supplier. Active in the Cornell Club of China and Cornell Club of

Hong Kong since his graduation in 1988, he received his bachelor's in history from Cornell University, where he completed the FALCON language program in Chinese. He received his MBA from the University of Southern California.

Bonnie G. MacDougall (d. 2017) was professor emerita of architecture, having joined the faculty in the College of Architecture, Art, and Planning at Cornell University as a visiting assistant professor in 1979 and served as associate professor of architecture and Asian studies from 1988 until her retirement in 2014. A cultural and architectural historian with teaching experience in anthropology and linguistics, she specialized in the architecture of South Asia, especially Sri Lanka. She also served as director of the South Asia Program from 1983 to 1988. She received her BA, MA, and PhD degrees from Cornell.

Kathryn S. March is graduate professor and professor emerita of anthropology; feminist, gender, and sexuality studies; and public affairs at Cornell University. Her research, teaching, and consulting have focused on gender, social change, and justice, notably in the Himalayas, where she has worked since 1973 and where, in 1992, she founded the joint Cornell-Nepal Study Program. Her books include *Women's Informal Associations in Developing Countries: Catalysts for Change?* (1985) and *"If Each Comes Halfway": Meeting Tamang Women in Nepal* (2002). She is the recipient of numerous grants and awards, including from the National Science Foundation, the Woodrow Wilson National Fellowship Foundation, the National Institute of Mental Health, the National Endowment for the Humanities, the Mellon Foundation, the Bunting Institute, and the Fulbright Scholar Program, and most recently she received the 2021 Sir Edmund Hillary Mountain Legacy Award.

Tsu-Lin Mei (d. 2023) was the Hu Shih Professor Emeritus in Chinese Literature. He taught in the Department of Asian Studies from 1971 to 2001, chaired the department from 1972 to 1977, and directed the East Asian Program from 1978 to 1981.

Jim Morris-Knower has worked as a librarian at Cornell University's Mann Library since 1997, when he graduated from the University of Michigan with his MILS and PhD. Some of his career highlights have involved personally delivering TEEAL (the Essential Electronic Agricultural Library) sets to libraries in Africa and Asia as part of his library work on grants to support researchers across the globe. When he is not at work, he enjoys building walls out of the native Llenroc bluestone in his backyard and playing his Telecaster to his dog.

Muna Ndulo is the William Nelson Cromwell Professor of International and Comparative Law and Elizabeth and Arvilla Reich Director of the Leo and Arvilla

Berger International Studies Program at Cornell Law School. He was formerly director of the Institute for African Development at Cornell University, dean of the School of Law at the University of Zambia, and has worked for the United Nations in various capacities.

Malden C. Nesheim is professor emeritus of nutrition and provost emeritus of Cornell University. He is the founding director of the Division of Nutritional Sciences at Cornell. His international work has included numerous studies on the relationship of parasitic infections to the nutritional status of children. He and his students have carried out research in Indonesia, Kenya, Panama, Papua New Guinea, and Venezuela.

Thomas Pepinsky is the Walter F. LaFeber Professor of Government and Public Policy at Cornell University, where he also serves as director of the Southeast Asia Program and associate director of the Modern Indonesia Project. A specialist in comparative politics and political economy, Pepinsky focuses his research primarily on maritime Southeast Asia and its connections with the global political economy, past and present. His current research investigates the political foundations of ethnic identity in the Malay world and beyond.

Judith Reppy is a professor emerita in the Department of Science and Technology Studies at Cornell University. She has been associated with the Judith Reppy Institute for Peace and Conflict Studies at Cornell University (formerly the Peace Studies Program) since 1973, serving at various times as director, assistant director, and acting director.

Norman Scott is a professor emeritus in the Department of Biological and Environmental Engineering at Cornell University, having joined the faculty in 1962 after completing his PhD at Cornell. He previously served as director of Cornell University Agricultural Experiment Station and vice president of research and advanced studies. Scott's research focused on thermoregulation in poultry, biomechanics of machine milking of dairy cows, electronic applications in agriculture, and sustainable development.

Anthony M. Shelton is International Professor Emeritus in the Department of Entomology at Cornell University. Shelton's research and extension programs were based at Cornell AgriTech, the New York State Agricultural Experiment Station. There he refined integrated pest management (IPM) tactics, including sampling and treatment guidelines, biological controls, host plant resistance, landscape management, biotechnology, and judicious use of insecticides. Shelton developed innovative management programs for major insect pests of vegetable crops nationally and internationally. Among the Entomological Society of America awards he has received are the National Award for Excellence in IPM, the National Recognition Award for Research, election as fellow, the National IPM Team Award, the L. O. Howard Award, and the Lifetime Achievement Award. He also received the Cornell (CALS) Award for Applied Research and served as the associate director of the Cornell Agricultural Experiment Station and the associate director of research from 1993 to 2001.

Arthur C. Smith is a college admissions consultant with Arthur Smith Advising. He previously served as the Alan B. '53 and Elizabeth Heekin Harris head coach of the women's track and field and cross country teams at Cornell University, where he managed the Transatlantic Series exchange between Cornell, Oxford, and Cambridge. Smith also served as admissions and advising dean in the College of Arts and Sciences and as an assistant director of admissions in the Office of Undergraduate Admissions, where he was the athletics liaison for varsity teams. He earned his BA from Cornell University, followed by an MA and PhD in history at Duke University.

William J. Sonnenstuhl is a professor emeritus in the Department of Extension and Department of Organizational Behavior of the School of Industrial Relations at Cornell University, where he taught courses on organizational culture, leadership, and change, and was associate director of the R. Brinkley Smithers Institute on Alcohol-Related Workplace Studies. As a young faculty member, he was fortunate to know many of the ILR School's founders and early faculty, including John Windmuller, and is grateful for their kindness, friendship, and mentorship. He received his PhD in sociology from New York University.

Patrick J. Stevens is curator of the Fiske Icelandic Collection and selector for Jewish studies in the Cornell University Library. He is also managing editor of Islandica: A Series in Icelandic and Norse Studies. From late 2021 into 2024, he served as acting director for the library's Division of Rare and Manuscript Collections.

Erika Styger is professor of practice in tropical agronomy and director of the Climate-Resilient Farming Systems Program at the Department of Global Development, Cornell University. Styger has more than thirty years of experience developing agro-ecological innovations together with farmers in Africa, Asia, and Latin America, with a focus on agroforestry and sustainable land management, and, for the past fifteen years, with the System of Rice Intensification. Her current work focuses on the scaling-up of the System of Rice Intensification at the global level.

Bill Summers is managing partner of the Summers Group, a communications consultancy based in Pinehurst, North Carolina. His team provides strategic and technical support to CEOs and other senior leaders. Summers has published ten books, both fiction and nonfiction, and has served as editor on four works of nonfiction. He received his BS from Cornell University in 1982.

Eric Tagliacozzo is the John Stambaugh Professor of History at Cornell University. He is the director of the Comparative Muslim Societies Program and runs Cornell's Modern Indonesia Project, as well as coediting the journal *Indonesia*. He is the author of three monographs (2005, 2013, and 2022) and is editor or coeditor of twelve other books.

Susan Tarrow taught French language and literature at Cornell and held the post of associate director of the Cornell Institute for European Studies from 1984 to 2005. She remains an active supporter of the institute and its students, helping to select candidates for the Susan Tarrow Undergraduate Fellowship, and continues to serve on the Fulbright Selection Committee for Europe. She received her BA and MA in modern languages at Oxford University and her PhD in romance studies at Cornell University and has authored work on Albert Camus and Primo Levi.

Terry Tucker is a professor of practice in the Department of Global Development at Cornell University. His work focuses on smallholder agriculture, especially farmers' adaptation to change, as well as their roles in research, innovation, and social learning processes. He also collaborates on institution-strengthening initiatives with universities and other postsecondary educational institutions in South and Southeast Asia, Africa, and Latin America. Tucker has held leadership roles with the Cornell International Institute for Food, Agriculture, and Development; International Programs–CALS; and the Hubert H. Humphrey Fellowship Program.

Jerry Wilcox spent twenty-seven years at Cornell's International Student and Scholars Office and ten years at the University of Texas at Austin overseeing the Study Abroad, English as a Second Language, and International Student and Scholars units. He retired in August 2008. Wilcox received his BS from Iowa State University in 1967. His Peace Corps assignment was in public health in central Thailand from 1967 to 1969. After receiving his master's degree from the University of Hawai'i as an East-West Center grantee, he became resident director of Cornell's International Living Center in July 1971. Throughout his career he was active in the professional organization NAFSA: Association of International Educators, holding many offices including that of president.

John Wolff is professor emeritus of linguistics and Asian studies at Cornell University, having taught from 1963 until his retirement in 2002. He was the director of the Southeast Asia Program from 1993 to 1998. Wolff has written books and scholarly papers on sociolinguistics, historical linguistics, and lexicography of the Austronesian languages and compiled dictionaries of Cebuano and Indonesian. He has also published pedagogical materials at all levels for Cebuano, Tagalog (Filipino), and Indonesian—languages that he taught at Cornell University in addition to Javanese.

Wendy Wolford has served as vice provost for international affairs at Cornell University since 2018. She also is the Robert A. and Ruth E. Polson Professor of Global Development in the Department of Global Development, where her research has focused on international development, land use and distribution, social mobilization, and agrarian societies with a regional concentration in Latin America—particularly Brazil. A member of Cornell's faculty since 2010, Wolford served as the faculty director of economic development at the Cornell Atkinson Center for Sustainability, where she co-led CARE-Cornell and Oxfam-Cornell collaborations.

Liren Zheng is curator of the Charles W. Wason Collection on East Asia at the Cornell University Library. He received his MA and PhD from Cornell University.

Larry Zuidema was associated with international programs in the College of Agriculture and Life Sciences at Cornell University from 1964 to 1995, ending as associate director with periods as acting director. From 1995 to 1998, he was a senior fellow at the International Service for National Agricultural Research, now a former institution of the Consultative Group on International Agricultural Research.

INDEX

Locators in italics indicate a figure. Individual countries are grouped by continent or region.